Pitt Latin American Series

PITT LATIN AMERICAN SERIES
Cole Blasier, Editor

Selected titles

Argentina: Political Culture and Instability

Susan and Peter Calvert

University of Pittsburgh Press

Published in the U.S.A. by the University of Pittsburgh Press
Pittsburgh, Pa. 15260
Published in Great Britain by The Macmillan Press Ltd

Printed in Great Britain

ISBN 0–8229–1156–6

LC 89–40048

Library of Congress Cataloging-in-Publication Data
Calvert, Susan.
  Argentina: political culture and instability / Susan and Peter
Calvert.
  p. cm. — (Pitt Latin American series)
  Originally presented as the author's Ph.D. thesis (University of
Southampton) under the title: Political culture and political
stability in Argentina.
  Bibliography: p.
  Includes index.
  ISBN 0–8229–1156–6
  1. Argentina—Politics and government—1810– 2. Political
stability—Argentina—History. 3. Political culture—Argentina–
–History. I. Calvert, Peter. II. Title. III. Series.
  F2843.C27   1989
  306.2'0982—dc20   89–40048
                                              CIP

To S.U.C.M and L.J.M.

Contents

List of Plates

Foreword

This book is based on Susan Calvert's PhD thesis for the University of Southampton which was entitled 'Political culture and political stability in Argentina'. Research for the thesis was conducted entirely by her over many years while working full-time as a schoolteacher in Dorset. In re-writing and revising it for publication, both of us wish first of all to express much gratitude to many friends in Argentina who spent many hours telling us about their country and taking us around it, not to mention sending published material and other information over a period of eight years. Thanks are also due to Dorset County Council and to the Ford Foundation who at different times gave financial support that made this work possible, and to Frank Colson, Walter Little and Raymond Plant for their advice.

Broadstone, Dorset
1988

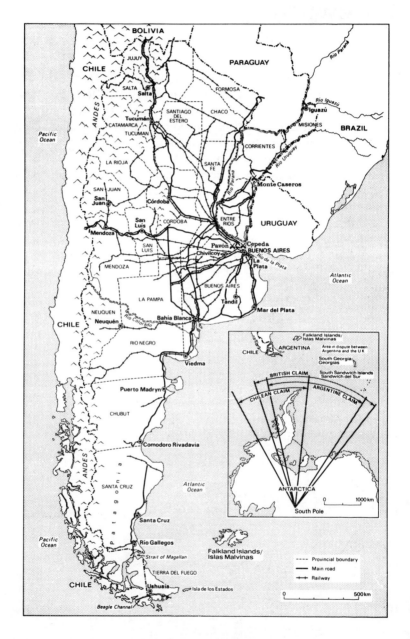

Map of Argentina

Chronology

ARGENTINA 1810 TO PRESENT

1810–29 Independence Era
1810 Provisional Junta
1811 First Triumvirate
1812 Second Triumvirate
1814 Directorate with series of Supreme Directors
1826 Presidency established by provincial representatives
1826–27 Bernardino Rivadavia
1827 Provinces reject new Constitution; President Rivadavia resigns

1829–52 Age of the Caudillos
1829 Juan Manuel de Rosas elected Governor of Buenos Aires
1831 Littoral Pact
1835 Rosas elected Governor with supreme and absolute power; result confirmed by plebiscite
1837–38 War with Peru–Bolivian confederation
1838–40 First Allied blockade of Buenos Aires
1845–48 Second Allied blockade
1852 Rosas defeated at Battle of Monte Caseros

1852–62 Post-Caudillo Instability
1853 1853 Constitution
1854 Presidency re-established; Buenos Aires independent
1854–60 Justo José de Urquiza
1859 Battle of Cepeda; Buenos Aires joins Confederation
1860–61 Santiago Derqui
1861 Battle of Pavón: forces of Buenos Aires defeat Confederation forces
1862 Provisional National Government

Generation of 1837

1862–68	Bartolomé Mitre
1865–70	War of the Triple Alliance with Paraguay
1868–74	Domingo Faustino Sarmiento
1874–80	Nicolás Avellaneda
1879–80	'Conquest of the Desert'

Generation of 1880

1880–86	Julio A. Roca: consolidation of oligarchy
1886–90	Miguel Juárez Celman
1890	Revolution defeated; Juárez Celman resigns
1890–92	Carlos Pelligrini
1892–95	Luis Sáenz Peña
1895–98	José Evaristo Uriburu
1898–1904	Julio A. Roca (second Presidency)
1904–06	Manuel Quintana
1906–10	José Figueroa Alcorta
1910–14	Roque Sáenz Peña
1912	The Sáenz Peña Law extends suffrage
1914–16	Victorino de la Plaza

1916–30 Radicalism in Power

1916–22	Hipólito Yrigoyen
1919	La Semana Trágica (Tragic Week)
1921	Argentina withdraws from League of Nations
1922–28	Marcelo T. de Alvear
1928–30	Hipólito Yrigoyen (second Presidency)
1930	Military coup

1930–43 The Infamous Decade

1930–32	José Felix Uriburu
1932–38	General Agustín P. Justo
1933	Argentina rejoins League
1938–42	Roberto M. Ortiz (powers delegated to Vice-President Castillo 1940–42)
1942–43	Ramón S. Castillo
1943	Military coups

1943–55 Rise of Perón/The Peronato

1943	General Arturo Rawson
1943–44	General Pedro P. Ramírez

1944	Break of diplomatic relations with Axis Powers
1944	Ramírez deposed
1944–46	General Edelmiro J. Farrell; Colonel Juan D. Perón, Vice-President
1945	Argentina declares war on Germany
1945	Perón arrested and forced to resign
1945	17 October: mass rally; recall of Perón
1946–52	Colonel Juan D. Perón
1949	New constitution
1952–55	General Juan D. Perón (second Presidency)
1952	Death of 'Evita' (María Eva Duarte de) Perón
1955	Military coup; return to 1853 Constitution

1955–58 Post-Peronist Demobilisation

1955	General Eduardo Lonardi (September–November)
1955	Lonardi deposed by anti-Peronist military elements
1955–58	General Pedro E. Aramburu
1956	Peronist revolt crushed

1958–66 Unstable Civilian Rule

1958–62	Arturo Frondizi
1962	Peronists win elections; Frondizi deposed
1962–63	José M. Guido; conflict between Colorados and Azules
1963–66	Dr Arturo Illia
1964	Perón's return from Madrid stopped in Brazil
1965–66	Peronists do well in elections
1966	Illia deposed; dissolution of Congress, etc.

1966–73 Military Rule: The Argentine Revolution

1966–70	General Juan Carlos Onganía
1969	The Cordobazo
1970	Kidnapping of General Aramburu
1970	(June) Admiral Pedro Gnavi
1970–71	General Roberto M. Levingston
1971–73	General Alejandro Lanusse

1973–76 Perón–Perón

1973	(May–July) Dr Héctor Cámpora
1973	(July–September) Dr Raúl Lastiri
1973–74	General Juan D. Perón (third Presidency)

1974   1 July: death of Juan D. Perón
1974–76 Isabel (María Estela Martínez de) Perón
1976   Military coup

1976–83 The Process of National Reorganisation
1976–81 General Jorge Videla
1978   The Beagle Channel crisis
1981   General Roberto Viola
1981   (November–December) Major-General Horacio Tomás Liendo
1981   (December) Vice-Admiral (ret.) Carlos Alberto Lacoste
1981–82 General Leopoldo Fortunato Galtieri
1982   Guerra de las Malvinas/Falklands War
1982   (June) General Alfredo Saint-Jean
1982–83 General Reynaldo Bignone

1983– Democratic Restoration
1983–89 Dr Raúl Alfonsín
1984   Referendum on the Beagle Channel dispute
1987   Easter Week Rising

1 Introduction

There has been general agreement amongst those writing about Argentina that her situation is unique and warrants special consideration. Argentina is seen as quite distinct from the rest of the Latin American countries. The possible exception, Uruguay, has usually been seen as too small to be effectively compared with her southern neighbour. The relatively early integration of Argentina into the world economy, her continued close relations with Europe, the wealth and immigrants she acquired through this trading relationship, the consequent growth of a large middle class and the higher level of development thus achieved, separate her from the other nations of South America. Likewise the strength of Argentine nationalism is unparalleled amongst the other republics of the region. This study therefore concentrates on Argentina and does not generally make comparisons with other Latin American states. But as Argentina is examined in the light of modern social science theory, it does note the comparisons made by other writers and by Argentines themselves with other countries of recent settlement.[1]

A similar consensus has been evident over Argentina's economic 'failure'. Again the comparisons on which this assumption of relative failure is based have not generally been made with other Latin American countries. Argentine expectations have been determined by contact with Europe, and economic comparisons were made with the level of development of Europe and/or North America and, more recently, with other countries of recent settlement which were formerly European colonies. Much work has already been done on economic factors, and the most prestigious and frequently cited explanations of Argentina's relative failure, especially those from Latin American academics writing in the 1960s and 1970s, stress economic factors, either alone as in the dependency model or in conjunction with the Iberian-derived corporatist tradition, as in bureaucratic-authoritarianism.[2] Whilst fully accepting the importance of such work, Argentine

1

academic interest in Australia, Canada etc., rather than in Chile or Brazil, is but one piece of evidence which suggests the need for a detailed examination of the Argentine cultural context.

Economic models of Argentine development have a great deal to offer, but the desire to preserve such models intact has tended to lead to unwarranted economic determinism and a reluctance to deal with the inevitable problems of applying ideological abstractions to specific instances. Weaknesses have been overlooked; hence models developed to replace ahistoric and unilinear modernisation theories exhibit similar features to those they replaced. Economic explanations cannot account for the enormous disparity in political development which characterises nations of the so-called 'periphery'. Nor in the Argentine case can the Revolution of 1930 – or for that matter the rise of Perón – be explained in solely economic terms. Many other writers, whether Argentine or not, have argued that Argentina's political disasters are not simple consequences of her economic history.[3] Her problems are cumulative and require a multidimensional explanation. There is no intention here to set aside economic explanations in favour of a simple cultural model. The view that people *act* as individuals and groups in accordance with perceptions of their world rooted in their experiences does not preclude the complementary idea that they *react* in accordance with their economic interests.

It has been argued that the *conventillos* (tenements) in late nineteenth-and early twentieth-century Buenos Aires synthesised gringo and *criollo* elements into a working class and that class struggle has been a permanent feature of Argentine politics since the 1890s.[4] Further, writing in the late 1960s, Torcuato di Tella suggested that Argentina was by then culturally and ethnically homogeneous, but divided by class.[5] However in conversation with the present authors in 1987, he emphasised the heterogeneous support bases and policies of the main political parties, as well as the unlikely coalitions they form, as evidence that contemporary Argentine politics could not be seen in simple class terms. The 1983 elections brought out the long-standing division between Peronism, as 'the people' confronting imperialism, and anti-Peronism, as liberty and democracy confronting demagogic dictatorship. Although possessing better 'leftist' credentials than his rival for the presidency, Alfonsín stressed the liberal rather than the welfare aspect of Radicalism, picking up the right-of-centre vote in the process. The nineteenth-century dichotomy of 'civilisation' against 'barbarism' was, quite deliberately, again presented to the electorate.[6]

It therefore seems appropriate to consider what Argentine culture offers to any explanation of political instability. Existing cultural models take a variety of forms. For some authors, democracy does not represent a foreign aspiration welded on to an indigenous reality in Spanish America. Rather, there is one single political tradition which has imported and adapted a European style, but which remains essentially Hispanic.[7] For others, the interaction of various historical forces, both indigenous and extra-national, generates the characteristic features of Latin American politics.[8] More specifically, the absorption of European democratic and political ideals has been held to constitute an obstacle to the 'institutionalisation and legitimacy of long-term dictatorial rule' in late industrialising nations such as Argentina.[9] The theme of cultural interaction, then, is fairly widespread, though by no means universally accepted. Nevertheless, it remains underdeveloped in much of the work that embraces it and tends to be rather simplistic. Moreover, there are three specific weaknesses in the various interpretations.

First there is the tendency to see non–Iberian (or, alternatively, non–Latin) influence as 'foreign' and something that may be dispensed with when Latin America again recognises and conforms to her 'true' identity.[10] In Argentina's case, this is unrealistic. Both Iberian American and non-Iberian European influences have become part of national reality. Secondly, there is the association of Iberian culture with tradition and the influence of non-Iberian Europe with modernity. Thirdly, there has been a tendency to build a rigid cultural framework seeing these two cultural legacies as distinct and separable.

The idea that traditional aspects of society resist modernity is widely held not only in studies of Argentina, but also in theoretical works concerned with governmental structures and styles.[11] For Martínez Estrada, the resistance of traditional culture is exemplified by Argentina. He sees the country otherwise as having all the necessary theoretical structures for the consolidation of a democratic state, which he equates with modernity.[12] The Hispanic/European distinction is not a simple division between traditional and modern elements. Both cultural aspects are traditions, but at the same time both have been reinforced, modified and modernised by historical experience and contact with each other. The Hispanic legacy was not transferred from the mother-country just to be retained in a cultural stasis. Nor can non-Iberian European culture be seen as consistently progressive, constantly promoting political and economic development. It has on occasion strengthened the 'regressive' elements of Iberian culture, as in the case of the impact of positivistic materialism on levels of corruption. It has also resisted potentially 'progressive' aspects of Iberian culture, as in the case of the proscription of Peronism after 1955. Peronism must be seen as displaying modern and rational aspects, not simply an emotive traditionalism, although it clearly exhibits features deriving from the Iberian legacy. Indeed regional variations in the nature of its support base after 1946 have exemplified the merging of Argentina's two cultural heritages.[13]

The dual-heritage theme in Argentina has to date been most explicit in the work of Milenky[14] and especially Sonego, though the former author is primarily concerned with foreign policy and does not develop the idea in the domestic context. Like Milenky, Sonego over-emphasises the distinctness of the traditions, recognising in them the existence of 'the two Argentinas'. He sees their alternation as the source of Argentine instability in a rather deterministic way, laying insufficient emphasis on their interaction with, and reinforcement of, each other and on the relevance of other non-cultural factors. His stress on the separable and distinctive nature of the two 'national designs' results in some odd assertions. For him, 1916 is seen as the rebirth of the *línea nacional*, whilst 1930 represents the restoration of the *línea liberal*.[15] In fact, the Radical victory in 1916 was the culmination of a crisis of participation, but it took an electoral form and Radicalism retained a liberal perspective. Nationalist rhetoric did not challenge the concrete benefits accruing from Argentina's export-oriented economy. Thus Radicalism, as with all movements and regimes, must be seen as a welding together of

Argentina's two cultures, though the form in which they coalesced was unique and destabilising. Similarly, Uriburu's coup, although an attempt to demobilise, set aside the institutional procedures established by nineteenth-century liberals. His brief presidency represents a struggle between the two cultures with the European or 'liberal' form only re-emerging with Justo's electoral victory in 1932. Even so, the ascendant Concordancia (conservative coalition) could not assume a simple non-Iberian form. The style during the Infamous Decade may have been 'liberal', but elections were won by fraud and the industrial capacity of Argentina was developed.

No culture is entirely consistent or internally coherent, and thus all are susceptible to modification. The broadly Hispanic culture of colonial society embraced conflicting elements: authoritarian and democratic, hierarchical and individualistic. The Church, too, combined medieval and Enlightenment thought. Values emphasising racial and cultural superiority, along with the loss of traditional authority in 1810, added to the vulnerability of Hispanic culture to non-Iberian European influence. But the impact of the European stream of culture operated on a pre-existing cultural base too strong to eliminate. Independence reinforced both aspects of culture and the rural/urban dichotomy emphasised and strengthened their ideological distinctions. The European tradition provided an institutional framework to replace that which had been lost, but those aspects which accorded with the Hispanic heritage were strengthened, thus reinforcing the alternative Iberian stream. The inevitable time-lag between adoption of institutions and absorption of the ideals on which they were founded resulted in a gap between theory and practice. So when these ideals were accepted, the institutions derived from them were not seen as fulfilling their proper functions. Other Iberian-derived features, such as strong kinship networks, were not only consolidated by the New World experience, but also reinforced by the impact of Europe. The position of notable families was enhanced by European culture, and such families embraced and benefited from the impact of one culture, but continued to derive influence and modes of behaviour from the other. The defensive function of kinship increased with urbanisation too. The affluence deriving from the trading relationship with Europe and the materialism brought by immigrants consolidated the sectoral structure and the zero-sum interpretation of economic and social power. The prestige of land-ownership may have been an Iberian trait, but it was operationalised by historical experience and especially by economic and cultural interaction with Europe. Similarly, other features such as disdain for manual labour, clientelism and an orientation to the past rather than to the future, were buttressed rather than eliminated.

Nevertheless, reinforcement of Hispanic culture was not the only result of the impact of European influence. If it had been, authors stressing one, primarily Iberian, cultural stream or those emphasising two distinct cultures would come closer to describing the situation. Modification and mixing of the two cultural patterns has occurred and continues to do so. Had the nineteenth-century dictator Juan Manuel de Rosas not bound together the nation, liberal centralism could not have gained the ascendancy in the way it did in the late nineteenth century. The liberal thinkers known as the 'Generation of 1837' had experienced the consequences of the failure of the liberalism of the immediate post-independence period. They knew well the practical weaknesses of the philosophy they espoused, and recognised the need to accommodate the Iberian legacy in the short term. These 'liberals' were the products of two cultures themselves and were willing to use methods derived from both streams of influence to retain their dominance and to pursue their ultimate goal of eliminating one culture in favour of the other. Liberalism, as absorbed by Domingo Faustino Sarmiento and his contemporaries, already had a positivistic orientation, initially stressing rationality and education. As such it was elitist and suggested limits on democracy at least in the short term, for fear of the return of 'barbarism' in the sense of mob rule. The impact of positivism changed over time, increasingly emphasising economic development, and the perception of mass participation as a threat strengthened amongst some sectors of the elite. Liberal constitutionalism placed weight on formal political procedure, but, as adopted and adapted, liberalism was used by elements not committed to participation. Liberal exclusion of the masses encouraged the development of the latent alternative political model. The weakness of institutions founded on a theoretical procedure which could and would be set aside when mass participation threatened dominant interests, led to the perpetuation and reinforcement of Hispanic-derived personalism. As with other Iberian features, the contradictions of liberalism led to the absorption by ostensibly liberal elements also of personalist politics.

Oligarchic fraud from 1880 onwards is an indication that liberal ideals were only partially absorbed. Its practice served to reduce the legitimacy of elections at the practical level. Liberal democratic procedure had been accepted as theoretically legitimate, but the continuance of democratic practice in the long term was seen as justifying its postponement in the short term. The conditional nature of the legitimacy of democracy in practice was both cause and effect of the continuation of an alternative political mode. The availability of other semi-legitimate methods did not necessitate unconditional ideological commitment to liberal-democratic political activity and, in addition, the lack of such commitment did not automatically stigmatise alternative methods. But at the same time, if support for European-derived political culture was conditional, so too was the possibility of employing Iberian-derived methods. Not only must those who use such means 'deliver the goods', i.e., satisfy in economic and political terms the various politically important sectors, they must also appear to embrace liberal-democratic procedures or at least the ideals behind them. Invoking the Constitution in justification of apparently unconstitutional succession is an instance of this, as has been the promise of elections after a crisis is dealt with, either after a specific period or at some unspecified future date. The consensus on the importance of elections is too great to ignore. Despite scepticism about government and high levels of political disinterest, voting remains an important indication that citizens are not alienated from the political system. The two great personalist leaders of the twentieth century, Hipólito Yrigoyen and Juan Domingo Perón, both depended on their capacity to generate electoral support. Indeed, the ability to mobilise votes is most often seen as a characteristic of the modern Latin American 'populist'. Although this emphasis on elections is conditional and therefore does not prevent the emergence of military regimes, it has contributed to their breakdown over time.

For Argentina, the dual heritage is pervasive. It is not that different sectors are socialised into one or other of the two cultures, although the operationalisation of alternative methods in political activity may in practice be class-related, since individuals are socialised to believe in one nation, but rather that they absorb often contradictory elements from the interlarding of both. This situation might be seen as providing a certain normative flexibility. When a means of resolving a problem fails another means is available. The fact that economic success and political stability have not resulted might therefore be thought to indicate that some powerful sectors have preferred frequent political change to a strong state. However, it is difficult to argue that any sector or sectors have consistently benefited from the paradox of Argentine instability. In practice the opposite seems to have been the case.

The dual heritage has not been functional. Polynormativeness has not promoted flexibility, but rather anomie. No clear identity has emerged to bind the nation together. The partial nature of each political culture results in the worst of both worlds. Argentina is confronted by 'political alternatives' in a form she has been unable to resolve or avoid.[16] The theoretical consensus on non-violent constitutional succession may be set aside in order to satisfy different interpretations of democracy, but, by definition, such a situation is a crisis measure which cannot endure. Indeed the availability of aspects of two cultures has historically made it possible deliberately to use one against the other, as with the enfranchisement of the *criollo* working class, who were seen as controllable, and their use against the aspirations of European immigrants. Further, the options available, even if not deliberately manipulated, keep alive and enhance the sectoral structure of society. The incapacity and/or unwillingness of either culture to eliminate the other and establish its own hegemony, results in a political system experiencing 'reciprocal interruptions'.[17] Worse still the impact of one culture may spur a cultural backlash from the other.

It has been suggested that the real enigma of Argentina is the question of why it forms one unity, when the different themes which make up her history do not suggest a synthesis.[18] Luna argues that such a synthesis is still lacking. Although for him it must be a welding together of civilisation and barbarism. The 'barbarous and elemental Argentina' of the nineteenth century has not disappeared, he says, but 'this current continues to flow on underground, in the most concealed [part] of popular hearts'.[19] Such a dramatic statement exaggerates the extent of separation between the two streams of culture which have from the outset been undergoing a process of homogenisation. In particular, immigration, internal migration and industrialisation must be seen as processes promoting a synthesis of the two Argentinas. Nevertheless, the entanglement of cultural features still enables a selective process which contributes to the lack of and/or distortion of those features which comprise the concept of political stability.

The absence of consensus on procedural means to achieve different substantive goals has promoted political violence. Although governments have not been as short-lived as in many other countries, the absence of agreement on succession procedure has resulted in the irregular termination of popularly elected governments. The latter have been few in number and their legitimacy circumscribed for certain powerful groups in Argentine society. Despite persistent aspects of the political system, profound structural changes have been attempted in accordance with different cultural perceptions: the integration of the working class by Perón, the subsequent demobilisation of organised labour by General Pedro Aramburu, the 'Process of National Reorganisation' by General Jorge Videla. Each provides an instance of government attempting to impose political reorganisation which in itself failed, but which reflected and subsequently accelerated the process of interlacing the features from the two cultural heritages. These two heritages continue to leave open a wide variety of responses to political and economic stimuli, a multiplicity of options for political action within the broadly nationalist capitalist ideological framework of modern Argentina.

These options affect three fundamental relationships, the relationships of government to the armed forces, the society and the nation, respectively. In relation to the military they permit 'temporary unconstitutionality', a succession process embracing coups *and* elections. They influence government

/societal relations in so far as *de facto* changes are accepted, government is seen as unpredictable, leaders are sometimes worshipped and sometimes despised and deep political cleavages remain. Most importantly, perhaps, in the light of the pervasive nationalism which characterises Argentina, the connection between government and nation is distorted. In Gramsci's terms, cultural hegemony is lacking. It is never clear what the national interest is, because the nation is not a clear concept and sectors/other subnational groupings are so important. Identifying themselves as separate groups, they develop their own perceptions of the nation and its situation; they lack a common history, apart from the initial act of independence and the common opposition to foreign incursion against Argentina's political sovereignty. Other people, be they outside or within the nation, may be classed together as enemies, and the extreme form of this perception is the destructive paranoia of the 'national security state'.

2 The Iberian Heritage and the Legacy of Catholicism

The modern political culture of Argentina, Kirkpatrick says, is a product of the nation's history.[1] For her, Argentina exhibits 'traditional Latin' politics, a term which she uses without clear definition to embrace such characteristics as oligarchy, democratic interludes punctuated by military coups, direct action and personalism. Lipset also emphasises that modern Latin American value systems are rooted in 'the institutions and norms of the Iberian nations' and were transferred during the colonial era.[2] As Latin America experienced the longest period of European colonisation of any area in the world, values stemming from the Iberian tradition were deeply internalised. The length of the colonial period is a factor for the persistence of its legacy, therefore, and may be seen as constituting an important explanation of the difference between the levels of European influence on Latin America and some emergent African nations. The extent to which the population was replaced by the colonisers also makes the Latin American experience unique. Burnett and Johnson write:

> ... the colonial period institutionalised modes of behavior and inculcated sets of attitudes that carried over into the republican era as barriers to reform and, consequently, as factors contributing to political instability.[3]

This view of Iberian features, as 'carried over' from the colonial era and comprising barriers to modernity, is simplistic and static, taking no account of the constant adaptation of cultural features in the light of historical experience and interaction with other influences. Nevertheless, Spanish American nations share too many features in common with each other and with Spain to ignore their common heritage. Some economic determinists argue that values were not transferred from Spain but that similar values developed in Spain and Spanish America. Authoritarianism, hierarchy,

11

fatalism and contempt for manual labour, they argue, favoured a dependent role in the international economic system.[4] To argue thus stretches the imagination somewhat and does not seem to accord with international comparisons of nations (notably the United States) with similar economic situations in the nineteenth century which had then very different cultural configurations and went on to develop in dissimilar ways.

The cultural legacy of the colonial period is partially derived from the purposes behind the Conquest of Latin America. The primary function of the Spanish colonies was to provide wealth for the Crown, though in addition they also served to spread Catholicism and to provide jobs for Spaniards abroad. Thus the importance of land was increased as it was won for the Crown and the process took on a moral aspect which was reinforced by the religious crusade. Christendom was seen as universal and Latin America as an unincorporated wilderness. Therefore the idea of conquest was that of spiritual incorporation.

The Spanish colonisation of Latin America took place at the end of the medieval period of religious wars and at the beginning of the expansion of Europe overseas. Many Spaniards had fought in the Renaissance wars in Italy and Spain had just reconquered the last of its territory from the Moors, and thus exported a crusading culture to its new conquest. In protecting and reclaiming their land from the infidel, the Spanish developed a strong sense of their racial superiority which they took with them to the Americas. As Hennessy notes:

> Victory against the Moors bred the conviction of righteousness and confirmed the Spaniards' view of themselves as God's chosen people with the right to reap an economic reward for doing His work.[5]

This victory also had the effect of reinforcing the Spanish class structure as it was the nobility who were seen to have defeated the Moors. Thus the defeat of the Moors established birth and race as the basis of social position, and the same ascriptive values passed into Latin American culture. The idea of racial superiority underlies both the nineteenth-century European cultural orientation and the later development of nationalism. More immediately, during the early colonial era, work came to be associated with the inferior races and this situation fed a strong contempt for manual labour. Moorish influence also contributed to the distinctness of Hispanic culture, which differed markedly from the traditions associated with the rest of Western Europe. Bunkley suggests that one important example of Islamic influence can be seen in the dominance of personal over objective values.[6] The strong individualism associated with the direct relationship between a man and Allah which developed in a nomadic culture, probably also influenced this aspect of the Hispanic tradition. Finally, the reconquest of Spain from the Moors contributed to the way in which violence in general and the military in particular came to be viewed. A culture which was itself a legacy of Roman imperial domination, and therefore with strong elements of discipline, order and military strength, came to be dominated by another displaying its most aggressive aspect, which could only be reconquered by force. Thus, as Hamill notes:

> The significance of the Reconquista, the eight centuries of intermittent border warfare between Moor and Christian (and just as frequently between Moor and Moor and Christian and Christian!) has been a favorite theme for historians. Military virtues, prowess at arms, and the psychology of the knight-errant were the lodestones of personal ambition.[7]

The example of the authority of the Spanish monarchy during the colonial period, despite its practical weaknesses, also contributed to the values which were to be inherited by the Latin American republics later. Personal absolutism, for example, was continued by *caudillos* (leaders of personal militias) such as Juan Facundo Quiroga, who brought eight provinces of Argentina under his domination until Juan Manuel de Rosas broke his power by superior force and unified the nation.[8] Writing in the late nineteenth century, Carlos Octavio Bunge pointed out that the Iberian absolutist heritage militated against the development of democratic attitudes and practices in the post-independence period.[9] The structure of political loyalties in colonial Latin America produced a problem of legitimacy in the post-colonial era. Individuals owed their loyalties directly to the person of the king, with no intervening hierarchy. Occasional uprisings occurred, but the absence of widespread revolt until 1808 when the king was removed from the throne, suggests that the authority of the king was not seriously questioned. Having developed no other legitimate institution, when the Spanish Crown was displaced, the source of legitimate authority was lost.

COLONIAL ADMINISTRATIVE STRUCTURES

The Spanish kings exhibited many of the features which Weber lists as characteristic of patrimonial rule, most notably the use of directive and the permitting of direct appeal to the Crown itself.[10] Under Spain, conflicts were mediated through the Crown and direct relationships between social and economic groups were therefore limited. Nor were problems considered in terms of the practicalities of solving them, but rather on the question of whether the king as moderating power would be supportive. Thus there did not develop a system of compromise between the interests and aspirations of such groups, as each could maintain its position intact and seek judgement from a final arbiter. The Crown became the 'source of all bounty'[11] and therefore provided a precedent for the fatalistic and statist attitudes which characterise Argentine politics. There remains a tendency to appeal direct to the executive in the expectation of material benefits.

The process of direct appeal to the king clearly weakened the administrative structure of the colonial era, as it enabled the formal hierarchy of power to be circumvented. Thus it contributed to the partial quality of the acceptance of law, obedience without compliance. From the thirteenth century to the fifteenth century, alongside the growth in the power of the monarchy, there had developed in Spain an emphasis on legal forms rather than legal purpose. Spanish law, with its roots in Roman law, was idealistic, in the sense that it sought to legislate problems out of existence; the mere act of ritualising an intention was supposed to resolve the problem. It was also universalistic in its application to the whole Empire disregarding the needs or unique conditions of particular areas. Jurists and theologians in Spain framed laws for colonies they had never visited. Moreno writes of this:

> The lack of correlation between what ought to be and what is, as reflected in the social and psychological patterns of the Roman–Spanish tradition, was transferred to the colonies. The geographic isolation of the new territories helped, if anything, to preserve the unreality of Spanish law.[12]

The isolation of the colonies, especially the River Plate area, added to the problem of formalism (i.e., law being enacted but not imposed). Violation was to be expected if Spain did not apply coercion to enforce the law, and Spain did not have the coercive power to apply in such a massive empire. After the risings of the 1780s, changes in the administrative structure, sometimes termed 'the second conquest', replaced civilian officials with both active and retired military personnel in an attempt to establish more effective local government in the colonies. The so-called 'Bourbon reforms' beginning in the mid-eighteenth century, were most strongly expressed in the establishment of intendancies. Eight of the twelve intendancies were created in the new Viceroyalty of the Río de la Plata in 1782. These relatively autonomous provincial administrators were supposed to ensure greater imperial control and more effective tax-gathering. Their introduction has been seen partly as a response to French Enlightenment ideas about administrative efficiency, but it was primarily a reaction to the military and economic pressure from non-Iberian Europe and the increased potential wealth of Hispanic America. Although theoretically a product of administrative rationalisation, the intendancies did not resolve and indeed actually reinforced many existing problems. Such reforms were limited by tradition and perpetuated Hispanic patronage, for example. They were most often simply changes in administrative style rather than institutions, and were thus insufficient. They came too late to contribute to the preservation of the Empire and were frequently misinterpreted or ignored anyway.[13] The formal structure of Spanish colonial administration included the *residencia*, a review of an official's work at the end of his term of office. Lambert argues that Spain did supervise her administrators and investigate complaints against them,[14] but *visitas* or inspections were probably very rare after the first period of conquest. Thus officials had a considerable degree of autonomy and were able to make decisions regarding whether or not to apply various pieces of often contradictory legislation. The failure of officials to implement all law contributed to the attitude that obedience to the law implied some sort of choice on the part of the colonial subject, and the failure to impose favourable decrees resulted in a tendency to blame officials rather than the system or the monarchy. A lack of respect for officialdom was thus generated.

The patrimonial ruler, according to Weber, retains power by means of tight control over his officials through such devices as limited tenure and not permitting the development of interests in their jurisdictions.[15] In a formal sense, despite the autonomy which distance from the centre of the Empire ensured, the Spanish monarchy operated in just such a way. Although the exclusion of *criollos* (those born in the Americas) from office was less marked in the River Plate region than in other parts of the Spanish Empire, peninsula-born Spaniards (*peninsulares*) dominated administrative offices and there was growing antagonism between the two groups from 1776 onwards. Spanish administrators often purchased their official positions (and also sold those within their gift), and were therefore frequently lacking in ability. They were allowed to remain in office only for relatively short periods, so that they could not build up a local support base which would make them less dependent on the Crown. As a result, such administrators did not become concerned with local matters and used their offices as a means to obtain wealth. The association of public office with personal gain was thus passed into the culture of the independent Latin American states.

Other cultural effects of the structure of colonial administration derive from the distinction drawn between *criollos* and peninsula-born Spaniards. *Criollo* resentment grew into hostility to the Spanish and thus laid a foundation for a more generalised xenophobia. It also provides an early source of a political zero-sum model, which is to gain importance later, in that the *criollos* came to see themselves as excluded as a direct result of the privileges accorded to the *peninsulares*. The dominance of *peninsulares* ensured the dominance of Iberian, especially Castilian, values and attitudes, However, the most obvious and direct consequence of the colonial administrative structure and functioning was the development of unworkable laws and formalistic attitudes which encouraged evasion and corruption.

Despite values operating against full compliance with the law, the Spanish Empire was essentially stable for a very long period; there was little evidence of tension within it. This apparent acceptance by its subjects of the imperial system leads Moreno to describe the Spanish monarchy as 'authoritistic' rather than 'authoritarian', because the latter term implies illegitimacy whilst the absolute powers of the Spanish Crown were accepted and seen as fully legitimate in this sense. He goes on to suggest that the legitimacy of Spanish absolutism indicates an inclination in imperial subjects towards absolutist and monistic arrangements. A culture had been transferred from Spain which was receptive to political organisation in accord with the tradition of strong paternalistic authority. The Spanish Empire was stable because the political system coincided with the inclinations of the ruled.[16]

The tendency to authoritarian domination was not destroyed when independence came to Latin America. The *criollos* who sought independence were comparatively few in number, and geographically concentrated. They did so, not because they wanted fundamental political change and a movement away from authoritarian government, but because, amongst other factors, they wished to supplant peninsula-born Spaniards in the most prestigious and lucrative governmental positions. Whilst the defeat of the British in 1806 and 1807 no doubt boosted the confidence of the *porteño* (Buenos Aires) elite that Spain could be beaten, the real impetus to revolution was the declining position of the colonial power. The immediate trigger to the independence struggle was the Napoleonic occupation of Portugal and much of Spain in 1807–8. Along with the seizure of the centre of the Empire went the capture of Ferdinand VII and thus the removal of the symbol of legitimate authority. The *estancieros* (landowners), to whom the Viceroy surrendered power on 25 May 1810, initially intended to rule on behalf of the Crown until such time as legitimate authority was restored.

A relatively small, comparatively weak and disunited

'revolutionary' *criollo* group therefore assumed control. Such independence movements were conservative in many respects, and the basic structure of society remained intact. Independence changed the personnel of government, though not the class structure or the role of the Church, for example. Thus many aspects of the colonial legacy survived. In particular the retention and, more importantly, the adaptation of traditional value systems contrast with the situation in recently emergent African nations where modernising mass movements have often been a feature of the independence struggle.

Even during the military struggle against the colonial power, the 'unity' of the *criollo* forces was strained, and conflicts flared between those from the areas of modern Paraguay and Argentina. With victory, the only binding force, a common enemy, disappeared and centrifugal forces became overt. The geographical weakness of the independent area was indicated in the secession of Paraguay in 1811 and the liberation movement led by General José Gervasio Artigas in the Banda Oriental (now Uruguay). More important still for the political stability of modern Argentina were the internal divisions the new state faced. These fissiparous tendencies showed themselves specifically in such occurrences as the fall of the First Triumvirate in 1812 as a result of Hispanic loyalist opposition and the declaration of an independent republic in Tucumán under Bernabé Araoz in the early 1820s,[17] and more generally in the period of *caudillismo* which followed independence. The nebulous quality of the nation left the need for affiliation which was met through fixing loyalties on individuals, and the failure of any national sense to override the parochial interest of the interior masses made them available for mobilisation by *caudillos* espousing local autonomy.

It is frequently argued that the legacy of Iberian domination and the wars of independence included the establishment of militarist attitudes in Latin American culture which have served to promote political instability.[18] Although it should not be suggested that modern militarism exhibits a direct antecedence in the 'militarism' of the colonial period, a form qualitatively different from that of the modern era, Hispanic values such as hierarchy, order and authority would prove to be conducive to militarism later.

The size of the Spanish Empire precluded the Crown's regular contact with all areas under its jurisdiction and therefore made defence impossible. Local militias were encouraged by Spain after 1762–64 when the British had occupied Havana, but they also reflected local interests. (For example, in 1752 the *cabildo abierto* (town meeting) of Buenos Aires met to establish a permanent rural militia as protection against Indian attacks.[19]) This led to the autonomous growth and development of private armies for protection, and thus control of rural areas such as the Argentine pampas rested with *caudillos* who, throughout the colonial period, were able to strengthen their domination of their localities. Such militias were developed in a very advantageous phase, when the Church as an institution had been weakened by the Crown and the Crown was about to be reduced in strength by Napoleon. The need for protection from the rich and strong contributed to the development of patrón–client relationships which would spread after independence. There being few other opportunities for advancement available to the most able and educated *criollos*, these militias established an association of leadership and the military which was consolidated during the independence struggle.

However, Spain did not militarise the American colonies. Armies served the king, and only after independence did militarism develop. It has therefore been argued that militarism was a product, a 'cultural residue', of the wars of independence and the internal conflicts that followed them.[20] The relationship between the wars of independence and the development of militarism is more complex than this implies though, as the subsequent extent of civil disorder was out of all proportion to the length and intensity of the independence struggle in many Latin American states. But the important consequence of the independence wars for Latin American militarism was the development of a concept of freedom won through military victory, to which the armed forces of the republics could later appeal in their quest for legitimacy for their political roles.

Besides the Iberian heritage should not be seen as monolithic. Both forces of progress and regression were inherent in it from the time of the Conquest. For example, there is an obvious area of contradiction in the purposes of colonisation, between the proselytising mission of Spain and colonial exploitation. This duality reflects the contradictory elements within fifteenth-century Spain, the military aspect of the Reconquista and the growing commercial importance of the towns. More importantly changes within Spain even during the colonial period caused local changes in the relative strength of aspects of the 'dual heritage'[21] which Spanish America had from Aragon and Castile, as well as modifications to the cultural legacy as a whole. The authoritarianism of the sixteenth and seventeenth centuries, the era of the Habsburgs, gave way to the 'enlightened despotism'[22] of the Bourbons in the eighteenth century. Enlightenment thought and the more liberal policies of the Bourbons did not change the underlying cultural legacy in the established areas of settlement such as the interior provinces of Argentina, but they were influential in the rapid late eighteenth-century development of Buenos Aires. Thus *porteño* culture acquired a more liberal streak which was to provide an impetus to independence, but was also to mark the cultural aspect of the cleavage which was to dominate the post-colonial period, the split between Buenos Aires and the interior provinces.

THE CONTRAST WITH NORTH AMERICA

It is difficult to see the Rosas era as simple protectionism, amounting to an attempted national capitalist developmentalist phase which failed. This view is implicit in the work of André Gunder Frank[23] and often explicit in the writings of Argentine authors of the left,[24] but nevertheless the nineteenth century marks the period in which North America forged ahead economically. Whilst the Unitarian–Federalist conflict was to waste much of the nineteenth century during which Argentina could have been developing economically, the Iberian cultural heritage was also a factor for the comparative economic failure of Latin America as against the colonies of North America. Until the eighteenth century, the Americas were dominated by the Iberian peninsula, not by Britain, which had, at that stage, colonised only the coastal regions of part of North America. Thus Latin America had a head start, and at independence Spanish America had some apparent advantages over the United States, at least in terms of impressive mineral resources, rich lands, greater wealth amongst the elite and more extensive colonial bureaucratic organisation. Argentina, in particular, and the United States share many common early experiences, but the Spanish legacy to the colonies was much more problematic than the British legacy to North America.

When the British colonised North America, northern Europe had been through and had already emerged from the feudal period. Spanish colonisation on the other hand occurred more than a century earlier and was, in any case, the product of an imperial power itself retarded by the struggle against Islam. Spain was still essentially medieval and the colonies founded in the New World were 'closed, corporate, elitist, authoritarian-absolutist, rigidly hierarchical, and premodern'.[25] The later settlement of North America took advantage of the changed global situation, especially in matters of trade, and in consequence the colonies of the north were less isolated from the outset.

The precepts guiding the Spanish Conquest did not contribute to development as those of the British settlement of North America did. The emphasis on plunder rather than settlement gave Spanish colonial society 'a character which lacked both the sentiment of equality and a respect for industry'.[26] The theme of assault upon and exploitation of an alien environment has continued to permeate Argentine politics, as has the impermanent orientation the *conquistadores* brought with them. The impetus of colonisation being the negative one of pillage, albeit for the greater glory of the Spanish Crown, rather than the positive one of permanent settlement, the Spanish colonies did not attract reforming, dynamic elements devoted to the establishment of new states as was the case in North America. The early and rapid colonisation process, along with the disposition to take advantage of the availability of indigenous populations which could be subjugated and employed, set limits on the extent of early European settlement in the Spanish colonies and encouraged the growth of large estates. Argentina was at the tail-end of Spanish colonial expansion. Her geographical isolation attracted few settlers in the colonial period. They tended to be of lower ascribed social status than those who were drawn to Mexico or Peru but they still sought a proprietorial role. North American settlers, in contrast, made the journey across the Atlantic with the intention of working their lands themselves and having a permanent stake in the future of a new area. This is not to say that these motives were the only ones which drove the North American colonists, and certainly cultural conflict did exist. However, the motivations of the settlers in New England were of this kind; the Civil War expressed, but effectively eliminated as a threat to stability, the cultural challenge of the Southern plantation owners. The different purposes of colonisation therefore produced different cultural patterns.[27]

The position of the respective colonial powers in the world order during the period of colonisation was also influential in determining their cultural patterns. Leopoldo Zea suggests that Anglo-Saxon America was an outgrowth of the victorious European culture which opposed and defeated the Hispanic culture from which Latin American culture was derived. Thus Hispanic America remains in conflict with the forces of 'modernity' which find cultural empathy in North America.[28] Whilst Spain led the process of European colonisation of the New World, Spanish literature and political thought acknowledged that other nations had overtaken her and that Spain was effectively in decline as a European power.[29] The Bourbon reforms were attempts to bring the Hispanic tradition more into line with the rest of Western Europe. However, they did not alleviate the sense of cultural failure and in some ways actually spurred the impetus to independence.

The Spanish colonies were also heirs to a 'rigid, unyielding' social structure[30] based on ascriptive factors and strengthened by the social positions of those who took part in the Conquest. The highest social stratum did not go to America and neither did they allow their estate workers to be recruited. Rather the Conquest was led by marginal aristocratic elements especially the younger sons of the upper classes. As a result, upper-class values and aspirations were transferred to the Spanish colonies in the form of 'a superior–inferior psychology which was not conducive to the development of political democracy.'[31] This social structure was reinforced throughout the colonial period by the establishment of a peninsular elite given *fueros* (privileges) in the form of tax exemptions, for example, and often seen as exhibiting their superiority through conspicuous consumption and contempt for the lower orders. A totally different social structure, 'more open, multiclass',[32] was established as a consequence of the different purposes behind the settlement of North America. Many English emigrants sought new opportunities and greater freedom in a system less elitist than the one they had left. These colonial structural dissimilarities were reflected in the different characteristics of the independence movements. The independence revolution in North America began with the people, whilst those of the Spanish colonies began with 'the civil protestations of an educated, well-placed elite'.[33]

The Spaniards sought to establish in the New World an extension of the Iberian peninsula, whilst the Anglo-American settlers were imbued with a sense of building something new. Thus an orientation to change was the legacy of the North American colonial era, whilst Iberian values involving 'hierarchy and order and absolutes' resisted social mobility, freedom and compromise in the Spanish colonies.[34] The *conquistadores* wanted to be *caballeros* (gentlemen) in a new Spanish nation and they created a 'rural and hierarchical' society.[35] Although geographical differences produced a plantation structure and alternative values amongst those who settled the southern areas of North America, the ethos of the dignity of work gave rise to the more egalitarian homesteading tradition of New England which spread to the Frontier and the American West.

Whilst the British colonies in North America moved from constitutional monarchy to republicanism, the Spanish colonies held to an absolutist tradition. Spain did not concede independence as Britain did to the United States and thus there was no legacy of goodwill. The liberated colonies could not expect such assistance from the mother-country as peaceably liberated colonies in the twentieth century have experienced. Even had Spain been inclined to assist her former imperial possessions, which she was not, long reliance on the fugitive riches of the colonial mines had made her weak and dependent by the beginning of the nineteenth century, whereas Britain, with a strong agricultural and rising industrial base, was wealthy and powerful and could offer financial help as well as a trading relationship to the new North American republic.

'Catholic hegemony and absolutism' was the legacy of Spain.[36] The extension of the Inquisition to Spanish America in the 1570s was expressive of a tradition opposed to the religious tolerance sought in some of the British colonies, for example, Maryland and Rhode Island. Religion was an important aspect of the cultural legacy in both areas, but the colonisation of Latin America was a religious crusade whilst the tradition amongst many North American colonists was one of non-conformity. The Anglo-American settlers were dissenters seeking refuge from intolerance, and thus the religious tradition remaining after independence was 'Protestant-pluralist'.[37]

THE CHURCH AND THE LEGACY OF CATHOLICISM

The bond between the Church and the Spanish monarchy preceded the Conquest and was exemplified in the long struggle to re-establish political and religious hegemony in the Iberian peninsula during the conflict with the Moors. Religious leaders had led armies against the Moors and monasteries had been turned into fortresses. The 1501 and 1508 Papal Bulls legalised Ferdinand's authority over the Church and conceded the *patronato real*, the right of the Crown to nominate to sees and benefices. Consequently the association of political and religious domination existed in pre-Conquest Spain. The military conquest of Latin America was therefore followed closely by the establishment of Church outposts, and Paraguay and, as its name suggests, what is now the Argentine Province of Misiones were both settled by Jesuit missions during the sixteenth and seventeenth centuries.

The colonial era was characterised by the binding of Church to state. In addition to establishing the political autocracy of the Crown in Latin America, the Habsburg period consolidated the spiritual authority of the Church. The monarchy and the Church were mutually reinforcing in that both were highly centralised and absolutist structures with strict, non-elective hierarchies and both required obedience from the population. The Church dominated the intellectual life of the colonies and thus the authority of the clergy was ensured by the religious and cultural gap between them and the people.[38] As well as these rather abstract supports the Church offered the monarchy, it also provided the more concrete benefit of supplying many colonial officials. Nearly all social services were the prerogative of the Church. Through close cooperation with the colonial authorities, the Church grew wealthy and powerful in Latin America as a whole, though in the Río de la Plata, unlike Mexico or Peru, its political influence exceeded its economic power in that the Church did not succeed in acquiring large tracts of land.

However, the Church was not monolithic, either in its influence over the colonial population or in its institutional unity. As Vallier points out, by the seventeenth century shortages of clergy and the gap between the Church hierarchy and the people meant that its failure to serve the needs of the mass of the population was becoming apparent. A clear schism developed between Catholicism in general and the Church in the Americas.[39] Although hierarchical in structure, lines of authority within the early Church were not always clear, communication channels were blocked, long-term planning and coordination were often weak, and internal divisions grew which prevented the dissemination of clear religious guidelines.

When independence movements became influential in Latin America, the threatened loss of the protection the Church had enjoyed under the Spanish monarchy, and fear that the greater freedom sought through independence would include more religious choice, led the Church hierarchy to resist the change. Some of the lower clerical orders were *criollos* from humble origins denied access to the higher Church appointments which were reserved for *peninsulares*, and they favoured independence. The wars of independence therefore saw the Church in the worst possible position; it was split, but would be damaged by the association of its hierarchy with the losing side. The subsequent weakness of the Church encouraged the growth of anti-clericalism.

The post-independence leaders of Argentina were not opposed to religion as such but wanted Church influence in secular matters reduced. Both the 1819 and 1826 Constitutions made Roman Catholicism the state religion and guaranteed the Church representation in the Senate. Nevertheless, Argentina was one of the first Latin American nations to take over social welfare from the Church. For example, President Bernardino Rivadavia (1826–27) confiscated the properties of some Church organisations involved in social welfare for not doing enough, and established La Sociedad de Beneficencia to control social welfare agencies such as hospitals and orphanages.[40]

The Church remained much more influential in areas of Indian settlement, colonised earlier when the crusading spirit of the Conquest was at its height, and thus was more important in the interior tradition than in the secular, commercial orientation of Buenos Aires. In addition, the Church was hardly likely to favour the establishment of a strong centralised state under liberal influence, and hence essentially anti-clerical, which would be powerful enough to counteract its influence. The great *caudillos* had, in any case, deemed it prudent to proclaim their allegiance to the Church despite the notable absence of religiosity amongst their followers. Indeed the Federalist forces adopted the rallying cry 'Religion or Death!' ('Religión o Muerte'). Thus the Federalist cause received the support of the Church and by 1852 Rosas' portrait was on all altars.[41] Rosas was not ungrateful and appropriated money to fund the building and restoration of churches, whilst closing schools ostensibly for reasons of financial stringency. He also ordered that theses must be presented in Latin not Spanish and thereby ensured that only theologians would receive degrees and Church authority would be maintained through the educational superiority of the clergy. Rosas' clericalism was not uncritical, however, and he did issue decrees to suspend, dismiss or imprison priests for immoral conduct. Similarly, after his initial encouragement of the religious activities of Jesuits, he expelled them in 1843 for apparently conspiring with his political enemies.

The long struggle between the forces of 'traditionalism', exemplified by Rosas' and liberal elements, led to considerable erosion of Iberian clericalism after the defeat of Rosas. Liberal leaders such as Juan Bautista Alberdi and Sarmiento emphasised the importance of religion, and the 1853 Constitution confirmed Roman Catholicism as the state religion and required the president to be a Roman Catholic.

However, the president was given powers of patronage over Church appointments and some control over the publication of Papal directives and expositions of doctrine. On balance, the new constitutional framework was considerably more secularised than that of Spain, but Church–state relations remained fairly peaceful until the first presidency of Julio A. Roca (1880–86), whose personal relations with the Church were turbulent to say the least, the president quite deliberately not attending Easter services in 1885.[42] While anti-clericalism was further encouraged by the influx of positivist ideas, the European-oriented forces of liberalism sought greater religious toleration in order to attract immigrants, and greater intellectual freedom after the years of persecution and exile that they had experienced under Rosas and the *caudillos*. Nevertheless, the Church reflected elite values and also helped to create them, so the conflict was limited. Church property was less of an issue in Argentina than in many other parts of Latin America, since the Church held less land and much new land was being won from the Indians. The limited struggle against the Church in Argentina (and also in Chile) has been seen as resulting in the more complete adoption of a more modern form of liberalism than was the case in areas such as Mexico.[43]

Roca's abolition of religious instruction in schools and effective establishment of secular state education in 1884, was followed by President Miguel Juárez Celman's introduction of the legal requirement of civil marriage. Naturally the Church, in the wake of the First Vatican Council, took steps to combat encroachments on its influence, especially the 1884 law, and this led to the setting up of the first Roman Catholic political party in Argentina, the Unión Católica. Many members of the Unión Católica left to join the newly formed Unión Cívica in 1890, but a split between the Church hierarchy and the politically active middle-class membership developed during the decade following. The decline of governmental anti-clericalism in the 1890s allowed the development of a new tacit alliance between the Church hierarchy and the ruling Oligarchy. Although the Church did not participate overtly in politics (and indeed was not to do so again until 1930), it offered no support to the growing political demands of the emergent middle classes and thus inspired later middle-class resistance to a secular Church role. Despite the tentative alliance of Church and state after 1890, the legacy of the 1880s is important to later political instability in that, since Roca's first administration, militant Catholic nationalists have seen liberalism as synonymous with anti-clericalism.[44]

Unlike other areas of Latin America where bitter conflicts often characterised the nineteenth-century relationship between Church and state, Argentina experienced relatively amicable settlements of disputes between the religious and secular authorities which postponed rather than resolved the question of the role of the Church. In the twentieth century more bitter conflicts were to emerge and to contribute to unconstitutional regime changes. The reduction of the influence of the Church as a consequence of late nineteenth-century anti-clericalism and the growth of other functional interests demanding access to social and political power left the Church weakened but still seeking a secular role. Argentine anti-clericalism has consistently taken a moderate form, trying to limit the role of the Church without reducing the importance of religion. The late nineteenth and early twentieth century saw anti-clericalism at its most radical due to the growing number of mainly Italian and Spanish immigrants who remained outside the formal Church. Many of them had been radicalised by the early anarchist movements in Europe and brought with them the ideological norms of secularism. Anti-clerical laws were passed, but often not enforced, which led to the strengthening of the process of secularisation, but at the same time did not contain a growing Catholic reaction. The latter trend produced closer bonds between Catholicism and nationalism and thus led to closer relations between religion and politics.

Despite the process of secularisation, which reduced the active Roman Catholic population to 10–15 per cent by the early twentieth century, and the anti-clericalism of the Unión Cívica Radical, relations between Church and state remained peaceful until well into the 1920s. Yrigoyen, during his first presidency (1916–22), did not move against the Church, indeed he resisted the 1922 proposals from his party to legalise divorce. But, in spite of government tolerance and the work of progressive elements within the Church in the 1920s, the growth of right-wing Catholic nationalism was proceeding apace. The domination of the right-wing was possibly shown in 1923 when the Marcelo T. de Alvear government nominated a progressive as Archbishop of Buenos Aires. The Vatican rejected the nomination. The following year, the same nomination was made and again rejected. It has been suggested that the Vatican rejections were a response to the right-wing Catholic nationalist protests.[45] During the 1920s, the Catholic labour union movement was formed and the Church took on a more active pastoral role. The Church hierarchy began to change its apolitical stance, becoming more sympathetic to nationalism. Some priests began to favour an alliance of the old 'cross and sword' kind between the army and the Church in order to attack the growing 'evils' of religious tolerance, democracy, North American materialism, Judaism and communism. Catholic nationalists saw the emerging secular nationalist groups as a means of stemming the tide of liberalism, which was still strongly associated with anti-clericalism. Thus the Church hierarchy and Catholic nationalist elements welcomed the 1930 revolution, General José F. Uriburu's strong pro-Catholic attitudes and his opposition to liberal democracy.

The period of the so-called Infamous Decade (Década Infame, actually thirteen years 1930–43) was marked by the Church's continued attempts to extend its pastoral role. The primary organisation through which this was attempted was Acción Católica (Catholic Action), which published the strongly nationalist newspaper *Criterio*, established as an 'adjunct' to the Church hierarchy.[46] Most important lay Catholics joined Catholic Action, which was in some respects a reformist group, but one which retained a traditional hierarchical and elitist structure which reduced its potential impact. Throughout the 1930s the political elements amongst the Catholic clergy were divided. The right-wing nationalist element comprised the vociferous majority, despite the official denunciation of fascism and totalitarian regimes. Nevertheless, a left wing did exist, though clearer demarcation of the two groups would not occur until the period of Perón (Peronato).[47] Relations between the army and the Church remained cordial during the 1930s, the governments of the Concordancia (1932–43) were sympathetic to the Church without wishing to increase Church power. Legalisation of divorce

was successfully resisted and the Church sought unsuccess-
fully to re-establish religious instruction in schools. The only
really anti-clerical political party was the Socialist Party which
had little power. Catholic nationalist elements resented the
increasing liberalism of the Roberto M. Ortiz administration
(1938–40 in practice, though Ortiz did not resign till 1942),
and tended to withdraw from politics until the events of 1943
brought them back.

With the 1943 revolution, the position of the Church in
politics re-emerged as a political issue. Catholic nationalist
support for the anti-liberalism of the Grupo de Oficiales
Unidos (GOU) regime was clearly expressed through *Criterio*
and other publications, though the hierarchy stressed Church
neutrality. Moreover, the GOU was anxious to extend
its support amongst the Church hierarchy and religious
affairs became more important. In December 1943, religious
instruction again became compulsory in state schools and
this measure has often been seen as winning the support
of the Church for the GOU and for Perón. In reality, the
pastoral letter instructing Roman Catholics not to vote in
the February 1946 elections for coalitions containing political
parties favouring the abolition of religious education merely
reiterated advice routinely included in such letters, but it
nevertheless may have been a factor in Perón's narrow victory
despite the support of the Catholic press generally for the
Unión Democrática.[48] Although fear of the growing influence
of the working class caused many Catholic nationalists to
begin to oppose Perón soon after his election, he continued to
woo the Church as an institution by granting it privileges such
as the appointment of religious advisers to some government
agencies and allowing religious processions in Buenos Aires.
More importantly, Perón controlled a labour movement which
was not anticlerical in the way that it had been prior to his
coming to power.[49] Not that the Church was by any means
united in its support of Perón. The hierarchy remained
officially independent and neutral; it had always had internal
divisions and within it there were elements for and against the
reforms he imposed.

Liberal Catholics, unlike Catholic nationalists and the
Church hierarchy, had been opposed to Perón from the
outset. Church opposition increased during the second Perón

government and was expressed in allegations concerning Perón's 'friendship' with Nelida Rivas and his possible activities with nubile young members of the Union of Secondary School Students as well as through opposition to the presentation of his late second wife, Evita, as a saint. This opposition was exacerbated by Perón's actions during the early 1950s which appeared as deliberate attempts to antagonise the Catholic Church. Snow suggests that the Church initiated the anti-clerical reaction of the Peronist government by moving into the opposition as early as 1951 in response to the teaching of Peronism as part of religious instruction in Argentine schools.[50] Whitaker sees the Church's refusal to canonise Evita as the initial provocation,[51] although he must be aware of the fifty years which must pass after death prior to canonisation. Alexander argues that Perón's actions were a response to attempts to form a Christian Democratic Party.[52] It has even been suggested that Perón was greatly influenced by Masonic elements, most notably the infamous Licio Gelli, the founder of the lodge Propaganda Due (P2).[53] It seems more likely that Perón was reacting to Church activity amongst 'his' labour movement, which he saw as a threat to the more secure of his two pillars of support. Certainly, he emphasised in 1954 that he had no quarrel with the Roman Catholic Church itself, only with those elements within it which had infiltrated labour organisations and which sought to undermine Peronist influence.[54] Whatever the reason, by 1954 the Peronist government's opposition to the Church was clear and a series of anti-clerical decrees began. In 1954 and 1955 prostitution and divorce were both legalised, religious instruction in state schools was discontinued and Congress passed legislation authorising arrangements to disestablish the Church including the procedure for a plebiscite to set up a Constituent Assembly with power to make the necessary constitutional amendments. A religious meeting held in June 1955 turned into a demonstration against the government and two leading churchmen (one a bishop) were expelled from Argentina.

The Church therefore supported the revolution against Perón in September 1955. Catholic nationalists dominated General Eduardo Lonardi's new cabinet, but contributed in turn to his ouster, as the extent of his clericalism proved unpopular with other military factions. Despite such military opposition, Church status was in general enhanced after 1955. Though some of the clergy had welcomed the social welfare benefits of Peronism, there was little Church resistance to their erosion in the post-Perón period and thus Church–state relations remained cordial.

Fresh attempts to organise a Catholic party began in the last years of the Peronato with a view to fighting the expected 1957 elections. The Partido Demócrata Cristiana (PDC) was founded in 1955–6, and Catholic nationalist elements began forming short-lived and largely uninfluential parties in response to Lonardi's replacement. The PDC averaged only 5 per cent of the popular vote in the period 1957–65 and this vote came mainly from upper-class and upper-middle-class districts, a characteristic the party retains today.[55] Whether because of the need to extend its working-class base for electoral reasons or because theological thought was becoming more concerned with the social and political demands of the masses, a trend reflected in the appearance of the first worker-priest in Argentina in 1960,[56] the PDC underwent a shift in its political position and was clearly more sympathetic to Peronism by the 1962 elections. By 1963, both Christian Democratic and Christian syndicalist groups had been radicalised and sought alliances with Peronist elements. The change to proportional representation in the 1963 elections assisted the election of several PDC Deputies who voted with the Peronist bloc more often than with the Radicals.[57] Indeed, Christian Democratic/Peronist coopera-tion has continued, exemplified in the electoral front the parties formed in the Province of Buenos Aires for the September 1987 elections.

At the same time that the Catholic Left was emerging, other religious elements were behaving in a very different way. Despite the July 1962 pastoral letter pleading for government action to alleviate the poverty of the masses, the Church hierarchy largely supported the continuing political exclusion of the working class and even lent overt support to federal government interventions in areas which had experienced Peronist victories in the municipal elections.[58] In that same year, right-wing Catholic nationalists founded a new political organisation, Ateneo de la República, which was militantly anti-communist. The 1966 coup was welcomed by both the Church hierarchy, some of whom took up important government positions, and the Catholic nationalists, the most militant of whom came to dominate Onganía's ministerial team.

Thus the Church as an institution tended to be politically conservative until the early 1960s, but then, whilst most of the hierarchy remained so, other elements became radicalised under the influence of the Second Vatican Council in 1962. This process was accelerated by the 1966 coup, which brought denunciations from the radical priests who used Vatican II to give their condemnations of Onganía a quasi-official appearance, and the 1966–70 period was marked by increasing Church conflict.[59] Not only were Catholic political elements split into right and left wings by the end of the 1960s, but these subsections were also divided amongst themselves. The Catholic Left was generally characterised by its connections with Peronism, but it ranged from moderate factions to extremists groups associated with the Montoneros, the main left-wing Peronist guerrilla faction. Right-wing Catholic nationalism was mainly of the old cross-and-sword type and traditionally anti-liberal democracy; but other groups such as Ateneo de la República were less extreme in this respect, having absorbed political thought derived from the influence of non-Iberian Europe. By the early 1970s, many Church elements were looking for a restoration of democratic politics.

The Church leadership, though generally conservative, showed some incohesiveness in this period with some members supporting radical priests, and it was in any case seriously weakened by divisions amongst Catholic political groups. The 1972 alliance with Peronism included only the 10 per cent or so of the clergy who made up the Argentine Movement of Priests for the Third World, which had been established in Córdoba in May 1968.[60] The divisions within the Church remained when this latter group declined as Peronism veered to the right. Thus much of the hierarchy welcomed the 1976 coup as a potentially binding force on the Argentine Church, but nevertheless sought apolitical status. The Church was again drawn into politics by Videla's appointment of prominent lay Catholics to his combined Ministry of Religion and Foreign Relations, which lent religious support to his conservative foreign policy.[61] The government also demanded Church support in its fight against communism, but such support remained ambivalent, violations of individual rights having prompted criticism in the pastoral letters of some of the bishops of Chile, Brazil and Argentina, until the Falklands conflict provoked the Church to subscribe openly to government policy, which had adopted a nationalist position appealing to the Iberian-derived tradition of the Church. Since 1982 criticisms of the Argentine Church have centred on its separation from the broad mass of Argentine Catholics, the closeness of much of the hierarchy to senior military elements during the 1976–83 regime and its reluctance to speak out against abuse of human rights by the military even when those being abused were priests of the Church.[62]

Although accusations concerning the role of the Church during the 1976–83 military regime have abounded and specific allegations against individual churchmen (most notably the late Archbishop of La Plata, Antonio Plaza) have recurred in the trials of military men concerned with the elimination of subversion, proposals to disestablish the Church were not taken up with the restoration of civilian government. However the Church's lack of contrition over its past political role, its attacks on the Alfonsín government since 1983 and its threat to refuse communion to Deputies who voted for the 1986 divorce bill (which was finally passed in June 1987 despite continued opposition from Christian Democrat and Orthodox Peronist congressmen), have led presidential advisers to recommend the disestablishment of the Church as an imperative for the preservation of democracy. This process has already begun at a sub-national level and the Province of Jujuy separated the Church from provincial state structures in early October 1986.[63]

Figures on mainstream religiosity suggest that Argentina is today a largely secular society. For example, in a survey of ten electoral districts, Imaz found that of his respondents, 81 per cent were baptised Catholics, but only 29 per cent were practising Catholics.[64] Nevertheless official figures issued at the time of the Pope's visit in April 1987 record that Argentina is 94 per cent Roman Catholic. The enormous turnout for Papal Masses in the interior cities, such as the two-thirds of the population of Salta, suggests that Catholicism remains an important aspect of Argentine life. It is clearly less influential in Buenos Aires and nobody who saw the crowds gathered for the Palm Sunday Mass in the city could fail to notice the mingling of races in Buenos Aires on that occasion. However, under normal circumstances the small number of practising Catholics has been taken as evidence that the Church is not a very important influence in Argentina. This is no new theme: at the beginning of the twentieth century Bryce wrote that Argentina, of all the Spanish republics, was the one in which the Church had least impact on politics.[65] Nineteenth-century liberalism effectively displaced the Church as a key protagonist in the political arena, ensuring that as an institution ' . . . the Church has failed to alter the trajectory of Argentine politics'.[66] Certainly this is also a view taken by many Argentines themselves, and very few of Kirkpatrick's respondents saw the Church (or indeed the upper class) as having much political influence.[67] However, religious values are largely shared in Argentina and are probably more subtly influential than crude measures of religiosity would indicate.

The Church has of course acted in a political manner on many occasions, sometimes with intent and sometimes inadvertently, and may thus have contributed to unconstitutional regime change directly. It is impossible to measure the extent of Church support for the 1955 revolution, for example. Similarly, and more pertinently, the development of Catholic nationalism was clearly important to the 1930 revolution, though again the extent of its contribution to that and other subsequent instances of instability is obviously immeasurable. Likewise, how far the Catholic Left's involvement with Peronism or the dissemination of radical Catholic theology, which began with the Second Vatican Council, contributed to the development of left-wing terrorism is difficult to assess, though Gillespie argues that new radical Catholic ideas were 'the single most important element' in radicalising the Montoneros in the late 1960s.[68] The indirect contribution of Catholicism to political instability is even more nebulous, but is potentially much more important. A number of themes emerge from the history of the Church, and these are indicative of a strong religious legacy working against a stable political system.

The association of religion and politics has had a direct impact on political behaviour. Political leaders, such as Yrigoyen and more especially Perón, have cultivated almost supernatural images which have made their political activities appear as moral crusades and have caused their legacies to be more divisive than mere secular politics might imply. This closeness of sacred and secular has left a crusading zeal in politics, dogmatic positions which militate against compromise and a tendency to see rules and norms as ethical rather than functional and therefore much more open to questioning and dispute.

Many indirect influences of Catholicism have been suggested. For example, the Church's emphasis on individual salvation resulting in a lack of national long-term programmes and the failure to develop an ideology of change. Similarly, the extent of cultural spirituality has been seen as an obstacle to the development of scientific and technological thinking. Also reinforcement of a psychology of looking to authority to solve problems is seen as having sapped individual initiative and responsibility. The emphasis on individual contact with God as opposed to religious ritual, which characterised the religious socialisation of the immigrants to New England, is believed by some authors to have been more conducive to the development of a high need to achieve.[69] The very fact of North American religious dissent is also supposed to have promoted industrial effort through the blocking off of alternative means to wealth and status. Finally, the pervasiveness of Catholicism, if not the Church as a formal institution, has been seen as promoting eternity rather than the secular long-term as the object of endeavour, thus reinforcing tendencies not to save or plan for the future.[70]

3 The Impact of Liberalism and the Orientation to Europe

The 'Black Legend' suggests that the colonial heritage operates against the development of constitutional forms of government in Latin America. But the legacy of Spain and Catholicism cannot by itself explain the pronounced instability of modern Argentina as it fails to account for the marked ideological adherence to democracy which promotes the oscillations from one form of politics to another. It has been argued that the Hispanic tradition did not absorb much in the way of Enlightenment thought. Yet post-medieval Hispano-Catholic thought did contain democratic as well as absolutist ideas. Latin American culture came from Europe, and the Bourbon period, especially, reflected the growing impact of mainstream European influence and the declining cultural separation of Spain. Latin America at independence was therefore receptive to European ideas. These alternative influences were to become a parallel aspect of culture with long-term political consequences for Argentina.

INDEPENDENCE AND THE FIRST LIBERAL PERIOD

As Sarmiento points out, the Revolution of 1810 meant little to the interior provinces of what is now Argentina;[1] it was essentially a result of decisions taken by the European-oriented intellectuals of Buenos Aires who failed to establish a modern state. The 1810 Revolution accelerated the onslaught of the European tradition against the Hispanicism of the interior, and in so doing it evoked a massive reaction from those who saw their culture as under attack.

Mariano Moreno and Rivadavia sought to model the post-independence Río de la Plata region on eighteenth-century

Enlightenment and French Revolutionary thought. Rivadavia, for example, encouraged the First Triumvirate to seek British support in 1811. In this way, they further alienated more conservative elements. Although he showed some awareness of the dual heritage of the area in excluding the main sections on religion, Moreno exemplified the gap between liberalism and Latin American reality when he distributed copies of Rousseau's *Social Contract* to the rural population.[2] Rivadavia also sought to extend the political revolution of 1810 into a cultural revolution against the Spanish legacy. Hence he, too, imported foreign books in the hope of changing *criollo* culture. Thus Sonego sees Rivadavia as seeking to consolidate the 'línea liberal', the elitist and dependent Argentine culture which had begun, he argues, with British involvement in trade and commerce in the Río de la Plata region.[3] Such liberal elements had been able to win popular support when they stirred up resentment against Spain, but, in despatching sophisticated, foreign-educated *porteños* as representatives into the interior in the post-independence period, they merely reminded the rural masses of the hated Spanish officials they had fought to remove.[4]

Liberalism, adapted from the most advanced nations of the world, clashed with the conservatism of the interior provinces where hierarchy and religion were the basis of the rural way of life. Liberalism was frequently seen as atheistic and thus the reaction to it of the rural population and their clergy took on the character of a crusade. Not only was liberalism imposed in a clumsy manner which alienated many of the lower classes, it was also used intentionally against the rural elite who then found in religion a cause which could win the political support of rural labour. The 1813 Assembly, for example, decreed sweeping reforms, including the abolition of entailed estates. Such changes offended traditional interests and were beyond the capacity of the Assembly to enforce. Attempts were made to win over the rural elite, such as the decision of the Congress to declare independence in Tucumán, but such ploys could not counteract the view of liberalism as a threat to vested interests.

In addition to its cultural strangeness, liberalism was weakened in its relation to the Iberian cultural current through its own internal divisions and inconsistencies. The early post-independence period was marked by not one but several different kinds of 'liberals' gaining ascendancy. Their views ranged from the classical rationalism of Moreno to the autocratic style of Rivadavia.[5] Liberalism could not insulate itself from the alternative culture by which it was surrounded, and personalism modified the rationalism which liberalism purported to represent. There was an emphasis on personalities even amongst the liberal leaders. For example, Moreno and Carlos Saavedra Lamas had different and competing personal support bases, as became clear in April 1811 when the first governing junta was dissolved.[6] Arbitrary and authoritarian methods persisted in the 'liberal' politics of the post-independence period. For example, Juan Martín de Puerreydón, as Supreme Director, forced loans to the government from his political enemies in 1817.[7]

The gap between Hispanic reality and the Enlightenment ideal was so wide that a reaction against liberalism soon occurred. By idealising the rural masses and by failing to acknowledge the existence of a distinct cultural pattern which could not simply be eliminated, the early liberals left the way open to the forces of what Sarmiento would later term 'barbarism'. Intellectual values involving 'order, stability and science' were in direct conflict with mass values embracing 'strength, freedom and superstition'.[8] The *caudillos* represented the values associated with the rural masses; they were understood by the people and therefore supported by them. Although the conflict between Unitarians and Federalists broadly, though by no means precisely, corresponded to a division between Buenos Aires and the interior and was rooted in divergent economic interest, it was also a cleavage between liberalism and the cultural legacy of Spain. As Sarmiento writes:

> There were in the Republic two parties: one in Buenos Ayres, supported by the Liberals in the provinces; the other originating in the provinces and supported by the provincial commanders who had obtained possession of cities. One of these powers was civilized, constitutional, European; the other barbarous, arbitrary, South American.[9]

The *porteño* liberals and their supporters made little attempt to reconcile their ideals with those of the masses.

In the 1820s, opposition to a unitary constitution brought the lower orders into the political arena for the first time. The excluded lower classes found their representation in the *caudillo* rule they generated. In this way, they effectively restored something more akin to the old anti-democratic, colonial and monarchical style of domination. The lower classes and their *caudillos* represented the victory of the interior and thus of provincialism which worked against the development of allegiance to the national state. The outcome of this was the early establishment of a latent model of political culture which would provide the basis for the later re-emergence of populist and personalist politics under Yrigoyen and Perón.

For Sonego, the *caudillo* era is a manifestation of the stream of culture which he calls the 'línea nacional', based on the values of medieval Spain.[10] The *caudillos* were the very antithesis of liberalism, standing for traditional values against changes and toleration. For example. Facundo Quiroga's motto presented only death as the alternative to religion. Likewise, Rosas' title 'Restorer of the laws and of public tranquillity' ('Restaurador de las leyes y del sosiego público') was confirmation of a return to the traditional colonial values and order which had been challenged in the immediate post-independence period.[11] European influence, if not halted under Rosas, was at least limited although such constraints as protective tariffs were inconsistently applied. Authoritarianism became the bond which united large landowners, the Church and the *gaucho* armies against that European-oriented elite which sought to establish liberal constitutionalism.

Liberalism had an abstract ideal to offer and, being out of accord with the reality of the dominant theme of the Iberian legacy, it led to conflict and confusion. In post-independence Argentina, the impact of liberalism contributed to virtual anarchy, and the Buenos Aires area experienced twelve political revolutions in 1820 alone. Rosas was able to take advantage of the chaos which ensued when he went off to fight Indians in 1833 and returned in 1835 as a national saviour. Through being able to offer a culturally viable alternative to liberalism, Rosas built up widespread personal loyalty and military might, and was thus in a position to counter the fissiparous forces and to hold the nation together. Liberal political arrangements were not rescinded, but their purposes were totally ignored. For example, the August 1821 law instituting direct elections and universal manhood suffrage remained in theory, but in practice lists of official candidates, who were property owners, were issued and local justices ensured that they were elected.[12] Rosas laid the foundations for a modern nation-state, and ironically enabled the liberal elements which followed him to create the structure they needed to establish their political hegemony for a considerable period.

THE GENERATION OF 1837

In 1837, Esteban Echeverría, Alberdi and other young intellectuals began meeting in a Buenos Aires bookshop, which became known as the Salón Literario de Marcos Sastre.[13] As nationalists, they were initially sympathetic to Rosas, only moving into opposition in 1838 when he broke off relations with France, the nation which was the source of their philosophical orientation. This led Echeverría to found his organisation for liberals opposed to Rosas, La Asociación de la Joven Argentina, which was forced underground in 1839, and to publish in that same year his own political programme for the post-Rosas era, with its positivistic emphasis on progress and democracy.[14] The Generation of 1837 were to remain the most potent intellectual opposition to Rosas. Writing in various parts of South America and Europe in the 1840s, they continued to criticise the Rosas regime and to construct their own plans for the regeneration of their country. The Constitution of 1853 had its basis in the deliberations of Echeverría and Alberdi, and in the years 1862–80, the first three presidents of Argentina espoused, and sought to put into practice, the ideas of the Generation of 1837.

Although the stronger cultural traditions in Argentina, especially the influence of religion, meant that Comtean positivism had less impact than in neighbouring Brazil, French and English positivist thought did modify the liberalism of the Generation of 1837. Positivist ideas such as that of the linear development of society gave liberalism an apparent practicality it had not had in the immediate post-independence period. These ideas explained popular support for Rosas and provided the intellectual justification for the liberal struggle against barbarism. The need for order preceeded the need for progress, but the two essentially went together. In the short term, the impact of positivism was advantageous, being reflected in the establishment – with new structures and philosophies – of what were to become some of Argentina's most prestigious educational institutions. But in the longer term, the impact of positivist ideas would also have repercussions for Argentine political stability. As a philosophy of progress through expertise and rationality, positivism confirmed the 'need' for elite rule and limits on democratic participation, it encouraged the development of an internationally-oriented economic model amongst the elite which would later conflict with the economic nationalism of other social groups and, through its emphasis on order, provided a cultural background conducive to the professionalisation of the armed forces. The Social Darwinist aspect of positivist thought can also be seen as contributing to the preservation of aspects of the traditional social structure, and thus to the continuation of challenges to it and resistance from it. The extent of positivist influence on all important political groups is emphasised by Whitaker and others, who see this as partially responsible for the orderly political development which brought the middle classes to political power in 1916, in contrast to the violence of the 1910 Revolution in Mexico, where positivism was identified only with the ruling group.[15]

The emphasis of positivistic liberalism on progress was taken up wholeheartedly by many of the young Argentine intellectuals who came to see the Hispanic cultural heritage as an obstacle to modernity. The Generation of 1837 saw Rosas as part of the colonial legacy, as a continuation of the colonial way of life. Echeverría, for example, held the lower orders responsible for the 'counter-revolution' which brought Rosas to power. His writings describe the conflict between the cultivated elite of Argentina and the anti-modern mass. Similarly, Sarmiento blamed popular ignorance for *caudillismo* and had doubts about the possibility of stability in a nation containing the contradictory elements of civilisation and barbarism, until the latter was eliminated.[16] The unfortunate combination of the native Indian and Spanish Catholic cultures, he argued, produced a feckless and indolent provincial population whose lack of industry contrasted lamentably with that of the German and Scots settlers in Argentina. For Sarmiento, the colonial heritage contributed to the low expectations of the rural population:

> The inhabitants of the city wear the European dress, live in a civilised manner and possess laws, ideas of progress, means of instruction, some municipal organisation, regular forms of government etc. Beyond the precincts of the city everything assumes a new aspect; the people wear a different dress, which I will call South American, as it is common to all districts; their habits of life are different, their wants peculiar and limited.[17]

This 'aristocratic disdain for the people'[18] which was widespread amongst the Generation of 1837 had two important consequences which would subsequently prove destabilising. First, it led them to believe that democratic participation must be limited, and this idea was later consolidated under the oligarchic 'liberals' of the Generation of 1880. They came to believe that the 1821 law giving the vote to all adult males in Buenos Aires Province had gone too far, and the Unitarian commitment to universal suffrage was seen by the Generation of 1837 as too idealistic. Secondly, the intellectual elite came to despise indigenous culture and to be tied to Europe in a way that alienated them from the mass of the population. On achieving positions of power, men like Bartolomé Mitre and Sarmiento sought to change Argentine 'culture'. In their attempts to do so, they widened the gap between the cultures and laid the foundations for the re-emergence of *criollo* nationalism in the twentieth century.

Despite the influence of European positivistic liberalism on the Generation of 1837, their philosophical orientation was at once more flexible and more ambiguous than it appears. Their formative years had been those in which the weaknesses of liberalism had become apparent from independence to the rise of Rosas. The Unitarian failure had alerted them to the dangers of theoretical positions which could not be converted into practice and they sought a temporary accommodation of indigenous mass culture until such time as appropriate modifications of it could be made. Alberdi, for example, recognised that it was not simply the barbaric countryside which was an obstacle to progress, but rather features of the colonial legacy in cities and provinces alike.[19] Echeverría was influenced by Argentine reality as well as French liberalism and emphasised the role of a strong, paternalistic *caudillo*. Like Sarmiento, he realised that it was Rosas who had unified the nation. Although he criticised the Iberian cultural legacy, Sarmiento himself was a part of that tradition. He did not sever himself from his Hispanic roots, which he acknowledged in his writings, and he retained a personalist style of politics. Not surprisingly he feared the potential power of the mob, and accepted election-fixing to ensure liberal domination. In addition to being a new kind of liberal '*caudillo*', he also took great pride in his honorary title of 'General'.[20] As Bunkley notes:

> Sarmiento . . . is a symbol of the agony of the Hispanic world of the nineteenth century, a world that existed in one way but felt that it should be different.[21]

When the liberal elite gained the ascendancy in Argentina it was as a consequence of the victory of the *caudillo* General Justo José de Urquiza at the battle of Monte Caseros in February 1852. The ideas of the Generation of 1837 were enshrined in the 1853 Constitution, but this was to some extent a compromise with the reality of Argentina. Despite the new theoretical supremacy of liberal political values, personalism and recourse to violence for political ends remained. For example when charges of fraud were brought against Sarmiento's chosen successor, Nicolás Avellaneda, during his presidential election campaign against Mitre, Mitre led a rebellion in 1874. Sarmiento declared states of siege in the provinces of Buenos Aires, Santa Fé, Entre Ríos and Corrientes and the forces of General Roca, amongst others, were used to suppress the rebellion.

The cultural division between the colonial heritage and the alienated forces of 'modernity', who saw themselves as having more in common with the more advanced culture of Western Europe and the United States, led to the extension of the gap between the theory and practice of politics through the adoption of a Constitution which owed much to foreign models. The abstract principles which formed the basis of the 1853 Constitution, as with other Latin American 'constitutional fictions'[22] of the period, were grafted on to the political system without changes in the underlying political culture.

Those liberals whose ideas were expressed in the 1853 Constitution were well aware of the gulf that existed between the ideals they intended to impose and the reality of the 'barbarism' of Hispanic American culture. They knew that the success of their new constitutional framework rested on the development of a sense of nation which did not at that stage exist. It had also become necessary to counteract the Iberian legacy by importing attitudes from the 'civilised' nations of Europe and the United States. Sarmiento, for example, saw the United States as the most potent model for Argentine development and therefore thought that progress towards civilisation would require a process of de-Hispanicisation. To this end, European immigrants were sought to populate the interior provinces in accordance with Alberdi's dictum 'Gobernar es poblar'.[23] Not only were the imported peoples expected to civilise the barbarous hinterland, but they would bring with them values which the native population lacked. The idea of racial regeneration as a prerequisite for economic development was later taken up and re-emphasised by the Generation of 1880.[24] Their developmental aspirations for Argentina were reflected in 'the project of the eighties' ('El Projecto del 80'), a plan which sought European immigrants and capital to assist in the building of ports and transport networks in order to extend the agro-export economy. The extent of the influx of immigrants generated by liberal policies, their concentration in Argentina's burgeoning cities and the political ideas they brought with them were later to contribute to instability.

The close identification of Hispanic America with Europe has several sources. In colonial times, the higher status accorded to *peninsulares* reinforced the cultural supremacy of the mother-country. In addition, the estrangement of the *criollo* from an alien environment populated by apparently threatening 'inferior' races must have increased the need to feel a part of an enduring and protective culture. Non-Spanish

European influences on Argentina began to be felt even before
independence, as in the case of British economic influence.
Later France became the focus of the cultural orientation
of Argentina's intellectuals, Italy supplied the majority of
her immigrants and Germany influenced the development
of her military establishment. As early as the middle of
the nineteenth century, Alberdi took pride in describing the
littoral provinces as ' . . . no more than Europe established in
America'.[25]

The Generation of 1837 liberals, especially Sarmiento,
had tended to identify with the United States and a
regionalist orientation remained amongst some elements
of 'The New Oligarchy' which succeeded them to power
in 1880. However, for the most part, the rise of the
Generation of 1880 represented a shift from Americanism to
a more universalist, primarily pro-European position. North
American influence would increase in importance again in
the twentieth century as British economic interests declined
in favour of US investments, and as US 'culture' was inter-
nationalised through the activities of her news collection and
distribution agencies and her film industry. This came much
later, however, and at the end of the nineteenth century, the
official culture of Argentina was elitist and pro-European, and
the literature of the period was 'positivista' and 'extranjera'.[26]
It is the legacy of this period which is suggested in Martínez
Estrada's comment that:

> in a special spiritual, historical and economic sense . . .
> Paris is closer to Buenos Aires than is Chivilcoy or
> Salta.[27]

This orientation of the intellectual elite to Europe, which
might be expected given the small cultural market in
nineteenth-century Latin America, has had a long-term
influence on the national psychology of Argentina. It has
contributed to the development of a pervasive national
pessimism, which is broken only by brief periods of unwarranted optimism which verge on the hysterical. The failure
to develop an authentic independent culture has perpetuated
the problem of identity. In political thought, Latin America,
generally, and Argentina, in particular, feature what Blanksten
terms 'ideological eclecticism' with contradictory elements,

notably democratic and authoritarian thought, coexisting.[28] These themes have been taken up by various sectors and used to justify their particular contributions to social disorder and political instability. The 'borrowed' quality of Argentine cultural activity increases the intellectual elite's sense of inferiority. This subordination to European culture, along with a sense of deficiency in contrast to US material development, has, according to Leopoldo Zea, extended to the general psychological climate of Latin America.[29] In Argentina, it results in a strong sense of failure and thus of pessimism, which lifts only temporarily with nationalist fervour and/or an economic boom.

Nevertheless, the Iberian influence on culture did not disappear. It remained, to re-emerge at various stages. During the periods of burgeoning nationalism in the twentieth century, uniquely Argentine aspects of culture have come to the fore representing the Hispanic legacy though modified by European influence. For example, the tango, which may well have had its origins in the popular dancing of the colonial period and the relatively isolationist era under Rosas, reached the height of its domestic popularity as Argentine nationalism grew in the interwar period. The growing nationalist reaction to the 'vendepatria' (i.e. traitrous) internationalism of the Concordancia governments during the Infamous Decade, also had its parallel in the intellectual alienation from Anglo-French culture.[30]

The influence of the European orientation of intellectuals in cultural matters may have both direct and indirect effects on political stability. The pessimism induced by the sense of inferiority thus generated, as well as the fatalism resulting from an existence outside the cultural mainstream, which have produced a sense of being acted upon rather than acting, fed into the general psychological climate. In so doing, it has affected the economic and political systems, and thus acted indirectly to promote unconstitutional governmental changes. But the military, as part of the same psychological environment, has also absorbed these attitudes. However, such general attitudes are less important than the more specific political ideals established as a consequence of the Argentine political elite's orientation to Europe.

THE IMPACT OF EUROPE ON POLITICAL INSTITUTIONS AND ATTITUDES

It was not the decision to adopt Western political models in Latin America which proved problematic – they were the only models available and were in any case adapted – but rather the way such models functioned in states where national social and economic systems did not at that stage exist. Moreover, the social and economic systems that did exist, as well as the values and attitudes derived from the colonial period, were out of accord with the spirit of the adopted political structures. It is argued by diffusionist theorists, such as Almond and Verba, that the belief-systems which underlie democracy diffuse more slowly than the institutions to which they gave rise in the Western liberal-democracies.[31] An inorganic constitutional structure – one that was not developed indigenously – cannot generate sudden changes in the political culture on which it is imposed. For the United States, which shared a similar cultural base with the nation from which its formal political arrangements were derived, this problem was less marked. The traditional Hispanic authoritarianism of non-political institutions as well as political culture, represented 'psychological reality', and was incompatible with the intentions behind the adopted structures. In the sense that legitimacy implies psychological acceptance of institutional arrangements and the structure of political authority, it was impossible for exogenously-generated models to acquire widespread legitimacy initially. By the time the theory behind the institutions had been internalised by the citizenry, the gap between that theory and governmental practice meant that the institutions were no longer clearly associated with the ideals they were supposed to represent.

Wiarda and others argue that these ideals were never fully held even by the nineteenth-century Latin American political leaders who adopted and adapted Western constitutional models. Sarmiento, for example, was well aware of the problems which the political culture bequeathed by Spain presented to the functioning of a liberal-democratic political system. In consequence, although sovereignty resides with the people, adaptations of the adopted structures reflected the Iberian legacy and included such features as greater authority for the executive and an enhanced role for corporate interests, especially the Church and the military.[32] These adaptations would later serve to destabilise the very structure they were designed to protect. Thus Latin American political modernisation in the nineteenth century cannot be seen as occurring in accordance with Western models because of the extent of adaptation in response to different culture and traditions.

An odd amalgam of traditional and imported features made up Latin American liberalism. They included statism from the Bourbon monarchy, anti-clericalism from France, federalism from the United States and *laissez-faire* economics from Britain. Thus the kind of constitutionalism to which this form of liberalism gave rise differed markedly from the type on which it was modelled. Dealy argues that Latin American political systems remained essentially 'monistic', that is, centralised and with competing interests controlled, as opposed to the competitive quality of liberal-democracy in the Western systems. As a result, a constitution became a means of ensuring consensus rather than serving as a means of arbitration between competing interests. Thus liberal constitutionalism in Latin America became an emphasis on procedure as an expression of unity. Unlike the liberal form, monistic democracy has tended to restrict individual rights for the sake of the consensus on which it has rested rather than to guarantee them. Because the two forms are fundamentally different, Dealy argues that Latin America cannot be seen as progressing towards pluralist democracy.[33]

Whilst it may be argued that such modifications represent adaptations to the existing political culture of Latin America, it must also be borne in mind that they have served the interests of those who took up the cause of liberalism. The political forms established by the application of the unique kind of liberalism developed by Latin American political elites emphasised constitutionalism over participation. In Argentina, as elsewhere in Latin America, the cause of liberalism was taken up by a landowning elite who favoured democratic choice in elections – if it were for people of high social standing choosing between candidates sympathetic to the existing social structure. (The 1869 census recorded some 333 725 Argentine men eligible to vote, whilst only about 10 per cent of these exercised this right in national elections.)[34]

The structure of democratic institutions was established by an elite and consolidated by another elite which saw its main function as protecting the privileges of that group. When this structure ceased to serve the purpose for which it was intended and became, through the mode in which it was used, a threat to the groups who had previously benefited from it, it was rejected in practice, though retained as a theoretical ideal.

The real separation between liberalism and the concept of democracy occurred during the period which began in 1880 and lasted until the Radicals achieved a massive electoral victory in 1916, though the destabilising effects of this situation did not become obvious until 1930. The landowning elite, who were politically represented by the Generation of 1880, had sufficiently close economic and social relations in addition to common attitudes and values, despite the existence of more conservative and more liberal factions which would diverge in time, to justify their frequent labelling as 'the Oligarchy'.[35] As immigration swelled the ranks of the popular classes, their comparative homogeneity increasingly set them apart from the masses. While the earlier Europe-oriented intellectuals sought political change, though not necessarily social change, the Oligarchy wanted economic growth without political or social change. Their European orientation was primarily economic, as was their liberalism. The impact of a combination of the Iberian legacy and positivist thought had now modified liberal values based on relative austerity, as exemplified by Sarmiento, to an ostentatious hedonism amongst some, though not all, sections of the elite. The emphasis on progress which positivism generated was marked among the Generation of 1837 too, but it was then less materialistic and placed greater stress on knowledge, science and, in essence, 'civilisation'. The Generation of 1880 sought progress primarily in terms of economic development which was to be achieved through attracting foreign capital. Democracy, beyond the limited sense of defending patrician interests, was seen by much of the elite as a threat to the stability necessary to attract foreign investment. Nevertheless, the holding of elections was part of the presentation of a progressive and 'civilised' image conducive to such investment, even if these elections were largely farcical. Thus political conservatism was developing under the guise of liberalism, and the Oligarchy were maintaining themselves in power by using 'democratic' institutions.

INTERPRETATIONS OF 'DEMOCRACY'

Despite using formal political structures and liberal-democratic theory to lend an aura of legitimacy to their political domination at least among their own ranks, the Oligarchy had not fully absorbed the ideals they professed to espouse. That much of the elite should have developed a concept of aristocratic republicanism reflects not only the inherent contradiction of a non-egalitarian economic structure and a democratic political order, but also the era in which they established oligarchic domination. Brazil was still a monarchy when the Generation of 1880 came to power and Chile was under aristocratic rule. More pertinently, the important European examples also appeared to justify such domination in that Disraeli as Earl of Beaconsfield had for the six years previously been Prime Minister of Britain, the quasi-aristocratic Marshal MacMahon had come to power in France in 1877 backed by conservative forces, and Count von Bismarck ruled Germany. However, under Juárez Celman (1886–90), the 'consolidator' of oligarchic domination,[36] the scale of electoral fraud increased massively and at this point democracy in Argentina began really to differ even from the still-exclusive systems of Europe.

The failure to internalise the ideal of liberal-democracy meant that the practice of constitutional democracy could more easily be set aside when it seemed to constitute a threat to the upper-class elements who supported Uriburu's coup. Moreover it was this failure which led to the rapid growth of electoral fraud to retain power, by means such as non-secret voting, removal of known opposition supporters from the electoral rolls, 'dead men voting', multiple registration of supporters, substitution of ballot boxes, intimidation and actual violence. Such methods dissociated democracy from elections and diminished the role of elections in the process of political succession. This dissociation occurred not only at a national level, but in provincial power struggles too, and amongst all political groupings. Thus, in the intense competition between the Partido Conservador and the UCR for control of the Province of Buenos Aires in the period 1912–43, or at least until the Partido Demócrata Nacional conservative faction split into liberal conservative and nationalist elements in the 1930s, both parties stressed constitutionality and the importance of democracy, but bought votes with funds acquired through gambling activities.[37]

Dahl's comparison of politics in Argentina under the Oligarchy with eighteenth-century Britain suggests that the extent of fraud and violence in the former was much greater. Ignoring both the constitution and the law, whilst claiming that governmental legitimacy sprang from them, negated electoral victory as a source of legitimacy. The absence of a transitional period between oligarchic rule and effective universal manhood suffrage, made reality by the restrictions placed on fraud and the introduction of the secret ballot by the Sáenz Peña Law of 1912, also meant that there was not time during which the legitimacy of elections could be established as a political norm.[38] (A related theme is taken up by Mouzelis, who sees this broadening of representation as occurring at a time when Argentina, like other areas of Latin America and the Balkans, had not achieved sufficient industrial development to promote a successful transition to democracy from 'oligarchic parliamentarism'.)[39] Thus later electoral rigging, such as that which occurred in 1932 and 1937 and which was justified as 'patriotic fraud', cannot be seen as aberrant. A pattern had been set whereby the opposition would not lose legitimacy if they by-passed the constitutional means of succession and sought military assistance to gain power. The military coup, or *golpe*, became an alternative means of political change rather than an inferior and illegitimate method. Dahl summarises the effects of oligarchic fraud on political culture thus:

> By their own conduct the notables taught the Argentinians that elections need not be binding on the losers or the potential losers.[40]

Despite widespread abuse of democratic institutions, Anderson sees Latin Americans generally as having a deep commitment, both intellectually and emotionally, to democracy.[41] However, it is possible to argue that different sections of the social structure hold diverse kinds of commitment and thus democracy is seen in dissimilar ways. Some authors are cynical about the professed adherence to democracy in Latin America, and find it a surprising feature in nations which they see as still politically 'immature'. Such a view fails to take account of the fact that in Argentina, as elsewhere, no alternative justification for the functioning of the political system could exist after the removal of divine authority in the person of the king. If God no longer provided the basis of government, sovereignty, by definition, must rest somewhere amongst the people, and indeed Article 33 of the Argentine Constitution makes this explicit.[42] In addition, the period 1880–1930 was the heyday of democracy and there is no reason to suppose Argentines were immune to this international ideological current. The victory of the more recognisably democratic powers in the First World War also reinforced its appeal.

The ideal behind the democratic form may not be wholly or universally accepted, but its procedural aspect clearly was. The desirability of a constitutional façade is entrenched, as was shown in the constitutional reform of 1949. Perón was a sufficiently potent political force to have completely disregarded the 1853 Constitution in establishing his new version, but instead chose to act within the procedures laid down in the existing document. Such a preference for acting within the constitutional framework has been common to most political sectors in Argentina, even to most of the military establishment. For example, General Alejandro Lanusse, on laying down the presidential office in 1973, felt it necessary to thank the Argentine people for their patience with his non-elected government.[43] But the advantages of operating in a constitutional manner are subject to measurement against the costs thus incurred. This situation, as we shall see later, reflects the zero-sum sectoral pattern of Argentine politics and is particularly marked in consequence of the differing interpretations of democracy held by the different sectors.

For the working class and some elements of the middle class, democracy implies mass political participation by whatever means may be available. In a sense, this attitude not only accords with rational interest, but also with Argentine political history. It was the support of the rural masses which maintained the *caudillos* in power and the establishment of liberal-democratic institutions which later excluded the lower classes from political participation. Direct action by the labour movement in the late nineteenth and early twentieth centuries reflected and reinforced demands for participation for those excluded from the formal political process, whether because of the elitist nature of the institutional structure before 1912 or by reason of their non-citizenship. The level of commitment to participation is indicated by the level of voting in presidential elections (88 per cent in September 1973), by the proportion of union members amongst the active labour force (34 per cent in the early 1970s), and by the continued independent action of organised labour under governments both sympathetic to and repressive of the Argentine working class.[44]

The early liberals, with their emphasis on education, may have intended eventual political inclusion of the masses once their capacity for manipulation by personalist leaders had been reduced. But much of the Generation of 1880 saw democracy as a means by which they could retain their own position in society. By their use of fraud, they made explicit a view of liberal-democracy which did not embrace mass participation. By the end of the Peronato, this attitude had spread down the social structure and much of the middle class, almost a half-century removed from their own struggle for access to political power, had come to believe that working-class electoral participation must be controlled. A deep commitment to the principles of liberal-democracy existed, but such principles were held flexibly, as a long-term goal. Technocratic attitudes developed out of the apparent failure of the political system to provide the sustained economic growth that the middle class desired. In 1966, for example, the democratic process was seen by many among the middle class as slow and riven by cleavages, and therefore as inappropriate for national development. Democracy was a luxury Argentina could not yet afford. The media encouraged these attitudes, with journalists such as Jacobo Timerman conducting an 'image-building' campaign for the military during the government of Arturo Illia.[45] Similar ideas were still being expressed by members of the middle classes in 1980.

Thus differing interpretations of what democracy means and how it should be put into practice led the different sectors to fear its 'misuse' in the hands of their political opponents. The competing political sectors with their contradictory images of democracy reflect the two aspects of Argentine culture which have their roots in the historical contributions of Iberian and European influences to the development of modern Argentina. Crawley, for example, suggests that in 1966, the nation was seen as comprising the two opposed sectors of small to medium-sized business interests allied with labour and, on the other hand, the agro-export sector allied with bankers, multinational corporations and large Argentine businesses with overseas connections. The former sector, which he terms 'nationalists', were seen as favouring mass participation regardless of institutional form; whilst the latter, the 'liberals', were regarded as 'formally adhering to democratic principles'. With such marked and contradictory interpretations of democracy, the military were able to present themselves as arbiters between the competing alliances and the sub-groups within them.[46]

INCOHERENCE IN ARGENTINE POLITICAL CULTURE

The survival of aspects of Iberian political culture can be viewed in two different ways. First, emphasis may be placed on the capacity of liberalism to adapt to the existing Iberian cultural pattern, initially under the influence of the Generation of 1837 who recognised the necessity of adaptation to reduce the incompatibilities which destroyed the immediate post-independence liberal experiment. Later the oligarchic brand of liberalism espoused by the Generation of 1880 sought to retain the traditional social structure whilst promoting economic growth. Secondly, stress may be laid on the flexibility of the traditional culture and its capacity to absorb necessary aspects of modernity without being destroyed in the process. This latter view would seem to present a challenge to those authors who suggest that Latin American culture resists modernity. The two explanations are not mutually exclusive and both have something to offer in the case of Argentina, though it must be emphasised that new ideas can only be accepted in so far as traditional culture allows them to be so in the absence of a complete rejection of the existing culture. However, the important point is not how the coexistence of different political cultures came about, but rather that it did, and that it has contributed to political instability.

All cultures comprise traditional and modern values and all experience some conflict in consequence, though the level will vary over time. However, the frequent use of the term 'fragmentary' to describe the Argentine political system implies a level of conflict within the political culture which is well beyond that found in many other systems. Amongst authors who see Argentina as characterised by cultural contradictions, Ricardo Rojas recognises two forces at work in Argentine society from independence. He sees the period 1810–29 as one in which the binding forces of civilisation which sought to establish democratic institutional structures dominated. The period 1830–52 represents the re-emergence of the centrifugal military forces which liberated the nation.[47] These two forces continue to exist and influence politics, each coming to the surface in turn in a modern guise. Similarly Sonego holds that two lines of political thought expressed in two different, mutually exclusive national designs, have coexisted since the beginning of the nineteenth century. Political instability is ensured through the oscillation of politics between these two blueprints. The dominance of the 'línea nacional' has brought to power *caudillos* and populist leaders, whilst the 'línea liberal' has produced leaders from amongst the urban, educated elite who have primarily represented the economic sectors linked to agricultural exports. Sonego sees 1916 as the rebirth of the 'línea nacional' after the period of oligarchic liberalism, whereas 1930 represents the restoration of the 'línea liberal'.[48] His interpretation of the differences between these political patterns is almost exclusively economic, expressing the cleavage between economic nationalists and internationalists. Thus other authors do not see 1930 in the same light. For example Martínez Estrada writes:

The year 1880 will appear in the awakening of new blood as a less authentic and less Argentine year than 1930, the year in which history is once again welded to previous eras in a continuous plane of feeling.[49]

Kirkpatrick gets closer to an accurate description of the parallel streams of culture in Argentina when she suggests that the Argentine people share a national and pervasive political culture not marked by deep cleavages, but not characterised by consensus and trust either:

> ... an integrated culture in which coexisted a number of shared and divisive purposes, understandings and demands.[50]

The acceptance of constitutional forms is shared, as is the belief in the ideal of democracy at a theoretical level. But different interpretations of what democracy means in practice and fear of its 'misuse' are divisive features of Argentine political culture. Both liberal internationalists opposed to working-class political participation and those modern economic nationalists who see democracy as resting on mass involvement have been influenced by European political thought and accept the theory behind the institutional structures derived form it. But such groups simultaneously reserve the right to fall back on other political methods derived from the Iberian cultural stream when Argentine political institutions fall into the hands of their political opponents and fail to function in the ways they would wish. Crawley rightly recognises that a 'parallel political system' exists in Argentina, although he is incorrect in his view that it was 'created' in the years 1955–65.[51] As he states, competition of corporate interests and recourse to military assistance are part of that system, but they are much older. Both have their roots in the Iberian legacy to Spanish America.

Thus, 1930 may be seen as the year in which a deferred instability actually emerged through the substitution of an alternative political model for the 'failed' democratic one. The retention of a reserve political mode is pervasive and has led to all manner of partial processes which are destabilising. The professionalisation of the military in accordance with liberal positivistic ideals did not preclude Radical appeals to the military for political support nor Conservative use of the armed forces in 1930; it merely made the military a more effective political force. The officer corps, like other political actors, used alternative methods when democracy 'failed'. In consequence, military intervention has most usually been justified in terms of the misuse of democracy by civilian politicians and the need for a period of military 'cleaning up' before constitutional forms could be restored. The exclusion of the Peronist movement by the armed forces in the period after 1955, whilst claiming to be ensuring democracy, illustrates a military view of democracy resting on institutional form not popular participation. Naturally, the Peronist interpretation of democracy during these years did not coincide with this position!

Explanations of authoritarian governments and corporatist structures in the 1960s and 1970s in Latin America have often rested on references to the Hispano-Catholic cultural tradition. Such regimes are seen as movements away from artificially sustained models to the essential underlying culture of Latin America. Technocrats are seen as preferring the authoritarian strain of culture to the democratic one, mass apathy to participation. In theory they do not need legitimacy as they can use repression to ensure compliance.[52] But these regimes cannot be stable in the long term because of the existence of the other stream of political culture which emphasises that theoretically legitimacy rests in constitutional forms. Therefore as repression eases over time, so the 'bureaucratic-authoritarian state' must give way to pressure for a constitutional restoration.

4 The Lack of Legitimacy

THE CULTURE OF VIOLENCE

An explanation of why legitimacy has not developed in the Argentine political system since the formal structure was laid down in the last half of the nineteenth century, is to be found in the different perceptions of function and effectiveness which spring from the two streams of cultural influence already described. Chalmers argues that Latin America's lack of political legitimacy is not a direct legacy of Iberian culture.[1] Horowitz makes a similar point in suggesting that the strength of the institutional framework and the authority of the Spanish monarchy during the colonial period were accepted by the masses rather than needing to be imposed on them.[2] Nevertheless with the collapse of the Spanish Crown, traditional legitimacy disappeared and the long dispute over the source of legitimate authority which has marked the nineteenth and twentieth century political struggles began. Morse writes that, under colonialism:

> The lower echelons of administration had operated by the grace of an interventionist, paternal monarch, thoroughly sanctioned by tradition and faith. His collapse straightaway withdrew legitimacy from the remnants of the royal bureaucracy. It was impossible to identify a substitute authority that could command general assent. Decapitated, the government could not function . . . [3]

Popular sovereignty was not established as the alternative legitimating principle because Argentina's two cultures interpreted its implications differently. Without a legitimate source of authority, the assertion of power was open to contestation. Thus it has remained. Those who wield power do so as long as others do not acquire sufficient motive and strength to supplant them.

The frequent association, and often confusion, of political violence and instability in much of the theoretical literature on political stability has provoked considerable criticism. However, it is hard to avoid the conclusion that a culture of conflict and violence is in itself socialising and will operate to prevent the development of a culture of consensus and constitutional change. In the relative absence of legitimacy, force is an alternative means of political succession and coercion a method of power maintenance. Political violence is much more likely where it is not stigmatised by the legitimacy of non-violent politics. Where crude power is wielded because there is no clear legitimate authority, this very process has the effect of preventing the development of such authority. Thus, because conflict and violence offer an alternative mode of conducting politics to what Kane calls a 'constitutional habit',[4] this aspect of Argentine political culture is important in its influence on stability.

Although it is possible to argue that the frequency of unconstitutional political succession has institutionalised illegitimacy and therefore reduced the actual violence associated with regime change, the threat of violence has remained, as has, in some cases, a high level of violence peripheral to the succession. In some examples of military intervention a much higher level of actual violence could well have been expected but, due to specific events, did not occur. Such was the case in 1955 when it was Perón's decision to go into exile rather than to muster his political support and fight it out. Similarly, in 1976, despite a low level of violence associated directly with the coup, the implication of violence was present in that the military took captive the Head of State. María Estela (Isabel) Martínez de Perón's ouster was also followed by political violence peripheral to the succession on an unprecedented level[5] illustrating the persistence of this aspect of Argentine culture. Lambert could have been writing about the Videla government's elimination of political opposition when he notes that the *gauchos* under Rosas' control:

> ... knew very well indeed how to make anyone who disobeyed disappear without leaving any doubt about where the punishment came from, but also without anyone's being able to prove anything.[6]

It must be noted that the terror under Rosas was much more centralised and organised than that experienced in the 1970s, both at the end of Isabel Perón's government and during the 'Process of National Reorganization'. In fact the lack of centralisation and organisation of the military regime's action against subversion may be seen as partially due to their inheritance of the Peronist infrastructure for elimination of the Left, complete with its anarchic qualities. However Alfonsín's 'Full Stop' Law, halting the trials of military personnel involved in the extermination of subversion, along with the principle of Due Obedience, suggests that a view of the Process as an organised product of military government has gained official credence.

A culture of violence, simultaneously resulting from and itself contributing to a lack of legitimacy, has marked Argentine political history. Stokes sees this as a consequence of Hispanic culture with its authoritarian institutions.[7] This is an incomplete, over-simplified view. It does not explain why instability increased after independence nor why Argentina has not achieved a period of stability under an authoritarian regime – as modern Paraguay has, for example. The Viceroyalty of the Río de la Plata may have been lawless in the frontier sense of the term, with a sparse population contending against hostile Indians, but before 1806 it was not unstable in the sense of strong challenges to the existing political structure, unlike either Peru or Brazil. Nor is Johnson correct in his assertion that the colonial era spawned no public opinion to question the policies of those in power once independence was achieved, thus making political ideology less important than force.[8] It was precisely a clash of ideologies reflecting different cultural influences as well as divergent economic interest which led to the establishment of a culture of violence and illegitimacy. Tensions in political relations after independence brought to the surface more brutal political behaviour than had been experienced in the colonial era.

It was the challenge to the existing order springing from the influence of non-Iberian Europe which caused the post-independence struggle. Rivadavia, as a representative of the European cultural stream, fell when the interior provinces led by *caudillos* rebelled, and order could only be restored by the use of force by Rosas' private army. By the 1820s authority had no other source but the exercise of coercion since the accepted imperial administrative structure had been demolished and the successor governments seemed totally out of touch with the realities of the area beyond Buenos Aires. Whilst some authors argue that legitimate authority disappeared with independence, an alternative view might be that it remained to some extent within the Iberian cultural stream as liberal elements sought and failed to establish the acceptance of their authority.

> Some have even claimed that the *caudillo*, as the military leader of independence, inherited the legitimacy of the Crown. It was then his to transmit to the civil government of his choice, and also his to take away. Certainly this was how the *caudillo* looked at it.[9]

As the two streams of culture competed to establish their hegemony, violence was used by both sides. The *caudillos* were not a barbaric force 'thirsting for blood' confronting peaceable and educated opponents. Throat-cutting was the favoured technique of both Unitarians and Federalists alike.[10] The culture of the slaughterhouse was pervasive.

It was Rosas' military success in the Desert Campaign of 1833, in pushing the Indians back as far as the Río Colorado and extending the ranching area, which ensured his recall and re-election in 1835, even though this success was primarily achieved by alliances.[11] Between 1835 and 1852, Rosas changed the nature of the Unitarian–Federalist conflict by forcibly unifying the nation under a federal system. Local autonomy was reduced. Some areas, such as the Province of Córdoba, under Facundo Quiroga until 1835 and then Manuel López until 1852, retained theoretical sovereignty, but they did so by their regional armies maintaining sufficient strength to dominate the locality without risking a challenge to the overall authority of Rosas. By using military might against liberal elements, Rosas consolidated a form of militarism and a pattern of political violence. Terrorism became an instrument of government, which itself devised the policy and selected opponents for elimination from a centrally collated black list. The violence reached its peak in the period 1839–42, and during October 1840 headless corpses were to be found lying in Buenos Aires every morning. It continued, however, though at a lower level, after the Sociedad Popular Restaurador, commonly known as the Mazorca (Rosas' terrorist organisation), was disbanded in 1846 having effectively diminished the opposition. By such means Rosas forced the integration and centralisation of the area by imposing his own authority. But his rule was a reaction against the challenge of liberalism and would have been less likely without the conflicting cultural heritage which inspired it.

In their struggle to assert the supremacy of the liberal elements they represented, both Mitre and Sarmiento contributed to corruption and violence as political practices. They were both brutal in their extermination of the *caudillos*, as is illustrated by Sarmiento's advice to Mitre not to spare the *gauchos'* blood at the Battle of Pavón in 1861 and his displaying of the heads of the dead *caudillos* on pikes in Buenos Aires. Sarmiento clearly recognised the importance of crude physical strength in his assertion that the national fate was decided at Pavón through the superior equestrian skills of the *porteño* forces over those of the Confederation army they defeated.[12] He also used fraud to win elections. Such methods assisted in the establishment of a political norm of illegitimacy, but again sprang from cultural conflict, not simply from the cultural legacy of Spain.

In 1880, Roca came to power partially on the strength of his role in subjugating the Patagonian Indians and partially as a result of electoral fraud and coercion. Although Roca consolidated the nation, strengthened government authority (especially the institution of the presidency) and made the country attractive to foreign capital, he also contributed to the growing tradition of governmental corruption and violence. Graham-Yooll speculates that some aspects of such violence may have even been a response to European pressure to stabilise the nation, but in the light of what went before this argument seems far-fetched.[13] Rather than seeking a permanent institutional solution to the problem of provincial dissent, Roca dealt with it by the expedient means of bribery and force. The 'stability' he achieved was based on a temporary sufficiency of resources for distribution amongst the varying interests within the upper class. Roca's hand-picked successor, his brother-in-law, Juárez Celman, was less fortunate in that the collapse of the economy in 1889–90 resulted in the re-emergence of conflicting interests within the upper class which, although generally short-lived, were sometimes expressed in violent power struggles, and forced his resignation in the 'Revolution of 1890'. These events illustrate a feature of Argentine politics which remains important today. To some extent legitimacy of a kind may be acquired on a temporary basis, and the deferment of instability achieved through the satisfaction of demands of politically important groups.

During the 1890s and 1900s a new sector was becoming politically active and its demands were not being satisfied by the existing system. Representing provincial dissidents and the emergent urban middle sectors, the UCR constituted the first real challenge to the conservative Partido Autonomista Nacional. The UCR could hardly be expected to respect and accept a political system based on a procedural interpretation of democracy which excluded the UCR from political office. In consequence, the UCR's initial political activities occurred outside constitutional channels, comprising abortive rebellions in which military elements were incited to participate. The urban artisan class, also excluded from participation and disillusioned with the formal political system, were exhibiting their disaffection through the direct action of the anarchist movement. Thus, by the time the Radicals came to power in 1916, a tradition of political violence had been established which erupted again in 1917–19 and would re-emerge in 1930 from a different quarter when constitutional government threatened important political sectors and when civilian politicians were experiencing a decline in the partial, tentative and highly personal legitimacy they previously experienced.

Kirkpatrick argues that there is a general consensus against the use of violence in politics in Argentina, and also against military intervention, although the latter is less marked.[14] Fernández' findings were similar amongst elites already active in politics, but amongst his student respondents, he found 70 per cent in favour of using violence to overthrow a government, though in an 'emergency' only.[15] Political exclusion of important sectors from participation in government, and/or the perception of the system itself as a potential threat when in the hands of those with a different interpretation of its political purpose, may make unconstitutional action the only apparent option available to certain political sectors at specific times. If other routes to the attainment of sectoral interests appear to be blocked, then the existence of a tradition of political violence makes action outside constitutional channels easier to justify. Thus Kirkpatrick shows violence is inherent in Argentine society, despite the theoretical consensus of opinion against it, and direct action is part of the political tradition.[16] This culture of political violence and illegitimacy results in a generalised expectation that the military will intervene to oust a government unable to assert its authority, or alternatively may be used to maintain a government against challenges to it.[17]

THE RELATIONSHIP OF VALUES AND EXPERIENCE

Expectations of political behaviour are clearly a product of the overall process of political socialisation. Beliefs about power and the conduct of politics not only influence the functioning of the political system, but are also influenced by it. Past experiences give rise to expectations of the future. Thus, amongst other criticisms relating to their failure to define clearly the concepts of 'civic culture' and 'democracy', and to establish the exact relationship between them, Barry questions Almond and Verba's emphasis on culture as a prerequisite of democracy because culture may reflect rather than cause institutional structure, a theme which Potter also takes up. Barry suggests that a democratic political culture may be the effect of democratic institutions and that a citizen's perception of his ability to influence the political system may be founded on his experience of the system rather than on an independent cultural variable.[18] Barry's argument is correct in the same sense that it is correct to argue that the chicken precedes the egg. The relationship between belief and reality is one of constant adjustment and reciprocity. In political terms, the interconnectedness of values and the functioning of the political system can be illustrated by the argument that certain values underlie the establishment of the actual constitutional structure of Argentina, the functioning of which then influenced political culture which in turn caused adjustments in the way political institutions operated, and so on. Likewise, it makes no difference whether the experience of spiralling inflation resulted in values which sustain it or vice versa; the problem for the Argentine economist is how to break into the cycle, adjust beliefs, restore confidence and reduce sectoral demands despite the permanent crisis of expectation. Beliefs concerning the legitimacy of certain forms of political behaviour remain an important influence on stability.

Both formal socialisation (being the transmission of beliefs to the child through the family and other primary groups) and informal socialisation (personal experience which consolidates or amends initial beliefs) are essential aspects of cultural development. What a child learns from his parents, other kin and peers will be the sum of their formal socialisation and experience. It could therefore be argued that political socialisation rests solely, though partly indirectly, on the way in which the political system actually functions. This, however, leaves aside the relationship between other aspects of culture and politics. For Kling, the socialisation process offers support to a culture of political violence through the other social relationships it transmits. He sees the authoritarian, male-dominated family structure, for example, as conducive to the acceptance of non-democratic political forms in Latin America.[19] Informal political socialisation through experience may be subdivided into the effects of system output and system management. System management by definition is influenced by beliefs about the purposes of the political system as well as being itself influential, and this also applies to system output. As Almond and Powell suggest, beliefs are among the supports which, along with demands, provide the inputs into a political system from which outputs derive.[20]

Although drawn from a different continent, Myrdal's concept of the 'soft state' in which policies decided upon are not enacted, or if enacted are not enforced,[21] could be applied to some extent to Latin America. It would be difficult to argue that Latin American governments do not follow policy decisions with legislative enactments, but many such enactments remain unenforced. Many authors explain non-compliance with laws in institutional terms; seeing inappropriate codes of law and legal systems derived from foreign models as resulting in impractical measures which cannot be enforced. Other explanations have included the inadequacy of administrators, who are selected on the basis not of merit but of political support in a clientelist system, and the impracticality of enactments, which springs from inadequate knowledge on the part of the decision-makers about what is possible rather than simply desirable. Obviously the failure to implement enactments can often be attributed to a shortage of governmental economic resources or their diversion to other activities. However, cultural factors are also seen as important in explaining this 'formalism'. Anderson, for example, emphasises the problems administrators face in achieving compliance.[22] Alba sees a psychological duality as characteristic of Latin America, whereby beliefs are not necessarily reflected in practice.[23] Thus even if a law is seen as just, there may still be a tendency to avoid full compliance. More significantly, the varying interpretations of the proper functioning of the political system and the lack of generalised legitimacy consequent upon these, have a marked effect on the way that system outputs are seen. Demands fed into a political system if not supported by belief in the legitimacy of that system will continue to be asserted if not reflected in the outputs of the system. A rejection of expectations believed to be just by a political system lacking legitimacy will lead to a generalised rejection of the results of the policy-making process. The same will be true if demands of other sectors seen as unjust are accepted by the system.

The effects of the state's problems of penetration in its failure to achieve compliance with the outputs of its governments, are a widespread contempt for law and a gap between apparent governmental intentions and actual performance. This latter situation leads to governments being seen as ineffective and thus to a further weakening of governmental authority. The result of this is a generalised lack of trust in government, illustrated in the case of Argentina by a Gallup Poll Survey of Buenos Aires conducted under the Illía government (1963–66). Only 4 per cent of respondents believed the government's statements that its authorised price rises would only raise the cost of living by 2 per cent; 86 per cent believed that living costs would rise more than suggested.[24] Years of experience of government ineffectiveness had taught these respondents not to trust their government.

A political socialisation which teaches that civilian rulers are ineffective and therefore illegitimate opens the way to military intervention.

Simplistic analyses suggesting that lack of experience of functioning democracy leads to a lack of understanding and valuing of it, are inadequate in the Argentine case. Democracy is valued, as was shown in the popular response to the Easter Week rebellions of 1987, but the preservation of it has, in the past, been seen as best ensured by its temporary overthrow. Nevertheless, no matter how noble the motive, the frequent use of unconstitutional methods has, through its socialising effect, encouraged expectations of further action of the same kind and thus reduced resistance to such actions in the future. O'Donnell sees the gap between the kind of political behaviour required by the formal institutional structure, and recognised as theoretically legitimate by the dominant democratic ideology, and the actual conduct of politics, as one of the 'constants' of Argentine instability. He considers this to be an historical legacy which has contributed to military interventions.[25] It is the tolerance of the gap between formal democracy and political practice which results in the partial quality of Argentina's acceptance of democracy. The attachment of conditions to the legitimacy of democracy undermines it by the failure to delegitimise all unconstitutional actions. Unconstitutional means and political violence then become self-perpetuating modes of political action; they are habit-forming and contribute to the political socialisation of active and potentially active political groups.

In contrast, in nations without a tradition of widespread political violence and unconstitutional change, political socialisation inculcates a non-violent political culture in which the electoral process is the sole legitimate means of political succession. Elections are seen as 'normal' and their results carry a moral obligation which falls on all citizens. Those who advocate violence challenge not only the formal procedure, but also its psychological support system. Thus violence in Britain and the United States, for example, is primarily aimed at non-political ends. Liberal-democracy is essentially procedural and it is from the limitations on procedures that limitations on other aspects of political behaviour derive. The acceptance of restricted means to attain power in the form of elections leads to limitations on the extent of change sought. In mass societies, the need to win sufficient support in an election implies moderation of goals and the need for political compromise. In many Western societies therefore limits are placed on goals to ensure that only legitimate political procedures are used. Goals which require deviant means become deviant goals. The 'attrition' of goals, in Kling's terminology, occurs for any group which wants to compete by legitimate means. Groups not prepared to moderate their aims are excluded from the political process. Revolutions, if they occurred, in such non-violent political systems would accompany profound structural change.[26]

In Latin America in general, and Argentina in particular, violence may be seen as a semi-legitimate means to acquire power in some circumstances, i.e. when the functioning of the system according to the prescribed procedures appears as a threat. In such a situation, the goals of competing groups are not moderated, but remain as ideological gulfs from which no compromise may be derived. The belief that the military should not intervene in politics rests on the assumption that political institutions are responsive to the non-violent demands of most groups in society. Where this is not the case, the ideological out-groups may perceive themselves as having inadequate access to influence government policies and may therefore revert to direct action. Small issues then become the focus of generalised discontent as they did in Córdoba in May 1969, when rises in student refectory prices and changes in Saturday working arrangements resulted in a wave of violence which eventually led to the overthrow of Onganía. Procedural legitimacy is further undermined by the effectiveness of the use of crude power. Silvert cites the case of the pay increase awarded to the Argentine Federal Police in mid-1961 after a contingent of officers had protested by firing on Congress.[27] The evident concessions to the military after the Easter Week rebellions of 1987 constitute a more recent example. Socialisation determines whether political violence and other unconstitutional means are seen as justifiable and effective. If this is the case, as it is in Argentina, then that makes the use of such methods more likely.

THE LEGITIMACY OF THE STATE

Political conflict and violence are reflections of the failure of Latin American political culture to develop the concept of the legitimate role of the state or to accord it mass support. Horowitz points out that some societies operate 'in Weberian terms' and the general perception of the state is as a service to its members with an administrative staff and a legitimate monopoly of force which is used to ensure order for the benefit of all. The state therefore has authority. Other societies operate 'in Marxian terms', with the state being perceived as having a monopoly of illegitimate power which enables the oppression of some elements of society by others. Such a state has power, not authority. In these terms, the state in Britain, the United States, the Soviet Union, etc., is perceived as legitimate, whilst in most Latin American nations it is seen as illegitimate. The sectoral nature of political conflict, the differing interpretations of how the political system should function and the frequency of unconstitutional political succession, all contribute to a perception of the Argentine state as, at least in part, a wielder of power not authority. Horowitz suggests that legitimacy, in the sense that a service state has it, rests on 'a common adhesion to either legality or mass mobilisation'.[28] Argentina does not have a generalised acceptance of either of these two legitimising principles, but rather has a sectoral (in the sense of temporary expedience on behalf of a particular sector) acceptance of them both.

The concept of the state as a power-wielding imposition may be seen as resting on a history of state ineffectiveness or irrelevance. For example, Johnson argues that the powerlessness of the Argentine state against Indian raiders in the mid-nineteenth century established a reliance on the individual rather than the state for protection of family and property.[29] With the enduring strength of loyalties to kin rather than nation, this frontier mentality could be said to have persisted. The state, with its limited funds, initially could provide little in the way of benefits to the people. The state was therefore reified, that is, viewed as a thing in itself, not as a sum of the social institutions which comprise it. Thus its attempts to raise the necessary funds appeared not only as irrelevant, but also as a positive threat. Despite the fact that the inflow of foreign capital in some senses served as a legitimating force for the state in Argentina in the late nineteenth century, it is still possible to argue that the early involvement of foreign capital in Latin America may also have undermined the development of a generalised concept of the legitimate role of the state. In fact, foreign capital set up a complex pattern of attraction and resentment reflected in Argentina's two cultures. The provision of railways and other utilities by outside investment and initiative may have caused producers and traders to develop international rather than national perceptions. (Of course, railway development was encouraged and partially financed by the Argentine state which, apart from building and operating an extensive network of 'feeder' lines in less-favoured areas, contributed government investment in the form of concessions, guarantees, some subscriptions and grants of land. But as Lewis points out, the bulk of the investment needed was British and most of the funds invested by the state were obtained from foreign borrowing anyway.)[30] Intellectuals also looked to Europe for their market and their inspiration. The state therefore was only relevant to certain groups who saw it as their means to power, wealth and social mobility because they were not successfully involved in the sub-national or supra-national systems. Thus it was an 'unnecessary' overlay on the system functioning on a different base. Nor could the state claim legitimacy in consequence of its constant defensive role against external threats, since in Argentina's case these were primarily mere boundary disputes.

Latin American value systems generally reduce the possibility of the state being seen as a locus of legitimate authority. The tendency to sub-national identifications indicated in the strength of individualism, kinship loyalties and personalism, affects the way in which national organisations are perceived. The state's activities are seen as restricting rather than enhancing aspirations associated with these identifications. Latin America appears to exhibit what Berlin terms 'the notion of negative freedom' in that the restrictions placed by the state on the behaviour of others, as well as oneself, are not seen as enhancing personal liberty.[31] This concept of freedom in its relation to the way the state is perceived may be partly rooted in the independence struggle which associated freedom with the overthrow of the existing state. Such an interpretation is clearly rational as the state does place restrictions on the individual and the groups to which he owes his loyalties; but in its failure to recognise the advantages of placing such restrictions on others, it links up, in Argentina's case at least, with a tendency to look on things negatively which amounts to a pervasive national pessimism. A state which is seen as restrictive is much more likely to be challenged than one perceived as ensuring freedom. As Horowitz notes:

> One of the prime features of instability in many Latin American regimes is the immature conception of consti-tutionalism as a juridical limit to personal sovereignty rather than as a device for guaranteeing maximum personal manoeuvrability.[32]

From its inception, the Argentine state has been seen as being used for sectoral purposes and therefore as open to challenge. Its decisions remain open to question because they lack legitimacy for large sections of the population at any one time and, in consequence, it is 'legitimate' to seek means to avoid complying with them. Silvert sees the clash between traditional loyalty to sub-national groups and the 'modern' need for loyalty to an impersonal institution, the state, as one of the important paradoxes which underlie the instability of Argentine politics:

> The narrowness of the loyalty horizons and the failure to accept the state as the ultimate arbiter of secular dispute weaken social institutions and invite autocratic personalism, whether directed towards change or the mere continuance of the *status quo*.[33]

ELECTIONS

Leaving aside the practical (if not theoretical) weakness of the Argentine Congress as an institution in comparison with the presidency, the general lack of legitimacy of the state also undermines the perceived importance of elections to determine who shall control it. Kirkpatrick's respondents showed a low rating of the vote as a means to influence government as compared with direct action. Political parties were seen as of limited importance in the process of political communication.[34] This tendency not to expect responsiveness from elected leaders is also reflected in Morse's view that, in Latin American politics generally, power is 'alienated' rather than delegated to leaders.[35] Miguens' work also suggests that Argentines feel impotent and frustrated as a result of the lack of responsiveness of elective governments and prefer authoritarian government as a more effective means of getting things done.[36] O'Donnell in summarising survey data on political attitudes and opinions in Argentina, emphasises the prevalence of scepticism about political parties, sectoral conflict and a willingness to see constitutional channels put aside to remove governments seen as unfit.[37] Retaliatory action, consequent upon the generalised lack of legitimacy, is not confined to domestic sectors:

> ... the reason behind the coups which establish military regimes is the revenge of those defeated by universal suffrage. However, those defeated by universal suffrage are not only local interests. Foreign interests have confronted every elected regime and have profited from all military regimes.[38]

Thus, explanations of instability in terms of political culture do not necessarily contradict explanations emphasising external factors; indeed it is the contention of the present work that explanations of all kinds may complement each other.

Where, as in Latin America, electoral mechanisms do not accord a government legitimacy because a *golpe* may be welcomed by large sections of the population when that government fails to satisfy expectations, constitutional procedures are tentative. Thus Onganía was able to stress in a speech in 1964 that the military owed obedience to the constitution and to the law, not to politicians and parties 'which circumstantially hold power'.[39] What initially appears surprising is that elections should be held at all, that there should be so much consideration of formal political arrangements. This anomaly has existed throughout the history of independent Argentina and was illustrated as early as 1835 when Rosas was begged by the ruling junta to assume 'supreme and absolute powers' but refused to do so until a plebiscite, which he won by 9315 votes to five, had been held to confirm his position. The desire for popular support springs from the absence of any other basis for governmental authority. The emphasis on the particular constitutional forms laid down in the mid-nineteenth century stems from the influence of the European stream of culture. Nevertheless, the simultaneous acceptance of and willingness to disregard procedures, whether relating to political or other matters, has a much older cultural base, though this has been reinforced by the interaction of the two cultures. It reflects what Camacho terms:

> . . . [the] paradoxical Spanish combination of legality and anarchy summed up in the phrase *obedezco pero no cumplo* (I obey but do not carry out) . . . [40]

According to Anderson, it is the survival and adaptation of other aspects of the Iberian heritage alongside the political forms adopted in the nineteenth century which produces Latin American instability. He argues that older and contradictory bases of political power have not been displaced. The absence of real political revolutions in most Latin American states, according to Anderson, means that 'power contenders' that cannot mobilise sufficient political support in elections have not been eliminated and continue to participate in politics. Winners of elections must negotiate with them to remain in power and will be displaced by them when government actions threaten older power groups. Thus democratic processes are only one alternative means of structuring power relationships.[41] There is considerable merit in Anderson's conclusion that other means of political succession remain as alternatives to electoral processes, but his explanation of why this is so has a number of weaknesses.

The main problem in applying Anderson's argument to Argentina is its failure to acknowledge the profound social change which occurred during the nineteenth and early twentieth centuries. The independence revolution can be seen as being as potent a source of political change as were those of Belgium in 1830 and Norway in 1905. Yet neither of these was followed by further social revolutions and both nations are marked by their political stability. Similarly, the 1912 Sáenz Peña Law had an impact on the extent of electoral participation equivalent to changes in the franchise in Britain in 1832, 1867 and 1884 combined (although not as extensive as that in France in 1848).[42] It is also difficult to decide what is meant by 'old power contenders' in the Argentine case. Presumably the term would be applied to landed interests and the military. Yet, it was the land-owning Oligarchy which consolidated the electoral process as a means to obtain power in the period after 1880, albeit on a very limited participatory base, and a military officer who won the election of 1880. The sectoral structure of Argentine society is such that it is hard for any power contender to put together a coalition sufficiently broad to win an election and sufficiently strong to retain its unity against an alliance of oppositional interests. It is frequently the increasing fragmentation and thus ineffectiveness of governing coalitions which leads many to tolerate or even welcome a *golpe*. Such was the situation in 1930 when Yrigoyen found himself incapable of ensuring the passage of legislation through Congress. Nor does Anderson's thesis explain the need of all power contenders to seek constitutional support for their actions. The Concordancia, representing the landed interests, sought the 'semi-legitimacy' accorded by elections through its use of 'patriotic fraud' in the years 1932–43 and, with the exception of the regimes which began in 1966 and 1976, military governments have always asserted their transitional nature between elected governments. Thus Anderson fails to recognise that all power contenders accept democratic procedures and electoral processes as the most legitimate means of political succession, but that at the same time this acceptance rests on differing interpretations of the proper functioning of democracy, and all power contenders therefore reserve the right to use different means when the system 'malfunctions'. As Guido di Tella notes:

> Elections have been tried over and over again as if Argentines were great believers in the electoral process, but the results have been deemed unacceptable by a substantial part of the power structure. In theory, democratic values have been flatly rejected. *De facto* violations of democratic procedure have been accepted on the assumption that they are unfortunate necessities, presumably temporary in nature.[43]

It is incorrect to argue, as Fitzgibbon and Fernández do, that alienation of the population from the political system works against its legitimisation in Argentina.[44] Despite scepticism about the effects of elections, Argentine citizens are not alienated from the political process. The level of participation in elections in Buenos Aires, for example, compares favourably with that in other Western urban centres. However Argentine political culture does reflect an odd mixture of formal participation, direct action and political passivity. The survey Imaz conducted in Buenos Aires under the Frondizi government showed 43 per cent of respondents were positively uninterested in politics, with a further 28 per cent showing little interest. Interest declined with social status and 62 per cent of working-class respondents were uninterested.[45] But it should not be forgotten that this same 'uninterested' working class was soon to vote for Peronist deputies and provincial governors in such numbers in the 1962 elections that military fears of a Peronist restoration led to Frondizi's ouster. Similarly, in March 1965, the extent of working-class support for Peronist candidates in the congressional elections was profoundly disturbing to the officers backing the Illia government. Also the willingness to use direct action, although circumscribed, remained and, for example, the stabilisation programme which formed an important part of Onganía's plan for Argentina was met with a general strike in March 1967. Labour militancy again increased in 1969 leading to Onganía's displacement.

Certainly Argentine attitudes to government are pessimistic and little respect is accorded to those in power. Kirkpatrick found that more than half her respondents believed that the ordinary citizen has little effect on government. The vote itself was not seen as an important mode of influencing national decisions. Such respondents were not alienated from the system, they did not require further influence but rather accepted that formal politics was too complex for them to participate more. Most respondents believed that participation was desirable, but did not themselves wish to take part in public affairs and did not admire those who did participate.[46] Such political apathy has been explained in terms of the establishment of the mass political culture at a time when the working-class population was largely transient, comprising an effectively excluded immigrant mass, and large sections of the middle class were employed in public services and thus had to consider their jobs.[47] But in addition these apparently contradictory attitudes are explicable in their derivation from two conflicting cultural legacies. The actual extent of voting derives from the European stream of influence as does the recognition that elections constitute the most legitimate form of political succession. On the other hand, direct action and political passivity express the perceived lack of responsiveness of the constitutional structure and thus the limits on its legitimacy, a perception deriving from the Iberian heritage.

THE MILITARY AND LEGITIMACY

The way in which citizens perceive their elected governments is, of course, only one facet of the relationship between legitimacy and instability, though it is also a determinant of both. A government that is seen generally as legitimate and effective is unlikely to be perceived differently by the military itself, since the armed forces are part of a wider society and have tended to act in Argentina on behalf of certain civilian sectors, as well as for their own interests. Indeed, as Habermas notes, movement away from competitive democratic legitimation is a means of resolving a legitimacy crisis.[48] If no such crisis exists, military intervention is unnecessary. Similarly, a society which recognises an elective government as legitimate is more likely to resist the usurping of that government by the armed forces. Civilians have powerful weapons they can use against military domination, but whether they choose to use them rests on the value they place on the civilian alternative. For example, the period 1976–83 in Argentina was marked by:

> ... the willingness of the general population to put up with abuses which would have spurred democrats elsewhere into noisy rebellion.[49]

A protracted general strike could have forced the military from power sooner but, in the end, it was military incompetence rather than social reaction which resulted in the recivilianisation of Argentine politics.

The military do have certain advantages deriving from Argentine political history which operate against the view that the armed forces should remain outside politics. At independence, the military was more popular than the revolutionary politicians and afterwards it was the only institution with any legitimacy, this being based on its role in the struggle against colonialism. The close relationship between politics and the military was maintained throughout the nineteenth century and the most important political figures were often soldiers. The connection was also made in small concrete ways such as the basing of new electoral rolls, drawn up by the military not the local civilian authorities following the electoral reform of 1912, on military lists of conscriptable citizens, in the tradition of Roman law. Appeals by political groups to the military have further strengthened this relationship in the twentieth century. Since the 1960s, the fear of communist subversion may also have had the effect of increasing the relative political legitimacy of the armed forces amongst some sections of the population, and this is a reason frequently cited by upper- and upper-middle-class Argentines to justify their support for the Videla government. Kirkpatrick's respondents viewed both landowners and communists much more negatively than they did the military.[50] Nevertheless, the massive public response to the Easter Week uprisings suggest that this view may have been changed by the experience of 1976–83.

Johnson points out that intellectuals have provided the main ideological opposition to the armed forces, and that for most Latin Americans they are simply there as part of the political system.[51] Beliefs about the relative power of politically active groups are important. Such beliefs may not confer legitimacy, but they do lead to a feeling of powerlessness in the face of what is perceived to be reality, and they may serve to further reduce the legitimacy of other institutions. The Seventh National Public Opinion Survey conducted in Argentina in December 1962 found that the majority of the 3290 respondents believed the armed forces were running the country despite rating military usefulness as lower than that of other important institutions.[52] Kirkpatrick also found that the military were seen as having greater social influence than any other group[53] Such beliefs were supported by expert opinion which, when surveyed, rated the armed forces as having greater political strength than any other group in Argentina.[54] Thus the assessment of the power of the military by citizens would appear rational and, since effectiveness of government is an inherent part of legitimacy, must therefore serve to undermine the legitimacy of civilian institutions.

The Argentine armed forces have not been seen as fully legitimately involved in politics, but the recognition of their political power points up the weakness of civilian institutions. This weakness and the varying interpretations of democracy operate against the development of a fully legitimate constitutional system. In such circumstances, some sectors turn against constitutional procedures when they appear to be betraying a particular view of how they should function and the limited legitimacy of the system allows the armed forces to assume a moral superiority and to intervene to restore the 'proper' functioning of the political system. Every such intervention makes the likelihood of future military involvement greater, since it provides precedents for future action and encourages civilian sectors to seek military aid to restore their particular perception of democracy. As the document issued in December 1985 to accompany the establishment of the Renewal Wing of the Peronist movement pointed out, even the more moderate and more electorally successful part of the major opposition party does not accept the basic procedural premises assumed by the governing party. It states of Peronism:

> Our political culture is different, our vision of democracy distinct.[55]

It is fortunate for President Alfonsín that the most recent military regime ended in such bad odour that military intervention may be, at present, an unacceptable alternative to his Radical government. The conduct of the military during the 'Dirty War' and the Falklands conflict has effectively reduced the 'semi-legitimacy' which is accorded to the armed forces in a political role.

5 The Personalist Political Tradition

THE ORIGINS OF PERSONALISM

As Weber points out, charisma may provide alternative grounds legitimating a regime where traditional grounds have disappeared and rational grounds have not yet developed fully.[1] Such is the case in Argentina, where traditional legitimacy disappeared with the overthrow of the Spanish monarchy and the survival of the Iberian stream of culture prevented the full absorption of institutional legitimacy. The semi-legitimacy of popular sovereignty results in a continuing quest for an alternative legitimising base and therefore leaves room in politics for the perpetuation of charismatic authority, and of personalism more generally. In Argentina, loyalties have often been divided between respect for the principle of government through abstract and impersonal institutions, and strong adherence to individual political leaders.

Weber's definition of charisma is very precise and this particular and extreme form of personalism rests on:

> devotion to the specific and exceptional sanctity, heroism or exemplary character of an individual person, and of the normative patterns or order revealed or ordained by him.[2]

Even in this specific sense, Argentina's history has exhibited a marked preference for charismatic leadership, and amongst the figures in politics and beyond who have displayed charismatic qualities rather than simply personalist support are José de San Martín, Rosas, Sarmiento, Yrigoyen, Carlos Gardel, Juan and Evita Perón. San Martín meets Weber's requirements for charisma in his exceptional heroism. He is commemorated with pictures hung on walls in classrooms and in the textbooks of Argentine schoolchildren. The anniversary of his death is celebrated annually as elementary school pupils queue to place flowers on the numerous memorials to him in

Buenos Aires and the provinces. Rosas' charisma, too, is of the heroic military leader type. He won the adoration of his *peon* followers and the respect of fellow cattlemen when, in 1820, he recaptured thousands of cattle stolen by Indians. Thus he acquired an heroic status which he never lost even though when, in 1833, the Buenos Aires legislature sent him to do battle with the Indians, he made treaties with his opponents and preserved the peace by his gifts to them. Later he fell from grace and there are no statues of him. A 'secular homage' is paid to Sarmiento's memory, resting on his revelation of a 'normative order', on his opposition to, and role in the defeat of, the *caudillos*. His house on the Delta of the Paraná is preserved as a national shrine. Yrigoyen came to symbolise the aspirations of previously politically excluded sections of Argentine society. Like Sarmiento, he is commemorated in the naming of streets and schools.

Carlos Gardel, as a successful tango singer, born in France but brought up in a working-class district of Buenos Aires, admired and accepted by wealthy Argentines and foreigners alike, provided a vicarious escape from poverty and symbolised the economic aspirations of many of those who lived grey colourless lives in districts similar to that from which he came. Even today tributes are left daily at his tomb in the Chacarita Cemetery, where a cigarette smoulders between the fingers of his larger-than-life-size effigy. What Yrigoyen did for those with aspirations to middle-sector status, the Peróns did for the working classes, going further in meeting working-class economic and political aspirations than anyone previously and, in the process, stirring up new expectations for the future. In addition, Evita's charismatic quality seems to have included, with hindsight rather surprisingly, an image of saintliness for some of her supporters, at least, though the basis for Peronism is a subject of fierce controversy. Certainly, the Peróns still inspire very obvious personal loyalty and their tombs are constantly decked in homage with flowers and other tokens of affection. The violation of Juan Perón's tomb in July 1987 was followed by massive demonstrations called by the CGT.

Personalism in the sense used here is a much less exceptional quality than Weber's concept of charisma and is in consequence much more widespread. All successful political figures display some charismatic qualities, though most, including many who would be defined as personalist leaders, do not meet the definition of the term used by Weber. Personalism will be used here to imply yielding support to an individual rather than an institution and possibly also accepting that the individual in question may use powers which go beyond the limits of institutional constraints. (Thus personalism may be associated in some cases with an acceptance of authoritarianism amongst supporters of a personalist leader.) Personal popularity, which does not imply that the individual is more influential than the institution he represents, cannot be seen as personalism in this sense. Such popularity exists in all systems even those with a more fully legitimate institutional structure. In Weberian terms, all political systems are mixtures of various kinds of legitimacy. No legitimating base exists in a pure form. It is therefore the degree to which a particular form of legitimacy exists relative to other forms which is significant, rather than the mere fact of its existence.

Some authors have argued that personalism was a quality of nineteenth-century Latin America, but has declined during the twentieth century. Even in its narrowest form, charisma, the list above suggests this is not so in Argentina. In the wider sense of the term personalism, there is even less reason to suppose that this feature has diminished. The preference for the personal over the impersonal remains a feature of politics and reflects the continuing interaction of Argentina's two cultures. A colourful figurehead is still the most effective means of mobilising widespread public support in Argentina, whether by electoral means or not, as the Peronist presidential candidate, Italo Luder, found to his cost in the 1983 elections.[3]

Explanations for the persistence of personalism in Argentina start with the cultural legacy of Spanish colonial rule. For example, personalism is seen as a derivative of the patrimonialism of the Spanish monarchy which associated the colonial territories with the person of the monarch. Alongside imperial patrimonialism, the power of the landowner developed in replication and was to some extent legitimised by the king's role of super-*patrón*. Paternalism became such a potent element of upper-class ideology that it is to be found in the writings of even those most influenced by liberal thought, such as Echeverría. It is a feature which has continued to characterise the words and actions of Argentine politicians, whether civilian or military. Since rural males were, until recently, the largest group of registered voters, the paternalist tradition has been electorally very important. In his 1973 survey, Turner found that Argentine rural workers continued to express the closeness of their personal ties to their *patrones*.[4]

In the post-independence era, Argentine political personalism took the particular form of *caudillismo*. North rightly points out that this term is used to describe two different political processes in Latin American politics. First it is the label used for individual military leaders acquiring and maintaining power over given, usually sub-national, territories through the use of personalist followings. Secondly, it is used to describe personalism in politics and a lack of institutionalised political structures.[5] The derivation of the term, from a Latin word meaning 'head', suggests that the first use may be seen as more appropriate. *Caudillo* will here be taken to mean the kind of military leader with a personal irregular army who characterised the second quarter of the nineteenth century in Argentina. Later political figures may have had features reminiscent of the *caudillos*, but they must be described as personalist leaders rather than *caudillos*. *Caudillismo* has a narrower meaning; it is only one type of personalism. However, the age of *caudillismo* in expressing the personalist tradition contributed to the wider concept and strengthened it.

There were four main indigenous reasons for the development of *caudillismo* in Argentina. First, the independence struggle had highlighted the role of military leaders such as San Martín and thus admiration for 'the man on horseback' was reinforced in a local context. Secondly, independence led to the removal of the symbol of institutional authority. This gave rise to political tensions and rivalries within an Argentine elite that comprised both urban and rural elements with kinship ties linking them. The weakness of the residual institutional structure derived from the colonial era led to the dissolution of central authority in the 1820s. The urban elite was so riven by internal rivalries that it could not effectively resist the transfer to provincial forces of the function of maintaining order. The provincial families who had retained the lands and influence they had amassed during the colonial era consolidated and extended their traditional roles. *Caudillos*, such as Facundo Quiroga, inherited not only land, but also regional policing and judicial powers. Thus surfaced the reality of dispersed power in its non-institutional form in the absence of some alternative legitimating base. Thirdly, the lack of identification with the geographical territory defined at independence could not counteract the strength of sub-national identifications. The nebulous quality of the 'nation' after independence may have further promoted *caudillismo* through the need for personification. It was the personal support and power of Rosas which held the provinces of what is now Argentina together, not common feeling. Fourthly, the latent economic problems of the colonial era surfaced with independence, and two separate and diverging economies were revealed. Buenos Aires no longer needed goods from the interior, but could acquire them more directly and cheaply from Europe. The interior also lost its markets to the north in Peru with the collapse of the Spanish Empire. Free trade was already beginning to force specialisation and it was clear that the littoral provinces were more advantaged in producing pastoral products for export. Thus, Halperín Donghi sees the revolutionary process as leading to 'the mutilation and fragmentation of the commercial hinterland of Buenos Aires' as a consequence of the legacy of a colonial structure which gave merchants primacy over domestic producers.[6] *Caudillismo* was therefore a defensive response from interior economic interests despite its primary association with the person of Rosas, a coastal landowner.

Caudillismo rested on charisma. The presumed exceptional personal qualities of the *caudillo* were the source of his support. For example, Rosas had the reputation of being more effective in the skills prized by his *gaucho* followers than were his men. No ideological base was necessary to this style of leadership and since pragmatism was the basis of alliances between the *caudillos*, none was developed. The state, such as it was, became an extension of Rosas' personal power. As Lynch notes:

> His state was the estancia writ large. Society itself was built upon the patrón–peon relationship.[7]

Rosas' ability to contain his rivals was the key to the perpetuation of his personal sovereignty and this capacity rested on individual agreements or the use of force. This manner of controlling dissident interests is directly contrary to the development of the power-sharing coalitions and compromises which form the basis of a political party system and to the emergence of legal forms to regulate political activity. The limited debate and repression of the *caudillo* era allowed no development of a political opposition, at least in the domestic context. Therefore the political party system and the formal constitutional structure developed late and in a distorted form. However, 'the *caudillos* exercised a kind of elemental democracy'[8] and only federalism could be seen as 'democratic' in the participatory sense of the term, since it was the option acceptable to the majority of the population.[9]

The end of the *caudillo* era, which enabled European influence to re-assert itself against the Iberian stream and led to the establishment of the formal political structure, was itself an example of *caudillismo*. It was Urquiza, the *caudillo* of Entre Ríos, who led the combined forces of Brazil, Uruguay and some Argentine provinces against Rosas and defeated him in battle at Caseros in 1852. In some areas of the interior this had little effect on the reality of political power. Considerable local autonomy remained until the end of the nineteenth century in the Andean provinces of Salta, Jujuy and Mendoza. Local politics passed into the hands of local *patrones*, who were frequently the old *caudillos*. This situation preserved personalism and prevented the development of national organisations by perpetuating a pattern of political loyalties which were not primarily owed to national institutions. The pattern of provincial autonomy and variation, thus retained, resisted the nationalising of provincial political practice. Fluidity, factionalism and personalism would survive the creation of national political parties and be expressed in some odd regional variants well into the twentieth century.[10]

Nevertheless, the decline of *caudillismo* made possible the beginnings of the development of political parties during the 1850s, but under Urquiza and his elected successor, Santiago Derqui (1860–61), these continued to reflect the Federalist/Unitarist division. Only after the defeat of the *porteño* forces by Urquiza's Confederation army at Cepeda in 1859 would Buenos Aires agree to become a party to the 1853 Constitution. However the state of virtual civil war continued until Mitre led the *porteño* forces to victory against Urquiza at Pavón in 1861 and went on to establish a provisional national government in the following year. The constitution adopted by Urquiza's Confederation, which became, with minor amendments, the formal political structure of the nation, reflected this surviving personalism.

The new constitution built certain weaknesses into Argentina's formal political structure which were to have long-term political consequences. Alberdi's major contribution to it meant that the constitution was theoretically essentially liberal, indicating the strength of non-Iberian influences. But as such it was seen by conservative elements as a threat to the old order and therefore encouraged the preservation of the semi-legitimacy of the Iberian cultural stream. The constitutional structure itself enabled the persistence of Iberian cultural traits such as legalism and, more importantly, personalism. It was modelled on the US constitution and contained the same basic elements such as 'popular sovereignty, separation of powers, federalism, limited government, national supremacy and the rule of law'.[11] However, the political structure created by this constitution was such that in practice all these ideals could be avoided whilst adhering to the letter of the document. For example, the provinces were given residual powers not specifically allocated to central government and this is what gives the 1853 Constitution its federal quality. But formal powers of presidential intervention enable the executive to undermine this. In addition, the president assumes all congressional powers when Congress is not in session and has the power to suspend Congress himself. He appoints all members of the national administration, though his judicial and diplomatic appointments require congressional confirmation. In practice, Congress has in many periods been largely a ratifier of presidential legislation despite the theoretical powers given to it by the constitution, and this creates a disproportionately powerful chief executive.

Two arguments surround this persistence of personalism in Latin America in the latter half of the nineteenth century.

They are not mutually exclusive and may even be seen as complementary. The first, and more frequently expressed, view is that Latin American culture remained essentially Hispanic and as such encouraged the personification of authority. Impersonal political institutions were to some extent incongruent with the cultural base of society and could not become fully legitimate in consequence. The second argument suggests that the character of 'liberalism' had changed even before Latin America became susceptible to its influence. Stokes writes:

> Latin American liberalism . . . was less that of the seventeenth century British social contract and natural law thinkers and more of the romantic, idealistic eighteenth and nineteenth century liberalism of Jean Jacques Rousseau . . . Latin American liberalism . . . almost immediately glorified the strong man who could and would use the power of government *for* the people, even at the expense of individual liberty, freedom and political participation *of* the people.[12]

There is a weakness in Stokes' argument which goes beyond the anachronistic and simplistic use of a nineteenth-century term to describe the antecedents of liberalism in the seventeenth and eighteenth centuries. Rousseau proposed no institutional structure for ascertaining the nature of the General Will and it is from earlier social contract thought that Latin American political institutions derive. However, this does not detract from the basic proposition that ideas of a General Will, ascertained by means other than counting heads, lent support to the personalist political tradition in Argentina. Shades of Rousseau can certainly be found in the paternalist thought of Argentine political leaders in the latter half of the nineteenth century. For example, Sarmiento believed that, when presented with a civilised example through education and urbanisation, the Argentine masses would realise what they really sought and forsake their mistaken orientation to indolence and barbarism.[13] The end of the *caudillo* era altered the form of personalism, but the establishment of impersonal political institutions did not eliminate it.

The 1860s saw the consolidation of this impersonal institutional structure, but it was also the era of what has been termed (erroneously in the narrow sense of the term being used here) 'the frock-coated *caudillo*'. After Urquiza's defeat, Mitre's Nationalists came to power, opposed by the Autonomists who wanted Buenos Aires to remain the capital of its province only, not of the whole nation. Thus, politics had become a competition between rival coalitions of economic interests but personalism remained a potent source of political support.

Both Mitre and his successor, Sarmiento, were examples of the mercantilist liberal element of the Argentine elite which espoused positivist ideas of order as a means to progress. Both feared that *caudillismo* could recur and were aware that the *caudillos* had enjoyed widespread support amongst the lower orders. Both saw the provinces as barbaric, a view powerfully reflected in the subtitle of Sarmiento's study of *caudillismo*. Both men therefore sought to civilise the nation. For example, Mitre established a judicial code and court system and extended postal and telegraphic services; whilst Sarmiento set up the primary education system. Sarmiento's emphasis on education suggests that *caudillismo* was seen as a function of the ignorance and manipulability of the masses. (This explanation was later revived for the personalism of the Perón period.) Both sought to attract immigrants who would bring European (civilised) ideas and would promote the development of cities in the interior ('civilisation' in the most literal sense). Such measures conferred a certain limited legitimacy on the state in the domestic sphere and much broader prestige in the international context, laying down the foundations for the influx of European capital in the 1870s and 1880s. But despite such attempts to depersonalise the state, political personalism survived. Using the term *caudillo* in the wider sense, Pendle notes that:

> The Argentines might be taught to read and write and to wear trousers, but they retained the traditional preference of the gaucho (to whose make-up the Spanish hidalgo, as well as the life of the pampa, had made a vital contribution) for personal independence and personal rule. They continued to be more ready to follow a leader than to give their allegiance to a political programme. The Argentine caudillo henceforth was dressed in a frock-coat – or in the uniform of

an officer of the national army – but he remained a caudillo at heart.[14]

Such was the way with men like Mitre and Sarmiento. Although espousing liberalism, they were products of the Hispanic tradition. As governor of the province of San Juan, Sarmiento declared a state of siege in 1863, indicating his willingness to elevate himself above the institutions of provincial government. As president he frequently chose to interpret the constitution in a personalist manner, using federal intervention against the provinces and governing by decree. These were the very methods he professed to oppose and which he earlier sought to replace by law. The opposition during Sarmiento's presidency was led by Mitre and was highly personal. When Sarmiento's term of office expired in 1874, he sought to impose the successor of his choice which inspired Mitre to lead the resistance to such a manoeuvre. The champion of the process of 'civilising' Argentina, a man who consistently opposed *caudillismo* and who probably did more to legitimate the newly-established impersonal political institutions, and the European stream of influence they reflected, than any other nineteenth-century Argentine leader, retained a personalist style of political leadership.

Avellaneda (1874–80), whose presidency constituted the transition between the Generations of 1837 and 1880, primarily concerned himself with encouraging immigration and the expansion of Argentina's agricultural land. Avellaneda's approach to national problems was an intellectual one, and he sought support for his schemes through rational argument rather than by rallying a retinue of personal supporters. (However, it should be noted that Avellaneda did work against Roca on a personal basis prior to the latter's assumption of power in 1880.) This style of politics was viable in consequence of the available resources and the growing strength of Argentina's position in the world, which conferred some measure of legitimacy on the regime. Politically-important sectors could be satisfied by the bringing into production of new lands and the expanding opportunities for trade. Appeal to a Congress dominated by the Argentine elite ensured that landed interests were not threatened by the enforcement of such progressive acts as Avellaneda's 1876 Land Law. The first frozen meat was sent to Europe during the Avellaneda presidency, and European capital and immigrants began to flow into the new nation, thus increasing her status abroad and also aspirations at home.

The Avellaneda administration laid the foundations for the dominance of the Oligarchy and the myth of a 'golden age', which Roca would then consolidate. Although his personal prestige was great as a result of his leadership of the Desert Campaign, Roca's presidencies (1880–86 and 1898–1904) were not essentially personalist administrations, despite Roca's use of force as well as bribery to quell provincial opposition. Intra-elite cliques would later form in some provinces around Roca and Juárez Celman, just as cliques had always formed around family and kinship groups, but Roca did not need to rally personal support as the Partido Autonomista Nacional dominated Congress and had the support of most politically-important sectors. Roca presided over the continuing expansion of the national territory and the beginning of an economic boom which was to last until 1889. An increasingly active state, legitimised by the inflow of European capital and immigrants, expanded its role by using European investment to develop the economic infrastructure. The improvement of port facilities, railway building and the provision of public utilities and other developmental schemes served to unite the elite elements who envisaged a bright national future from which they could all benefit. Under such circumstances, Roca was able, temporarily, to reduce to a level manageable within the institutional framework the competition between the different politically-active interests which comprised the Oligarchy. Through the process of professionalisation and grants of new land won from the Indians he maintained military adherence. In consequence, he extended the institutional strength of the presidency rather than having to seek personal political support. However, Roca did, in accord with the personalist tradition, pick his own successor and Juárez Celman was 'elected' president in 1886.

The reversion to an inconvertible paper peso in 1885 and the reduction of its value in the years following because of inflation, hit European investors in Argentina's rapid economic development. Embezzlement, corruption and general economic incompetence reached new peaks in Juárez Celman's administration making the inflationary spiral more intense, and by 1889 a serious economic crisis loomed with European credit no longer available. As the national economic 'pie' now seemed unable to satisfy the various important interests, internal elite rivalry increased in the late 1880s. However, on this particular occasion, factions developed along geographical lines rather than strictly personal ones, despite the adoption of names derived from the leaders. Roca tended to represent the Buenos Aires faction and Juárez Celman that of Córdoba. Juárez Celman did seek to establish a personal support base by putting his own appointees in key positions but he ran out of time, and elite factionalism was dissipated by his resignation after the abortive rebellion in 1890 and 'rocquismo' was to dominate Argentine politics into the early years of the twentieth century. The emergence of a new threat reduced the tendency to personalist cliques amongst the elite. Disaffected elements began to align themselves with the growing urban middle sectors in the Radical Party which emerged in 1891. Personalism in politics had to give way to some element of elite unity. The Oligarchy feared losing control of the national government which was their main source of credit, and governmental instability would in any case be unattractive to the foreign investors and immigrants they needed. By 1912 the more liberal faction of the PAN which favoured expansion of the suffrage, which was in accord with certain positivist tenets, had come to dominate and the Sáenz Peña Law was the consequence.[15]

RADICALISM AS PERSONALISM

Whilst charges of nepotism and personalism were levelled at the Oligarchy after 1890 by the emergent opposition groups, these features – especially personalism – were to become much more important characteristics of the electoral coalition which developed out of these dissident elements. With Yrigoyen's unexpected elevation to the presidency in 1916, a new form of political personalism was soon to develop. Conniff sees the 'populist' leader as an urban product in contrast with the rural and military *caudillo*,[16] and Yrigoyen's personal support base lay primarily amongst the urban middle sectors. Yrigoyen's style of politics is also clearly distinguished from the personalism of the immediate post-Rosas years in that it rested on emotional attitudes whilst Mitre and Sarmiento were much more concerned with a programme of cultural and economic development.

Yrigoyen's career was marred by corruption (though it has been argued that he was himself an honest man who simply did not recognise the corruption of those around him)[17] and he built up an extensive system of personal political debts. He placed great emphasis on personal loyalty and personal relations in organising from a selection of disparate elements the first mass party in Argentina's history. His political style was essentially an adaptation of traditional political methods to the 1912 electoral reform and the increased number of politically active sectors articulating demands. Thus the organisation of mass political activity became necessary, and Yrigoyen achieved this by continuing an adherence to the formal institutional structure with elements of political practice derived from the Iberian stream of culture and reflecting the constraints placed upon him by continuing conservative domination of Congress. In his combination of some of the ideals and practices associated with the liberal stream of influence and some of those connected with Hispanic culture, Yrigoyen's dominance of Argentine politics reflects the failure of either cultural pattern to achieve hegemony in a society with two parallel semi-legitimate traditions of political activity. Gallo and Sigal alternatively see the synthesis achieved by the UCR as one expressing the dichotomy between traditional and modern political practice.[18]

From its inception the Unión Cívica Radical was forced to use unconstitutional tactics as a consequence of relative elite unity. This unity enabled the effective exclusion of the UCR from the formal political process by the use of just such methods. In response, the UCR's first leader, Yrigoyen's uncle, Leandro N. Alem (1891–96), tried to organise a rebellion which would sweep away the government of 'El Régimen' (the Oligarchy). Provincial rebellions occurred in 1891 and 1893 and the UCR did acquire some factional support amongst army officers. This was still insufficient to counteract the strength of upper-class support in the military so soon after Roca's stabilisation of the armed forces and the benefits they had received from the extension of the national territory during the Conquest of the Desert. Subsequently, Yrigoyen as leader tried to use the same methods, planning a coup in 1905 which was also unsuccessful as a result of continued officer loyalty to the conservative regime. Only 6.46 per cent of army officers were involved and none of these held a rank above colonel. Yrigoyen's appeal to the military 'mission' as justification for revolt in support of the Radical cause would be used against him in 1930.[19]

Exclusion, both effectively imposed and, after 1898, chosen, from the formal political system provides an important key to the personalist quality of Yrigoyen's regime. Apart from the psychological conditioning of institutional impotence forcing personal action which in turn enhances popular support, the legacy of exclusion for the political programme of the Radical Party was a largely negative one. Although the Radical elite were largely derived from traditional economic activity, the UCR built up its middle-class membership in the years 1906–12 from amongst those groups frustrated by what they saw as blocks on the achievement of their personal aspirations. Urban professionals, middle-class students, middle-class junior army officers and the sons of immigrants who had been upwardly mobile, were examples of groups with expectations in excess of their opportunities, perceiving themselves as excluded from assuming their rightful place in Argentine society. What such groups had in common was an awareness of what they were opposed to, but they had no shared vision of the future. As Rock puts it:

> The positive content of Radical doctrine and ideology was very limited. It was little more than an eclectic and moralistic attack on the oligarchy, to which was appended the demand for the introduction of representative government.[20]

Just as the absence of a positive programme left a need for some alternative source of appeal, so too the nature of Radical support encouraged personalism. The opposition to Juárez Celman which came to comprise the Unión Cívica had been a catholic selection of oligarchic, mercantile, clerical and urban middle-class groups both in the littoral and in small towns in the provincial interior. The UCR itself was born out of a split which occurred in this coalition and has remained actually or potentially fragmentary since. In 1894, Juan B. Justo's faction formed the Socialist Party, and Alem and other leaders vied for leadership of the UCR. Yrigoyen plotted against his uncle until the latter committed suicide in 1896. It was in consequence of a further schism that Yrigoyen was confirmed as the party's leader in 1898. The most important division within the Radical movement lay between patrician interests and the urban middle sectors, a rift which would re-emerge during the 1920s with disastrous consequences for the UCR. Radicalism remained a tenuous coalition representing different class and regional interests. As such, it could not afford to develop a specific programme which would narrow its support base; the Radical Party had to remain pragmatic when in power, providing benefits to its various sectors in order to retain their support. Thus unity was provided, not by a political programme, but by an emphasis on Yrigoyen as the movement's leader. His character and emotional rhetoric bound together the various elements of the Radical coalation.

The selection of Alvear as Radical candidate for the presidency in 1922 reflected Yrigoyen's growing fear of losing the support of upper-class elements. He therefore chose as his successor a patrician without a personal support base, in the expectation that he himself would be able to retain indirect control of the party. However, the schism in the UCR deepened as Alvear attacked the very basis of Yrigoyen's personalist middle-class support by limiting state spending on benefits to UCR activists. By 1924, the UCR had split again and the more conservative anti-personalist wing had been formed. This failed to eliminate Yrigoyen's influence in the UCR and he was able to regain the presidency in 1928 with 57 per cent of the popular vote. But it did weaken the party and placed more emphasis on personal, rather than institutional, support which was to dissipate rapidly in 1930.

In addition to the problems confronting Yrigoyen in holding together his party, he faced political opposition from all sides outside the UCR. The judiciary and Congress remained conservative-dominated. Despite his 1916 presidential victory, the Senate opposed Radical policies and, although he achieved the largest single party representation in the Chamber of Deputies, the opposition joined together against Radical legislation. In addition, Yrigoyen's own cabinet was dominated by representatives of the powerful patrician elements in the Radical movement. Outside the formal political structure, Yrigoyen faced labour unrest which culminated in the violence of 'Tragic Week' (la Semana Trágica) in January 1919. The perceived leftist threat led to the formation of right-wing paramilitary groups and most notably the creation of the Liga Patriótica Argentina. The use of the army as strike-breakers contributed to further factionalism within that institution. Opposition both within and without the formal political structure made Radicalism essentially institutionally impotent. Policies could not be realised if they challenged conservative interests and thus Yrigoyen's middle-class support base was under threat. Yrigoyen had therefore little option but to extend his system of patronage and his personal influence in the Radical Party. Rock notes that:

> In 1920 Yrigoyen began to enjoy the period of his great personal dominance in Argentine politics. But it was dominance without real power, since final authority lay in the hands of the conservative coalition, which was dominated by big business and the army.[21]

Radical rule in Argentina embraced and strengthened both the European and the Iberian streams of political culture. As a result of the Sáenz Peña law of 1912, political participation was greatly increased and the election of a non-oligarchic government effectively destroyed the *acuerdo* (consensus) system of obtaining agreement in Congress. Thus was political contestation in the legislature heightened and the role of Congress enhanced. However, the impotence of Radicalism in the face of opposition from all sides, but especially conservatism within the Radical Party itself and in the wider political context, forced Yrigoyen to resort to political methods which reflected and reinforced the Hispanic cultural legacy. The resort to personalist appeals for support and the use of political patronage are examples of this.

The personal quality of Yrigoyen's power is further indicated by his willingness to use the executive powers given to the president by the constitution for his own narrowly-defined political ends. It is true that federal intervention was an established practice, having been used 82 times in the 51 years from 1860 to 1911. But Yrigoyen's first six-year term as president saw 20 such interventions and they were of a more overtly political nature than had previously been the case.[22] He used intervention in some opposition provinces prior to elections in order to ensure subsequent Radical victories, but he also used this device against Radical factions seeking provincial autonomy, more concerned with democratic participation than procedure, and seen as too anxious to distribute benefits to the lower orders or *chusma* ('rabble').[23] It was by means of intervention that Yrigoyen had achieved a Radical majority in the Chamber of Deputies by 1918. He was less successful in the Senate, but never gave the method up. When the Senate refused to consider Yrigoyen's oil nationalisation proposals, the continuing need for a Senate majority inspired Radical intervention in the provinces of San Juan, Mendoza, Corrientes and Santa Fé in 1928–9. Further, Yrigoyen allowed members of his congressional faction to indulge in direct action against those who opposed him through their establishment in 1929 of a pro-government paramilitary group, the Klan Radical.

Finally, and perhaps most importantly, Yrigoyen encouraged the politicisation of the armed forces. Not only did he use them as strike-breakers and seek their support for his oil nationalisation plans, but he also personally interfered in internal institutional matters. By elevating those who had responded to his personal requests for military support in the period of electoral abstention until 1912, he offended those who were senior for promotion purposes, undermined the unity of the officer corps and reduced its institutional distance from politics. Following the Alvear interlude, Yrigoyen did not meet the promises of military equipment made by his predecessor, but instead returned to his preferred methods of personal meddling in assignments and organisation, and nepotism in appointments. Yrigoyen was not alone in using personal influence in the military, but his involvement came at a crucial stage in Argentine history when the newly-professionalised armed forces needed to be brought under effective government control if the principle of civilian supremacy was to be established. By his actions, Yrigoyen paved the way for military involvement in his overthrow in 1930:

> Yrigoyen intervened in military affairs *before* the army intervened decisively in politics, and the officers responded in *reaction* to his interference.[24]

Personalism in the Radical movement was not confined to the national level, but could also be seen in the kind of support built up by provincial factional leaders such as José Nestor Lencinas and his son Carlos Washington in Mendoza, and Federico Cantoni in San Juan.[25] Nevertheless, Yrigoyenism was a product of an unstable coalition of oppositional elements and in turn it contributed to the internal fragmentation of Radicalism during the course of the 1920s. It produced a style of leadership which was not well-suited for the expanded role of government in the twentieth century. Yrigoyen's highly personalist rule failed to build up a middle-class political philosophy or establish viable institutions for the continued political involvement of newly mobilised groups. His individual stubbornness, reflected in his odd and unnecessary personal crusades, despite criticisms from within the UCR and outside it, prevented him changing his political style and his unpopular personal retinue. Because an effective institutional structure for middle-class representation had not been established when the aged, reclusive and reputedly senile Yrigoyen could no longer generate sufficient personal support, nationalist elements, factions of the army and the conservative elite were able to displace the constitutional government, despite the continuing, although somewhat diminished, support for the Radical cause; support which remained latent and re-emerged in the gubernatorial elections in the Province of Buenos Aires in 1931. However, Yrigoyen's importance did not end with his overthrow. He was the first popularly elected Argentine president, and, after his death in 1933, consistent with the Weberian concept of charisma, he was accorded the spontaneous tribute of a splendid funeral and became a myth, a symbol of the aspirations of the middle class.

THE CONCEPT OF POPULISM

Clearly, Yrigoyen's style of politics was personalist and paternalist, but whether Radicalism can be correctly described as 'populist' depends on which definition of populism is used. How, and indeed whether, the concept of populism can be used in a wider comparative context is debatable, but it has acquired some fairly specific and generally agreed characteristics in its application to Latin America. Drake notes that Latin American authors tend to see populism in three different, but connected, ways: as political mobilisation by a charismatic leader, as a multiclass coalition with emphasis on working-class support, and as developmentalist and integrative reformism.[26]

Although it has been suggested that 'populism' originated as a term applied to a nineteenth-century, anti-industrial phenomenon and that an alternative term such as 'popularism' might be more appropriate in describing a movement such a Peronism,[27] many authors have pointed to the urban character of twentieth-century Latin American populism, as contrasting with the essentially rural quality of movements defined as populist in other areas and at other times, for example 'classic' nineteenth-century agrarian populism in North America and Russia. Dix, distinguishing between what he terms 'authoritarian' and 'democratic' forms of populism in Latin America, points out that even the authoritarian variant, which is likely to be the more urban of the two kinds, also receives extensive rural support. He notes that Peronism, for example, has enjoyed considerable strength in some rural areas as is shown by the high percentages of the national vote it has achieved there when Peronist candidates have participated in national elections. Little points out, however, that effective penetration of rural areas was only achieved after the Peronist assumption of power.[28] Alternatively it has been suggested that populism is neither inherently urban nor rural, but arises out of an awareness of economic and political deprivation. For a variety of reasons such deprivation may be more keenly perceived in an urban context in Latin America, but in addition, the 'mass' quality of modern populism implies an urban background. Certainly the sparse population and traditional structure of much of the Argentine interior would make rural populism less likely, although Rodríguez does define Lencinism in Mendoza and Bloquism in San Juan in the 1920s as examples of 'populism', and Dolkart suggests that Manuel A. Fresco as Governor of the Province of Buenes Aires from 1936 to 1940 was seeking to establish a 'populist' working-class coalition of the right.[29] As Skidmore, writing of Brazil, points out:

> The term 'populist' is an imprecise term, which has come to be used to describe a style of politician produced in a situation where a mass urban electorate is receptive to a colourful leader who relies on a direct, emotional appeal, based on economic issues of varying ideological sophistication.[30]

The implication of Skidmore's definition is that populism, at least in Latin America, can only occur at a certain stage of economic and political development. This idea is central to most of the work on the concept of populism as it has been applied to Argentina. For Germani, populism is frequently a by-product of the modernisation process, an attempt to integrate groups whose demands for participation exceed the level which is acceptable in the existing society.[31] For di Tella too, national popular movements arise when mobilisation precedes economic and political integration and thus the presence of large numbers of internal migrants who have not been assimilated into formal working-class organisations is central to the development of the national popular movement.[32] This new, recently displaced and marginal working class is seen as manipulable, as a 'disposable mass'. Such a fragmentary and marginalised working class is incapable of developing autonomous institutions and is thus open to emotional appeal. The association of populism with a particular stage of development is criticised by Laclau, who points out that examples of the phenomenon termed populism have occurred in developed societies as well, though less frequently. For Laclau:

> ... populism is historically linked to a crisis of the dominant ideological discourse which is in turn part of a more general social crisis.[33]

Laclau's analysis has the virtue of much wider application, but it does not negate the work of Latin American theorists who see populism in Latin America as deriving from a certain stage of development, since what they are effectively describing is a 'crisis of transformation' accompanied by a 'fracture' in the dominant power bloc brought on by the conflict between traditionally oriented economic interests and those favouring autonomous industrial development supported by excluded working-class elements. Germani himself acknowledges that the 'disintegration' which may lead to the development of a national populist regime is experienced by all societies, but adds that this is more likely and more potent at certain stages of development.[34]

The third characteristic generally associated with Latin American populism is also criticised by Laclau. It is the idea that populism necessarily involves a multiclass coalition and de-emphasises social class. This is central to the analyses of authors such as Worsley,[35] Conniff,[36] Germani[37] and di Tella. For the last it constitutes the basis of his definition of populism as:

> . . . a political movement which enjoys the support of the mass of the urban working class and/or peasantry but does not result from the autonomous organisational power of either of these two sectors. It is also supported by non-working-class sectors upholding an anti-status quo ideology.[38]

Laclau sees the support base and the ideology of populist movements as class-based, and criticises theorists who deny this. He argues that defining populism in terms of its direct appeal to the people is essentially tautological and that an appeal to 'the people' may also be an appeal to a certain social class. The problem is the absence of definition of the terms 'class' and 'people'.[39] Laclau's criticisms are useful but exaggerate the weaknesses of the ideas he attacks. Latin American populism occurs in what amounts to an unresolved and continuing crisis of national identity and, as such, expansive ideologies claiming to represent all social groups are therefore explicable. Indeed, in any polity where mass electoral support is required, consensual appeals will be heard from time to time. Such appeals, however, are frequently more for the consumption of supporters, who require justification for their continuing support than for opposition elements who are unlikely to be won over. Similarly, all political movements encompass elements from different social classes, though the most class-bound may feel the need to confer 'honorary worker' status or use some other such device to retain their apparent purity. The strength of the 'multiclass' analysis is that it reflects the heterogeneity of the groups which supported populism and the fluidity of the social structure which worked against the previous autonomous development of class consciousness and enabled charismatic leaders to stimulate it.

The fourth widely agreed characteristic of Latin American populism is clearly related to the absence of pre-existing autonomous institutional development amongst groups which support the populist movement. It is the hierarchical quality of populism. Dix suggests that some populist movements, those he calls 'democratic', are less hierarchical than those he terms 'authoritarian'. Acción Democrática (AD) in Venezuela, Alianza Popular Revolucionaria de América (APRA) in Peru and the Movimiento Nacional Revolucionario (MNR) in Bolivia fall into the first category, in contrast with Carlos Ibáñez del Campo in Chile, Gustavo Rojas Pinilla in Colombia and Perón in Argentina. Democratic populism is still led by elite groups, though these are more likely to be professional politicians or intellectuals, and such a movement is less tied to one leadership figure.[40] There is little disagreement on the hierarchical nature of populism generally, however, though Laclau, amongst others, questions the explanation of this quality in terms of traditional values brought to urban areas by internal migrants.[41] Most authors see the hierarchical characteristic of populism as being in accord with Latin American culture. In Argentina, it is a reflection of the re-emergence of the Iberian cultural stream in response to a crisis in the European stream of influence. The failure to include emergent political sectors into the formal structure stimulates recourse to a modern form of the alternative political mode. Hennessy argues that the populist leader is like the *patrón* in rural areas, and appeals to internal migrants socialised in such dependent relations. The importance of primary relationships, the distrust of impersonal institutions, machismo and the admiration of the strong man remain parts of Latin American culture and have carried over into the modern urban setting.[42]

Populism contains many apparent contradictions and perhaps the most obvious is that despite its hierarchical quality, its tendency to reflect the Iberian corporatist legacy by the establishment of a one-party system or at least the identification of the populist movement with the state itself and its use of cooptation, it relies on mass participation through the electoral system. The mass quality of Latin American populism and its support base amongst newly mobilised groups precludes dominance by force or repression and therefore widespread electoral support is required. It is this need which gives populism its unique style of leadership combining controlled mobilisation through a hierarchical organisational structure and charismatic appeals for electoral support. The populist leader's rhetoric must appeal to recruits from different sectors and this therefore militates against the development of a formal ideology, at least until the support base is established. Emotive issues and symbols are often more potent sources of support than political programmes. In particular national unity is promoted by nationalistic appeals that shift popular disaffection from internal issues to external ogres. In combining a respect for tradition with the demands of emergent sectors, populism needs to achieve some change, but is not usually revolutionary. It has been defined as 'the promise of progress without upheaval',[43] and tends to promise more for all within the existing structure of society. Populism is usually seen as being concerned with redistribution of resources rather than economic development, though this is questionable in the case of Perón and inaccurate in the case of Kubitschek (1956–61) in Brazil.

In assessing the extent to which individual Argentine leaders were populist, it is necessary to measure the characteristics of the movements they led against the features of populism as listed above. Of the three national leaders of the past who sought mass support, there is little controversy about the populist credentials of Rosas and Perón. Lynch points out that Rosas was 'a leader of the masses, a precursor of the populist dictator', but he was clearly not a populist himself.[44] Peronism, on the other hand, is often, though not always, seen as 'the typical example' of modern Latin American populism; it is frequently the model from which the characteristics of Latin American populism are derived. Radicalism remains an area of dispute.

RADICALISM AS POPULISM

It is only the qualities of Radicalism after the beginning of the twentieth century which are controversial, since only then did it begin to acquire its mass character as a coalition of sections of the elite with the middle class. Following Yrigoyen's ouster in 1930, Radicalism continued to function as a primarily middle-class political party but lacked a charismatic leader and was clearly not a populist movement. The era from 1900–30 remains the period at issue. This era falls outside the time-span usually allocated to Latin American populism, 1930–60, but Argentina's greater development would explain this apparent anomaly. For various reasons, some authors have described Radicalism as 'populist'; Remmer, for example, because it lacked a concrete programme;[45] Rock because it fitted the general sense of the term 'populism', though he emphasises the problems associated with the term and states that he is not using it in a technical sense.[46] For other commentators, Radicalism 'came close'[47] to the populist pattern or was 'potentially populist'[48] but never completely fitted. Germani sees Radicalism as having many of the features of populism, but it is distinguished from the national populist movements by its essential liberalism; he therefore terms it 'liberal populism'.[49] In similar style, both Conniff and Tamarin distinguish between 'reformist era' populism, which characterised the interwar period, and 'national developmentalist era' populism, which is seen as typical of the period since the Second World War. Radicalism is seen as an example of the former kind, Peronism the latter.[50]

Certainly Radicalism was primarily, though by no means entirely, an urban movement and thus fits the first characteristic of populism. The UCR between 1912 and 1916 was strongest in the littoral provinces outside Buenos Aires and, within that area, the bigger the centre of population the higher was the Radical vote.[51] Whether it arises in the way suggested by the model employed by authors like Germani and di Tella is more questionable, however. As with Peronism, Radicalism did reflect new demands for participation, all of which, given their varied roots, the existing political system was unable to satisfy. Thus it could be said to represent an excess of mobilisation over integration. Nevertheless, Germani points out that Radicalism may have represented a middle-class challenge for political power, but not really an attempt by the middle class to assert itself economically. The middle classes had benefited to some extent at least from the existing economic structure and thus, he argues, did not have a vested interest in making fundamental changes to it. The traditional elite who retained their economic power, did not therefore really resist the rise of the Radicals.[52] If the UCR was not a real alternative to the older conservative parties, and certainly it had some of its support base and policies in common with them, it could be argued that it did not constitute a sufficient challenge to the existing system to be seen as populist. Laclau, for example, sees Radicalism as the cooptation of the middle sectors and the consequent neutralisation of popular resistance. Yrigoyen merely forced the expansion of the participatory aspect of liberal democracy.[53] The benefits of liberalism were not being questioned and thus the content of Yrigoyen's Radical regime was never as offensive to the traditional elite as was his style. In the end it was not the changes he was seen as making which led to his ouster, but rather the political impotence of his government.

According to Rock, the use of mass mobilisation techniques, the 'polyclass' and 'integrative' character of Radicalism and the attempts to maintain unity by emphasising Yrigoyen as the leader of the movement, all accord broadly with the general use of the term populism.[54] However, whether Radicalism was 'polyclass' is debatable. It certainly was not in the sense of the term multiclass usually adopted, that is, implying a primary support base amongst the working class with additional support from the lower middle class and other sectors, as suggested in di Tella's definition of the concept of populism. Germani points out that in the early years of the twentieth century such a large proportion of the Argentine working class were immigrants, and either politically apathetic or sympathetic to direct action,[55] that there was therefore relatively little potential working-class electoral support for Radicalism. (Although Cornblit suggests a slightly higher figure, 1.4 per cent, Bagú states that by 1914 only 0.9 per cent of immigrants had acquired Argentine citizenship and were therefore able to participate in the formal political system.)[56] Tamarin sees Yrigoyen as initially constructing a highly personal relationship with Argentine labour, but choosing to retain his middle-class and upper-class support at the cost of such working-class support as he may have acquired by 1919. He suggests that Yrigoyen's style of personalist leadership worked against the development and maintenance of a broad multiclass coalition. It built up opposition to him within the upper-class elements of the UCR leadership and led to the emergence of Anti-personalist Radicalism. Similarly, Yrigoyen's regional policy preferences led to the decline of his provincial support and to the development of local personalist Radical factions. Therefore, having lost his support in the working class, the Radical upper class and the provinces, he was left with a relatively narrow support base amongst the urban middle class.[57]

The hierarchical quality of Radicalism must also be seen as only partially conforming to the quality suggested as inherent in populism. Whilst it remained a movement directed from above with a highly structured political machine organising parish-level committees involved in welfare as well as political matters, it nevertheless retained liberal and pluralist elements in its ideological aspect and displayed marked regional variations. Similarly, whilst Yrigoyen's conception of his role as leader was essentially hierarchical, the institutional opposition he faced limited his capacity to realise this form of leadership.

Yrigoyen also lacked that appeal of a strong, macho leader which is often associated with Latin American populism. Indeed, his popular nickname was 'El Peludo', a kind of armadillo which rolls into a ball when attacked. (It is also small, hairy and bad-tempered.) He has been described as an 'enigma', displaying introversion and hesitation to an extent unusual in a political figure. Remmer points out that he did not have the qualities usually associated with charisma and was not a good public speaker. This might equally have been said of Rojas Pinilla of Colombia, but in his case he did have the macho appeal of a soldier as well as an articulate daughter who spoke for him. However, Yrigoyen's strange personality is not without parallel in Latin American politics. For example, the tiny, reclusive lawyer Augusto B. Leguía who came to power constitutionally in Peru in 1919 was able to retain power until 1930 despite lacking the colourful personal style usually associated with personalist rule. The fact is, Yrigoyen was a shrewd politician and deliberately fostered a mysterious image which complemented the quality of a 'moral crusade' which Radicalism under his leadership acquired in place of a more concrete political programme.

The 'quasi-religious' aspect of Radicalism described by Tamarin is certainly in accord with the emotional rhetoric usually associated with populism. However, Radicalism failed to use the most potent source of emotional appeal. It did not embrace Argentine nationalism in the way that Peronism would later. Although Gallo and Sigal argue that a strong nationalist tendency was part of early Radicalism, Yrigoyen's nationalism took a moderate, rhetorical form which was most pronounced with reference to petroleum and most often exhibited at election times.[58] This must partly be seen as a consequence of the higher proportion of immigrants in the population at the beginning of the twentieth century, but it also reflects Radical commitment to aspects of the European stream of influence. As Germani suggests, Radicalism attempted to weld together liberal–democratic aims with a personalist style.[59] The orientation of Radicalism to liberal democracy clearly reflects its electoral base in accordance with the characteristic associated with populism, but it must be remembered that, despite franchise extension, that base was still very small. The number of people voting in 1916 only amounted to about a quarter of the number who took Perón to power in 1946, and less than one tenth of the number who re-elected him in 1952. The expanded electorate which heralded the rise of Peronism reflected a population which had doubled in size and which contained a much smaller proportion of immigrants.

Radicalism, therefore, fits the model of Latin American populism only partially. Laclau may well be correct in his assertion that the UCR in the first three decades of the twentieth century was a popular party rather than a populist movement. Laclau further suggests that there are limits on the extent to which Peronism may be seen as populist,[60] but most other authors have tended to see it as the archetypical form of Latin American populism. Certainly Peronism had features in common with the rise of Yrigoyen's Radicals. For example, both movements were initially much clearer about what they opposed than about what they proposed. However, such similarities are superficial and perhaps the most important aspect of Radicalism in a study of Argentine populism is the contribution it made to the later emergence of Peronism. Thus Germani and others see Radicalism as integrative, but this process certainly was never completed. This and demobilisation during the period 1930–43, in consequence of the failure of conservative elements to generate a single charismatic figure who could weld together a national electoral coalition, increased the politically marginal elements in Argentina and led to the second and deeper crisis which gave rise to Peronism.[61]

PERONISM

Despite winning much support from peasants and rural workers in the interior provinces, Peronism was initially primarily an urban movement and it was in Buenos Aires that Perón began building his support base by receiving union delegations at the Department of Labour in 1943–44. Although he took up the interests of rural workers by promotion of such legislation as the Statute of the Peón, signed in November 1944, later hinting at far-reaching land reform during his election campaign, and spoke to mass gatherings of workers in provincial towns and cities such as Tucumán in February 1945, it was in Buenos Aires that the mass rallies so characteristic of Peronism occurred, most notably that of 17 October 1945.

Also in accordance with the characteristic features of Latin American populism, Peronism occurred in its urban context at least as a consequence of the process of development. Throughout the Infamous Decade, both industrialisation and the reactivation of excess industrial capacity had been expanding the urban working class, creating a mobilisable mass excluded from political and economic participation. The withdrawal in 1943 of military support for the exclusionary conservative regimes, which reflected Argentina's modified European/liberal culture, made possible the later re-emergence of the Iberian cultural stream which encompasses the personalist political tradition. The popular demands for participation were not new, they had been expressed in a variety of ways since the beginning of the twentieth century. What was new was the depth of the crisis of institutional legitimacy being experienced by the European aspect of Argentine culture, a crisis for which the only precedent was the immediate post-revolutionary period which led to the rise of Rosas. This crisis coincided with the economic boom resulting from the Second World War which di Tella sees as leading to the emergence of disaffected groups willing to support the demands of the popular sectors.[62] Certainly, Argentina's renewed affluence enabled Perón to increase the rewards received by the working class, to extend national investment in industry and to expand the public sector. Thus he could, at least temporarily, satisfy the expectations of both sectors of the working class and middle class and had therefore the basis for a multiclass coalition.

The extent to which Peronism was a multiclass movement is a matter of some debate, which hinges on the confusion associated with the term 'polyclass' and reflects wide regional variations in the social spectrum of Peronist support. Certainly figures from the Secretaría Electoral de la Capital Federal show voting for the Perón–Quijano ticket in 1946 as being strongest amongst blue-collar workers and lowest amongst professionals.[63] Likewise, Germani's own analysis of voting behaviour in the 1946 election suggests that the *porteño* electorate cast their votes along distinct class lines. Districts in Buenos Aires dominated by manual workers tended to vote Peronist, whilst those of both lower-middle-class and middle-class character tended to support the Unión Democrática. Despite such findings, Germani still maintains that Peronism was a multiclass movement representing two mobilised masses: the new (i.e., expanded) working class and the urban middle class. The catalyst mobilising both groups and creating the potential for a multiclass alliance was, for Germani, the process of internal migration which had expanded not just the working class, but also the lower middle class.[64] Other authors have alternatively suggested that the polyclass nature of Peronism is not expressed in its urban context where its support was essentially 'clasista', with a syndicalist base. Rather it is the heterogeneous mobilising movement appealing to the lower orders more generally and picking up traditional conservative support in its opposition to the Radical Party in some of the interior provinces which is seen as the polyclass and 'populist' aspect of Peronism.[65] It is certainly true that Perón sought to appeal to both *obreros* (blue-collar) and *empleados* (white-collar workers),[66] but Tamarin asserts, that, whilst middle-class opposition to Perón rested more on the trappings of his movement than on any real hardship experienced as a consequence of his policies, Peronism was essentially a working-class movement. The working class were the cornerstone of Peronism.

Like other authors who argue a similar case, Tamarin is wrong in stating that Perón never suggested that a classless society could exist, as is shown by such speeches as those of 14 August 1944 and 1 May 1947.[67] Similarly, in populist style, Perón constantly emphasised harmony, especially between 'honest' (non-exploitative) capital and labour. However, Tamarin rightly points out that Perón also stressed that the state should act on behalf of workers to secure social justice.[68] Di Tella also sees lower-middle-class and intellectual support for Peronism as less extensive than that for populist movements in less developed societies. He too recognises its essential class base and sees this as being the reason for its eventual loss of such middle-class support as it enjoyed at the outset. Indeed the influence of the labour movement was a factor for Perón's ouster in 1955.[69] But by 1965 Peronism seems to have acquired widespread support amongst Kirkpatrick's lower-middle-class respondents, with a sizeable minority identifying themselves and being identified by interviewers as at least sympathetic to Peronism.[70] However, several factors had probably worked to increase such support: the consistent failure of governments since 1955 to deliver economic and political stability, the influence of the period of union 'resistance' 1955–58, the productivity offensive which formed part of Frondizi's *desarrollismo*,[71] the frequent electoral proscription of Peronism since Perón's ouster and the consequent division of Argentine society according to attitudes towards Peronism. These contributed to the myth of Peronism as a golden age for the lower orders of Argentine society.

At the activist level, Peronism initially seems to have encompassed a much wider social spectrum. Apart from labour support through the Partido Laborista, Ciria sees two other groups as important bases of Peronist activity. The UCR–Junta Renovadora, established in October 1945, brought together middle-class Radical youth groups and became the main organisation of former Radicals who had moved to Peronism.[72] Blanksten also sees the 'Collaborationist' Radicals led by Juan Hortensio Quijano, who became Perón's Vice-President, as the most important other base for Peronist electoral organisation, though he does point out that they constituted a small fraction of the Radical Party and thus a rather limited base in terms of electoral support.[73] The third arm of Peronist activism was a varied selection of nationalists, retired army officers and other middle-class elements, the 'Centros Independientes'. All three groups were welded together in May 1946 when Perón established the Partido Unico de la Revolución Nacional, which later became the Partido Peronista. By the end of 1947, a centralised party structure had been established and the possibility removed of an independent political party dominated by organised labour.[74]

Di Tella further points out that, despite the strength of its working-class base, Peronism was supported by several elites, most notably elements of the armed forces and the clergy, marginal elements of the upper middle class and some new industrial groups, whom he sees as providing much of the leadership, financial backing and ideology of the movement.[75] Though divided, the military mainly supported Perón. Indeed military officers served in Perón's Cabinet and as Peronists in Congress. But such backing at the institutional level reflected pragmatic self-interest. Fears of social unrest led elements of the armed forces to see Peronism as the means to contain working-class mobilisation. In addition, the alternative to Peronism, the Unión Democrática, was not a happy option for the military. Not only did it include the Communist Party, but also there were fears that such a coalition of political parties would seek to reduce military strength and particularly the possibility of future military intervention in the political system. With its internal divisions evident even before achieving power and its penchant for philosophical debate rather than concrete proposals, the Unión Democrática must have seemed to the military to imply the continuation of weak, vacillating and therefore unstable civilian government. Representing as it did the European stream of influence, being comprised of electoral groupings many of which had imported philosophies, it constituted a challenge to the Iberian strand of culture which had gained the ascendancy within the armed forces and which was reflected in the increased nationalism of the officer corps. The support of the clergy is debatable as has been discussed above in Chapter 2. The marginal upper-middle-class elements referred to by di Tella were few amongst Perón's supporters, since Perón at least rhetorically challenged the 'oligarchy' at every opportunity and even hinted that his supporters would favour their physical extermination. However, there were some landowners amongst Peronist Congressmen.

The view that Peronism represented the interests of a new entrepreneurial elite which emerged either as a consequence of industrialisation during the 1930s or as a result of the growth of industry during the Second World War, suggests that a coalition of labour and national bourgeois elements confronted the old conservative agricultural elite and together resisted the return of a primarily agro-export orientated economy.[76] It has been further suggested that Peronism was an implicit alliance of the Argentine working class and the national bourgeoisie, both of which sought increased domestic consumption. Perón prior to gaining power certainly emphasised that wage rises would produce a larger internal market and thus be beneficial to industrialists. He made overtures to industrialists, but found them to be mainly pro-Radical, believing that the GOU regime was a temporary anomaly. Eldon Kenworthy questions the extent and the potency of this supposed alliance:

In the light of the general characterisation of Latin American industrialists as an ineffective political group, unwilling or unable to play the role of a national bourgeoisie, this ready acceptance of the Argentine industrialists' contribution to Perón's rise to power is surprising.[77]

Peronist economic policies in the late 1940s redistributed income from the agricultural sectors and from property-owners to the whole industrial sector, though especially to labour. However, this does not prove a conscious alliance between industrialists and workers. As Kenworthy notes, motives cannot reliably be inferred from policy outcomes. Apart from this limited coincidence of economic interests and a few individual industrialists who became important figures in the Peronist hierarchy, there is little evidence of a coalition between labour and industrialists.[78] The pro-industry policies supposed to imply Perón's seeking of support amongst industrialists were firmly established prior to his coming to power. The 1930s saw the protracted use of governmental policies favouring, perhaps largely unintentionally, industrial modernisation (though this was to be achieved with the involvement of foreign capital), most notably the use of exchange controls and import restrictions. Perón's pro-industrial policies require little further explanation than that they promoted the industrial development needed for increased military self-sufficiency, they seemed to make economic independence possible and they appeared to be a means by which working-class living standards could be raised. Perón did not make kind remarks about Argentine industrialists with a view to winning their support, indeed he accused employers generally of using their wealth to weight the scales against their employees.

Whilst many industrialists did not actively oppose Perón for fear of their companies being either closed or confronted with unexpected obstacles, there is no reason to suppose that such threats made them actively supportive of Peronism. In addition, relations with labour became much more difficult; every change in job specifications and procedures required union agreement in a way that it had not done prior to Perón's rise to power.[79] Some industrialists, particularly the larger ones who were members of the Unión Industrial Argentina (UIA), which had helped fund the Unión Democrática campaign, opposed Perón, causing him to intervene in their organisation and close it in May 1946. He then began an attempt to combine the various entrepreneurial groups into a single, more manipulable, structure which would represent industrial interests. The Association of Production, Industry and Commerce was established in late 1946, and reorganised as the Argentine Economic Confederation in 1949. When, in 1952, the General Economic Confederation (CGE) was formed it was the relationship of this organisation with the Peronist government which is frequently taken as indicating the close attachment of industrialists to Peronism. Certainly the president of the CGE sat in on Perón's Cabinet meetings, and the CGE, like the CGT, was represented on the National Economic Consultative Commission which was created in August 1949 and which advised the Perón government on economic policy. However, the extent of CGE support for Perón is questionable, its lack of opposition to him may rather reflect the heterogeneous interests it represented which prevented it devising a clear policy. In addition, as Imaz shows, the proportion of businessmen among the governing elite in 1946, though slightly higher than the figure for 1941, was considerably smaller than had been the case in the mid-1930s. This business involvement dwindled further under Peronism and burgeoned after 1955.[80]

Thus, despite its middle-class dominated leadership with some 60 per cent of the governing elite being drawn from military, legal and business backgrounds, Peronism rested largely on the support of manual workers. The question of why the movement took the particular populistic form it did, therefore, requires an explanation in terms of the characteristics of the Argentine working class. The most obvious factor for the rise of Peronism was the absence of an already established working-class party. Labour was clearly excluded from the political system in that the main electoral opposition to the Concordancia remained the UCR. Secondly, there was the underdevelopment of the labour movement before the 1940s, although some authors claim that this has been exaggerated and that organised labour was numerically very strong. In fact Yrigoyen's initial '*obrerismo*' had increased labour activity and unionisation peaked in 1920 at some 700 000. But the long process of demobilisation effectively began with Yrigoyen's actions in 1919 and the 1920 peak would not be reached again until Perón's first presidency. The very fact of the lack of common origins produces an atomised workforce, lacking any real sense of national, let alone class, identity. The sheer number and small size of enterprises worked against labour organisation, although this situation was changing by the mid-1930s, but in addition the incentive to build a strong labour movement was lacking. Social legislation, both under the Radicals and during the period 1930–43, had been passed, often as a result of Socialist Party initiatives, but not enforced and the Department of Labour, as a small, relatively unimportant part of the Ministry of the Interior, had few powers. Working-class wages in the 1930s were low in comparison with what they would be later under Perón, and certainly in comparison with what they were for some industrial workers in Buenos Aires before 1930, and living standards declined markedly in the late 1930s. The labour movement was essentially defensive. Tamarin may be correct that wages for workers in Greater Buenos Aires may even have compared unfavourably with some other countries which had been hit hard by the Depression.[81] However this was not so in the case of the nations from which immigrants had come or the areas outside Buenos Aires whence the internal migrants hailed. Sectoral bargaining had not yet developed in consequence of the number and size of urban businesses and perhaps also as a result of the legacy of anarchist activity. Negotiations occurred between individual employers and their workers. Most strikes were lost by workers in the period 1930–34. Wide differentials in wage levels within the working class further undermined any sense of common interest. Although Rock, amongst others, suggests that Argentina experienced a relatively low level of urban unemployment during the 1930s, the rate was rising. Tamarin argues that official figures only included a small proportion of those who were actually unemployed and, of course, disregarded the question of underemployment. Guido di Tella estimates unemployment at about 28 per cent of the workforce.[82] Given these obstacles, the rate of organisation amongst industrial workers, between 20 per cent and 30 per cent in 1941, was not remarkably low, indeed it may be seen as a considerable achievement,[83] but the organised labour movement itself was politically inexperienced and characterised by internal divisions. In March 1943, the CGT had split into two parts, one comprising some socialist unions, the other a mixture of socialist and communist elements. Some unions remained outside either CGT bloc, in the Unión Sindical Argentina or as independent organisations. These labour organisations continued to be marked by minority ideological positions, with some union leaders more tied to their political factions than to their members' perceived interests.[84]

Perón, in accordance with precedents established by right-wing nationalists in the 1930s, made appeal to the popular sector and was able to weld together much of this fragmented and excluded working class, but explanations of why and how he managed to do so differ. The debate revolves around the changing nature of the urban population and the question of 'working class dualism'. In 1914, the population of Greater Buenos Aires had been 49 per cent foreign-born and only 9–11 per cent had come to the city from within Argentina. By 1947, 26–28 per cent were foreign-born with 29–32 per cent internal migrants.[85] Dispute over these figures forms part of the debate between what has been termed the 'orthodox' view of a large anomic in-migrant population held by Germani and the 're-visionist' perspective of Halperín amongst others.[86] Further controversy remains over the extent to which the working class could be seen as comprising two distinct groups and the characteristics of the expanding in-migrant population. Germani in his earlier work sees Peronist support as resting on these internal migrants who constituted a 'disposable mass' of uneducated, unsophisticated people open to emotional, nationalist and stylistic appeals, whose support created an artificial movement which would become real in time.[87] (A similar, though more sympathetic, argument is implicit in Guido di Tella's analysis of Peronist support too, although he is concerned with the Peronism of the 1970s. He suggests that the continuing expansion of Peronism rested on continued rural migration until the mid-1960s.)[88] Others see support for Peronism as being more widespread amongst the working class and being based on instrumental factors. Some authors believe that both emotional appeal and instrumentalism must be seen as contributing to the rise of Perón,[89] For example, Anderson suggests that mass political activity in Latin America generally was partly due to the raising of domestic lower-class expectations by external factors but was also probably partly a result of 'longings for personal identity and pride, relief from monotony and the appeal of the dramatic'.[90] Likewise Fillol, writing specifically about the emergence of Peronism, asserts that the Argentine working class needed Perón for psychological as well as material reasons.[91]

Displacement from the land, as agricultural production declined in the late 1930s, coincided with an increased demand for industrial labour and thus internal migrants were drawn to Buenos Aires as European immigrants had been prior to 1930, according to Germani. By 1947, as a consequence of upward social mobility and differential fertility rates, 50–70 per cent of the old working class had been replaced by internal migrants, especially in semi-skilled and unskilled occupations. Germani further claims that most of these in-migrants came from rural areas or small towns:

> ... in the years 1935–46 the great majority of internal migrants were drawn from persons whose previous situation was characterised by a less modern and non-industrial lifestyle and work experience, both in the agricultural and non-agricultural sectors.[92]

Other authors have also held similar views, for example suggesting that the size of estates and the radial pattern of communications based on Buenos Aires led to isolation in the Argentine interior which worked against the development of cohesive rural society and thus contributed to the paternalist mentality of internal migrants. In-migrants are seen as having been disorganised and authoritarian in outlook in contrast with the older Buenos Aires working class. Being willing to sell 'their freedom for a dish of lentils',[93] they provided the basis for a national populist movement with a reformist programme rather than a working-class political party.

But is this correct? The 1936 census of the city of Buenos Aires showed that 70 per cent of the 360 000 recently arrived internal migrants had come from the relatively developed littoral provinces, and amongst these many were from medium and large towns.[94] The same could be said of those internal migrants who supported Perón's rise to power. Indeed it has been argued that many were the same people, as in 1947 more than a third of such 'migrants' had been resident in the city for longer than eleven years.[95] The social diversity of their backgrounds and their considerable experience of life in an urban setting precludes the general description of such in-migrants as 'traditional' in their attitudes in contrast with the rest of the urban working class. In any case, as Doyon points out, much of the Argentine interior could not really be seen as traditional since modern production methods prevailed. Also, in some areas, provincial political variants of a populist kind may have undermined deferential attitudes. Such data undermine the idea of an unsophisticated, ill-educated disposable mass ripe for mobilisation by a self-seeking hedonist with only an image of national greatness to offer. The older working class comprising a larger proportion of recent immigrants from Europe, cannot be seen as much more organised, more literate and more educated given the fairly low level of unionisation in all sectors of industry except transport and given the origins of many immigrants in the poorest parts of Southern Europe. Further, it is by no means clear that migrants constituted an easily delineable separate working-class sector. They seem to have entered the well-established construction and service industries and so enjoyed some social mobility.[96]

In addition, the apparently less traditional older working class also supported Peronism, as is shown by Germani's own work in correlating votes cast in the 1946 elections with the social class of polling districts.[97] Other authors also confirm from electoral data that the 'old' and 'new' working class in the large Argentine cities were equally supportive of Perón. The new working class was by no means as important to Peronist electoral victory as some would suppose. Many internal migrants were women and therefore could not have voted for Perón in 1946 since 1952 was the first year in which women were able to vote in a presidential election.[98] Also many internal migrants were registered in the areas from which they had come and returned there to vote because of the complexities of re-registration. Kenworthy further suggests that these migrants were the group most likely not to have voted in a situation where the national vote, despite compulsion, was only 83 per cent.[99]

Although the importance of in-migrants must not be overlooked, the activity of the 'old' working class unions is key to the rise of Peronism. The Partido Laborista of which they comprised the greatest part, was initially the main pillar of the emergent Peronist movement. Both the 'old' and 'new' working class had been excluded from political and economic participation whilst the process of industrialisation accelerated, at least relative to other sectors, between 1930 and 1943. Not only did both parts of the urban working class therefore share a common grievance against the way in which the political system had operated to exclude them, but in addition there is little evidence of different values leading to conflict between the two sectors. Indeed, the process of industrialisation in the 1930s integrated into a working class a variety of new groups from diverse backgrounds, both rural and urban.

Although there was opposition to Perón amongst the working class, this did not reflect a cleavage between old and new elements of it. It existed amongst some communist, socialist and syndicalist dominated unions in the period 1943–6 and reflected the ideological orientations of the leadership rather than the background of the members. Opposition also continued amongst some craft unions after 1946, but there was no significant opposition to Peronism from the working class as a whole nor from one distinct sector of it, and disaffected union leaders for the most part proved unable to mobilise their members against Perón. Indeed there were very good reasons why labour generally should support Peronism. Perón offered state protection to the unions and thus sustained the strong syndicalist tradition of Argentina. Ideological schisms had weakened the labour movement during the 1930s and early 1940s and the resistance of the conservative elite to labour demands had thus undermined the support for ideologically-oriented union leaderships. The opposition to Perón was not willing to take up union demands and, most importantly, Perón had already shown himself to be a source of material benefits, even if these were limited.

Opponents of Peronism from both the left and the right have taken comfort in explanations of Perón's rise to power in terms of 'irrationality'. Such an interpretation can be seen as a defensive reaction in a situation in which an alternative explanation of a phenomenon appears more threatening to dominant sectors than the phenomenon itself. Peronism is seen as an anomaly, as a deviation from the course of liberal–democratic development, explicable in terms of 'psychological abnormalities'. As part of the backward culture of the Argentine interior, it is seen as an aspect of traditionalism and therefore irrational in the modern context.[100] But Peronism is not simply traditional, it is part of a modern culture derived from the Iberian legacy though adapted and reinforced since. It emerged because an aspect of the supposedly modern European stream of influence failed to adapt. The exclusion of the working class from the political system, dominated as it was in the 1930s by members of the elite military club, the Círculo de Armas and traditionally powerful families, many of them members of the Jockey Club[101] (the most prestigious social and sporting club in Argentina), made Peronism rational in political terms. As Perón increased the working class share of the national wealth from 38 per cent in the early 1940s to 46 per cent in 1948, it must also be seen as rational in economic terms. The fact that provincial support grew most profoundly in the least developed regions of the country after 1946 would seem to add further weight to this line of argument, although such support may sometimes have originated in traditional local political rivalries.[102]

Both Kirkpatrick and Miguens assert that the essential rationality of working-class support for Perón and the lack of supernatural beliefs about him or a mystical relationship with his followers suggest that he cannot be described as charismatic in the Weberian sense.[103] But Weber does not see such characteristics as essential requirements for a charismatic leader, as 'specifically exceptional powers or qualities' will suffice in the absence of supernatural ones. He goes on to suggest that whilst charisma may rest on magical powers of divine origin, it may also be accorded to secular leaders.[104] However, the emphasis on the rationality of Peronist support is justified. Indeed, Taylor's study of the relationship between the memory of Eva Perón and working-class Peronists questions the idea of irrationality at what should be its strongest point, at least in its urban form. Amongst those of her working-class informants who were recent migrants from rural areas at the time of the rise of Perón, there was little evidence of mysticism and fanaticism in their image of Evita. Rather they assessed her achievements on their behalf in realistic terms. Some militant factory workers saw her as revolutionary, as did Peronist student groups, but the myths of saintliness were manufactured and sustained amongst middle-class supporters. Taylor's findings conflict with the assumption of working-class quasi-religious attitudes to Peronism expressed by middle- and upper-class opponents of the movement.[105] Since Taylor's research was conducted in the 1970s, it could be argued that only those concrete elements of working-class support would have survived the intervening years. Questioning in 1980 suggested that the rallies and fervour of the early days of Peronism were clearly remembered by older urban Peronists, but what determined their support was nevertheless the material benefits received or perceived as received. What had been passed to younger Peronists was a belief in these material gains. Perón was described as a 'good man' who provided housing and increased status, in that order. Miguens remarks that only with a rational base could Peronism have survived the years of Perón's exile.[106] Turner's 1973 study similarly calls into question the idea that the Argentine working class is irrationally inclined to the admiration of individual figures. He found this trait no more developed amongst rural working-class respondents than amongst the middle class. The urban working class did display this characteristic more than other groups, but it was specifically Perón who was admired, and workers who expressed loyalty to him emphasised material benefits as the reason for their attitudes.[107]

For authors like Kirkpatrick, Perón's rise to power is explicable in terms of the economic benefits he offered, his personal political skill and his being in the right place at the right time. Little also stresses that Perón's hold on the working class was weak initially, being strengthened by some lucky events. Therefore psychological explanations in terms of working-class authoritarianism are unnecessary.[108] However, the view of the Argentine working class as exhibiting authoritarian attitudes derived from authoritarian family structures and therefore as responsive to paternalism and charisma, is significant because it is in accord with longstanding beliefs about the different natures of masses and elites. Writing in the late nineteenth century of Latin America specifically, Bunge suggested that the mass were essentially apathetic and wanted the burdens of responsibility taken from them.[109] In the early twentieth century, generalising from his study of German trade unions and the Social Democratic Party, Michels wrote of 'The Political Gratitude of the Masses . . . felt by the crowd for those who speak and write on their behalf'.[110] The 1962 reprint of Michels' *Political Parties* contains an introduction by Lipset who himself includes a whole chapter on 'Working Class Authoritarianism' in *Political Man*.[111] If such authors are correct, then seeking to explain authoritarian regimes should not occupy us, but rather we should put our efforts into explaining why authoritarian regimes break down and why some societies do not experience them at all. Explanations of support for regimes in terms of working-class authoritarianism cannot explain why different kinds of politics emerge in different societies nor why such support dissipates over time.

The evidence that the benefits of Peronism outweighed the costs for the Argentine working class does not diminish the importance of the personalist and authoritarian characteristics of Perón's rule. The gains in real income were both rapid and evident, if short-lived, but Peronism itself would not have had such pervasive and long-lasting impact, had it not been presented by a leadership that was colourful, dramatic and inspiring of national fervour and confidence. These features derive specifically from Argentine political culture, not from some assumed quality associated with the general nature of political masses, although Germani's 1961 study of Argentine authoritarianism suggests authoritarian attitudes are class-related.[112] The emphasis on strong individual leadership, being as it is a legacy of Iberian colonialism, gives rise to what Lambert describes as: 'the propensity of Latin American populations to view power as embodied in a man and their inability to understand it as an abstract concept'.[113]

Although Kirkpatrick's evidence suggests that Peronists were more favourable to strong-man politics as a means to effective government and had less sympathy with political discussion than other social sectors, more than a third of her respondents in all sectors exhibited such attitudes. Similarly, seeing the government as controlled by and for special interests and themselves as victims of the system was common amongst all groups, and the stronger association of this characteristic with Peronists could be seen as a realistic assessment of the situation of the Argentine working class. As Kirkpatrick points out, the tendency to authoritarianism in other social sectors is indicated by the support enjoyed by a variety of authoritarian regimes.[114] The tradition of seeking benefits direct from the executive derives from Spanish patrimonialism and is a feature of Argentine politics, not uniquely of Peronism.

Despite Neilson's comments on the tractable qualities of the Argentine people and their failure to resist the abuses of the 1976–83 regime,[115] and the apparent similarities between the features of the authoritarian personality as described by Adorno *et al.*[116] and aspects of Argentine political culture, it is by no means clear that uncritical submissiveness was in evidence in the relationship between the working class and Perón. James notes that spontaneous rank-and-file struggles after Perón's overthrow cannot be explained if lack of working-class autonomy is assumed.[117] Germani's suggestion that liberty was sold for a dish of lentils wrongly assumes that liberty existed for the working classes before Perón. The degree of autonomy enjoyed by individual unions before Perón's consolidation of his support base was less than Germani's analysis suggests, and so too is the extent to which it was undermined. When Perón took formal office in 1946, the institutional structure for administering labour had been established for some time, albeit most recently under his direction as a member of the military government. The November 1943 elevation of the Department of Labour had brought regional and provincial agencies under national control and provided the means effectively to enforce existing labour legislation. This reflected both the slow increase of state involvement in all social areas and the syndicalist tradition of seeking state protection. It was not, therefore, a change in the nature of the working class which led to the hypothetical willingness to sell itself to the highest bidder.

Even though labour did not have as much independence to lose as is frequently implied, there was no question of the existing working-class organisations submitting freely to the will of Perón. The means Perón had to employ in his attempts to control the mobilised working class are evidence of this. He did not initially control either the CGT or the

Partido Laborista. In fact, the Labour Party remained a threat, including as it did some powerful labour leaders who wished to maintain the independence of the labour movement. Indeed, Navarro suggests that the party was created by the CGT after 17 October 1945 specifically for the purpose of avoiding the surrender of the labour movement to Perón. Precisely because the uncritical submissiveness often assumed to explain Peronism was lacking, Perón, by a variety of means, sought to establish a vertical structure controlling labour from above.[118]

The Labour Party was dissolved in May 1946 to be replaced by the Partido Unico de la Revolución, a change Perón achieved by putting pressure on selected Labour Party Congressmen effectively using the technique of 'divide and rule'. Although he received the critical support of mature unions affiliated to the CGT Number 1 and the Unión Sindical Argentina, as well as that of the autonomous unions, the CGT Number 2 remained communist and socialist dominated. As a consequence of this, Perón's expansion of the organised working class with the establishment of new unions particularly took the form of creating *sindicatos paralelos* which would poach members from the other unions remaining outside his sphere of influence. The state alone had the power to register trade unions, and registration was imperative for successful negotiations. Although the creation of parallel unions preceded Perón's rise to power, the extension of this policy after 1946 was assisted by the 1943 regime's closing of some of the more militantly independent unions, leaving space for the creation of new, though by no means tame, organisations.[119] Old *laborista* leaders opposed to the Peronisation of labour, including those who actually organised the demonstrations in support of Perón on 17 October 1945 (such as Cipriano Reyes, leader of the packinghouse workers, and Luis F. Gay, of the Labour Party, who was elected General Secretary of the CGT in November 1946 as a deliberate assertion of independence from Perón) were circumvented as far as possible and then displaced by Peronists such as José Espejo who assumed control of the CGT in December 1947. Thus, amongst labour, Peronism established a hierarchical structure in accord with the populist model.

Despite Perón's dissolution of the Labour Party and

creation of his own political structure, the main institutional part of Peronism remained the unions. However, the labour movement did not become a puppet of the state and displayed a variety of different attitudes to Peronism. Little identifies six such different views of the Perón regime amongst Argentine unions in the period 1946–55. He terms them, in ascending order of the extent of their Peronist support: 'oppositionism' which was found amongst craft unions; 'labourism' reflecting support qualified by a belief in the need for powerful independent unions as found amongst the metal workers and meatpackers; 'liberalism' or cooperation until a point of principle produced conflict which typified printers and railwaymen; 'independent Peronism' or support tempered by the retention of the capacity for independent action as in the case of bank employees; 'opportunism' such as that displayed by commercial travellers; and finally 'loyalism'.[120] Even this latter category does not imply unconditional submission to Perón. The absence of uprisings in the wake of Perón's ouster in September 1955 suggests that whilst loyalty to the man himself survived, and little decline in his electoral support occurred, his reduced capacity to protect and reward his support base worked against the positive action necessary to preserve Peronism as a political movement at that time.

To argue that Perón enjoyed the submission of the working class and with such support could dominate Argentine politics, is to underestimate his skill as a politician. Such a simplistic explanation of Peronism also leaves difficulties in accounting for his ouster, his long years of exile and his inability to control the divisions within his movement when he returned to power in 1973. Perón's failure to achieve unity within the Peronist movement in 1973–74 reflected his forced abandonment of the methods of control he had used between 1946 and the early 1950s. Perón's first period of office had been characterised by his skilful manipulation of Argentina's sectoral structure, but the economic advantages he enjoyed as a result of Argentine neutrality during the Second World War enabled him to achieve this. He was able to indulge his preference for the carrot over the stick and to build an 'inclusionary corporatism' based more on negotiated inducements to labour than on constraints.[121] By 1973, the massively deepened cleavages between the sectors and years of economic stagnation prevented a repetition of such a performance, even if, at the age of 78, Perón had still had the capacity and the will to achieve unity.

Perón built up his mass support from a position of power within the 1943–46 military government. Actions associated with him as Minister of Social Welfare, such as rent reductions and, most importantly, the *aguinaldo* or annual bonus equivalent to a thirteenth month's pay, provided the basis for this support, which therefore must be seen as both rational and conditional. However, these qualities of Perón's political base do not detract from the personalist, or indeed populist, features of his movement. He was able to become the leader of Argentina without being associated with any of the traditional political parties, none of which, despite negotiations, would field him as their candidate in the 1946 elections. This argument has been contradicted by the suggestion that Perón actually gained from this independence of traditional parties as he alone was untainted by association with electoral fraud. But more importantly, the compromise candidates, Dr José P. Tamborini and Dr Enrique P. Mosca, put up by the traditional parties in coalition, were bland figures whose lack of charisma probably also contributed to the electoral defeat of the Democratic Union. Perón remained the 'single adhesive agent'[122] which held Peronism together, though with diminishing success, until his death in July 1974.

Few would dispute that Perón's style was personalist, though whether he fits Weber's model of charismatic authority has been the subject of some debate. Perón's delegation of his personal authority first to Evita and later to Isabel, suggests that he intended his movement to be dominated by just one name and that he would allow no rivals to emerge. It has further been asserted that the continuation of the same form of authority after Perón attained power is a contradiction of Weber's concept of charisma which undergoes a process of 'routinisation' in order to manage everyday affairs and to ensure the succession.[123] Navarro points out that Perón was able to avoid this process through the sharing of his authority with Evita who remained outside the institutional political structure.[124] Also it can be argued that Perón, whether for reasons of egotism or the absence of dynastic possibilities, avoided naming a protégé who might succeed him or become a rival. His choice of Isabel as his running-mate in the 1973 elections can only be assumed to reflect his own fears of being superseded in historical import-ance. Such a choice echoes his comment in 1956: 'My anxiety was that some clever man would have taken over.'[125]

The emotional content of Peronism certainly accords with the style expected of the charismatic leader and/or populist leader. The emotional appeal of a popular hero restored to his proper place by the ordinary people and then forgiving and embracing his former persecutors on the balcony of the Casa Rosada is unparalleled in Argentine political history, with the possible exception of President Alfonsín's appearance in the same place at 6 p.m. on Easter Sunday 1987, to announce the surrender of the rebels at the Campo de Mayo. (Professor Torcuato di Tella confirmed to the present authors the similarities to the events he remembered as a teenager in 1945.) Not only grand spectacles like those of 17 October 1945, but also small gestures, constantly reinforced on every public occasion, gave the working man a new status and a new pride in himself. Perón's frequent reference to himself as a *descamisado* or a worker, albeit the 'first worker' in Argentina, and his habit of removing his coat and rolling up his shirtsleeves, placed him amongst the people who supported him. He glorified and gave dignity to those who had never before been so honoured. Evita's emphasis on herself as a conduit to Perón reassured his followers of their access to him but at the same time emphasised further his position of leadership.

Though his supporters (and opponents) may not have seen it as such at the time, his attacks on the Oligarchy were largely symbolic, accompanied only by the occasional expropriation comprising property of marginal quality usually in some remote region and belonging to a generally unpopular victim, as in the 1949 expropriations of *latifundios* in Salta and Jujuy, many of which belonged to Robustiano Patrón Costas, local patriarch and former Governor, Senator and Acting President. Under severe personal provocation more controversial expropriations sometimes occurred, as in the case of the 40 000 hectare Pereyra Iraola *estancia*, originally given to the family for supplying provisions to Rosas in 1832, which is now a public park just off the main road to La Plata. Such actions constituted a reminder to the faithful of how they had been elevated and of the need for continued support. Perón's style in building an emotional bridge to the working class was wholly new. Rosas' winning support by exhibiting skills associated with *gauchos* never implied that he was one of them; his style was not egalitarian. Yrigoyen could not have made such appeals either, as to have done so would have offended his primary support base amongst the middle class, just as the trappings rather than the content of Peronism alienated sectors of the middle class. No previous political personality had had the common man touch which Perón was able to utilise to great effect:

> He used a radical language previously unheard in government officials but appreciated by the workers because it was their own.[126]

As a consequence of the extent of the crisis in the European cultural stream, which had excluded the working class from political participation, and the relative temporary economic independence of Argentina, Perón was able to make emotive appeals to now strongly developed Argentine nationalism in a way that Yrigoyen was not. He could emphasise 'Argentine methods for Argentine problems'[127] in the economic sphere and Argentina's independence of the two major power blocs in the international political arena. Thus Peronism won the support of some nationalists of both the left and the right, despite its anti-intellectualism and initial lack of an ideology. When Justicialismo was constructed, to bind together elements of the already established Peronist movement, it took a vague and philosophical form, seeking a universal explanation of social and political differences in terms of countervailing ideological forces. That the intellectual content of Peronism was much less important than the personalist and emotional aspect is indicated by the popular survival of the name Peronismo, rather than Justicialismo, for the movement, despite the formal title of the party.

PERSONALISM AND POPULISM SINCE PERÓN

The survival of Peronism despite the overthrow of Perón has been the most important feature of Argentine politics since 1955. By that year, economic stagnation and conflict with the Church, amongst other factors, had so undermined, if not the extent, at least the intensity of Peronist support, that no mass uprising in defence of 'El Líder' occurred. However, the movement had constituted the most profound critique of the European stream of cultural influence since Rosas and had made apparent the limited and defensive nature of liberal democracy through the increased, though controlled, mobilisation of the Argentine working class. Thus, in Castles' terms, temporary changes in 'the nature of social, economic and political organisation' led to changes in 'the expectations held by political actors of the appropriate nature of social, economic and political actions' and to the establishment of a widespread oppositional 'image of society'.[128] In more concrete terms:

> The major legacy of Peronism has in fact been an intransigent and highly articulate labour movement under its own independent leadership . . . [129]

Castles suggests that when such an oppositional image of society arises, there are three possible outcomes. The development of a third image of society which becomes the new dominant image is one possibility. This has not occurred in Argentina because the two competing images are products of two cultures which are firmly ingrained having been operative since before the beginning of the national period. A second possible outcome is that the former dominant image may re-establish its hegemony through concessions to the oppositional image and the use of political socialisation. This has singularly failed to happen in consequence of the depth of crisis and as a result of the failure to achieve an element of compromise between internationally oriented sectors and labour. The third and most destabilising outcome of two conflicting images of society, according to Castles, is fragmentation.[130] This has been the bitter harvest of Peronism for Argentina's already sectoral society.

It cannot be argued that attempts to integrate the Peronist

movement and thus to defuse popular resistance were not made. Military elements did seek an accommodation with the working class both through limited negotiations with unionised labour and in allowing elections to occur in which it was hoped that non-Peronist parties would be able to capture Perón's support base. However, the strength of hardline anti-Peronist factions in the armed forces, known initially as *gorilas* and then as *colorados*, limited the degree of compromise with the working class which could be achieved. Staying in power, or even achieving it (in the case of Onganía), required appeasement of the military hardliners. General Lonardi's brief tenure as president is evidence of this, and it was followed by three years of attempted de-Peronisation under General Pedro Eugenio Aramburu (1955–58). Aramburu then permitted controlled elections in which Peronist candidates were proscribed but on Perón's advice Peronists reluctantly supported the UCRI, resulting in the presidency of Frondizi (1958–62). But the new civilian president's attempts to integrate Peronism with his Intransigent Radicals went beyond what the hardliners considered acceptable and eventually resulted in his displacement. By the time Onganía seized power in 1966 attitudes had hardened and the possibilities for compromise had receded. Onganía confronted a divided but broadly Peronist labour movement, dominated by bureaucratic and anti-liberal leaders, and attempted to try to control it by systematic intervention.

When the economic nationalism, albeit partial, of the Iberian cultural strand had broken down in 1955, the European stream had reasserted itself. The preference for industry of the early Perón years, especially expressed through the expropriation of agricultural profits by the Argentine Institute for the Promotion of Trade (IAPI) and their redistribution to the industrial sector, encouraged internationalist-oriented sectors to reassert themselves. Aided by the boom of the mid-1950s, they successfully sought foreign investment and tried to impose the austerity measures needed if the popular classes were to bear the costs of economic development. But the legacy of Perón's personalism was a mobilised working class with an increasingly militant wing against whom repression was needed to contain popular resistance. Democracy, although the theoretical ideal of such sectors, had been reassessed in the light of experience. It had been allowed to spread too far and would, if put into practice again, produce dangerous results. Nevertheless, repression cannot be maintained indefinitely when seen as ideologically illegitimate, and as the level of repression under Onganía eased over time, so unrest re-emerged. When it did so it took an increasingly threatening form as young men from both left- and right-wing Catholic nationalist groups joined with others from the traditional left and from the anti-Vandorist, Framini faction of mainstream Peronism to form the Montoneros in March 1970. The Montoneros were not the first such guerrilla group formed, nor would they be the last; the process of polarisation was accelerating.

In the wake of increasing public disaffection, Onganía was replaced first by General Roberto M. Levingston (a man so unknown that his photograph had to be displayed when his presidency was announced); then by Lanusse himself. During the period from Onganía's departure to the election of Héctor Cámpora, the military sought to negotiate a dignified and less than absolute abdication from power. But the extent of the crisis in the internationalist-oriented sectors in consequence of their economic failure resulted in the eventual return of Perón without the opposition of those who had stood against him for such a long period.

In a society torn by two conflicting, if increasingly over-lapping political cultures, personalism had failed, and so had anti-personalism. Perón's populism had been a product of a particular time and could not be replicated. Returning with his military rank restored, no longer a *descamisado*, and clearly not the socialist that in exile he appeared to some to be, Perón found it increasingly difficult to hold together his heterogeneous movement, some of which had welcomed him back as a personalist leader whilst other elements had come to see Peronism as an ideological force of the left, the anti-imperialist means of mobilising the population without which 'liberation' could not be achieved.[131] Perón stressed cooperation between the classes and introduced a programme of national reconstruction based on a social pact between national industrialists and labour. Attempting to build such bridges forced him to choose between the competing factions of Peronism, all of which he had been able to appease when he was stationed in Madrid. Perón chose the right, and the left marched out of the Plaza de Mayo on 1 May 1974 when he made his choice explicit and criticised their tactics. Although Isabel Perón displayed personalist behaviour, trying to win support by dressing in military uniforms and saluting her audiences, she lacked the charismatic qualities of Perón. After Perón's death, the effect of her personalism was schismatic. Peronism divided into groups who were for Isabel (*verticalistas*) and groups who opposed her. The loss of such a key figure in a relatively weakly organised structure made the Peronist movement more subject to attempted takeovers by its extremes and the process of fragmentation quickened.

The failure to reconstruct populism did not, however, signify the end of personalism in Argentine politics. When personalism has emerged in Argentina historically, it has been essentially a response to political and/or economic exclusion of certain sectors. It is not only populism, which is one particular form of personalism, which constitutes a response to perceived deprivation. All forms of personalism reflect deprivation, though the particular form may vary with the sector perceiving itself as deprived. Thus economic exclusion of interior interests led to *caudillismo*; the political and economic exclusion as a result of *caudillismo* led to the rise of the 'frock-coated *caudillos*'; political exclusion by the Oligarchy resulted in Yrigoyen's Radicalism; and political and economic exclusion of the working class led to the rise of Perón. As an element of the Iberian legacy, personalism usually, though not always – as can be seen in the emergence of post-*caudillismo* personalism – occurs when the European-oriented sectors of Argentine society are ascendant and excluding other sectors. In consequence personalism has remained as a response to a crisis generally in the European stream of culture and thus can be seen in the style adopted by General Leopoldo Galtieri in 1982. Economic chaos and disaffection amongst excluded elements caused an internationalist regime to take up a nationalist cause, one long associated with Perón and reiterated in Peronist publications since the 1940s. Galtieri when addressing the public assumed a style reminiscent of Perón, the Montoneros in exile offered to return to fight, the crowds outside the Casa Rosada sang Peronist songs, and the drums, primarily a symbol of Peronism, though now taken up by the new Radical youth groups too, returned to the Plaza de Mayo. The crisis of losing the war also produced elements of political personalism in the direct sense of President Alfonsín having a more colourful image than his opponent, without which his faction of the UCR could not have hoped to win the presidency. This feature has led to a virtual cult of personal support for the Radical leader which has been termed 'Alfonsinismo'. It has also had an impact in the indirect sense of the reluctance of Isabel Perón to lead the Peronist Party, at least as a committed figurehead. Her indecision and apparent support for Alfonsín contributed to the electoral defeat of her late husband's movement. Vicente Saadi, leader of one of the two most important factions of the orthodox wing of the fragmented Peronist movement was made President of the Peronist Party in November 1986, with Isabel demoted to Vice-President. He has since been succeeded by Antonio Cafiero, Governor of the Province of Buenos Aires.

Elite recruitment patterns are to some extent self-perpetuating, since they not only reflect, but also reinforce value systems. In addition, they have important effects for the stability of the political system. Although it can be argued that charismatic leadership, like nationalism, performs a valuable role in societies marked by divisions, in that it may transcend them, this has not proved true in Argentina except in the short term. In this case, the interaction of the two conflicting strands of Argentine political culture, from which, on the one hand, personalism and, on the other, formal impersonal institutional structures derive, has produced not compromise and stability, but rather conflict and governmental incapacity. Aspects of these two cultures are in many ways diametrically opposed and each is sufficiently strong to weaken, but not destroy, the other, and elements of each thus remain in reserve to alternate in Argentine politics.

In addition, personalism is inefficient both at the national and sub-national levels, both in politics and beyond. For example, a lack of charismatic qualities has hindered some politicians who might otherwise have been able to contribute to long-term stability. The attempts of Ortiz to restore constitutionalism were thus weakened, and Horowitz cites Frondizi's lack of charisma as a factor for his party's defeat by the Peronists in the 1962 elections. In both cases the outcome was military intervention.[132] More obviously, personalism operates against meritocratic modes of advancement both in the governmental structure and in business. Likewise, status being accorded to a person and not to an office can lead to a reluctance to delegate as well as a failure to relate one's role to the wider organisation. Personalism is neither an isolated nor an isolatable aspect of political culture. It is related to the emphasis on the individual and on kinship on Argentine society; also to distrust of strangers, to machismo and to clientelism.

6 Kinship and the Zero-sum Model of Politics

HISPANIC INDIVIDUALISM

Argentine politics has been seen as dominated by individuals and Argentines as lacking confidence in impersonal organisations and people they do not know personally. Both traits are commonly related to the individualist aspect of Hispanic culture, both in Spain and in Latin America, characterised by fatalism, hierarchy, *dignidad* and male superiority. These features clash with 'modern' values favouring political development such as belief in the possibility of changing things and advancement on merit. Such values stem from and/or comprise a society's 'world view', which is in turn derived from its geography, history, economic situation, etc., but which nevertheless determines its options in the present and future.[1]

Such views are criticised as culturally determinist. Criticisms of this kind ignore the obvious impact of experience on perceptions at every level, from the individual to the societal. If attempts to change things are consistently unsuccessful, for whatever reason, and if the individual's life-chances are seen as determined by the status others accord him/her, people will recognise what is happening and act accordingly.

Resting as it does on the idea of compromise and the counting of heads, the democratic aspect of liberal democracy which is an Argentine political ideal, conflicts in its very essence with that particular kind of individualism which characterises Iberian culture. Ortega y Gasset sees individualism as the root of what he calls 'particularism' in twentieth-century Spain. This phenomenon is similar to the sectoralism of Argentine society, the apparent incapacity of social groups to compromise with others so as to attain some element of their goals.[2] Like other authors, Ortega y Gasset is suggesting that a particular sort of individualism is a traditional Hispanic characteristic. As Hamill points out, the pride and individualism of Spanish culture is reflected in the old adage '*del rey abajo ninguno*'.[3] This Spanish trait is seen as having been transferred to Latin America during the colonial era, and reinforced by the independence struggle. It has remained a feature of Argentine society and is illustrated in such *porteño* sayings as '*Yo primero, mi familia secundo, el mundo tercero*'.[4]

Individualism may have encouraged the acceptance as an ideal of European liberalism and thus strengthened the non-Hispanic stream of cultural influence, but its content has been consistently seen as hostile to democracy. Individualism in Hispanic nations rests on *dignidad*, the pride of an individual in himself and his right to assert himself against others, but it does not imply compromise between the rights of one individual and those of others. In this sense, Hispanic individualism is unlike the North American variant and not conducive to social, or indeed political, stability. Individualism in North America has been described as a 'political and social and economic concept' in contrast with the 'ethical and religious and personal' individualism of Latin America, where:

> Individualism dictates not so much an equality of opportunity or obligation in relation to others as a fulfilment of one's own inner integrity, one's *dignidad*, one's honor, one's *alma* [soul].[5]

Different kinds of individualism are presumed to have different social effects, destabilising ones in the case of the Hispanic form. De Madariaga suggests that, although Spanish culture is marked by psychological emphasis not just on the individual, but also on the other extreme, the universe, this still means that the middle range of social and political communities is insufficiently valued. Social cooperation would tend to reduce individual liberty in the sense prescribed by Hispanic culture, rather than enhance it as in the North American form. Therefore individualism tends in Latin America to lead to the development of vertical structures, where authority flows down a hierarchy, rather than to horizontal structures built on cooperation.[6] The high value placed on the individual similarly leads to the lower valuation of abstract principles and to the disposition to vote for a person rather than a political programme. Thus it undermines the development of impersonal loyalties to political parties and institutions.

Regrettably much of the evidence for the nature and strength of individualism in Hispanic culture is impressionistic. Extensive comparative psychological studies are not available and would in any case be suspect, as the concept of individualism would be especially difficult to measure.

THE EMPHASIS ON KINSHIP

As with the emphasis on the individual, the strength and other characteristics of the Hispanic family are seen by some authors as contributing to social and political instability. Two main areas of destabilising influence are assumed. First, the strength of kinship ties is thought to be a factor operating against the development of wider loyalties; loyalties to impersonal principles and institutions, to community and to nation. Thus de Madariaga, for example, argues that the family is stronger, more extended and more self-sufficient in Hispanic culture, and that this leads to nepotism and to hostility to those outside the kinship network.[7] Secondly, the structure of the Hispanic family and its style of socialisation are seen as inculcating values which are essentially authoritarian and thus lack congruence with the values on which the formal political structure is based. However, the reasons for the continuing importance of the family in modern Latin America lie not only in the transfer of Iberian culture during the colonial era, but also in the historical experience of the New World. This not only reinforced, but even increased, the central importance of kinship networks.

From the Conquest onwards, the Habsburg monarchy granted legal privileges to certain families who performed services for the Crown. Such families often controlled local offices and therefore patronage networks at the municipal level. The local Church establishment and notable families supported one another, and remoteness from the centre of the Empire ensured their power:

> Since the post conquest period, the family has been an important organisational form in Hispanic-American society. It was the strongest organisation in society when all other state structures were too distant (overseas in the peninsula) or too weak ... Individuals working in a loosely organised association had largely accomplished the conquest of Ibero-America, but families acquired the wealth and power and status that accrued from it.[8]

The power of many of these families peaked in the early eighteenth century and was diminished, in some cases eliminated, by the Bourbon reforms at the end of the century which resulted in the rise of a new elite of notable families in the old areas of Spanish America, as well as in newly important areas like the Viceroyalty of the Río de la Plata. Important trading families which would later become the backbone of the landed elite, such as the families Anchorena and Martínez de Hoz, were represented. The second generation of this elite, whilst diversifying and acquiring land, had absorbed elements of Enlightenment thought and they favoured economic liberalism. Acting as an elite rather than as individual families, they began establishing both formal and informal social and economic institutions. Despite this liberal orientation, elements of this elite were amongst those who provided the rural military support for Rosas at a later date.

The early nineteenth century saw an expansion of the economic interests of these notable families and the extension of their political power beyond their localities. Some of them, as members of the Cabildo Abierto, took part in the process of voting for independence in 1810, and after it was achieved the weakened post-independence state left them more influential. They retained their patronage networks after the collapse of the Crown and used them for electoral and/or military purposes. In consequence of the demise of Spanish government, members of important families sought public office as a means to assert their trading, commercial and exporting interests. The new centralised state structures were emerging at a time when only the notable family networks had the potential for concerted action because only they had been able to retain and extend the social dominance which they had established in the colonial era. When land became valuable in the 1820s, the dominant families already held large tracts, or were in a unique position to acquire them, through leases granted under Rivadavia's 1826 Law of Emphyteusis. Carving up the available land in this way would serve to limit the growth of an internal market and determine the direction of Argentine economic policy for more than a century. Indeed, this was how the Anchorena family originally acquired a landholding.

The divisions of the Rosas period were followed by a new period of family prosperity and the notable family networks achieved the peak of their power in the late nineteenth century. Their support for the extension of the national territory, especially through the Conquest of the Desert, won them new lands and the integration of Argentina into the world economy strengthened their economic position still further. Their dependence on foreign markets changed, but did not destroy, the insecurity the Argentine elite felt in a hostile environment so far from the centres of 'civilisation'. The family therefore retained its role as a defensive organisation. This role was also somewhat strengthened by the increasing orientation of the elite to Europe and North America. This orientation led to an increased separation from the rest of society as new residential areas and exclusive schools were established. In addition, family power was extended by the responsiveness of government to the wishes of the most prestigious families, even to the extent of the cooptation of important provincial families by governments in the post-1852 period and the representation of provincial interests through the selection of non-*porteño* presidents. Further the economic elite was more actively involved in politics and not just in supporting the government. For example, the Cesares banking family, which had given staunch support to conservatism through its role in welding together Mitre's Partido Nacional with the Partido Autonomista, also provided the treasurer for the newly formed Unión Cívica.

The notable families dominated positions in the executive, including ministerial offices and the presidency itself. In so doing they set a pattern of control of public offices which the military would assume in due course. In 1930 military political power was enhanced, so that family power was proportionately decreased and only with the tacit agreement of the military could the agro-exporting elite dominate Argentine politics in the 1930s. Industrial development and Perón effectively destroyed the importance of the family networks. In the latter case, this was done not so much by deliberate attack, but rather by unleashing the collective strength of the working class and thus 'necessitating' the further political involvement of the military in the process of demobilisation. Although the influence of notable families was thus generally reduced, some individual families have been able to retain their disproportionate access to political, as well as social and economic power.[9]

However if the influence of notable family networks has declined, their success in protecting and promoting the interests of their members has strengthened the importance of kinship in Argentine society at all social levels, not just amongst the elite. The Latin American middle class is generally seen as having absorbed values associated with the traditional upper class including an emphasis on kinship. The lack of other defensive organisations such as unions or cooperative societies amongst rural *estancia* workers has resulted in continued reliance on kinship systems. The process of modernisation may also have contributed to, rather than detracted from, familism amongst the urban masses in that the extended family's defensive function becomes more necessary in the free-for-all of the city. The bulk of internal migration to Buenos Aires took place sufficiently long ago for extended families to have re-established themselves. Urban existence, in the poorer quarters of the city and in the shanty towns around it, meant very close proximity of relatives, if not actually co-residential extended families.[10] A similar extended support pattern remains in rural areas although most residential units are nuclear, since they are frequently tied to occupational roles. Silvert, amongst others, has suggested that new loyalties, such as nationalism, are reducing the emphasis on kinship, especially amongst the middle class. He further argues that the process of urbanisation has led to the development of nuclear family forms.[11] However, Argentine nationalism is a long-standing phenomenon and there is no reason to suppose that it is not a binding rather than divisive force within families.

There has, of course, been an increasing trend in some areas of Buenos Aires to nuclear families defined by the formal structure of the household. Amongst people questioned about this, most stressed apartment size as the key factor for this development in the Capital Federal district, and emphasised continuing frequent contact with the wider kinship network. In the case of middle-class housing developments, the value of real estate in the city has decreed the building of high-rise blocks, and the 'monoblocks' built by Perón for his followers were constructed for cheapness and high-density housing. However, older working-class residential areas such as Avellaneda and Morón retain larger family units, as does the old and new housing occupied by the middle classes in the more outlying suburbs. There is little evidence of family isolation even amongst those living in structurally nuclear families in Buenos Aires.

So in Argentina there remains a very strong emphasis on family. Some commentators have seen this as providing protection and stability through political crises, but as working against economic development because work needs are subordinated to the family institution. The effects of the emphasis on kinship and style of socialisation on economic development is very difficult to quantify, despite studies by authors such as David McClelland, who emphasises the economic value of universalistic values, functional specificity, meritocratic advancement, a collective orientation, affective neutrality and so on.[12] A strong emphasis on kinship both reflects and reinforces particularistic values and is therefore seen as operating against the development of values which would favour long-term national economic prosperity.[13] Despite a high level of differentiation in the economic sphere, in the sense that a monetary value is placed on most goods and services, familism is still strong in Argentine business. Amongst the entrepreneurial middle class, the tendency is strong for all members to contribute whatever time and skills they can, whether on a full- or part-time basis, to the family business. In much larger businesses, familism has also been well-developed and is in some cases highly successful, for example in SIAM (Sociedad Industrial Americana de

Maquinarias), prior to its sale to IKA-Renault in 1965.

The values relating to enterpreneurial activity transmitted through the family have been subject to much examination, but such studies suffer from inevitable weaknesses given the nebulous quality of what they attempt to test. McClelland himself gives little attention specifically to Argentina, and such evidence as he does provide assumes that an analysis of children's books reflects the process of socialisation generally. Limited as it is in its usefulness, his study suggests that children's books in countries which could be seen as having elements in common with Argentina (Brazil, Mexico and Italy) tended to display low 'achievement', but high 'affiliation' imagery (friendship, bonds to people not things or principles). Argentine schoolbooks examined in 1950 displayed more achievement imagery than subsequent economic development would suggest, but McClelland asserts that such imagery was exaggerated by the impact of Peronism. These books also contained a high level of 'power' imagery (relationships based on force and domination) and were less likely to have references to peers, which can be seen as an orientation to other people, than books used in more rapidly developing authoritarian countries such as the Soviet Union, Greece and Spain.[14]

What then is the relationship between the values inculcated during the primary socialisation process and political stability? It has been frequently said that all agents of socialisation in Latin American nations are essentially authoritarian. For example, Moreno, with experience of both cultures, argues that subordination to the family is much more common in Latin America than in the United States.[15] But congruence theory (that politics will reflect the characteristics of other social institutions) over-simplifies matters. In Argentina, families may broadly exhibit Hispanic structures and be authoritarian, schools may emphasise discipline and signal lesson changes with excerpts from the national anthem, political parties may resist compromise and make appeals to the military, but despite all this there still remains an ideology of liberal democracy. Argentine culture generally can never fully be 'congruent' with either a democratic or authoritarian government, because its dual aspect precludes this.

Perhaps the most important feature of the emphasis on

kinship is the impact this has on attitudes to other people and other institutions. The family as 'an offensive and defensive alliance'[16] may be so because it is the only institution on which its members can depend. But, even if loyalty to the extended family is an effect, rather than a cause, of the distrust of people and institutions outside it, the 'offensive' element of the extended family must be seen as reinforcing and strengthening, if not creating, distrust of other people and institutions. Petras may be right in his assertion that informal bonds (including those of kinship) actually enhance class consciousness in Argentina and strengthen class affiliations. If so, this integrative function is very limited. Such bonds do not reduce the nation's sectoral structure, nor do they contribute to a sense of identity wider than that of class. Primary cleavages generally tend to operate directly against loyalties to the wider community, to public duty and to nation.[17] This idea constitutes one of the many bases for comparison of the relative development and stability of Australia with the Argentine case. Australia is seen as having a stronger sense of community in consequence of the fact that the extended family ' . . . is not a prominent feature of Australian life'.[18] In contrast, in Latin America, as Anderson notes:

> . . . the individual goes out from the family into the larger society to enhance the position of the family, rather than viewing the family as a base supporting the individual's commitment to larger social systems.[19]

DISTRUST OF OTHERS

Distrust of other people is frequently cited as a trait generally characteristic of Latin Americans which does constitute an obstacle to development. It has been variously described as a lack of 'collaborative spirit'[20] or 'interpersonal cooperation'.[21] Its existence is rarely questioned, though its importance has been disputed. It is generally seen as a longstanding characteristic, being reflected in Bolívar's famous dictum:

> There is no faith in America, between either men or nations. Treaties are papers; constitutions, books; elections, combats; liberty, anarchy; and life, a torment.[22]

This trait, too, is generally believed to derive from Hispanic culture as is indicated by Ortega y Gasset's emphasis on the incapacity of the individual in twentieth-century Spain to understand and make allowance for ' . . . the ideas and desires of others'.[23] Nevertheless, the strange interaction of European influence with Iberian culture in strengthening the family and contributing to destabilisation of politics, has probably reinforced if not actually deepened this characteristic.

Scepticism over the effect of distrust of others on Argentine political stability is expressed by Kirkpatrick. She acknowledges that a lack of trust and mutual hostility are frequently seen as national characteristics. On the other hand, her figures suggest that other nations, notably West Germany, exhibit similar attitudes, but do not face the same political problems. However, in making her cross-national comparisons she is using figures from Almond and Verba's study and taking on board all the weaknesses of that study. As a pioneer work, Almond and Verba's study reflected the prevailing lack of experience of comparative empirical social surveying. The small samples they used and the difficulties of ensuring the same interpretation of a question amongst respondents from different cultures and with different languages, are obvious problems. In addition Kirkpatrick herself notes that this particular comparison may be weakened by the methodological differences between her work and that of Almond and Verba. But Kirkpatrick does argue that mutual distrust contributes to institutional weakness which she sees as the main reason for instability, although she does not consider it sufficient explanation in itself. She goes on to suggest that the inability to compromise, the incapacity to share political power and the widely-held zero-sum model of politics may provide a fuller explanation.[24] In so doing, though, she fails to acknowledge the indirect contribution of mutual distrust to instability, in that those 'other' factors to which she accords importance are intimately bound to a lack of trust in others. The interrelation of cultural factors precludes explanations in terms of one value; rather, a multiplicity of cultural aspects interact to provide a backdrop for instability.

Although Kirkpatrick suggests that such influence is limited, most commentators on the lack of trust in other people see it as a feature working against political stability. It does so both indirectly, by operating against economic efficiency, and directly, by its impact on political behaviour. Fillol asserts that the Argentine population is a 'conglomeration' not a 'community' and that this limits the capacity to work together for development.[25] Anderson suggests that distrust operates against economic efficiency in transitional societies generally because it results in unwillingness to delegate tasks and a low capacity for teamwork if this is based on non-primary groups.[26] Primary loyalties reduce the possibility of making the most rational choices in consequence of 'the necessity to distinguish in any decision between those one knows and those one does not know'.[27] Mutual distrust also reinforces and perhaps increases the tendency to despise long-term hard work as a means to success. *Picardía criolla* (literally, 'native trickery') has become part of Argentine culture, and the socialisation process includes the learning of the necessity to put one over on other people before they do the same to you. The ability to get away with things and to make a fast buck through trickery is admired and the person who is successfully tricked gets little sympathy.

The failure to understand and relate to people outside primary groups can be seen as having direct impact on political stability too. Snow suggests that political culture partly rests on beliefs relating to political identity. Such beliefs have two levels, national identity and horizontal identification. The latter rests on trust of others and its absence increases reluctance to hand over power. Not only do incumbents stand to lose the advantages of office themselves but they do not trust their opponents with the governmental apparatus.[28] Again the contradictory forces of elements of two cultures can be seen: an ideology which emphasises procedures to be followed by all incumbents interacts with a fear that the procedures themselves are insufficient to constrain people and a belief that to allow others to operate those procedures is a greater threat than the loss of the procedures themselves. Dahl summarises such attitudes:

... conflicts are more threatening among people who distrust one another. Public contestation requires a good deal of trust in one's opponents: they may be opponents but they are not implacable enemies.[29]

MACHISMO

Political competition may also be seen as more ferocious and compromise less likely when a gladiatorial attitude is inherent in the concept of masculinity exhibited by a society. The strength of machismo in Argentina, like the emphasis on kinship, does not simply reflect the transfer of the characteristic from Spain, but also its reinforcement and strengthening by historical experience. From the outset, the settlement of Argentina was the conquest of a hostile environment and the *gauchos* formed a barrier between the towns of the littoral and the pampas Indians. The heyday of the *gaucho* in the late eighteenth and early nineteenth centuries coincides with the peak years of the pastoral economy, when hides were in much demand to supply European armies. But, more importantly, this was the period in which the most productive land was won and patterns of development established. During those years, the foundations of the independent nation were laid and the association of nationhood with male might was established.

The term '*gaucho*' had originally been a term of abuse, but was first used in a favourable manner by the Salteño hero of independence, Martín Miguel de Güemes (a man whose memory has been recently evoked by Major Jorge Durán, who led the Salta barracks uprising in Easter Week 1987).[30] During the liberation struggle, his *gaucho* armies, in black and red ponchos, defeated Spanish attempts at reconquest from Upper Peru (now Bolivia). This resistance to Spain has since been romanticised in Argentine popular films as well as in her literature. Not only in their military function, but also in their general lifestyle, the *gauchos* developed a culture based on individualism and male dominance. By the very nature of the isolated and dangerous lives they led, the *gauchos* were independent and armed, they submitted to no hierarchy or discipline save that of the *caudillos* who could rule them only by force. As Rennie notes:

> All that the *gaucho* had of the democratic spirit was a sense of personal liberty that was anarchic.[31]

Martínez Estrada describes the *gauchos'* cattle herding 'as a form of big-game hunting'[32] and thus the male role of mighty hunter subordinated women in rural Argentina.

It has been suggested that male dominance is the natural outcome of male conquest. Conquering males, unaccompanied by European women, taking native and therefore racially 'inferior' women, established a pattern of male dominance in Latin America generally. Certainly on the pampas, the *gaucho* lifestyle can only be seen as reinforcing such a situation. Their isolation meant that most relationships were neither sanctioned by law nor by the Church and in any case the independent *gaucho* earning a living from seasonal and migratory work would have been hard to tie down. Sarmiento noted the strict division of labour by sex and that women assumed all the domestic role.[33] Other authors assert further that *gaucho* men held women in contempt.[34] This contrasts markedly with the Northern United States where small farmers held values which emphasised the dignity of hard work and the worth of women who no doubt assumed the bulk of the domestic role but who nevertheless took part in the process of production too. Such values would appear to reflect historical experience rather than the simple transfer of different values from Britain as the mother country, since different attitudes to work and women developed in the Southern United States despite the similar ethnic backgrounds of settlers. (The late nineteenth- and early twentieth-century rewriting of Southern history continued to exhibit such values, a feature which may be termed the 'Gone with the Wind' syndrome). It should be noted however that Australia appears to provide a rather different picture, suggesting that a combination of cultural legacy and historical reinforcement provides a fuller explanation. Although, like Argentina, Australia had what has been termed 'a big man's frontier' from which the Australian form of machismo is believed to derive,[35] cultural factors seem to have mitigated the effects of this as regards the importance of women, especially within the family.

Australian women make most decisions within the context of the family. The paternalistic character of the Latin American family, however, is probably also class-related,[36] and derives from the paternalism of both the family and the estate which characterised pre-Conquest Castile.

It has been suggested that male dominance is breaking down in Argentina, both in the economic and political spheres. Alba notes that by the end of the 1960s, 25 per cent of jobs were held by women.[37] However, he offers no breakdown of the kinds of occupations these were. Austerity measures during the latter part of the 1960s may have forced working-class women especially to seek economic roles to supplement family incomes. Since 1980 as the economic position of the middle class has declined, many middle-class Argentine wives have been seeking part-time work, but this is seen by them and their husbands as a temporary expedient detracting from their 'proper' role, and the present authors have discerned little evidence of symmetry evolving in conjugal roles in their admittedly limited experience of middle-class Argentine families. A recent ILO survey of working men and women in Greater Buenos Aires shows that, as elsewhere, women do housework in addition to their paid occupational roles. Such women worked an average 90 hours a week, compared with 40.3 hours for men.[38] Aviel argues that women are active in professional bodies and that 39 per cent of university students in Argentina are women.[39] However, the number of women active in such bodies is very limited, and university education and entry to the professions is highly elitist and should not be assumed to reflect changing attitudes in society in general.

In Argentina, unlike other Latin American nations (except Uruguay) women register to vote in numbers comparable with those of male voters. However, active participation in politics, despite the involvement of women in guerrilla operations – which were in any case another example of primarily elitist activity – is dominated by men; especially so if the periods of total male government under military regimes is taken into account. It is indicative that the two most important women in Argentine politics in 1988, Adelina d'Alessio de Viola and María Julia Alsogaray, are Deputies in the liberal rightist, upper-middle-class Democratic Centre Union Party led by the father of one of them, Alvaro Alsogaray. Further the recent establishment of a government department to protect women's rights required the Radical government to appoint a Christian Democrat Deputy to head it, as the UCR had no suitable female politician within its own ranks.

This limited female involvement is generally seen as beginning with Evita's launch into public politics on 17 October 1948, when she addressed the crowds for the first time. (The earlier role she has since been accorded in rousing sentiment amongst labour in support of the imprisoned Perón in October 1945 is highly suspect.) The Partido Peronista Femenino was established on 26 July 1949 and women first voted in the presidential elections held in November 1951, 63.9 per cent of them for Perón, slightly above his national 62.5 per cent support. This pattern was repeated in the 1954 congressional elections when Peronist candidates received 65.23 per cent of the female vote compared with 60.69 per cent of the male vote. However, to see these developments as indicative of the beginnings of a breakdown of male domination of politics is erroneous. Perón himself is seen by Naipaul as 'the greatest macho of them all'[40] and Evita's influence derived from him, as she never failed to emphasise. The whole symbolism of Peronism, the workers with sleeves rolled up and tools in hand, smacked of machismo. Indeed it still does. Herminio Iglesias, for example, until November 1986 General Secretary of the Justicialist Party and leader of the orthodox FREJULI faction of the Peronist movement, regarded by his political opponents and genteel society as a gangland thug, is but one example of the brutal male strength that Peronism appeared to wish to preserve in its image, at least until his recent expulsion from the Party. Other 'hard men' remain.

Though possibly less potent than it once was, machismo remains and has an impact on stability in both indirect and direct ways. Its indirect influence is through its effect on development. At the most general level, being masculine is an ascribed feature and its emphasis reinforces ascriptive values which undermine the orientation to achievement. More concretely it gives a man pride in himself without the need to develop it, to work hard, for example.[41] In the direct sense, machismo causes the externalisation of violence and aggression and this carries over into politics. Because all men are assumed to be macho until they prove themselves otherwise, it operates against the art of compromise. It is significant that Alexander Haig, himself a top-ranking soldier, should have remarked upon the strength of machismo he found amongst the Argentine military government in 1982 and the malign influence he believed this had had on the junta's foreign policy.[42]

RELUCTANCE TO COMPROMISE

The effect of the orientation to self and family is reinforcement of an inherent weakness, the inability to make political compromises, which is part of the wider incapacity to share power with political opponents. Individualism and machismo operate to make compromise an affront to personal pride. Distrust of those outside primary groups contributes to distrust of political opponents. Argentina is 'a society that considers compromise a questionable trait of human character'.[43] Two beliefs are necessary if negotiation and compromise are to be developed. First, problems must be seen as soluble, but they are frequently not so seen in Argentina in consequence of the pessimistic and fatalistic attitudes which prevail. Secondly, both sides in any dispute must see themselves as benefiting from such negotiation. Where distrust of others is well-developed, a zero-sum model of society in general, and politics in particular, operates, and benefits to someone else come to be seen as costs to the individual:

> The almost universal view in Argentina is that no public measure can be good for almost everybody, that the benefit of one group is the automatic detriment of all others.[44]

Compromise is only possible when those who disagree see their disagreement as a greater threat than the object of their disagreement. Thus shared values must be more potent than differences if compromise is to be achieved. Particularism works against the development of shared values, by constantly emphasising distinctions between people; an example being whether they are within or without one's own kinship network. However, the direction of causality is by no means proven. It is equally possible to argue that the existence of a zero-sum model of society gives rise to particularism, since under such circumstances it is necessary to establish who can be trusted in a defensive alliance against the rest of society. It seems most probable that the two aspects are too interrelated to be separable and that they reinforce and strengthen each other, to the ultimate detriment of Argentine political stability.

Again historical experience has reinforced an existing Hispanic characteristic, and the interaction of Iberian culture with that of Europe has exacerbated the operation of the trait. Compromise is frequently seen as backing down, as something immoral because it involves shifting from a position one knows to be correct:

> In Latin America . . . compromise as a political craft has little prestige and scant effectiveness. Indeed compromise has clearly derogatory overtones. The verb *transigir*, broadly meaning 'to compromise', implies giving in, in a prejudicial sense.[45]

This attitude is shown to be very powerful by Moreno who, despite being a sophisticated and objective observer of Latin America, argues from his personal experience that willingness to accept a contrary view because it is that of the majority in any group is alien and incomprehensible to the Latin American. The tendency is to see the majority as wrong.[46]

Clearly economic scarcity contributes to the development of a zero-sum model, but this explanation is inadequate alone since many nations experiencing scarcity do not develop such negative images of society. The alternating periods of prosperity and retrenchment may be a factor which causes economic matters to take on an importance greater than the preservation of the political system since sectoral interests are anxious to maintain their previous gains. However, the implication that a zero-sum model is something relatively new to Argentina, deriving from her poor economic performance since 1930 does not seem to be borne out by the historical evidence.[47]

Argentine history is permeated by examples of failures to compromise and intolerance of opposition, which must be seen as providing from the outset the basis for a zero-sum model. Rivadavia, as president of the United Provinces from February

1826, refused to visit the interior provinces and made known his utter contempt for the *caudillos* and their *gauchos*. In return, their hatred for him and refusal to accept his presidency made compromise between Unitarians and Federalists impossible and contributed to the rise of Rosas. Rosas' regime would not compromise with any of the aspirations of Rivadavia and ' . . . the entire Rivadavia model was rejected as irrelevant'.[48] Rosas controlled all the institutions of state and society and would tolerate no opposition. Order was ensured by the suspension of political liberties. To control the Federalist cause despite divisions between Federalist groupings, he assumed absolute powers and issued laws by decree; he made and confirmed judicial decisions and controlled the legislature and bureaucracy, having purged his opponents. Although judicial procedures were available to him, Rosas used terror precisely for the purpose of discouraging opposition. Indeed there could be no such thing as 'opposition'. Argentines were either pro-Rosas or 'traitors to their country'.[49] Variants on 'Death to the savage Unitarians!' appeared as salutations on all official letters and proclamations. Hardly surprisingly, his opponents did not believe either that compromise was possible. Sarmiento saw the forces of 'civilisation' and 'barbarism' as diametrically opposed. When he and Mitre had their chance in turn to eliminate their opponents, they were ruthless.

In one sense the adoption of the 1853 Constitution could be said to represent the supreme compromise, since it evolved from the interaction of the two cultures. Yet the Iberian strand of culture did not compromise with the new ideological overlay, but rather remained as a fallback position. The liberal–democratic theory behind the constitution emphasises the operation of the political system within defined procedural limits. It thus implies compromise amongst politically-competing groups and therefore toleration of opposition and dissent. Some of the features of the constitution, most notably the power of the presidency, discourage power-sharing, again illustrating how Hispanic and European cultural elements combine to strengthen pre-existing traits which act against stability. In addition, the constitution is sufficiently flexible to allow its use as an eliminator of opposition through mechanisms such as federal intervention and the state of siege. This reflects the 'monistic' concept of democracy which prevails in Latin America. Power-sharing is not part of this concept and consensus is achieved, not by compromise between competing groups, but by the elimination of competition. The political institutions which have been adopted do not exist to resolve conflict and thus there is no need for a separation of powers along the lines of those adopted with similar constitutions elsewhere.[50] When these formal political structures fail to eliminate conflict, alternative devices such as the military coup are available to do so.

During the nineteenth century in Argentina, opposition groups were denied representation and political conflicts occurred outside the institutional structure. Even during the period of oligarchic domination, which marks the beginnings of the development of national political parties, competition within institutional structures was kept to a minimum:

> No opponents to the policies of the oligarchy were allowed to share in the government. Power was transmitted from one president to his successor in a close caucus, and elections were controlled.[51]

The development of political parties therefore took a very different form from that occurring elsewhere. In the United States, which had the additional advantage of both traditions and competing institutions which encouraged compromise and dissent, political parties had acquired their basic form earlier. From 1795 to 1814 they represented intense ideological cleavages but these gave way through the Era of Good Feelings (c. 1816–24) to compromise solutions on which broad electoral coalitions could be built. The structure of party was well established before the issues of slavery and secession came to the fore. In contrast, in Argentina political parties did not develop out of the institutionalised competition of rival political groups and eventually emerged as challenges to government authority which were confronted by elite resistance. In consequence, Argentina, like other Latin American nations, did not develop a concept, in the style of Britain or the United States, of the victorious political party working for the nation as a whole. The immigration and economic development generated by the policies of the elite itself caused it to seek to protect its own interests. Even if a capacity to compromise were well-developed, democracy then would have appeared as a threat due to the coincidence of a new era of prosperity with the emergence of groups demanding access to power and economic opportunities. Thus it is possible to argue that the zero-sum model was consolidated in the period of oligarchic rule, partly as a result of elite intolerance of opposition and partly as a result, not of economic scarcity, but of prosperity.

That such a model was also entrenched in the attitudes of opposition party activists by the end of the nineteenth century is illustrated by the situation in the Socialist Party. At its Second Congress in June 1898, only four years after its foundation, the Socialist Party was already fragmented, with nine different factions being represented. Just one year later elements within the party were criticising the leadership for their preoccupation with electoral politics.[52]

This is not to say that the elite did not use compromise to achieve consensus within their own ranks. They even went so far as to attempt to coopt Radical elements into the Cabinet, the legislature and sub-national institutions. Roca offered Yrigoyen an electoral pact which could have made him president, but Yrigoyen refused and fraud was used to elect Roque Sáenz Peña in 1910. The new president made further overtures to the Radical elite, who themselves imbued by a the zero-sum model, again refused. The electoral reform of 1912 did not constitute a compromise, but rather was a result of the belief of the then dominant elite faction that they could win elections despite an expanded franchise, coopt Radical elements and thus preserve the existing situation. When the 1914 congressional elections showed they could not, the Socialists and Radical parties were labelled extremist and attempts were made to abort the electoral reform. The rump of the PAN refused to compromise and join an electoral front against the UCR for the 1916 elections and thus helped ensure Yrigoyen's victory. Conservative and Radical intolerance of each other during the period of Radical rule and the incapacity of the two political forces to make the necessary compromises must be seen as contributing to Yrigoyen's ouster in 1930.

Yrigoyen and his supporters, 'whose mentality towards politics had been shaped by their twenty-six years as an opposition force',[53] did not seek a rapprochement with the opposition when they gained power. Indeed Yrigoyen increased the level of political conflict by viewing his victory in 1916 as the first stage of a revolution which would lead to the destruction of the Oligarchy which he proceeded to attempt. This attitude 'could hardly be expected to convert the conservative politicians of the oligarchy into a loyal opposition'.[54]

In Congress, partisanship was strong and strict party alignments marked voting. Debates became personal clashes. Instead of reducing antagonism by coopting conservative elements into his government, Yrigoyen exacerbated the situation by his interventions in conservative provinces. Likewise cooptation of Anti-personalist Radicals during his second administration could have worked against the declining legitimacy which the UCR was experiencing as a consequence of its split. Without compromise and cooptation, the weakening effects on the government of a Senate dominated by conservatives, Anti-personalist Radicals and Socialists were magnified. The lack of political negotiation and institutionalised competition within the formal structure encouraged the growth of extra-institutional conflict and political violence in the form of paramilitary groups such as the Liga Republicana and the Liga Patriótica Argentina opposing the government and the Klan Radical supporting it.

The end of the Radical era did not mean an end to political intransigence. After his initial association with Anti-personalist Radicals against Uriburu, General Agustín P. Justo, once in power, had the Radical leaders arrested. (In doing so, he illustrates the tendency throughout Argentine history for alliances to be built, not on compromise for the purpose of constructing a positive programme, but on common differences with a shared enemy.) However, despite such treatment, Radical elements refused to join with the Socialists and Progressive Democrats to form a middle-class political front against the Concordancia (which was itself divided) and militarism. Political realities could not overcome the strength of the zero-sum model. The Radicals continued to see themselves as the sole heirs to power and conservatives on the other hand, ' . . . viewed their war against the Radicals as a crusade for the fatherland.'[55] Later, Castillo would also refuse to entertain any power sharing and would provoke a political crisis which paralysed the legislative process by allowing the re-introduction of electoral fraud to prevent Radical victories in important provinces in the gubernatorial elections in late 1940. In 1941 he dissolved the Socialist- and Radical- dominated Buenos Aires Municipal Council by presidential decree, and also continued the pattern of using the state of siege to repress criticism.

For some, Perón appears as the supreme Argentine pragmatist. He is seen as a man willing to compromise any principle to stay in power. Thus Blanksten describes the Perón regime as a 'balancing of forces' and Justicialismo as 'a juggler's act'.[56] But Peronism can hardly be seen as heralding a new capacity for political compromise in Argentina. Perón's primary power base, the trade unions, were available to him largely as a consequence of the incapacity of the labour movement to cooperate amongst itself. His strength between 1946 and 1955 rested on his ability to control the various sectors of Argentine society, his playing off of one sector against another. When he lost this capacity, when he seemed no longer to have the will to control opposition, he fell. He suppressed dissent through a variety of methods including the closing of *La Prensa*, his *desacato* (disrespect) law which was introduced in 1949, and a spy network which is still recalled by the middle classes in comments to the effect that it was impossible even to trust one's own maid. In the years following his ouster, his very existence polarised Argentine society. Unlike the North American situation where a 'multiplicity of affiliations' or 'cross-cutting solidarities' reduce an individual's stake in any one group,[57] the inability to compromise both strengthened and was itself reinforced by continuing loyalty to, or hatred of, Perón. The ability to see history as one believes it should have been helped produce social and political fragmentation in the years after 1955. No compromise was possible between diametrically opposed beliefs. Perón was *either* a saint *or* the man who destroyed the old Argentina.

The brief Lonardi government (1955), which sought to begin the re-integration of labour, found itself confronted by hardline military elements opposed to compromise. The *'revolución libertadora'* (Liberating Revolution) was the result of the coalition of nationalists such as Lonardi himself and his Minister of Foreign Affairs, Mario Amadeo, and 'liberals' determined to take a firm line against the vestiges of Peronism. The former group reflected aspects of Iberian-derived culture and therefore were willing to make concessions to the participatory interpretation of democracy. No such compromise was possible for the liberal faction led by Aramburu who took power from Lonardi. An immediate demobilisation process began with the dissolution of the Peronist Party and the intervention of the CGT.

Frondizi (1958 – 63) is the rare exception, a man remembered as someone who tried to achieve some element of consensus in Argentina's fragmented society. In seeking and gaining Peronist support in the 1958 elections by promising to protect the rights of the workers, he was compromising with another political group. Certainly Frondizi had been amongst Perón's staunchest opponents whilst he held power, so his deal with Perón in exile must be recognised as compromise and as such came as a considerable surprise to Peronist labour too.[58] Likewise his efforts to integrate divergent political groups by selecting his presidential advisers from all sides of the political spectrum, should be construed in this light. However, once in power, these policies produced military opposition and Frondizi was forced to change tack. Thus he won the hostility of all sides and, lacking sufficient popular support, he had to use the divisions amongst his enemies to his advantage. It was Frondizi's attempts at conciliation with the left, both at home and abroad, which brought him down and thus reinforced the idea that compromise, at least with other civilian political groups, is a dangerous device for the Argentine politician.

Arturo Illia (1963 – 66) similarly suffered from the operation of a zero-sum model in politics. O'Donnell shows that few Argentines believed that the Illia government acted primarily for the benefit of their own social group or of all social groups. A Gallup Poll survey of the Buenos Aires area showed that only 7 per cent of respondents believed that the whole population benefited from Illia's policies.[59] Some of Illia's policies seem, to the external observer, to favour each social group. They were broadly nationalist; some were pro-labour, for example ending political proscription and introducing a minimum index-linked wage; others were anti-labour, such as reform of the trade unions; some were pro-Colorado, including the restoration of purged officers; others were pro-Azul, for example, subordinating the military to constitutional authority. In another society, Illia might have been seen as offering something to everybody. In Argentina, the zero-sum model meant that every political force had something against him.[60]

Fernández found the political elite to favour compromise in a survey conducted just prior to the 1966 coup.[61] However, this response may represent desperation given the situation prevailing and there is little evidence of similar responses from other political groups in more recent surveys. In his 1973 survey, Turner found that despite what they have in common (elite backgrounds, anti-Peronist attitudes and internationalist orientations), large-scale business executives did not associate closely with *estancieros*. He suggests that such a division within the economic elite may reflect the zero-sum model in that businessmen may feel that the *estancieros* get disproportionate rewards from the economic system as well as the social status associated with land ownership. For their part, the attitudes of *estancieros* did little to encourage common feeling; they did not see the economic development of the entire nation as a priority.[62]

The return of Peronism in 1973 did represent a compromise by just such groups as business executives and *estancieros*, as well as a far wider section of the middle class who had consistently opposed Perón. However, Perón's return did not mean that he had learnt the art of compromise whilst in exile. He failed to achieve this even within his own movement. Indeed, the term '*verticalismo*' was adopted to emphasise the hierarchical quality of the movement. Peronism remained absolutist. Compromise was impossible since Perón himself by 1973 was virtually 'sacred' and could not therefore be wrong. This feature is illustrated by the reluctance of leftist elements within the Peronist coalition to take political action opposed to the wishes of Perón himself, although rank-and-file union activity increased.[63] After Perón's choice of the right wing of the Peronist movement and his incapacity to compromise with the left wing, his death in 1974 removed the binding force of Peronism. Under the influence of José López Rega, Isabel Perón exacerbated the situation by moving further to the right rather than seeking some compromise with the left. Intolerance of opposition led to the establishment of paramilitary groups for its suppression, most notoriously the Argentine Anti-Communist Alliance (AAA). As successive sectoral demands for wage and price rises were met, inflation soared and the economic situation declined. The worsening political situation is shown by Jacobo Timerman who, interviewing a Peronist senator in early 1975, asked why Congress did not pass the necessary legislation to empower the army to crack down on subversion whilst maintaining constitutional authority in Congress, thus restricting military excesses and preventing the coup which was beginning to seem inevitable. The senator replied:

> 'Once we allow the military to step through the door, they'll take possession of the entire house. This would be tantamount to a coup, leaving us on the outside. Furthermore, right-wing Peronists who support right-wing terrorist groups that assassinate leftist Peronists, will not vote for the laws; and leftist Peronists who support leftist terrorists who assassinate rightist Peronists will not vote for the laws. Moreover, the army will suppress only one sector of violence and not the other. It will pit one against the other, thus assuring its own survival.'[64]

The senator's latter point, illustrating as it does that the army is also part of a zero-sum model of political power, was further confirmed by Timerman's interview with an officer of the Army General Staff. When asked why the army did not seek to eliminate all forms of violence, the reply was: '"Do you expect us to fight so that they [the Peronists] can continue to govern?"'[65] 'They' were, of course, the democratically elected government and an army elsewhere, not prey to a negative, zero-sum model of power and an only partially legitimate concept of democracy, might have felt it incumbent upon it to protect constitutional authority.

The extent of intolerance of dissent during the military regime which supplanted Isabel Perón in 1976 does not need labouring. The regime clearly illustrated the military's incapacity for compromise with the 'plebeian-populist and immigrant' aspect of Argentina. Society was to be penetrated totally and reformed in a manner which would ensure forever that order was not subverted again.[66] As President Raúl Alfonsín has stated:

> 'The military rulers in Argentina had a messianic vision of their role – they identified the military with the state. They treated politics and politicians with utter contempt'.[67]

Having lost the capacity, and perhaps the will, to suppress dissent in the manner achieved by Videla's government, the Galtieri junta lost the Falklands War and thus their last ditch attempt to reduce opposition.

The Multipartidaria in the period after the Falklands defeat showed that the political parties recognised the need to compromise in the transition to civilian government. Once the electoral campaign got under way, however, this spirit of cooperation was less in evidence. Alfonsín presented his campaign as 'civilisation' in opposition to Peronist 'barbarism' and stressed the liberal aspect of Radicalism rather than social welfare. In so doing he succeeded in winning sufficient right-wing support (variously estimated at between 10 per cent and 17 per cent of voters) to gain the presidency with 50 per cent of the popular vote (52 per cent excluding blanks and null votes). The coalition he built thus is seen by Democratic Centre Union activist Manuel Mora y Araujo as expressing the division between the nationalist/corporatist sector of Argentine politics and the internationalist/democratic sector.[68] Since the military withdrawal from government, Munck sees a new emphasis on compromise and negotiation emerging to replace the zero-sum model of politics which has dominated for so long, and a belief that the process of politics should be conducted by political parties in Congress.[69] Nevertheless, sectoral demands have escalated as groups have sought to protect their own positions against the imposition of austerity measures. Strikes and political unrest have re-emerged, necessitating the use of one of the president's most potent weapons against dissent, the state of siege.

Thus Argentine history exhibits numerous instances of destabilisation through an incapacity for political compromise and the operation of a zero-sum concept of both politics and economics. In fact, Guido di Tella sees political instability as Argentina's unique adaptation to the pressure for representation of various sectors in a context characterised by those features.[70] These aspects of political culture are very debilitating, especially so if a liberal-democratic ideology has been absorbed as an ideal to which the nation should aspire. Autocracy, as Kirkpatrick points out, requires little 'compromise, conciliation, and cooperation'. It is therefore again the interaction of Argentina's two cultures that is destabilising. Argentines are simultaneously convinced that government should be above sectoral wrangles and independent, but concerned that it is not, with some 75 per cent of the population believing government to be subject to the influence of special interests.[71] Distrust of others in contributing to distrust of political institutions helps to undermine the semi-legitimacy of the formal political structure.

The zero-sum view of power has meant that established elites have tended to try to incorporate new interests if they do not seem to constitute too great a threat, but have reserved the option of displacing them if they prove to be so. This was what occurred in 1930. Alternatively, if emergent groups are perceived as a threat, they are likely to be seen as subversive and excluded from the formal political process. In such circumstances, the demands of excluded groups become politicised and thus all the more threatening and the zero-sum model is reinforced.

In emphasising the competition of groups and thereby enhancing the role of sectoral structures, the zero-sum concept partially supports and reinforces the tendency to corporatism, which is however of a limited and fragmentary kind. At the same time, the zero-sum model operates against the development of full vertical structures in the various sectors ensuring that the advantage claimed for corporatism by some commentators, that of bringing together all levels within a sector to express their common interests, is not achieved. For one institution, the military, corporatism does imply in times of relative institutional unity, in the classical sense, the functional representation of sectoral interests in government. For other sectors, Argentine corporatist tendencies comprise vertical cleavages cutting across horizontal divisions, and representation of such civilian interests in government depends on the particular position of the regime in power. Corporatism of this kind works against the development of class consensus or indeed any kind of 'shared consensual perceptions'.[72]

The failure of the main political sectors, the landed, industrial and commercial elite, the urban middle class and the urban working class, to cooperate has resulted in civilian incapacity to rule without recourse to the military. Power has been so dispersed amongst civilian groups that no group has been able to contain the other groups or counterbalance military power. Cooperation has not been achieved within the various sectors either; distrust of others and the incapacity to compromise contribute to factionalism since, as soon as different interests become apparent, the crack becomes an unbridgeable chasm. Thus coalitions have been temporary, united only by what they oppose, and have not been able to alleviate the chronic civilian political impotence. Social fragmentation gives rise to a multiplicity of smaller political parties, again illustrating the interaction of two cultures, on the one hand the incapacity to compromise and on the other the belief that representation should occur through political parties. These parties are hostile to each other and therefore largely impotent, they have acted as 'mutually exclusive forces'[73] weakening each other by their conflicting aims. The anomic quality of Argentine society, stemming from the emphasis on the individual, kinship networks etc., instead of national identification, and the bitterness of sectoral wrangles, are therefore pervasive, even penetrating the military itself. Amidst this chaos, the armed forces or elements within them, may see themselves and/or be seen by civilians, as the only organised group capable of stabilising the situation.

These cultural aspects pull the armed forces into politics in two main ways. First, the effective exclusion of opposition drives it outside the formal rules of the political game and invites the military to appear to be responding to a challenge to the constitutional order. Thus one culture, the Hispanic, provides the means to achieve the other, the liberal-democratic. Secondly, the belief in not sharing power has given rise to an emphasis on political differences. Divisions have been allowed to remain and encouraged to deepen, thus allowing the military to appear as a force for national unity and stability in a situation of semi-permanent catastrophe. The year 1916 represents a unique case of transfer of power from one civilian regime to another. Exclusion of opposition has meant that, since then, Argentine politics has been dominated by one main political party, first the Radicals and then the Peronists. The existence of two alternative potential civilian governments is new. In the past, alternatives have been so involved in in-fighting, that the military has been able to present itself as the only effective opposition.

However, these same characteristics also cause civilian sectors to push the armed forces into the political arena. The zero-sum model makes losing more important and therefore encourages civilian groups to seek military assistance rather than risk the effects of a regime under their civilian opponents. Similarly, the incapacity to compromise and intolerance of opposition may necessitate military support if any civilian group is to gain the ascendency. Once the military are in power, civilian groups have supported them again for fear of the effects on their interests of a civilian government dominated by those they oppose. Without such support from certain key economic groups and the bureaucracy, the armed forces could not put their policies into practice.

The traits described above also influence political stability indirectly, through the effects they have on development opportunities. The expectation of injustice inherent in distrust of other people leads to corruption and nepotism[74] in business as well as politics. The zero-sum model not only provides a justification for fraud in elections, but also in economic activities.

7 Economic Values

The most cursory view of Argentine history suggests that economic crises and political instability are related. Colonial restrictions on trade and economic opportunity contributed to the development of the independence movement. Divergent economic interests were a factor, some would say *the* factor,[1] for the Unitarian/Federalist conflict and for the rise of Rosas; and changes in the relative strength of those interests made his defeat possible. The instability of the period from the overthrow of Rosas to 1880, though manifested in the dispute over the federalisation of Buenos Aires, primarily expressed the disagreement over who should benefit from port revenues. The apparent stability of the era from 1880 to 1930, which led many European observers to conclude that Argentina had all the vital prerequisites for development and stability, reflected rapid economic growth which made possible the satisfaction of the most important sectors of society. Unrest was limited to the political sphere, concessions were eventually made and the period of deferred instability extended.

Although Argentina probably did not experience the full effects of the Great Depression until later, and then not as severely as some other nations which remained politically stable, the 1930 Revolution did reflect the end of the period of rapid outward-oriented economic growth. And, even if Potash is correct that Justo's later confirmation of the military role in politics was more important in setting the pattern for political intervention by the armed forces in the next half-century,[2] 1930 made this possible by bringing the army directly into the political arena. In the post-war period, deteriorating economic prospects contributed to Perón's ouster, and Argentina's 'stagflationary' economy has usually been cited as a factor for her political problems ever since. Likewise disaffection with the economy destabilised the Galtieri government and provided a spur to the invasion of the Falkland Islands. Economic problems have also provided the greatest political problems for the Alfonsín government.

If economic development is seen as related to stability, then factors which encourage or discourage development are indirectly factors for or against stability. Since Weber, many authors and institutions have accepted that cultural features may contribute to or work against economic development.[3] Given appropriate structural conditions, an ideology which explains economic success or failure in national terms and values which promote industrialisation and development may be necessary preconditions for sustained growth. Values which work against consensus and cooperation in behaviour patterns not only operate against political stability directly, but also militate against development and thus may indirectly promote instability. In summary:

> Structural conditions make development possible; cultural factors determine whether the possibility becomes an actuality.[4]

Many Argentine intellectuals have alternatively come to accept an explanation of national underdevelopment which locates the causes of Argentina's problems outside the nation. Dependency theory, which was largely developed in Argentina to explain the apparent anomaly of Argentine economic failure, is an acceptance of the role of victim. It sees external forces as determinants of national performance and is thus an aspect of the pervasive fatalism of Argentine society. However it should be noted that Argentina's era of closest integration into the world economic system (1880–1930) coincides with her fastest period of growth and, further, the 1880s saw considerable industrial development prior to the slump of 1889–90, which suggests that recession is not the spur to industry which dependency theorists believe it to be.[5] British trade with, and investment in, the United States, Canada and Australia during the same period led to sustained development, not to dependent stagnation, as the theory suggests it should. Obviously domestic structural differences may account in part for this distinction, but the different cultural legacies of these other nations may also partially explain the alternative and more successful routes to development upon which they embarked.

The primary problem in seeking cultural explanations of economic development is the question of the direction of causality. It is possible to argue, as the UN Economic Commission for Latin America (ECLA) has done, that Latin American values are not wholly compatible with development, but that:

> . . . these shortcomings are not so much a basic cause of underdevelopment . . . as they are subordinate factors produced or confirmed by the combination of circumstances that make up underdevelopment.[6]

Certainly, values and attitudes are modified by historical experience. Rapid economic change may give rise to a sense of insecurity and a reluctance to take risks or innovate. An inflationary situation may promote the desire for a quick profit rather than long-term investment. The incapacity of the economy to meet all demands may encourage the development of a zero-sum model. However, it is equally true that the values may precede the event. Thus, it will be argued here that values and experience interact with events modifying or more frequently reinforcing and strengthening values to create a vicious circle of economic underachievement which has proved very difficult to break.

The interaction of culture and experience may explain the differential development of nations with similar structural advantages and historical experiences. Such explanations also avoid the implication of cultural inferiority since a similar pattern of values and attitudes may have different effects in other circumstances. Despite similar value systems, Mediterranean countries, for example, have fared better in terms of development than many of the nations of Latin America. Indeed Italy and Spain today exhibit very striking economic growth, indicating that it is not a Mediterranean heritage alone which resists development. For Argentina, however, developmental problems, like other influences on her political stability, reflect the interaction of two cultures. Non-Iberian influences have raised expectations, especially during the 'Belle Epoque' of export-led growth, whilst some Hispanic attitudes may tend to reduce national potential for satisfaction of such demands. Economic policies have reflected these two streams of cultural influence, and partial implementation of alternating nationalist and internationalist policies has contributed to economic underachievement. This has in turn reinforced economic nationalism whilst increased contact with the non-Hispanic cultural model has also strengthened the internationalist tradition. Development strategies are therefore subject to reversal as dominant attitudes alternate and consistent long-term economic mobilisation is difficult to achieve. As Anderson rather simplistically suggests, official economic policy has tended to follow the Western model, since the West offers the foremost example of economic success, but this may not be supported by underlying values in Latin America:

> ... Western public policy assumes the prevalence of such values as industriousness, entrepreneurship, individual profit motivation, and a high degree of economic 'rationality' within a general understanding of the system and a willingness to play by its rules.[7]

These underlying values (which include the propensity to spend rather than save and a tendency to choose business partners on the basis of kinship) resisting Western-style development are frequently seen as deriving from Hispanic culture, being transferred to the New World during the Conquest and the colonial era which followed. That the late development of industrial activity in Latin America may be associated with the cultural legacy of Spain is indicated by the experience of the mother country herself. Outside Catalonia, there was relatively little industry in Spain until the mid-twentieth century. Structural factors alone, although undoubtedly significant, do not appear to account satisfactorily for this situation. Subsequent Spanish industrial development suggests that although badly distributed, resources were present which could have led to earlier industrialisation. It is also relevant that in Mexico, which uniquely in Latin America had satisfactory resources of both coal and iron ore, the early development of these took place under the influence of Americanised entrepreneurs and the culture of the region around Monterrey has continued to be strongly permeated by North American values.

Argentina's developmental problems have therefore been seen as a function of weaknesses inherent in the cultural legacy of Spain. The persistence of such defects is thought to be at the root of economic underachievement in the modern period. This argument implies that culture is static, but the Hispanic tradition interacted not only with the environment into which it was transplanted but also with the influence flowing from non-Iberian Europe in the nineteenth century.

RACIAL EXPLANATIONS AND IMMIGRATION

The idea that Spaniards degenerated in the Americas is a frequently recurring theme in the literature on Argentina. W.H. Hudson, for example, suggests that the decline of Hispanic culture is evident in the change which took place in the nineteenth century whereby an active and industrious agricultural society gave way to the indolence and anarchism of the *gaucho*.[8] Hudson, like other authors, sees this as the result of the abundance of Argentina: life simply became too easy. Bryce writes of the Argentine:

> He is seldom a hard worker, for it has been his ill-fortune to be able to get by sitting still what others have had to work for.[9]

Of course, Bryce's comment has never been applicable to the nation as a whole. As elsewhere, most poor Argentines have always had to work hard and have lived simply. However, it does reflect the myth of plenty exemplified by tales of *gauchos* killing cattle for the tongues alone – an image so potent that even Marx recorded a variant of it in one of his rare comments on Latin America.[10] Expectations of abundance may not have had much meaning for most *peons* and their families, but they had for the elite who held the key to Argentina's economic development, those who owned the pampas land and profited from its fertility. Thus there is some truth in Alberdi's belief that Argentina's backwardness rested on the expectation of wealth without effort,[11] at least on the part of the leading sectors.

The interaction of Spanish and indigenous influences is also powerfully expressed in racial explanations of Argentina's underdevelopment. Such theories reflect traditional ascriptive attitudes deriving from the Reconquest of Spain, but they were reinforced in the latter half of the nineteenth century by the impact of the Social Darwinist brand of positivism.

They suggest that the particular racial mixture in Spanish America is a very unfortunate one, that the *mestizo* is 'inferior' to both the Spaniard and the Indian.[12] For Sarmiento the combination of Spanish, Indian and Negro races produced a people which was:

> ... characterised by love of idleness and incapacity for industry, except when education and exigencies of a social position succeed in spurring it out of its customary pace.[13]

Sarmiento saw the absorption of the native Indian culture as the main cause of this lethargy, but also found fault in the Spanish cultural legacy which he compared unfavourably with the dynamic culture of the German and Scots settlements in Argentina. Although explanations of laziness and dishonesty in racial terms are unacceptable, such explanations may be and often are internalised and thus become a self-fulfilling prophecy.

For Sarmiento, the indolence of the *mestizo* was due to the lack of a civilised example which resulted in low expectations. He believed that cultural contact with 'civilisation' and the importation of European immigrants and Protestantism would promote development. Alberdi, too, believed that the same fertility which caused Argentine underdevelopment would attract to her the means of development, foreign immigrants and capital. However, the interaction of Hispanic tradition and contact with Europe in the nineteenth century did not, at least in the long term, have the desirable effects envisaged by Argentine liberals. Indeed by the early twentieth century, immigration was being blamed for all manner of social problems, including the rising urban crime rate, prostitution and the white slave trade. A reversal of pre-existing racial attitudes occurred and the immigrant was increasingly seen as inferior to the native population.[14]

The similar cultural backgrounds of the majority of immigrants produced just the opposite effect to that which Sarmiento and Alberdi had in mind. The mingling of immigrant and traditional cultures, especially amongst the lower-middle sectors of Argentine society, did not alter the latter in the manner expected. Rather, traditional upper class values became exaggerated; for example, not having to work became a more important mark of status. In the late nineteenth century many immigrants came from peasant societies, bringing with them cultural traits which were not conducive to development, including passivity, hierarchy, low achievement motivation, low need for autonomy and high dependency, with the notable exception of Italians from Northern Italy with strong traditions of craftsmanship and industry.[15] The Generation of 1837 had hoped that immigrants from north-west Europe would be attracted to Argentina and thus included religious toleration in the constitutional structure they established. However, Argentine immigration legislation, which began in 1876, did not put geographical restrictions on immigration, as happened elsewhere, and very few non-Latin immigrants settled. Solberg suggests that Canadian immigration policy, in contrast, was selective, and southern Europeans were amongst the 'non-preferred races'. With the exception of those from Ireland, Australian immigrants in the late nineteenth century also come from higher income areas than those in Argentina. Díaz Alejandro notes that Australian immigration was restricted early in the twentieth century in numerical terms in order to protect existing working-class living standards, and this may be seen as a spur to development through higher expectations based on existing standards and through the absence of a large pool of cheap labour.[16] In the United States the cultural pattern of northern Europe was thoroughly established by the mid-nineteenth century when the first waves of immigrants from southern and eastern Europe began to arrive. Thus, although immigration into the United States was not restricted before 1924 (except for Orientals), immigrants were absorbed by a pre-existing ethos conducive to productive effort and industrial enterprise. None of these factors operated in Argentina.

EUROPEAN INFLUENCE

The impact of non-Iberian Europe has also been marked and, contrary to the assumptions of theories which seek a simple explanation of Latin American economic failure in terms of the Hispanic tradition, it has contributed to the

Argentine economic malaise. Clearly, contact with Europe has influenced the economy of Argentina from the outset; initially, for example, by providing the market for coastal interest which widened the gap between the two divergent economies of the Río de la Plata region and led to the Unitarian/Federalist division. However, through its effects on culture, such contact has also worked against development. This has occurred in two main ways, though both are essentially concerned with economic expectations and are interrelated. First, the Western economies offered a model and, through demonstration, especially as a result of later working-class contact with Anglo-American culture,[17] raised expectations as well as influencing economic attitudes and thought. Secondly, the very success of the attachment to Great Britain limited the possibility of an alternative form of development.

The demonstration effect of British-manufactured goods and the example of rapid North American economic development led to the adoption of some Western economic attitudes. These borrowed modes of thought had unintended consequences in Argentina. For example, beliefs in the virtue of private enterprise and the distribution of public land to private interests cannot promote increased agricultural activity if land remains a status symbol. Free trade, by encouraging Argentina to specialise in agricultural products, increased the value of land and thus the prestige of owning it, and the new lands taken over after 1880 went to supporters of the ruling elite. Similarly, economic liberalism carried with it implicit distaste for personal taxation. Given the land-based wealth of Argentina, the most potent source of revenue from taxes would have been the taxation of land ownership. However, the land-owning elite were too powerful to submit to this without perceiving how they would benefit. More nebulously, the effect of Western economic success has been a certain cultural ambivalence. The geographical isolation of the nation from the centres of the world economy, comparable to that of Japan where different attitudes prevailed, tended to be taken as confirming Argentina's economic marginality and has promoted a psychological conflict which encourages both a resentment of other more central nations and half-hearted attempts to imitate them.

With no major international conflicts and economic prosperity resulting from the international trading boom in the late
nineteenth century (which Díaz Alejandro sees as producing
in Argentina a much more efficient allocation of resources
than could have been achieved as a consequence of autarkic
policies),[18] there was little external need in the short-term to
build a modern domestic economy. In Argentina the value
of exports increased sixfold in the period 1880 to 1910. The
trading relationship with Britain reinforced the anti-industrial
tradition Argentina had inherited from Spain and affected attitudes to tariffs. These may have achieved similar theoretical
levels in Argentina, Australia and Canada, but it has been
argued that, through the distribution of such duties between
raw material imports and finished goods, they offered much
less protection to some Argentine domestic manufacturing
industry. This is disputed by Díaz Alejandro who sees tariff
levels in the first four decades of the twentieth century as
comparable with those of other countries. He suggests that
higher duties on inputs than on finished goods in some
areas may have been offset by lower duties on some of
the other inputs to the same product. Further, he claims
that instances of negative effective protection have been
greatly exaggerated. The effects of the tariff structure are
therefore very controversial, but tariffs remained unpopular
in Argentina.[19] The prosperity of the period from 1880 to 1930
has had important effects on values and attitudes since. The
Golden Age has become part of the mythology of dependency,
contributing to a past rather than future orientation. It is also
a contributory factor to the pessimism which has accompanied
twentieth-century economic stagnation. The close association
with Europe has also subscribed to the ambivalent national
identity which has resulted in a failure to cooperate with
neighbouring countries to achieve external linkages compen-
sating for relative shortages in some natural resources and to
develop a complementary productive system.

The Belle Epoque also influenced economic expectations
and values directly, in promoting satisfaction with the existing
structure and reinforcing Hispanic clientelism. The era is
generally seen as one of high social mobility for immigrants.
Amongst the millions of new arrivals in Argentina in the
period from 1870, of those who remained, 30.4 per cent

could be classified by 1914 as middle class, in the sense of having taken up non-manual occupations. Of these, 66 per cent had come from working-class backgrounds. The rate of upward mobility amongst immigrants in Australia was much lower. Amongst those members and supporters of the UCR who were not connected with the elite, many had also been upwardly mobile. Thus satisfaction with the existing export-oriented economic structure sapped the dynamism of the middle-class Radical movement. The Radicals were primarily concerned with distribution not reform and with consumption rather than industrialisation. Unlike the Australian Labour Party, which forced the conservative Country Party to make concessions on economic diversification in return for a share in political power, the UCR did not want structural change. This is reflected in Gallo's comment that tariffs increased until 1913 under the Oligarchy, but further protection was resisted after 1916, although he stresses that Argentina, unlike Australia, had not suffered the levels of unemployment which might have made tariff protection more attractive.[20] The Golden Age had promoted expectations of increasing benefits within the existing economic framework. The Radical era therefore was concerned with the division of the spoils and encouraged sectoral expectations without official promotion of entrepreneurial capacity. Economic contraction therefore undermined the very foundations of Yrigoyen's regime.

CLIENTELISM

Clientelism, ' . . . a pattern of relationships in which goods and services are exchanged between people of unequal status',[21] is essentially an economic value. It may have reached its apogee under Radicalism, but it was an important aspect of colonial society and has survived since, being reinforced by the European stream of cultural influence. Clientelism is clearly related to a distrust of impersonal authority and to a preference for dealing with those one knows. It has both direct political impact and indirect consequences through its negative effects on the capacity for national development.

The Iberian cultural legacy to Latin America included

clientelism at both the individual and the collective level. Economic dependence was a feature of Spanish colonial society:

> Spaniards had a special word, *paniaguados* (from *pan y agua* . . .), for those who received their sustenance from a patron.[22]

The administrative structure of the Spanish empire was clientelist from the outset. But at the same time, the remoteness of the colonial government encouraged the growth of another form of clientelism, the personal dominance of the *estanciero*. The development of the *latifundia* and its isolation from wider society promoted paternalistic and dependent relationships between a *patrón* and his workers. Again the unique historical experience of Latin America served to reinforce a value derived from the Iberian legacy. (This trait has remained and, in his 1973 survey, Turner found surprisingly high levels of mutual respect and affinity between Argentine landowners and *peons*.)[23] *Caudillismo* was essentially clientelist, with benefits given in return for loyalty.

Clientelism has survived into the modern period and patronage has been emphasised as a characteristic of Argentine communities even among the urban poor, who might be thought to constitute its weakest link. But the form of its survival and its effects are of greater consequence to stability. As O'Donnell points out, Latin America has always been essentially corporatist[24] and corporatism, the organisation of economic production under vertical corporations officially recognised by government, is a collective form of clientelism. Just as interests were mediated through a patrimonial monarch under Spain, they now seek redress through the modern executives of republican governments. Such a system may have worked well in the past, avoiding conflict by the accommodation of emergent groups through political cooptation and marginal economic benefits. In the longer term, however, this method of resolving sectoral disputes weakens non-executive powers and makes control of the executive a central political aim. The sectoral economic structure is encouraged and expectations raised since modification of demands through compromise between sectors is not part of the processing of economic inputs. As more sectors have become active and their expectations have been strengthened by the knowledge of past prosperity, so their demands are increasingly difficult to fulfil. Satisfaction of such demands may negate long-term economic planning, and failure to meet such demands may mean that an economic crisis becomes a political one.

Ultimately the state has become the *patrón*. This role it always had in theory, but now has in practice as a result of the increasing size and complexity of government. Kirkpatrick's respondents showed class differences over what they considered to be the proper economic role of government, but there was consensus on the idea that economic problems should be resolved by government.[25] The role of the state in fostering economic development has been important elsewhere, for example in France, and expectations of state initiative might therefore be thought to be conducive to development. In Latin America, however, the state has dissipated resources in maintaining disproportionate armies and bureaucracies, and assumptions about its role have limited productive enterprise in the wider society. The state has traditionally been seen as a source of initiative and all Argentine governments have paternalist features.

The clientelist role of the state as provider defuses political opposition to some extent. Opposition to certain policies becomes a saleable commodity which may be traded off for sectoral benefits in the short-term. The solution of disputes by appeal to the state rather than by compromise or collective bargaining places the onus of processing demands on the state itself and thus provides justification for maintaining coercive means to control such demands and the use of such means when demands are deemed unreasonable. In addition, private initiative may be distorted and philanthropy undermined by the emphasis on the state as provider where little ideology of personal effort and collective good exists to offset such negative effects.

Perhaps more significant than this is the other key role of the clientelist state, that of employer. The expectation that the state will provide not only material benefits but also jobs saps the dynamism of those sectors of Latin American society which might elsewhere be expected to provide some measure of entrepreneurial impetus. In this way the benefits of an active state are reversed. Instead of positively benefiting society through the provision of public services which are essential to the quality of life of all citizens or which private enterprise would not find profitable, the state has become a drain on the productive capacity of society by providing jobs for the clients of the governing elite. Clientelism works against efficient administration in that appointments are made as rewards for political support rather than on the basis of merit. Despite the development of competitive entry, the Argentine bureaucracy has nevertheless been described as being largely 'a political spoils system'.[26] Such appointments carry with them the expectation of loyalty amongst appointees who are therefore vulnerable to pressure from those who appointed them or alternatively those who can ensure their occupational survival. Likewise appointments and promotions of this kind do not encourage occupational effort since this is not the feature which is rewarded.

The employer state also encourages, through over-staffing which leads to low wages and therefore to poor quality personnel, moonlighting and corruption. In 1958 Frondizi stated that 1 800 000 people were employed by national, provincial and local government in Argentina. From this figure he calculated that some 7 million people, or 30 per cent of the population, were directly dependent on the state.[27] This level of non-industrial state employment, which is much higher than that found in Western Europe, the United States and Japan, places a heavy burden on resources available for the economic development of the nation. The present Minister of the Economy, Juan Sourrouille, is well aware that the huge costs to government generated in this way are simply not available for more productive investment. It is, however, no simple matter to reduce civil service numbers without losing the most able elements. Decrees which became law in November 1986, removing differentials for workers in different sectors of government whilst increasing differentials within the hierarchy of individual departments, are expected to resolve this dilemma.

Expectations of state provision may derive from the Iberian stream of influence, but they have been reinforced by historical experience. Initially the importance of the non-state *patrón* was increased by the isolation of the individual in a hostile environment against which protection was sought. However, the influence of non-Iberian Europe has also had an impact in raising expectations. In addition, the overlaying of liberal democracy on to the Iberian heritage has reinforced clientelism in the twentieth century by increasing the need to mobilise mass support which must later be rewarded. Anderson implicitly recognises the interaction of the two cultures when he notes that:

> Patronage, nepotism, the multiple career pattern, and a desire to realise the promise of modernisation, at least in externals, for that urban middle group that lusted after a Western way of life, all contributed to chronic overstaffing of public offices with redundant employees.[28]

Clientelism reinforces other economic values which have survived to work against development. Through the attachment of one's prospects to those of someone else higher in the status hierarchy, individual effort is undermined and thus entrepreneurial capacity reduced. Similarly the passivity of waiting for benefits from the state, and the opportunity to acquire increased status through work of an unproductive nature available through the state, both derive from and serve to reinforce a marked disdain for manual labour.

ATTITUDES TO WORK AND INDUSTRY

It has been suggested that the Hispanic tendency to despise manual labour was a product of the Reconquest of Spain, which established the dignity of battle rather than work. At best work was a 'necessary evil', a way of making a living which lacked nobility and dignity. In Argentina, too, manual labour was looked down on and tended to be associated with 'inferior' races. Indeed recent ethnographic evidence demonstrates a relatively high proportion of black and mulatto artisans in Buenos Aires in 1778. Conversely, status was accorded to the professions and to those with a 'humanistic' education, and the administrative sector and professional services began to grow in the late eighteenth century.[29] Again the Spanish inheritance interacted with the hostile environment of the New World to produce adverse consequences in the long term. For the Spanish in the Viceroyalty of the Río de la Plata:

> To work, to yield a little to the demands of nature, was
> to be defeated, barbarised. Thus a false scale of values was
> born, and men and things moved by different routes. By the
> classification of tasks into servile and free, the old system
> of the hierarchies of haves and have-nots was re-initiated.
> The pinnacle was represented by landownership, which
> meant submission to that which was easier to acquire and
> demanded less intelligence to retain.[30]

The Hispanic disdain for manual labour was therefore
largely reinforced by the historical experience of the New
World, though it was given an unusual twist in Argentina,
where manual work was accorded some respect provided that
it was associated with horsemanship. The nineteenth-century
trading relationship with non-Iberian Europe, especially
Britain did not alter this trait, but rather lent it further
support. The lack of status accorded to work was confirmed
by the fact that the landed elite tended to inherit rather
than earn their wealth. Although it is true that trade in the
early national period was dominated by Basque and Catalan
families who provided the backbone of what was to become
the Oligarchy, it was from their ownership of land not their
personal entrepreneurial efforts that later generations of the
Oligarchy derived their income. (A notable exception to this
situation was to be found in nineteenth-century Córdoba,
where elite economic power derived primarily from control
of public administration and dominance of the liberal
professions. *Estancieros* constituted only the second tier of
the Cordobese status hierarchy.)[31] The *estancieros'* capacity
to control their *peons* meant that labour was performed
by others. In confirming Argentina's role as a primary
agricultural producer, her participation in the international
division of labour reinforced the existing economic structure
of the nation and ensured the survival and strengthening of
extensive farming and ranching. Similarly, the prosperity of
the late nineteenth and early twentieth century established
a 'quondam' orientation, a tendency to look to the past
rather than the future, which saps the motivation to hard
work. Only a future emphasis can supply the incentive for
sustained economic struggle.

Fillol argues that Argentine economic values are basically passive and apathetic and thus unconducive to development. Economic success in bursts followed by periods of stagnation is possible, but long-term development would require a fundamental change in such values.[32] That disdain for manual labour survives is indicated by the number of servants and domestics still employed by middle-class Argentine families,[33] despite the rising costs of doing so. Thus is the same attitude transmitted to the next generation. In more concrete terms than Fillol's general statement, this may have a number of repercussions. For example, it provides the basis for the division of *trabajadores* (workers generally) into *empleados* and *obreros*, which contributes to the sectoral structure of society. The concern for status further implies a reluctance to perform tasks associated with subordinates. The idea of a 'free' man as someone who does not work may mean that the discipline of working company hours is resented and avoided where possible. This trait relates to, reinforces and is reinforced by the fatalistic feature of Argentine culture. The desire for a leisured existence without working for it is reflected in the popularity of lotteries, for example. Finally, contempt for manual labour may be seen as working in favour of the military, who are not seen as parasitic despite their non-productive role.

Related to attitudes to manual labour is the status accorded to entrepreneurial activity. Development may be seen as a function of the capacity for entrepreneurial activity in society which in turn derives from the attitudes to such activity. Motivation may be religious as described by Weber, or social as in the work of McClelland,[34] but the level of motivation is key to the process of development. For Weber, technical possibilities are a prerequisite of capitalist development which itself increases technical possibilities through the growth of modern science, for example. However, technical opportunities are not always utilised and therefore capitalist development does not occur, at least not as rapidly and extensively as elsewhere. Capitalism becomes self-generating over time, but it has to start somewhere and does so amongst groups of people. Thus ideology is seen by Weber as the force promoting entrepreneurial activity, not as the outcome of such activity.[35]

It is alternatively possible to argue that entrepreneurial

I (a) Juan D. Perón, President of Argentina 1946–1955 and 1973–74.
(b) (below left) President Leopoldo Galtieri, addressing the Argentine people, condemning the "attack by the British" on the Malvinas Islands.
(c) (below right) Raul Alfonsín, President of Argentina since December 1983.

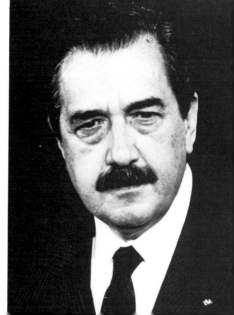

II(a) (left) Basilica at
Luján.

II(b) (right)
Güemes looking towards
Salta and the mountains.

III Colonial Buildings: (a) (above) The Cabildo, Buenos Aires.
(b) (below) Old Cabildo, Luján.

IV The Pyramid, monument to independence, Buenos Aires.

V Wall Politics. (a) (above) Perón–Perón, still visible, Buenos Aires 1980.
(b) (below) Peronist slogans, Salta, 1988.

VI Grave of Rosas, the Old Cemetery, Southampton.

VII Relics of the Welsh pioneers at Puerto Madryn in Patagonia.

VIII (a) (above) Congress.
 (b) (below) Telecommunications building with statue of Almirante Brown,
founder of the Argentine navy.

activity increased in status in Argentina as industry expanded in the late nineteenth and early twentieth centuries and that the relative lack of it in modern Latin America rests on the failure of governments to encourage such activity as successive governments in the United States, for example, have done. Certainly Argentine governments did not use the fiscal measures available to them to encourage the development of non-traditional exports until Frondizi came to power.[36] However there may be little entrepreneurial motivation in society for a government to encourage. Indeed the very expectations of the role of the clientelist state may detract from such motivation in the wider society. All development-orientated sectors in Latin America see the state as a prime mover in the development process. Further, the absorption of marginal groups into dependent state activity may reduce the capacity for entrepreneurial activity of the most potentially dynamic sectors. Much industrial activity has been directly promoted by Latin American governments, especially so in the area of heavy industry. For example, in Argentina, Fabricaciones Militares remained, in 1983, the largest national industrial enterprise, though by 1986 it had been displaced by Yacimientos Petrolíferos Fiscales (YPF), with an annual deficit of US$697 million, producing what is rumoured to be the world's most expensive petroleum. (In fact the combined losses of state-owned enterprises would meet more than half the service charges on the national debt.)[37] The most successful businessmen have tended to have close contacts with government. But the business community generally comprises individuals who often have other sources of income and invest outside the domestic economy. Their lack of commitment to their own industry is indicated by the readiness of domestic entrepreneurs to sell their industrial interests to multinational corporations. A small proportion of Argentina's largest companies remain in private domestic ownership, heavily outnumbered by those which are internationally owned.

One cultural explanation of the lack of entrepreneurial capacity in Hispanic societies is that suggested by Ortega y Gasset who sees Spanish pride as working against novelty and innovation. He believes that there is a reluctance to accept that the existing situation is imperfect and that improvements are possible.[38] More substantial in its explanatory power is the idea that the status and wealth attached to entrepreneurship in any society will determine how much of it there is. This explanation is only partially cultural in the sense that the past economic experience of entrepreneurs will influence present and future activity and this experience is itself also determined by structural and conjunctural factors. However, since culture and experience are intimately bound together the cultural aspect of this explanation is important. When applied to Argentina this does not necessarily suggest a low achievement motivation. Whether in Argentine society the actual level of the need for achievement, 'n.Ach', the measurement of which remains the subject of much controversy, is high or low is not central to this explanation. McClelland's analysis is that a person with high motivation to achieve will aspire to the highest status occupation they can hope to attain and maintain successfully.[39] In Argentina, as in Latin America generally, high status is accorded to non-entrepreneurial activities, a feature Riggs too recognises as characteristic of developing or 'prismatic' society and which partially explains the high proportion of immigrant elements in entrepreneurial activity. Hispanic values, again reinforced by the experience of America and the interaction with Europe, have tended to make those with capital to invest contemptuous of entrepreneurial activity. Investments in land, which confers status, were favoured over stocks and shares in domestic enterprises even before land became the only reliable hedge against inflation.[40] The fact is that much entrepreneurial activity, it seems, is to be found among the relatively poor urban sectors and either takes the form of involvement in the black market or finds its outlet in essentially unproductive activities, such as opening taxi doors. Above all the status of those who have not had either to work in or to manage their own businesses has been higher than those who have had to be so involved.

That the allocation of status militates against entrepreneurial activity is indicated by the disproportionate number of immigrants who have been involved in industrial and commercial enterprises.[41] Imaz' analysis of the backgrounds of 286 Argentine entrepreneurs in 1959 found that 130, or just over 45 per cent, were foreign-born. His further study of 119 'important' entrepreneurs is still more revealing. The business of 50 per cent of his respondents were founded by newly-immigrant ancestors, and a further 14 per cent of the sample were Anglo-Argentines. Only 10 per cent were descended from the old families of the traditional upper class. Much of their entrepreneurial activity was land-related, being concerned with meat-processing and the marketing of other agricultural products. (This distortion of investment is also recognised as a problem for Latin America generally, by authors who emphasise dependency as an explanation of underdevelopment.)[42] The attachment of status to non-entrepreneurial activities has also diminished the dynamism of successful entrepreneurial elements who have risen up the social hierarchy. In order to be absorbed into the upper class, Imaz sees this bourgeoisie as having to adopt the anti-entrepreneurial values of the existing social structure.[43]

The success in business of the British in Argentina is reflected in the following comment about the 1930s: 'The city of Buenos Aires business directory reads almost like that of a British colony'.[44] But even with the decline of specifically British involvement, the influence of those of British descent remains disproportionately high, as Imaz' figures suggest. This may be explained in terms of the reluctance of Anglo-Argentines to lose their identity through the absorption of Hispanic-derived values and ' . . . a Protestant dedication to work, to reap slow, secure profit.'[45] The suggestion that Protestantism is more conducive to entrepreneurial activity than Catholicism is a reiteration of Weber's view of Calvinism as an ideology likely to promote capitalist development. Weber held that ascetic Protestantism recognised worldly success as indicative of having been chosen by God. The short time available in which to prove one's election caused disdain for time wasting and luxury. Work was the means by which advantage could be taken of opportunities in order to concur with God's will. He states that Protestants, whether of the same culture or not, whether in the majority or as a minority, were much more likely to be economically dynamic than Catholics. Therefore Weber's explanation for the development of capitalism is seen as resting on religious differences not historical circumstances.[46] In consequence, historians and social scientists have criticised both the apparent cultural determinism of Weber's model and the empirical basis for it. Kautsky, for example, defends the Marxian view of the relationship between the economic infrastructure and the cultural superstructure. He argues that Calvinism was a response to, not a cause of, early industrialisation, developing as an ideology of legitimisation amongst capitalists.[47] Weber himself pre-empted this criticism. He was aware that historical circumstances were important to capitalist development and that capitalist development may itself influence religious affiliation.[48] To see Weber's work as a one-sided culturally deterministic model is to ignore the acceptance by Weber of much of the Marxian economic model, which he did not consider wrong, but rather inadequate. The interaction of culture and economics is the important feature of Weber's work and this element is applicable to Latin America generally and Argentina in particular. Whether in consequence of Catholicism specifically or, more probably, wider Hispanic values strengthened as a result of historical experience and the influence of non-Iberian Europe, the 'capitalist spirit' has not been marked amongst those with accumulated resources in Argentina.

A central feature of the low level of 'capitalist spirit' in Latin America is the widely remarked upon reluctance to take risks in investments, and the entrepreneurial tendency to favour short-term gain over long-term profit maximisation. Numerous historical examples of this trait may be found. The isolation of the Río de la Plata region gave investment there a further quality which required high profits from the outset. The high profit, low turnover model of business practice was established very early indeed. At the end of the eighteenth century and the beginning of the nineteenth, allegations against Buenos Aires merchants suggested that they traded at a low level for high profit margins.[49] Similarly, asked whether Argentine landowners would favour nationalisation of the railways, Ezequiel Ramos Mexía, a member of the Cabinet in the years 1911–14, replied that the 4–7 per cent return which could be expected on railway investments would compare unfavourably with the 30 per cent profit per annum they were earning on their existing capital investments. Alba notes the lack of interest in long-term low profit investment which has tended to characterise the national period expressed in colossal interest rates in Latin America of 15–18 per cent compared with the usual rates of European bankers of 5–8 per cent.[50] Even taking into account the prevailing rate of inflation, this seems a substantial difference. In recent years, the same problem faced the Videla government which began to shift national income in favour of the pampas bourgeoisie in the hope of building a more dynamic rural sector which could then become one pillar of the capitalist reorganisation programme. However, the landowners of the pampas used the additional profits from the change in government policy for financial speculation not for agricultural reinvestment and modernisation. The current Radical government's policy of issuing state securities at interest rates which make investment in industry unattractive is a further aspect of the problem of attracting funds to entrepreneurial activities. Moreover state debts are being increased in the process.

The marked unwillingness of Argentine entrepreneurs to take risks and their requirement of high profit margins have a number of detrimental effects. The availability of credit for short terms at high rates of return limits investment capital for productive ventures. Cheap loans and venture capital are not available. Investment on the local stock market is seen as tantamount to gambling. Brazil with a GNP only five times greater than Argentina's has a stock market which moves 150 times as much capital. Seeking large returns per unit rather than a mass market also results in uncompetitive goods. Some authors have argued that these traits are simply cultural, reflecting a desire to avoid sustained privation and effort. Such explanations are inadequate as these attitudes are inseparable from local economic conditions. Cardoso argues that state protectionism and foreign capital involvement limit risk-taking possibilities and thus a basic difference in Latin American entrepreneurial mentality cannot be assumed.[51] Cardoso is correct as far as he goes, but he is treating entrepreneurs as passive and he fails to answer the economic motivation argument which stresses that 'entrepreneurial' individuals actively seek risk-taking opportunities because these may provide them with concrete indications of what they interpret as success. Cardoso tends to imply economic cause and cultural effect, again a partial explanation. Fillol presents a more balanced view. He acknowledges that political instability gives rise to fears of governmental policy changes and that inflation makes short-term investment and the buying of land a rational pattern of behaviour. But he also holds that a short-term advantage mentality exists and contributes to the economic circumstances which reinforce it.[52] Even if it is held that economic history is the key to economic attitudes, it is difficult to avoid recognising that the relationship between the two becomes reciprocal over time. Past economic experience may be seen as determining economic attitudes and expectations, but these contribute to future economic experience. However, the contribution of cultural factors is greater than a simple absorption and reinforcement of economic experience. For example, the concept of nobility, and the emphasis on ostentatious living as an indication of it, must be seen as contributing to underinvestment, but this cultural value does not derive from political instability and inflation. Likewise, land-ownership as a source of status is not simply a response to the insecurity of other investments, though of course it is reinforced by economic experience.

EDUCATION AND ATTITUDES TO WORK AND INDUSTRY

In similar vein, it is impossible to ascertain the exact relationship between education and economic values. Clearly the two are interrelated rather than one causing the other, and they comprise part of the relationship between education and political stability. This exists in more concrete terms than the controversial 'education for democracy' thesis. Comment on Argentine education broadly stresses three aspects: availability, the content of courses and the independence of educational institutions. The first of these is at once a structural and a cultural explanation, as well as being a function of instability, since political and economic crises have had marked effects on educational funding. The last is relevant because the priority of, and priorities within, education reflect cultural features. The second suggests the dominance of cultural factors over structural requirements. However, it may be argued that historical inertia is also a key feature here. The lack of educational autonomy similarly reflects historico-cultural factors rather than instrumental considerations. All three aspects of education may be argued to act directly on political stability, but they more clearly operate indirectly through their sustenance of economic values and thus their contribution to economic development.

The marked decline in illiteracy during the latter years of the nineteenth century and the first half of the twentieth century is testimony to the expansion of elementary education. However, during the same period, the increase in the proportion of students completing the second cycle of secondary education was much less spectacular[53] and remains a problem. The difficulties of encouraging attendance of youngsters beyond the age of fourteen in the public schools in less prestigious residential areas is plain. In addition, the quality of teaching in such institutions reflects not only the low status attached to school teaching, but also the training of teachers in evening classes after their normal day's work, and the low salaries which necessitate holding two, or even three, teaching posts. In contrast, high salaries are available for employees of some private schools, and private education burgeoned to cover an estimated 50 per cent of students by the mid-1960s.[54] The proportion who have actually completed the second cycle of secondary education (ages 15–17) in public schools still clearly affects the intake of institutions of higher education and, despite the high proportion of students in secondary education claimed by some official sources, this percentage remains low.[58] State university places have increased by more than 1000 per cent this century. The University of Buenos Aires, since Perón's expansion of it, is one of the largest educational institutions in the world. Despite this, and the fact that fees payable by students have been generally lower than in 'other [sic] European countries and the United States',[56] expenditure on higher education and research has been inadequate, a feature reflected in the low levels of academic salaries necessitating supplementary occupations, the very small proportion of full-time staff (about 4 per cent at Buenos Aires in 1965) and poor student–teacher ratios.

The difficulties of obtaining sufficient secondary education to enter university, along with the cost and length of courses and the relatively low chance of actually graduating, have perpetuated the elitist nature and image of higher education. The historical legacy of universities for the upper class established long before elementary schools for the lower orders, the prestige of education, which is apparently especially valued in the interior, and the status of the title 'Doctor', an attribute which determined access to the Cordobese elite until the early twentieth century and which has been virtually indispensable for those seeking high-level political careers during some periods, have remained.[57] The University Reform Movement, which began in Córdoba in 1918, did achieve the opening up of bastions of upper-class privilege to the emergent middle classes as well as some rationalisation of academic appointments. The URM, in the form in which it began in Argentina, was therefore an attack on the Iberian cultural legacy, but, at the same time, it constituted a critique of what was perceived as European cultural imperialism. Its long-term impact may be seen as a contribution to the diffusion of Iberian-derived, European-reinforced, economic values down the class structure to the urban middle classes who now dominate state university admissions. As a method of social mobility, a university education became a means of entry to the traditional professions for a broader section of the population, and the content of courses continued to reflect this function.

The early Latin American universities were founded soon after the Conquest and modelled on those of Spain, performing the function of 'custodians of pre-established knowledge',[58] which was of course determined and constrained by the Inquisition. They were not research institutions. The only university in modern Argentina which predates independence is Córdoba, which was founded in 1624 and concerned mainly with the study of ecclesiastical literature. The University of Buenos Aires was not established until 1821 in a period of chaos which generated few students. By 1828 the institution was apparently moribund and only one professor remained in post still teaching his classes. Its initial liberalism was dissipated by the Rosas era when the function of training priests was strengthened. The University of Buenos Aires was able to recover largely as a consequence of the appointment of Juan María Gutiérrez as rector in 1861. Gutiérrez saw the Spanish academic tradition as restricting the development of new scientific, philosophical and literary work. He therefore restored a positivistic, liberal orientation to the institution, opposed political intervention and favoured meritocratic appointments. Mitre as president emphasised the importance of scientific study in accord with the prevalent positivistic philosophy of the liberal elite and in 1866 engineering degrees were instituted at Buenos Aires. In 1909 a third national university was created at La Plata, with a clearer scientific and research-based orientation. Nevertheless, until 1918, all three national universities remained primarily geared to training aristocrats for the professions.

The association of education and social status of colonial times has remained. Business success is valued less than intellectual development, a feature reinforced by the impact of Europe which resulted in rapid economic growth in Argentina without resort to extensive entrepreneurial activity on behalf of the traditional elite. Many commentators argue that the content of Latin American education continues to reflect (and it must therefore also reinforce) values diffused from the landed upper class. Prestige has traditionally been disproportionately attached to the broad arts faculties of universities; the size and situation of the central institutions of the Faculty of Law at Buenos Aires provides an example of this characteristic. There is widespread agreement that the legal and medical professions have remained the most prestigious occupations in Argentina and the proportions of registered students reflect this.[59] The corollary is the relative unpopularity of technical subjects such as engineering. In Argentina's case, O'Donnell has dissented from this view and emphasised the number of students enrolled for engineering and natural science courses. He argues that education in Argentina does reflect the nation's industrial needs.[60] O'Donnell's argument is questionable, however, in that the instrumental value of a natural science education is itself unproven, especially when the sciences being studied remain unspecified. Secondly, engineering courses in Latin American universities, according to Edelmann, tend to be theoretical rather than practical, and qualification in the subject tends to lead to emigration as pay and status are lacking in the domestic context.[61]

The lack of autonomy of Argentine institutions of higher education has weakened not only research, but also on occasion the content and standard of teaching. Unlike the situation in some industrialised nations where increased political intervention in education has been justified by apparent economic needs, interventions in Argentina have been cruder and more overtly political in intention. University autonomy was progressively undermined in the nineteenth century and Law No. 1597, adopted in 1885, gave the federal government the right to appoint professors and enabled it to intervene in the universities in times of crisis. The URM was partly a reaction to the diminished independence of these institutions.

The 1943 Revolution was accompanied by student protests which led to the purging of both university staff and students. Student support for the Unión Democrática brought retaliation after Perón's election and all six state universities were intervened and purged. In May 1946 between a half and three-quarters of professors were replaced by Peronists and in October 1947 university administrations were put under the control of presidential appointees. Scholarships and even admission to classes depended on political activity. Their opponents were quick to respond, and Peronist appointees were purged in 1955. Student opposition to Onganía's coup was again met with intervention of all the national universities. Cámpora began a further wave of purges in 1973, the most notable consequence being the appointment of the left-wing nationalist Peronist historian, Rodolfo Puiggrós, as rector of the University of Buenos Aires. The content of courses changed; many took on overtly nationalist forms. Sociology, which under Gino Germani had been strong until Onganía's time, was virtually destroyed in this process. Torcuato di Tella recalls the replacement of Parsonian social science with courses on the complete works of Perón! The quality of teaching declined as many of the best academics were fired, especially those with foreign training, and unrestricted entry led to quite untenable student–teacher ratios. Research virtually stopped. In 1976 the Videla government promised the restoration of university autonomy, but proceeded to purge not only social science courses, but also the Faculty of Natural and Exact Sciences at Buenos Aires, for example. From that faculty alone some 60 students and professors were numbered amongst the 'disappeared'.

The return of civilian government again saw the opening up of university education. Open entry since 1984 has, according to Professor di Tella, brought some 60 000 students a year into the *ciclo básico* at Buenos Aires alone and necessitated the requisition of old factory buildings and warehouses as lecture halls for the university itself and the five new satellite centres that have had to be established, where teaching is conducted with the aid of video recordings. In reaction to the military ideological penetration of Argentine society, compulsory courses on social science methodology and democracy have been instituted and similar courses have, for the same reasons, been introduced at high school level.

ATTITUDES TO WEALTH AND CONSUMPTION

The importance of existing cultural values and their modification through contact with other cultures may be further illustrated by a brief survey of attitudes relating to the acquisition of wealth and its disposal. The influence of European positivist thought in the late nineteenth century not only contributed to the development of education but also brought with it a new emphasis on material gain and economic progress. This was reinforced by immigration from Spain and Italy which combined a strengthening of Iberian values with the materialism of modern Europe, the purpose of such immigration being economic advancement. The economic booms of 1884–9 and 1905–12 consequent upon the trading relationship with Europe increased the importance of wealth as a mark of status. Ancestry remained the most important measure of status, but material wealth came to compensate to some extent for inferior birth and education. By the early twentieth century, materialism was an important feature of the Argentine upper class and Bryce notes that the dominance of this trait was very apparent to visitors to the country during that period.[62]

Cardoso sees the absorption of materialism a factor strengthening Argentine entrepreneurship. He argues that entrepreneurs in Argentina are more modern in their attitudes with financial incentives being much more important than elsewhere in Latin America, where industrial groups have tended to adopt 'traditional' values in order to be assimilated into traditional society.[63] But traditional values have been modified rather than eliminated by 'modern' influence. Again the two cultures appear to have interacted in a way which leaves Argentina with the worst of both worlds, as is shown by other authors who are less enthusiastic about Argentine materialism. Implicit in Romero's analysis is the idea that materialist attitudes have reinforced the zero-sum model of competition of various sectors of society. Fillol argues that instrumental attitudes detract from vocational orientation and Randall takes up a similar theme. She suggests that there is no emphasis on non-monetary incentives for Argentine workers for the simple reason that they do not respond to such incentives.[64] Thus any developmental scheme which calls for a period of national austerity has little chance of success.

It seems clear that any society will be more receptive to cultural influences which complement rather than contradict existing values and attitudes. In 1970, ECLA argued that Latin America is absorbing economic values derived from the United States and north-west Europe, but adds the rider that:

> . . . the consumption values appropriate to post-industrial societies seem to have been incorporated much more readily than the production values needed for the stage of industrialisation itself.[65]

The absorption of materialism and European patterns of consumption fits neatly with values derived from the Iberian legacy. The traditional means of acquiring status through consumption is reinforced by materialism. Money is sought avidly because status may be enhanced by appropriate spending patterns and work may be avoided. Status is not attached to simply being rich; how one's wealth is consumed is central. This Hispanic-derived trait was reinforced by the concentration of wealth produced by Argentina's historical experience in its primary productive relationship with Europe. This pattern of behaviour contrasts with Weber's notion of capitalism, the main principle of which he sees as accumulating more and more wealth but not enjoying costly pleasures. The Hispanic-derived acquisition of status through consumption has more in common with what Weber describes as the most important hostile force resisting capitalism, 'traditionalism', which consists of the desire to earn sufficient to live in the style to which one has become accustomed.[66] Materialism may have increased the motivation to earn, but it has not decreased the capacity to consume. It has in fact strengthened the tendencies to unproductive investment, conspicuous expenditure and inflation.

The emphasis on consumption has been enhanced for some sectors by cultural contact which has raised expectations, but it has always been an important feature of the Argentine elite. For example, appearance is still central to expectations of respect accorded by others. A strong fear of being thought to be lower class has encouraged an emphasis on formal dress. Pride in apparent wealth became more formalised in the years after the fall of Rosas:

> It even became a civil offence to appear in the parks of Buenos Aires without a jacket, collar and tie. Fashionable churches, fashionable theatres, fashionable tea-rooms, and fashionable clubs flourished to emphasise the pride of riches and position . . . [67]

This situation reflected Sarmiento's association of civilisation with the frock-coat. (Perón, almost a century later, tried to turn this sign of status on its head by imbuing the term 'descamisado' with a new dignity and by removing his own jacket to identify with his followers.) Bryce in the early twentieth century, remarked upon the status attached to consumption and recorded that Argentines exhibited a high propensity to spend and a strong desire to be seen doing so.[68] The French have an expression 'as rich as an Argentine'. Amongst more recent writers, Stokes has noted the continuing relationship between status and conspicuous consumption and the 'ostentatious use of leisure'.[69] Likewise, Díaz Alejandro notes that devaluations aimed at encouraging increased investment by redistribution to non-wage earning sectors have led to the increased consumption of consumer durables.[70] Certainly an emphasis on consumer goods as a mark of success has spread down the class hierarchy. The *fotonovelas* which became popular among lower-middle and working-class women in Argentina in the 1950s and 1960s encourage such attitudes.[71] At the peak of the boom under the 1976–83 military regime, Calle Florida was packed till late every night with shoppers buying massive quantities of records, clothes and other items. Particular pride was taken in being able to show that a purchase was imported from Europe. Foreign holidays were much in demand and a favoured middle-class entertainment was the holiday slide-show.

For Weber, a combination of acquisitiveness and asceticism promotes capital accumulation,[72] and an elite's propensity to spend must be seen as working against capitalist development rather than for it. Several authors suggest that economic values in Latin America militate against government attempts to encourage saving and investment, that immediate gratification is favoured over deferment, and that higher per capita income gives rise to higher spending not increased saving. Merkx argues that the balance of payments is squeezed from two different directions when the general level of prosperity rises because wealthier sectors tend to purchase imports, and exports are wage-goods tending to be consumed in greater quantities domestically if wages increase.[73] Of course, low levels of savings reflect economic experience too. The instability of currency values and prices leads to money being seen as a means of immediate exchange only and promotes land-ownership as a safe investment. Although Solberg argues that saving has not historically been part of *criollo* culture, there is evidence that saving has not been consistently at a low level, though there may be specific reasons for this, and indeed high domestic savings rates (about 10 per cent of GDP) in the first three decades of the twentieth century may reflect the greater propensity of immigrants to save, which Solberg notes. For example, the Patriotic Loan floated in the 1930s by the Argentine government brought almost immediate national solvency through the contribution of small-scale, private savings accumulated during the 1920s.[74] This period preceded the stagflationary experience of the post-1930 era and was perhaps that in which the middle class were most able to achieve personal savings. The high rate of savings accompanied by high inflation characteristic of the period 1950–61 suggests to Díaz Alejandro that the former was to some extent forced.[75] In addition, Ferrer notes that the savings rate in relation to GDP was 20 per cent in 1984,[76] which appears high if account is not taken of the colossal interest rates which had to exist in order to attract savings in a situation of high inflation. The inflation rate for 1984 was over 680 per cent. Such savings must in any case be seen as insecure. This was shown in June 1985 when Alfonsín's announcement of IMF austerity measures necessitated the declaration of an extra bank holiday to stop the rush to withdraw savings in order to buy dollars and consumer durables. At the beginning of 1988 the twice-daily fall in the rate of the austral against the dollar again gave rise to lengthy queues outside the money-changers, and many of those who waited were working men with quite small sums to change.

PRESTIGE AND LAND-OWNERSHIP

The association of prestige with land-ownership is generally seen as part of the Hispanic legacy. Southern Spain at the time of the Conquest had a land tenure system similar to that adopted in much of Latin America. Unlike the northern area which was comprised primarily of *minifundios*, in the south *latifundios* were established by grants of land to people from further north as the Moors were driven out of southern Spain. This pattern of landholding was especially pronounced in Andalusia. This land tenure system is thought to have been transferred to Latin America and consolidated during the colonial era. Other aspects of the colonial experience are seen as reinforcing this transfer. Colonial occupation, for example, rested on a series of urban centres to which power was delegated for administrative purposes. Thus agriculture existed to supply these centres; production and marketing were therefore relatively large-scale operations requiring extensive units of production. A land tenure pattern of *estancias* rather than smallholdings was established accordingly. In addition, the Iberian conception of the leisured gentleman and the hierarchical character of Hispanic society are seen as supporting the *estancia* structure. The emphasis on urban living is also thought to have worked against the development of lower-class enthusiasm for smallholdings, though Halperín argues that aspirations to build a nation of independent farmers were more widespread than is usually assumed and surprisingly resilient, lasting into the twentieth century, despite the dominance of the land-owning class.[77]

The simple transfer of Hispanic culture is questionable, however, as Halperín is implicitly suggesting, though for other reasons too. At the end of the eighteenth and beginning of the nineteenth centuries, wealthy *criollo* merchants of high social standing in Buenos Aires invested their capital in trade-related activities such as retailing and meat-salting. They did not generally buy rural land, which, being unfenced and uncharted, did not become an attractive proposition until after independence. Brown argues that rational socioeconomic reasons promoted the growth of *latifundia*, not 'a kind of sociopsychological lust for land by a native gentry'.[78] These arguments suggest that either the accordance of status to land-ownership is not an Iberian trait, or that this trait was not initially absorbed or, at least, not acted upon. The latter explanation seems the most appropriate. The ideal of the land-owning *caballero* needed the reinforcement of historical experience in the Americas and the influence of Europe to assume the importance it later acquired.

The growth of the *latifundia* system in Argentina was therefore the product of a cultural legacy sympathetic to such a development and unique historical circumstances which promoted it. In the first forty years after independence, government policies, whether intentionally or otherwise, tended to encourage the development of *latifundios*. In January 1816, under Supreme Director José Rondeau, a law decreed a minimum size for *estancias* in order to prevent the encroachment of farms on cattle land. Later, Rivadavia's Law of Emphyteusis introduced a system of renting out public lands for twenty-five years. The measure was supposed to provide the dual benefits of productivity and government retention of the land as security against foreign loans. No size limit was set on the rented land and the system encouraged the growth of *latifundios*. By the 1830s, some 21 million acres of public land had passed under the control of a mere 500 individuals.[79] In 1836 ranches of more than 5000 hectares comprised 77 per cent of provincial landholdings, compared with those of less than 2500 hectares which made up less than 5 per cent of the total.[80] The period

1830–52 further concentrated the ownership of land, as Lynch notes:

> ...the Rosas regime left an indelible imprint on the agrarian structure of Argentina. The countryside was given its social and economic form before Argentina received its massive immigration, underwent a revolution on the pampas, and became a major exporter of grain and meat. Before modernisation even began, the system of landholding, the size of estates, and in many cases the personnel, all had been permanently implanted.[81]

By the end of the Rosas regime, the land-owning elite had consolidated a system of large production units, but production per acre was low until the needs of Europe enabled Argentina to reap the rewards of comparative advantage. The land most suited to export production was clearly that closest to Buenos Aires, and therefore inequality of development increased. For geographical reasons, much of Argentina was not developed, in contrast with the extension of the farming area in Canada and the United States, for example. However, with pampas agriculture as the basis of an apparently very successful economy, land increasingly became the primary source of wealth and status, although just when land values began to increase is disputed. Family relationships between Buenos Aires bankers and pampas land-owners, some of whom may have been displaced from urban mercantile activities by foreign traders in the years immediately following independence, ensured that the former were willing to provide loans for further land purchase and for some improvement of existing estates. Export gains were generally not used for development. Thus wealth from commercial activities was made available for further land accumulation.

One of the consequences of the manner in which European needs reinforced the existing land tenure system was that the pampas had an established elite prior to its development. This contrasts not only with the situation in the United States, where many poor settlers moved West to acquire smallholdings, but also in other lands of recent settlement such as Canada, where the central government had control over public lands and planned the development of the prairies. Government policy in Canada

promoted owner-occupier farms under the 1872 Homestead
Act. In Argentina the 1853 Constitution gave the individual
provinces control over public lands, which would have made
a coordinated land settlement policy difficult, even if cultural
values had promoted such a programme. The combined effect
of the increasing value of land and the poverty of provincial
treasuries was the sale of large tracts of public land to *estancieros*
or to entrepreneurs who then rented it to immigrants, with
the consequence that the majority of agricultural units were
rented family-sized concerns, especially in the littoral. Land
settlement programmes which did exist had been virtually
abandoned by 1895.[82] Thus, when families such as the di
Tellas arrived in Argentina in 1895 with the intention of
buying land, the best was already consumed by existing
estancias. The continuing affluence of Argentina as a primary
producer further enhanced land values, which rose fourfold
in the first decade or so of the twentieth century, promoting
much speculation. In 1928, 11 million acres or 13 per cent of
Buenos Aires Province was still owned by fifty families and
the six largest landowners in the Province had a combined
annual income in excess of the budgets of the Ministries
of Foreign Affairs, War, Agriculture, Public Works and the
Treasury. This land tenure pattern has proved remarkably
resilient, despite the inevitable subdivisions occurring as a
result of inheritance and rising land prices.[83]

There can be little doubt that land has acquired what
has been termed 'a psychological overvaluation',[84] that it
is a mark of status in modern Argentina and that the
ownership for leisure purposes of a *quinta* within commuting
distance of the city is the ideal of most middle-class *porteños*.
The numerous construction programmes on the pampas to
the south of Buenos Aires (the north-western side of the
city having been fairly effectively occupied by older and
more prosperous families for the same purpose) and the
quantity of traffic leaving the city on a Friday evening for
the south and returning on a Sunday, bear witness to this
fact. Whether this value was a simple transfer from Spain or
a development over time reflecting the interaction of Hispanic
culture with historical circumstances and the influence of
Europe may be a matter for debate, but the impact of this
trait has been generally agreed to be negative in terms

of economic development and thus of political stability. Large-scale landholdings are not intrinsically detrimental to development. Some parts of the United States, Canada, Australia and New Zealand have similar land tenure systems to that of the Argentine littoral provinces, but there large holdings have promoted mechanisation and increased efficiency to a greater extent. Indeed in Australia government encouragement of rural sector modernisation and expansion of agricultural production occurred in the 1920s, some thirty years before similar processes happened in Argentina. It is the values attached to landholding, and the way that the land tenure system interacts with other values and attitudes, which reduce its developmental effectiveness. E.R. Wolf eloquently describes some of the ambiguous characteristics of large estates in Latin America which, although based on his meso-American experience, have surprising relevance to the *estancias* of the Argentine littoral:

> Organised for commercial ends, the hacienda proved strangely hybrid in its characteristics. It combined in practice features which seem oddly contradictory in theory. Geared to sell products in a market, it yet aimed at having little to sell. Voracious for land, it deliberately made inefficient use of it. Operating with large numbers of workers, it nevertheless personalised the relations between worker and owner. Created to produce a profit, it consumed a large part of its substance in conspicuous and unproductive displays of wealth.[85]

Land in Argentina has provided for the most part a safe investment in times of social upheaval and inflation. It supplied a sense of permanence and security in a society which has seen itself as being at the frontier of civilisation, isolated and remote from its spiritual home in Europe. In addition, it was the source of social prestige. If land is valued for these reasons, it does not require development: it meets the needs of its owners without further effort on their part. Thus land was frequently bought and left uncultivated. Excess capital which might have been used for land development was spent or exported for securer investment abroad. Some commentators assert profit maximisation and efficiency amongst nineteenth-century *estancieros*. This view echoes the argument found in the 'development of underdevelopment' model of Frank and also later dependency theory, which holds that *latifundia* were not semifeudal structures but rather rational commercial, entrepreneurial responses to the needs of world capitalism.[86] But the under-utilisation of pampas land is marked and Wolf's view is more applicable than such authors suggest. It was not until the mid-1920s that mechanisation really got going and this neglect made equipment very expensive by the 1930s as a consequence of the collapse in primary export prices.[87] As late as 1969 only 7 per cent of Argentine farms had electricity supplies, a feature which inspired the rural electrification project begun in 1974.[88] Government attempts to encourage more efficient production are clearly evident at events such as the annual show of the Sociedad Rural Argentina (SRA) in Palermo each August. The preference for land as an investment has increased the need for foreign capital involvement in Argentina. The association of prestige with landholding likewise sapped the dynamism of the middle class at a key stage of development. Whilst urban industrial elements were growing in political and economic power in Australia and Canada, for example, the Radical regimes stopped short of seeking fundamental economic change.

CORRUPTION

Just as the purchase of land has diminished resources available for development, so too has the prevalence of corruption. This is a double-edged problem in that 'an exchange of political action for economic wealth'[89] not only reduces available resources through their consumption by corruptible officials but also distorts political action and may thus affect developmental potential. Again, this is a feature which has often been seen as a simple cultural transfer from the mother-country, but the American experience, the process of modernisation and the influence of non-Iberian Europe on that process have been creative of new forms of graft and have certainly reinforced traditional ones.

The lawlessness and dispersal of power in the early national period reinforced the use of position for material gain. Facundo Quiroga is an example and it is known that his estate on his death was much more substantial than that which he had inherited from his father.[90] Roca's presidencies consolidated the power of centralised government, but they also confirmed corruption as a feature at the highest administrative levels. Government trading accounts were falsified. Loans sought from Europe, especially Great Britain, for development purposes were frequently consumed as graft. The influence of non-Iberian Europe on the development of corruption went further than merely supplying funds, it had a cultural aspect too. Besides the simple raising of indigenous expectations as a result of contact with more materially advantaged cultures, the postivistic emphasis on economic progress and financial gain had influenced the attitudes of the immigrants whether from Spain or Italy. Disregard for the law was already an established feature of Argentine society when immigrants arrived seeking material advantage. An unfortunate combination of a tradition of moderate corruption and a new materialism therefore worked to increase the quantity and modify the quality of corruption. Scobie argues that *coima*, or bribery as a specific form of corruption, was virtually unknown in Buenos Aires before 1880 when immigrant-imported materialism began to have an impact. But by 1904 the equivalent of a quarter of the national budget was estimated to be spent each year in Buenos Aires on bribes.[91]

Corruption did not diminish in the twentieth century either. Gross over-manning of the government sector and the consequent corruption of officials was evident under the Radical regime of Yrigoyen, especially so in his second presidency. Although this is a standard charge on such occasions, this was one reason cited by the military for the 1930 coup. Economic avarice is one of the primary accusations made against Perón and Evita who were reputed to have spent enormous sums on personal possessions (including some 7 million pesos in Buenos Aires jewellery shops) and to have amassed fortunes in foreign banks. Indeed Alexander believes the extent of these transfers of funds to European accounts to have been sufficient to be actually damaging to the Argentine economy.[92] Although in exile in Panama Perón lived simply, his accusers claim this was due to his inability to get his hands on his extensive bank deposits in Switzerland and Spain. Certainly much that was left behind in Argentina was publicly displayed by the new military governments after Perón's ouster, incidentally refuting the arguments of international communist conspiracy theorists such as de Villemarest.[93] Although Perón's personal activities during his third presidency have not been subject to many such criticisms, the period after his death is seen as one of rampant corruption. Most allegations were levelled not at the president herself, but at her Minister of Social Welfare, López Rega, whose dubious activities in a printing company run by ex-police officers had caused comment in the early 1960s, prior to his gaining influence over the Peróns. While a part of the Argentine government he is reputed to have been a member of P2, a 'distinction' he shares with Admiral Massera.[94] Corruption was again a reason given by the military for their takeover in 1976, but the new regime could hardly be said to have a clean sheet itself. Some US$10 billion from the foreign debt of US$40 billion accumulated during the military regime remains unaccounted for in government spending figures. Most recently rumours abound concerning the alleged purchase by National Deputies and Senators of real estate in Bahia Blanca, shortly before the announcement of the relocation of the Argentine capital at Viedma. Bahia Blanca's situation, approximately equidistant from the proposed new capital and the beaches of Mar del Plata, has led to a massive increase in land values there.

Corruption has been alternatively explained in developmental, structural and cultural terms. In the first type of explanation, it is seen as either a product of underdevelopment, as few demands on state funds allow personal gain from public office or as a consequence of the process of modernisation. The modernisation process, Huntington suggests, encourages corruption in three ways. First, it separates public roles from private interests and thus makes corruption possible. Secondly, it establishes new sources of wealth and power not covered by traditional norms. Finally, modernisation produces a rapid expansion of government activity and regulation.[95] Such developmental explanations are, nevertheless, in part cultural in that they imply some sort of anomic breakdown, or inadequacy as in Huntington's analysis, of the old norms and values. Other authors reject the idea that corruption is clearly a consequence of modernisation.[96]

Structural explanations of corruption emphasise the weakness of political institutions and the nature of government administrative structures. Corruption is seen as a product of weak governmental authority which undermines the government position in relation to the individual. Similarly, large bureaucracies paying low salaries in consequence of over-manning, comprising political retainees for whom graft as a means to amassing wealth is a rational alternative to tenure, promote corruption. However, the causes of the structural conditions which are seen as the source of corruption are, at least in part, the consequence of cultural factors.

Direct cultural explanations emphasise that Latin American value systems maintain corruption in government and in the wider society. There is a danger in such theories that they may be assumed to be implying the moral inferiority of societies which exhibit a high level of corruption, that such societies are simply more dishonest than those where graft is less common. Although such explanations are unacceptable, cultural explanations in terms of the desirability of detection of corruption and the consequent effectiveness of sanction do have merit. Greater tolerance rather than greater improbity is the main theme in these explanations. Since evading the law is tolerated, officials are paid to assist in the process. Fillol sees the acceptance of corruption as part of human nature as a feature of Argentine society.[97] This is supported by religious belief, according to Wagley, who sees Latin American Catholicism, as being of the southern European kind and, compared to the northern European and US forms, '... more understanding of the lesser vices of men.'[98]

It has been argued that, at least at the theoretical level, corruption is not necessarily conducive to political instability either directly or indirectly through negative effects on development potential. Ake suggests that rather than weakening effective administration, corruption may actually serve to consolidate an elite in power.[99] Certainly this could be said of the establishment of oligarchic hegemony in Argentina after 1880. The deferment of instability thus achieved must be weighed against the unproductively consumed resources which were lost through economic corruption and the damage done to the legitimacy of democratic procedures by political corruption. Anderson argues that it is possible to view corruption as redistributive because payments flow from the more wealthy to petty officials who are less so. He further suggests that the possibility of private gain may make public officials more dynamic, that 'political entrepreneurship' may be conducive to development.[100] Anderson is, however, very cautious in so saying and rightly so, as much stronger arguments, at a more practical level, can be made for the deleterious effects of corruption.

Anderson himself acknowledges that large-scale private accumulation of public funds can have the obvious effect of reducing national economic resources. The effects may be more powerful than this implies since graft can distort an economy out of all proportion to the actual sums involved; for example, through the inefficiency of inappropriate construction schemes adopted as a result of corruption. (As recently shown by the Mexican earthquake of 1985, corruption may literally undermine the foundations of society, and can lead to high costs in terms of lives and rebuilding and compensation payments.) Very recently, widespread allegations against Argentine government officials have surfaced which have suggested that several important agreements have failed owing to personal financial demands being made of international companies.[101]

Corruption is also a self-perpetuating problem. Even if it is viewed as having a non-cultural explanation it becomes an expected pattern of behaviour over time and is therefore difficult to eliminate. The expectation of corruption is weakening for all institutions and, for example, governmental authority generally is undermined whether or not a specific government is actually corrupt. Similarly, the force of law is reduced as the power of money is increased. As part of this process wealthier sectors of society become more powerful in relation to other sectors and to institutions, including government. Pressure for institutional and procedural change is diminished by the individualisation of demand satisfaction. Contrary to Anderson's suggestions that the most able elements in the political and administrative hierarchies may be made more dynamic by corruption, the opposite may be the case if ability and corruptibility do not coincide in the same personnel. Able, but honest, people will be displaced in favour of the most corrupt who rise to the top, but whose authority will in any case be weakened by the low level of public trust they are capable of generating.

A generalised fear of contact with officialdom may be the outcome of such a situation, not just a fear of officials themselves but also of the complex regulations they administer. Fear of corruption by officials may generate more complex regulations in accordance with the Hispanic tradition and as this happens so corruption increases because more people are encouraged to try to buy a short cut through the red tape and because greater complexity of rules necessitates more bureaucrats. In fact corrupt officials have a vested interest in the proliferation of regulations.

TAX EVASION

The experience of corruption in government contributes to the reluctance to pay taxes. The knowledge that other people are not paying their taxes and that such money may be misused anyway must work against any idea of duty in matters of taxation. The possibility of avoiding sanctions through waiting for a tax amnesty or bribery if discovered in the meantime (the present authors are informed that the going rate in Argentina at the beginning of 1988 was 10 per cent of the possible fine) has the same effect. The evasion of taxes limits development potential in more than one way. Besides simply reducing the revenue available to the government, it also means that money which is collected is wasted, frequently being paid as bribes. Further, capital which is retained through non-payment of taxes tends to passive, rather than active and therefore visible, uses, especially so amongst an elite which already has a tendency to hoard rather than invest. This has impact not only on capital which should have been paid as taxes, but on all capital since wealthy sectors tend to conceal their wealth generally if they fear disclosure (hence the additional benefit to lottery winners of being able to sell their winning ticket at a premium to someone wishing to reactivate illegally-held capital). This reluctance to pay domestic taxes may contribute to the widespread tendency of elites in Latin America to act as potential exiles, not identifying with the nation and keeping investments and accounts abroad in more secure capital markets. (In 1986 some US$28 billion was estimated to be held abroad, a sum in excess of half Argentina's foreign debt.)[102] The shortage of government funds has partly been made good by foreign loans which incur interest charges and therefore reduce development potential. In addition in Argentina, instead of taxing real income, the state has tended to raise revenue through increasing money supply and thus has contributed to the inflationary spiral. That attitudes to taxation vary is illustrated by the different reactions in Argentina, Canada and Australia in the 1930s to the need to raise taxes and balance budgets in order to retain national credit-worthiness. It is not possible to argue that these differing attitudes were simply the product of different cultural bases as historical experience in the three nations varied. Canada and Australia already had some direct taxation, whilst Argentina had traditionally relied on customs receipts for government revenue. Nevertheless, the impossibility of separating culture and experience has already been emphasised. In Argentina it was much more difficult to collect revenues domestically than in Canada and Australia. Argentina's first income tax was announced in 1931 and came into force in 1932. In late 1932 when the 1933 budget came up for debate in Congress, the SRA anti-taxation campaign began. Tax strikes were threatened on a national scale, commercial and industrial organisations protested, and retailing outlets held wildcat strikes. In contrast there is little evidence of unrest over taxes in Canada or Australia.[103]

The Alfonsín government's continuing incapacity to balance its budget and pay its debt service charges led in 1986 to an official campaign to reduce tax evasion. The announcement in August of measures to simplify the tax system was accompanied by Treasury Secretary Mario Brodersohn's statement that some 40 per cent of names on official tax registers have false addresses which correspond to churches, public parks, rivers and so on. La Dirección General Impositiva (National Tax Board) estimated evasion at 50 per cent for some taxes and reported that only 13 per cent of registered Argentine citizens actually pay the taxes they should.[104]

THE ECONOMIC EFFECTS OF PERSONALISM
AND PESSIMISM

Reluctance to pay taxes to impersonal institutions is clearly supported by the generalised distrust of those outside the sub-national groupings to which a person belongs. Distrust of others affects stability indirectly through its economic implications as well as directly. Personal dependent relationships characterise many business and entrepreneurial activities as well as political ones, although in specific cases these have proved highly successful. This can lead to over-manning of financial institutions and to higher costs for the services of financial intermediaries. These extra costs of borrowing are estimated by Ferrer to be about 20 per cent, and they contribute to inflation.[105] Personalism in business means that credit depends not on rational economic factors, but on connections. Fillol sees personalism as the source of over-centralised authority in Argentine enterprises. He sees the accordance of respect to the person not the office as leading to three related problems. First, the hierarchy of persons rather than positions leads to a sense of personal superiority which makes subordinates unlikely to challenge decisions taken by their superiors. Secondly, the personalisation of an office causes reluctance to delegate authority. Subordinates are given little responsibility and therefore display little initiative. Thus overlapping functions or those not specifically allocated are often neglected. Finally, because it is not a person's position which is accorded status this results in a failure to relate that role to the wider organisation.[106]

Distrust of other people is part of a more generalised lack of confidence which Merkx has termed 'a pervasive desconfianza'.[107] Again, this trait may be seen as a rational response to the reality of the stop–go economic cycles Argentina has experienced since 1930, but such a lack of confidence has become a cultural factor which contributes to that reality. As Ferrer notes:

> The economic agents have such negative expectations that any attempt to stimulate the economy by fiscal and monetary policy leads to prior upward adjustment of prices, combined with capital flight.[108]

The whole process of the interaction between expectations and experience is cyclical. The lack of confidence contributes to the structural weakness of a domestic capital market which encourages inflation by increasing money supply to cover government deficits and foreign loan repayments. Further inflation then in turn encourages the short-term emphasis which is the result of a lack of confidence. Ferrer argues that the cycle must be broken into, that confidence is needed to reduce interest rates and sustain an accord on the division of income which will prevent sectoral spiralling. How this is to be achieved remains an enigma in a nation where pessimism has reached such a level that a magazine poll finds 53 per cent of its respondents wishing to emigrate.[109]

8 Nationalism and its Antithesis

At the theoretical level many commentators see nationalism as something that helps, and so is characteristic of, development. It is thought to be a potentially integrative force, focusing all loyalties on the state and binding together developing nations which lack other means of cohesion. Its primary function is therefore domestic, the provision of a point of agreement in an otherwise fragmented society. It provides a basis for consensus and thus has even been seen as a precondition for the development of democracy. Summarising themes from other writers, Silvert offers a definition of nationalism as: 'the acceptance of the state as the impersonal and ultimate arbiter of human affairs'.[1] In so doing, Silvert is suggesting that nationalism gives the state the capacity to settle disputes; it rests on 'acceptance', and it overrides all sub-national forms of identification because the state is 'impersonal'. Such a definition is more in accord with the concept of legitimacy than it is with nationalism and certainly cannot be seen as applicable to Argentine nationalism. Nationalism is not about 'states', but about 'nation'; it is not concerned with things 'impersonal', but is rather emotional and subjective. It may be defined as a devotion to various intuitive understandings of the symbolic elements which comprise national identity.

The sectoral structure of Argentina, the lack of consensus (even on the question of nationalism) and the persistence of sub-national identification suggest that according to Silvert's definition Argentina does not exhibit nationalism. Few writers would agree with this. On the contrary Argentines are invariably seen as fiercely nationalistic. Whitaker argues that one of the traits which is so widespread in Argentina as to be considered national is 'ebullient patriotism' which he sees as accompanied by ' . . . excessive sensitivity to criticism that easily becomes resentment and xenophobia'.[2] Argentina's particular forms of nationalism do not fit Silvert's definition and, as will be shown, have rather more negative features than functionalist views of the phenomenon would tend to suggest. As K.R. Minogue says: 'Nationalism . . . appears to be a love for an abstraction of the nation, and that abstraction may have none but the most tenuous connection with the concrete national life.'[3]

Nationalism rests on values and attitudes and in turn expresses them. Argentine nationalism might therefore be expected to reflect the two cultures which have influenced national development. Two main streams of 'nationalism' can indeed be recognised: one deriving from the influence of non-Iberian Europe and the other from the Hispanic tradition. But as with other cultural features, the national experience has contributed to the unique evolution of these themes and their interaction has modified both. Yet again Argentina has tended to develop contradictory elements which contribute little to national stability.

THE FRONTIER AND NATIONAL IDENTITY

The geographical location and isolation of the area which is now Argentina might be expected to have encouraged the growth of nationalism. In fact this process did occur, but in a distorted form which did not promote the development of a sense of national identity. At the same time, a unique aspect of the Argentine concept of the frontier is that it has encouraged the growth of internationalism as well as giving nationalism an odd pessimistic and fatalistic quality.

The Río de la Plata region was not only separated by huge distances from the mother-country, but was also the periphery of the Spanish Empire, so much so that, until the late eighteenth century, the Spanish Crown did not even send *corregidores* to administer the area. This neglect by the imperial power and the primitive quality of frontier life could have led to the development of a strong sense of regional identity, but other factors worked against this. Most importantly, the viceregal boundaries established under Spain, including as they did Paraguay, part of Uruguay and much of what is now Bolivia, were an administrative convenience, they were not an expression of regional unity. In addition, the

Hispanic traditions of individualism and localism, transferred by colonisation and reinforced by the experience of isolation and remoteness from the imperial power, worked against the development of viceregal identification. Nationalism of a kind may have prevented the complete fragmentation of Spanish America after independence, but the absence of regional identification corresponding to the viceregal boundaries allowed centifugal forces to break up the old viceroyalties. Even Bolívar's Confederation of Gran Colombia lasted only eighteen years. Thus as the boundaries of the new nations took shape, localism remained stronger than common interests; the nation was an 'abstraction' and mere national survival was the priority.[4]

Although the experience of the physical frontier in Argentina had much in common with that of similar regions in Australia, Canada and the United States, it did not have the same impact on the development of a sense of national identity that it appears to have had elsewhere. In North America, the frontier experience is seen as contributing to the development of democracy through its encouragement of individual freedom. The frontier became a source of national identity through the pioneering urge to settle new regions and establish a great nation. By contrast, in Argentina, extending the available cattle-raising area was the main pressure on the frontier and there was no concept of free land to attract settlers as in North America. In consequence, few immigrants were drawn into the frontier experience. Where the frontier was pushed back successfully it was as a consequence of state initiative but in response to the needs of an external market and frequently with the involvement of foreign investment capital, as in the case of the pampas railways. Of course, foreign capital contributed to the expansion of the frontier in North America too, but there the general theme of settlement and nation-building was more widespread. For some, these were the benefits the Argentine railways offered, but for others, enhancement of land values was the key.

Although the independence era is associated with revolutionary, nationalist thought, rejecting the colonial past and seeking a new national identity, a parallel internationalist perspective was also strong, as were traditionalist ideas. The isolation of Argentina from the important nations of the world contributed both to 'nationalist' and 'internationalist' orientations. Her geographical position made her 'psychologically as well as physically peripheral',[5] and this had two related effects. First, it encouraged a sense of isolation and fatalism which became part of the nationalist perspective. The development of the concept of Argentina as a victim of forces beyond her control has sources in her remoteness. Secondly, national location gave rise not to a rejection of some of the old values of Europe as irrelevant and to the development of a new and distinct identity, as in the case of North America, but rather to a clinging to Europe as a source of identity. Argentina was a frontier, certainly, but a frontier of Europe which must seek to preserve her identity from the encroachment of the Americas. This latter perception of Argentina's place in the world as Europe's most remote outpost has developed over time to create an image of the nation as a kind of outlying citadel under attack from hostile forces. The interpretation forms part of the modern internationalist belief, widespread amongst some military factions, that international communism has begun an ideological battle against Western civilisation.

The concept of the 'enemy within' may reflect the absence of a more tangible enemy without. Her remoteness has protected Argentina from involvement in international conflicts. In addition, as the second largest republic of South America, she has been reasonably secure within the region. Thus there is little objective physical threat to Argentine security in the sense of her national territorial integrity. It has been suggested that this weakens Argentine nationalism and makes emphasis on its economic aspects inevitable. However, territorial nationalism has always been strong in Argentina, as was shown in the nineteenth century in territorial disputes which Ugarte sees as Argentina's tendency to 'a policy of frontier strife'.[6] It continues to be so, as is indicated by the Beagle Channel dispute and popular reaction to the Falklands invasion. This form of nationalism may be an expression of the continuing quest for national identity. A recent British study of the attitudes to the Falklands War of 300 British and Argentine boys aged seven to seventeen suggested marked national differences in territorial awareness. The greater Argentine emphasis on 'sovereignty' as the reason for the war as compared with the British boys' most frequent explanation in terms of 'people' may have reflected the rhetoric of respective political leaders, but further evidence suggests that territory is a much more important aspect of Argentine identity than of British. The Argentine boys had much greater national geographical knowledge and were far more effective at completing an unfinished outline map of their country than were their British counterparts. The average level of national geographical awareness achieved by the British seventeen-year-olds was lower than that of the Argentine ten-year-olds. Territory was also seen by the Argentine sample in a more political way:

> . . . while in England inclusions [on the unfinished map] seemed to depend on the *size* of the omitted area, in Argentina the *political* importance was more crucial. The Malvinas (and the Antarctic territories) were frequently drawn in by the Argentine boys. But the English boys did not often draw in Northern Ireland.[7]

Argentina's sense of identity expresses both nationalism and a strong attachment to Europe, as was evident in Foreign Minister Dante Caputo's attempt to define her position in the world to the UN General Assembly as ' . . . a Western, non-aligned developing country'.[8] This cosmopolitan mixture is nowhere more in evidence than in the narrow cultural sense of art and personal commodities. Whilst Buenos Aires shops have become increasingly interested in selling Amerindian products since the end of the import boom in late 1980, young *porteños* continue to seek to identify themselves with their North American counterparts. According to Jorge Estomba, an artist and adviser on cultural affairs to the Radical Government's Foreign Ministry, Argentina is a 'bastard land' lacking the cultural direction and national identity of other countries like Brazil.[9] It has been further suggested that in terms of her cultural identity:

> . . . Argentina is a headless chicken, scurrying about in quixotic search for an identifiable future . . . Given . . . the impossibility of getting a trio of Argentines to agree about anything, creating a new sense of Argentinity, without demogogic gobbledygook or political partisanry, seems utopic [sic].[10]

The quest for cultural identity has been a recurrent theme in Latin America, as has the wider quest for identity generally. This may suggest that Alba is correct in his assertion that the Latin American republics are not really nations in the widest sense, in that they still have not come to terms with what they are.[11] It certainly does lend weight to Zea's argument that Latin American nationalism is essentially 'defensive' in that it does not seek imperial expansion, but encourages the quest for identity and resists foreign incursion.[12] This particular form of nationalism can exist alongside an internationalist perspective and in Argentina does so to the detriment of political stability. But the lack of national identity contributes more directly to instability because there is nothing to override the emphasis on sub-national affiliations which reflect the sectoral structure of society. In such circumstances, order is imposed rather than derived from common interests and therefore is associated with authoritarian government.

THE DEVELOPMENT OF INTERNATIONALISM

Internationalism may be seen as a liberal form of nationalism or as a kind of anti-nationalism. If the latter view is taken, then as a negative concept it should be presented after nationalism. However the relationship between nationalism and internationalism is not a simple dichotomy in Argentina. The two may be theoretically contradictory, but neither may in practice stand alone. In Argentina the internationalist perspective was established in a form closer to its present one at an earlier stage than nationalism. Nationalism in its modern form grew out of a reaction against the late-nineteenth-century view of the *estancia* and the international market as the source of Argentine wealth, status, progress and development. It was a response to liberalism, the consequent immigration and working-class political activity.

The colonial heritage is usually seen as promoting nationalistic fervour in Argentina, but it also contributed to the internationalist, pro-Western perspective. Not only did Hispanic culture emphasise order and hierarchy, characteristics sympathetic to the modern anti-communist aspect of pro-Western internationalism but, more importantly, the fact that Spain was the colonial power provides the most long-standing connection with Europe. Independence from Spain was not simply a nationalist revolution; it was sought, at least in part, as a means to extend trading links with Europe, especially Great Britain. Argentina's close relations with Europe in the immediate post-independence period and after the defeat of Rosas helped to establish a strong sense of Europeanness, of superiority to the rest of Latin America. She came to see herself as destined to be the regional leader, being culturally and economically more advanced. The importance of British trade, which made Argentina in effect 'a Spanish-speaking appendage of the British Empire',[13] the admiration of French culture, the adoption of a formal political system bearing considerable resemblance to that of the United States, the influx of Italian immigrants and the influence of German military training, all add up to the early establishment of ties with the states which now comprise the most important parts of the Western political alliance. Such strong historical connections cannot easily be put aside and they provide the basis for the belief that Argentine greatness rests on an alliance with the developed West.

The development of the Western world provided the only model available for Argentina's aspirations to greatness and, for a considerable period, a taste of the important role she hoped to assume. Great Britain's need to feed her growing industrial labour force and to acquire a market for its products, along with the availability of capital accumulated through industrialisation which could be invested abroad, resulted in a reciprocal economic relationship which put Argentina only slightly behind the United States in per capita wealth in 1916 and ahead of France,[14] inspiring much optimism in Argentina and amongst observers such as Lord Bryce:

> All is modern and new; all belongs to the prosperous present and betokens a still more prosperous future . . . It is the United States of the Southern Hemisphere.[15]

British investments in Argentina burgeoned from the 1870s onwards, followed by German and North American capital involvement in the early twentieth century. By the First World War, Britain was being pushed out of the Argentine import market by other European nations and by the United States as Argentina's trading relationships became more multilateral, but she remained Argentina's biggest customer and investor until the Second World War. (Indeed the special relationship between Britain and Argentina continued well beyond this period. Only in the late 1960s did Argentina cease to be Britain's foremost Latin American supplier and the largest receiver of her investments.) Britain remained more liberal in economic practice than most other nations during the 1920s and thus Argentina experienced more free trade in the period 1914–30 than was the case elsewhere. In this way Argentina's protracted period of economic prosperity and apparent development, which lasted, with a few minor hiccoughs, from the 1870s to the 1930s, became clearly associated with economic liberalism and with integration into the international economic system which at that time meant association with the nations of Western Europe and the United States. Further evidence of the relationship between economic development and connections with the West could be seen in the uneven development within the nation. Those productive areas which were most intimately bound to the West, ranching, farming and food processing, were the most developed and prosperous economic sectors. Similarly, Buenos Aires, that geographical area which was most prosperous and which dealt most directly with Argentina's trading partners, came to represent Argentina's developmental aspirations.

The influence of the United States on Argentine culture, economics and politics, became important during the 1930s and 1940s. Argentina pursued an independent foreign policy during the Second World War and for some time afterwards, but on some of the most important international issues she showed herself to be clearly within the Western sphere of influence and, more particularly, within that of the United States. For example, Argentina's admission to the United Nations Organisation was blocked by the Soviet Union and, in order to avoid a Soviet veto, needed US concessions (although these were probably forced from the United States by the other Latin American republics).

The armed forces have been subject to the often contradictory impact of the two cultures just as have other aspects of Argentine society. The military role may be seen as essentially nationalistic, but the Argentine military was professionalised under an outward-orientated internationalist regime. In consequence the attitudes of the armed forces were formed at a time when European influences were dominant, when the Indians were defeated and the *gauchos* were contained. French army influence, and German military missions from the era of Prussian dominance in the late nineteenth century on, consolidated 'European' attitudes.

In Argentina generally and amongst the armed forces in particular, national pride is associated with a powerful military establishment. The sub-continent was conquered by military means and independence won by armed force, though this was on a very limited scale in the case of Argentina. National prestige is therefore reflected in military might which, through the example of Britain, France, Germany and the United States, is seen as a sign of development. At first sight this would appear to suggest that nationalist thought should dominate the officer corps. But the ideological orientation of any external power which contributes to the boosting of national status through its support of the armed forces is likely to be sympathetically received by many officers. As it replaced Germany as the dominant influence on the Argentine military, the United States later found itself in just such an ideologically advantageous position. Direct US involvement in Argentine military affairs began with attempts to counteract Axis influence in the officer corps during the Second World War. Argentina's agreement to the establishment of the first US military mission was secured in October 1948. These early examples of US involvement were not met with resistance by a unified nationalist military because an internationalist, pro-Western orientation was already well developed amongst elements of the officer corps. Since that time, the Argentine military has become increasingly tied to the West through its partial dependence on Western, and especially US, financial assistance, weapons technology and training of personnel.

Before the Second World War, New Deal Policy was opposed to military aid. During the Lend–Lease era Argentina scarcely benefited, especially in comparison with neighbouring pro-Allied Brazil. After the end of Lend–Lease, in 1946–47, the US Congress refused to pass military aid bills. The way in which the State Department concurred with Ambassador Braden's call to cancel arms shipments to Argentina in 1945 was characteristic of the general attitude of the immediate post-war period. However, as concern over Soviet intentions grew, US concern with hemispheric defence consolidated in the signing of the Inter-American Treaty of Reciprocal Assistance (or Rio Treaty) in 1947 and was reflected in her allowing Argentina to purchase more than $2 million worth of military equipment at cost or surplus property prices by April 1949.[16] The more extensive aid provided by the United States under the Military Assistance Program during the 1950s, especially after 1953 under Eisenhower, was also accorded justification in terms of hemispheric defence and increased the ideological ties between the Argentine armed forces and the United States.

The extent to which the United States has contributed to the strengthening of the Argentine armed forces has been a matter of considerable controversy, not least because the US federal government, according to Needler, issues at least four sets of figures on Latin American military assistance which are not only not the same, but are mutually contradictory.[17] It has been argued that US military assistance to Argentina has been negligible in proportion to the national defence budget. For example, figures have been produced suggesting that during the years 1952–62 the US provided less than $5 million or only about $40 per member of the Argentine armed forces.[18] However for a variety of reasons such figures do not represent the full picture. Horowitz argues that some US financial assistance for specific purposes has been covert and cites the example of sponsorship for the 1955 coup which ousted Perón.[19] It must be said that such involvement in this particular instance is by no means proven. But it would be consistent with a pattern of covert US funding which began with the sponsoring of the overthrow of Mossadegh in Iran in 1953 and Arbenz in Guatemala in 1954. Alternatively, some emphasise much higher overt US assistance over the longer term; for example Wynia gives the figure for the period 1946–73 as $174 500 000.[20] In any event, the protection implied by the Rio Treaty means that the aid which is given disproportionately strengthens Latin American military establishments in their domestic context because it is spent on cheaper counterinsurgency weapons and equipment. Moreover, the granting of licences for local production by the United States and some Western European nations is effectively a subsidy to the Argentine military through Fabricaciones Militares. Argentina has built up a sizeable arms industry, producing destroyers, helicopters, tanks, missiles, etc., but she is still heavily dependent on Western technology for this production. The domestically-produced Pucará counterinsurgency aircraft, for example, has a French engine and utilises much US equipment. Western European nations and Israel have become increasingly involved in supplying arms to Latin America since 1970 for a variety of reasons including the drain on US production of the Vietnam War and the Carter Administration's reluctance to do so. But it was during the period of US domination of arms sales that the important shift from arms ostensibly appropriate for hemispheric defence to the provision of counterinsurgency equipment occurred.

Fear of the Left is clearly a feature of nationalist thought since it involves a response to a threat perceived as having an international source. Indeed this was perhaps the most marked feature of the elitist right-wing nationalist groupings which developed during the 1920s and 1930s. It was in fact perceived by them as a direct consequence of the immigration encouraged by liberal internationalist policies. As a threat to order, political dissent conflicts with the hierarchical and ordered cultural values derived from Spain. In addition, reinforcement of such values amongst officers undoubtedly occurred in a manner which encouraged the growth of opposition to leftist political activity during the 1930s. To the Argentine army, the humiliations suffered by the Spanish army after the abortive uprising by General Sanjurjo in 1932 must have served as a warning that the Left should not be allowed to take control of the state. Officers in Argentine military academies would no doubt have felt much sympathy for the Iberian values held by the Nationalist forces which included traditionalism, nationalism and the idea of a strong state.

However, the perceived threat began with the European stream of influence, has been nurtured by Western influences and remains an essential part of the internationalist perspective. It was the outward-orientated development process in the late nineteenth century which brought to Argentina not only European capital but also immigrants who carried with them aspirations derived from European socialist and anarcho-syndicalist thought. The military perception of the Left as a threat has been reinforced by contact with the United States. The suppression of leftist dissent has been most coordinated and effective in regimes with a primarily internationalist orientation in recent years. Both the 1966 military government and the 1976 regime sought to eliminate leftist opposition, though with varying degrees of commitment. Although the more nationalist government of Isabel Perón laid down the organisational structure for rooting out subversion in the foundation of the AAA, which operated from the Ministry of Social Welfare under López Rega, this process reached its peak under her successor, General Videla. The Process of National Reorganisation over which he presided was justified in internationalist, pro-Western terms:

> ... the armed forces saw themselves as not merely engaged in a strictly military operation but locked in a virtual crusade as the lonely and misunderstood guardians of 'Western Civilisation'.[21]

That the Argentine military should have seen the elimination of subversion in this way is the logical outcome of the strength of the national association with Europe and the role of the United States in promoting amongst officers a conception of the global struggle based on an East–West division. Through the transfer of values inherent in US training for counterinsurgency, the Argentine military came to define its dominant role in terms of resistance to an international communist conspiracy. The belief held by many Argentine officers that the Third World War had begun and was being fought on their national territory is clearly shown in the statement made by General Galtieri whilst visiting Washington early in 1982:

> The First World War was one of armies against armies, the Second World War was one of weapons against weapons, the Third World War is one of ideology against ideology.[22]

Europe was seen by the United States as the main arena of potential confrontation with the Soviet Union immediately after the Second World War. But when the Korean War began in 1950, fear of communism in Latin

America was already evident in US policy. For example, US arms sales to Argentina, despite her failure to cooperate with the United States during the Second World War, reflected the fear that Argentina would seek military assistance elsewhere and thus shift her ideological position. The United States had initially refused to supply the arms sought by the Perón regime, but, when Perón threatened to buy military equipment from Czechoslovakia, Ambassador Bruce put pressure on the State Department. By the end of 1947, the US War Department had made the required arms available.[23] Similarly, it was US reluctance to risk the anti-communist aspect of the Rio Treaty, which led to the United States opposing the proposal made in 1948 by the democratic governments of Guatemala, Uruguay and Venezuela to introduce a clause calling for inter-American action against dictatorial governments in the Americas.

The anti-communist aspect of US policy towards Latin America which existed throughout the Cold War period was deepened as a result of the Cuban Revolution of 1959. The first wave of insurrection imitative of the Cuban Revolution was of the rural kind and occurred from 1960 on in the Caribbean region (including Venezuela and Colombia, though not North-East Brazil until the late 1960s), Peru and Bolivia. In 1962 internal security and counterinsurgency became the main focus of US policy when Robert McNamara, as Defence Secretary to the Kennedy Administration, developed the doctrine of 'flexible response'. In that year, the US Armed Forces Southern Command School of the Americas was established at Fort Gulick in Panama, where Latin American officers were trained and assistance was given in identifying subversive elements. Fort Gulick retained this function until it was closed in September 1984. With the exception of the Carter Administration, and the recent US about-face over the Noriega regime in Panama, the idea has continued of Latin American military elements as stabilising forces and bastions against communism.

Argentina experienced some insurgency in the early 1960s in the north-west of the nation, but this was effectively eliminated in 1964. She was much more subject to the second wave of insurrection, this time of the urban kind, which spread through Latin America beginning in Guatemala in 1967 and the Southern Cone in 1968. The armed forces were geared up in counterinsurgency before the state began to experience widespread insurgency. A question therefore arises concerning why elements of the Argentine armed forces should have been so receptive to the anti-communist aspect of Western ideology when the state appeared so far removed geographically and culturally from the initial centre of insurrection. In fact military absorption of a counterinsurgency role only fully developed in the 1970s. Guido di Tella sees the hesitation of the Onganía regime in suppressing the Cordobazo violence of 1969 as evidence of this.[24] Anti-communism provided a common orientation for both nationalist and internationalist elements within the armed forces. Both modes of thought were susceptible to the perception of the political Left as a threat to national security for a variety of reasons, not least because it provided a basis for unity and a role which could justify the costs of the military establishment.

From the professionalisation of the Argentine army in the late nineteenth century until the Falklands War in 1982, the military have constituted a permanent force essentially underemployed. A comparison with Britain illustrates this point. The regular army in Britain in 1983 numbered some 139 000 personnel out of a total population of 55 million and reflected an active military role in NATO and elsewhere. The Argentine army numbered some 80 000 in 1979 from a population of 28 million[25] and had no such role. In Europe generally, external threats have given national militaries a role in defending their nations. Under the subsidiary provisions of the Rio Treaty, the United States could come to the assistance of Argentina (or one of her neighbours) in a regional dispute (though these provisions have only been successfully invoked twice and neither case involved Argentina). But comparative peace has been achieved amongst the states in the Southern Cone. Any threat from outside the Americas (the primary provision of the Rio Treaty), would be subject to US intervention, and in such circumstances the Argentine armed forces would lack the equipment, training and discipline available from US forces. As a consequence of the lack of a sufficiently consuming military role, many Argentine officers have assumed an active political function to which the US emphasis on counterinsurgency has lent a certain legitimacy.

A role is needed not only as a justification for the existence of such a large and expensive institution, nor just as an explanation of its activity within the sphere of domestic politics, but because, without a role, discipline and order within the Argentine officer corps itself declines markedly. The first military lodges were formed during the independence struggle and a strong tendency to factionalism has survived within the professional army. When officers are not kept busy and united in purpose, they conspire. Examples of the military proclivity to conspiracy are numerous, but by way of illustration of this trait during the period of civilian government under Frondizi from 1958 until March 1962, there were some 35 plots against the elected government by the *gorila* (hardline anti-Peronist) faction of the army.[26] Periods of unity within the officer corps have been rare and short-lived, but have also been associated with performance of a function perceived generally by officers as important to national security. The restoration of order through the suppression of the Left is a role which has proved able to unify the officer corps. Such unity was achieved temporarily at the beginning of the Onganía regime in 1966, but was lost through the re-emergence of public disaffection. Unity was likewise achieved in 1976 and the immediate goal of the elimination of subversion obscured factional disputes during the late 1970s.

Both the 1966 and 1976 military takeovers combined anti-communist ideology with a primarily internationalist form of developmentalism. Such a combination is rational because the crushing of leftist opposition is seen as a prerequisite for the political stability essential to economic development. However, the weighting of these two related orientations differed in 1966 and 1976. Onganía's more short-lived and much less bloody regime was initiated largely as a response to the demands of business interests. General Videla's accession to power in 1976 came as a relief to a much wider section of the civilian population, since political violence had reached unprecedented levels with an assassination every five hours and a bombing every three hours.[27] The new regime's belief that the Left constituted a challenge to the very basis of traditional Argentine values, which were in turn synonymous with those of the capitalist West, was indicated by Videla's description of the former leftist Peronist president, Héctor Cámpora, as a 'political delinquent' and his statement that:

> a terrorist is not just someone with a gun or a bomb but also someone who spreads ideas contrary to Western and Christian civilisation.[28]

That the armed forces should see development as important is in accord with the military ethos which emphasises national status and security. Obviously an economically successful nation is seen as less vulnerable to internal and external threats and is therefore perceived as more secure. At the same time the military recognises the intimate connection between public order and development, the coincidence of public unrest and economic troubles. The armed forces see the economic aspirations of the working class as part of the inflationary spiral which has led to economic stagnation rather than development. Military self-interest requires development both because only a wealthy nation can afford to maintain a large and well-equipped military institution and because the armed forces want national self-sufficiency in the raw materials they require. They began to acquire their own productive base when the First World War cut off some of their essential supplies. In 1922 Alvear formalised this process by his appointment of General Mosconi as director of the newly-formed state oil company. The Second World War accelerated this trend. For example, the military took control of domestic iron and steel production in 1941, having argued that this was an essential aspect of national defence. Thus the Argentine military have both ideological and instrumental reasons for simultaneously seeking order and modernisation. Since the latter goal sets in motion forces which may threaten public order, the military have seen themselves as having an important function in containing unrest while promoting development. Such a role has been dubbed 'technocratic militarism'.

The economic orientation of the military has been primarily to the West, as would be expected from the coincidence of military professionalisation with the political dominance of the agro-exporting Oligarchy in the late nineteenth century. The military-supported, internationalist-orientated regimes of General Roca (1880–86) and General Justo (1932–38) provide illustrations of the way in which such an internationalist perception was established amongst the armed forces. This orientation again became dominant amongst officers, though in a modified form, after Perón's overthrow as a reaction to the nationalist statism of his regime. It has since been encouraged by US and Western European policy towards Latin America, in particular by the aid offered by the United States in the 1960s to military civic action programmes and through the transfer of technology. One example of such technical aid perceived by officers as important to national development (as well as to potential military strength), is the training of Argentine nuclear scientists in the United States and Western Europe. Most importantly, when the military regimes of 1966 and 1976 sought capital for developmental schemes, it was from the capitalist West that such funds came. Similarly, the loans needed to deal with the inherited economic crises were secured through Argentina's membership of the IMF, the most important contributors to which are the OECD nations. Both regimes further opened up Argentina to foreign capital, both appointed Ministers of the Economy with internationalist perspectives, well-known and respected in Western financial circles, who emphasised comparative economic advantage rather than extensive autonomous industrialisation as the best means to achieve the development sought by their military employers. (It should, however, be stressed that nationalism was also inherent in these regimes and their internationalism was a relative rather than an absolute feature.)

Liberal internationalism derives from contact with Europe, especially Great Britain, during the Belle Epoque of primary export production. However it has re-emerged with every economic crisis since 1930 despite the growth of economic nationalism. Those crises have been marked by heightened political activity by the military and therefore the dominant mode of thought amongst senior officers must be seen as circumscribed internationalism. This form of economic analysis, based on an acceptance that national resources and the domestic market are too limited for autochthonous economic growth necessitating the import of foreign capital and production for the international market, provided the theoretical basis for the economic policies of the 1976–83 regime. It had, through the protracted period of relative failure of the Argentine economy, the turbulent political situation and its compatibility with fashionable monetarist explanations of economic underachievement, acquired a certain 'scientific-technocratic legitimacy'.[29] However, as with political institutions and procedures, such legitimacy remained partial, since alongside internationalism another mode of thought coexisted, having sources more specifically within the Hispanic cultural tradition, though also subject to reinforcement and modification through historical experience.

THE GROWTH AND REFINEMENT OF NATIONALISM

Despite Argentina's ideological ties to the West, she, at the same time, sees herself as a potentially great power thwarted by external, primarily Western, forces. She has tended to exhibit what Snyder terms 'integral nationalism' which has ' . . . rejected sympathy for and cooperation with other nations, promoted jingoism, militarism and imperialism'.[30] This has led Argentina to favour relative isolation in her foreign policy and to assert her independence on many international issues throughout the national period. In the twentieth century it has encouraged the growth of aspirations to autonomous development and led to the establishment of a history of opposition to the United States unparalleled amongst the other capitalist states of Latin America.

Latin American nationalism is frequently seen as deriving from the Hispanic legacy. For example, de Madariaga argues that the individualism and egotism of Iberian culture lead the individual to see the nation as a kind of extension of himself; the nation belongs to him rather than he to it.[31] More frequently such explanations rest on the degeneration of Iberian pride of race into xenophobia. The Reconquest is seen as having produced an emphasis on pure blood. Whilst most peoples are ethnocentric, the long Iberian experience of foreign domination increased this feature. Rouquié notes the continuing reluctance to acknowledge the *mestizo* aspect of Argentina.[32] Certainly the present authors have been conscious of Argentine racism both in attitudes and in the allocation of social prestige in social encounters in Argentina.

Clearly such attitudes were in evidence in the extermination of the Indians in the late nineteenth century, though it might be argued that the particular tribes found in the national territory were less compliant than those in many other parts of Latin America. It must further be pointed out that the elimination of the Indian threat was not simply a response to racist attitudes derived from Spain, since the influence of non-Iberian Europe also contributed to the process. Not only did the needs of the British market increase the value of land and necessitate the extension of the agricultural frontier but, in addition, positivist thought justified such actions in the same Social Darwinist terms used to explain the extermination of the Tasmanian Aborigines and the subjugation of the Yaqui in northern Mexico. However, what does suggest that Hispanic pride of race may have been absorbed is the absence of any self-criticism such as was a feature of Peruvian literature in the late nineteenth century and emerged in Mexico before the Revolution of 1910:

> Perhaps . . . there should be a literature of self-rebuke in connection with the subjugation and final extermination of these natives, but Argentines have not thought so.[33]

The process of achieving independence contributed to the growth of nationalism, although it encouraged contact with non-Iberian Europe and thus also contributed to pro-Western internationalism. Despite the relative ease with which Argentine independence was achieved, the fact that Spanish authority was not willingly conceded and that the independence movement followed successful resistance to British incursions, established a certain pride in the attainment of nationhood against obstacles. Argentina's initiation of and major contribution to the liberation of all Spanish America ' . . . gave the Argentine people a continent-sized pride and faith in their national destiny'.[34] Thus nationalist feeling, albeit of a partial kind existing alongside a European orientation, was established much earlier in Argentina than in some other Latin American nations.

As early as 1825, when governed by ostensibly outward-looking, pro-European liberal elements, Argentina displayed the modified isolationism which has expressed nationalist aspects of her political culture and characterised much of her political history since. In reluctantly agreeing to take part in the Panama Congress in order to avoid conflict with the other new Latin American republics, she simultaneously made it clear that she did not want regional commitments.[35] In the period 1825–28 territorial nationalism was strengthened in confrontation with the imperial aspirations of Brazil which was seeking long-term control of the Banda Oriental. The recognition of Uruguayan independence was a double defeat in that it meant the loss of a rich area and the creation of a rival port to Buenos Aires, and it angered those who had sought to bring Uruguay under Argentine domination and led to military support for the centralist leader General Juan Lavalle against the autonomist governor of Buenos Aires, Manuel Dorrego, in December 1828.[36]

Integral nationalism, though modified and reinforced in the twentieth century, was most clearly illustrated in the nineteenth century by the long period of domination by Rosas. Although *caudillismo* was a sub-national phenomenon, it has been seen as masking rather than inhibiting the development of nationalism.

> In a perverted way, [nationalism] was expressed even by the caudillos, for they represented as close an approximation to the paternalist nation-state idea as was feasible in those tumultuous times.[37]

Some *caudillos* were not explicitly nationalistic. Amongst these was Rosas himself. Yet his brutal welding together of the disparate provinces effectively created the nation. The period was not consistently nationalistic, but Rosas did encourage his followers to make distinctions between nationals of Argentina and other countries by his differential treatment of Indians from within the national territory, with whom he negotiated, and 'foreign' Indians, whom he killed.[38] Such attitudes were clearly absorbed by the *gauchos* and survived beyond the fall of Rosas. As late as January 1872 a *gaucho* massacre of foreigners occured in Tandil.[39] Sarmiento sees the independence of the *gauchos* under Rosas as a possible source of Argentina's inflated sense of national importance.[40] The Rosas era, despite some internationalist features, was essentially introspective. Rosas used nationalist feeling to ensure his own popularity, invoking foreign threats when his regime was under pressure.

Despite the consolidation of liberal internationalism after the fall of Rosas, Argentina continued to exhibit integral nationalism, which was strengthened by boundary disputes with Chile in the late nineteenth century. She continued to assert her political independence of all other powers whilst her economic dependence on the trading relationship with Britain increased. The 1880s saw a growing hostility to the United States as intellectuals condemned US influence and in December 1889 *La Nación* published two letters from José Martí expressing his fears concerning the power of the United States and his suspicions about US motives in calling the Pan-American Conference in Washington that year.[41] The first Pan-American meeting was held in 1889 and Argentina began as she was to continue, with her diplomats opposing US schemes for closer hemispheric links. Since that time, Argentina has, at subsequent meetings, consistently questioned US intervention in Latin America, sought in particular to prevent closer cooperation between the US and Brazil and stimulated opposition to US policies amongst other Latin American nations.

This antagonism to the United States is not simply explicable by reference to Argentina's close relations with Europe and especially Great Britain, to her traditional economic rivalry with the United States, to envy of US international economic (and indeed political) success, nor to US use of various measures to protect her markets against Argentine penetration. Argentina also sought to remain independent of her most important trading partner, refusing to give exclusive trade and tariff concessions to Britain in the period 1881–1929.[42] Internationalism cannot explain many of Argentina's foreign policy manoeuvres. Nationalism with imperialist overtones, which must be seen as deriving in part from the European stream of influence, since Argentina's view of her fitness for regional leadership rested substantially on her greater Europeanness, may in part do so. The greatest Argentine contribution to international diplomacy at the beginning of the twentieth century – the Drago Doctrine – illustrates anti-European nationalism seeking US support against European hostility.

There is much dispute concerning the quality of, and reasons for, the changes which have occurred in Argentine nationalism during the twentieth century. Some resentment of foreign capital involvement, and particularly British ownership of the bulk of the Argentine railways, was expressed in the last decade of the nineteenth and the first decade of the twentieth century. There was also growing opposition to immigration, primarily amongst elite elements in the years before the First World War. However, it is broadly agreed that the 1920s and the Great Depression constitute a watershed in nationalist development. Yrigoyen's election in 1916 is frequently seen as the emergence of a more nationalistic regime than the oligarchic governments that preceded it. His policy of neutrality during the First World War had considerable popular support even after the United States and many other Latin American republics had either entered the war or at least broken off diplomatic relations with Germany. Although it could be argued that Argentina, with her various European immigrant communities, would have found it difficult to take part in the war and that Britain needed Argentine neutrality to ensure her food supplies, neutrality is usually seen as evidence of Argentina's determination to remain independent. The isolationism of Yrigoyen's first presidency is further emphasised by his precipitate withdrawal from the League of Nations in 1920. Nevertheless, the nationalist quality of Radical government was limited in comparison with the new forms of nationalism which emerged from the period of Radicalism. It took a moderate, largely rhetorical form, only producing concrete actions against foreign-owned railways, for example, at election times.[43] Radical nationalism lacked a full economic aspect since Radical aspirations rested on retention of the existing economic structure relying on agrarian exports to Europe. Although national resources, such as oil, were seen as requiring protection, international trade remained the means by which Argentine greatness was to be achieved. Nevertheless cultural nationalism formed part of provincial electoral politics for the UCR, as it did for their conservative opponents too.[44]

The 1910s and 1920s saw the first important stage in the development of what has been termed 'modern', 'dynamic' or 'integral' nationalism.[45] Labour unrest 1909–10 inspired retaliatory violence by student and paramilitary groups during the May 1910 centennial celebrations. This constituted the first elite resonse to the perceived immigrant threat to order in the form of the existing social structure. But more extensive polarisation of Argentine society occurred in consequence of the unrest of Tragic Week in May 1919, which left 700 dead and 4000 injured. Dolkart sees this as heralding the end of the 'liberal consensus' in Argentina. The formation of the Liga Patriótica Argentina (LPA) in early 1919 expressed the schism developing within the elite between liberal and nationalist elements. Although the LPA was not itself anti-liberal in policy initially, being primarily anti-worker and pro-order, it became more opposed to Yrigoyenist 'demogoguery' in time. Strands within the LPA were more extreme, containing anti-semitic and corporatist elements. Hence the LPA laid the foundations for more aggressively nationalist groupings to follow.[46]

To cultural nostalgia and the emphasis on national independence shared by all groups was added anti-liberalism and a concern for economic independence and development, which brought nationalism into direct conflict with the internationalist perspective. This new form of nationalism had internal sources deriving from the Iberian legacy and expressed in the nineteenth century by the isolationism of the Rosas era. But at the same time both Hispanic and non-Hispanic external intellectual currents contributed to its development. The late 1920s in Europe saw widespread disillusionment with political parties and representative democracy which appealed to elements in Argentina for whom semi-legitimate democratic structures had produced an unacceptable elected government. Anti-democratic examples in nations with close cultural connections with Argentina, such as those of General Miguel Primo de Rivera in Spain, and Mussolini in Italy, encouraged such disillusionment.

Nationalism with strong economic overtones had been evident as early as the 1870s and 1880s when some individuals and organisations began calling for tariff protection.[47] However, economic nationalism did not become influential until after the First World War when intimations of economic vulnerability converted some disillusioned intellectuals from their cultural nationalist orientation to a wider nationalism emphasising economic independence. The disruption of trade during the war years had promoted the desire for self-sufficiency and, in the 1920s, 'petroleum nationalism gained widespread political support as well as ideological currency'.[48] Development was seen as desirable and external dependence as an obstacle to it. Though beginning among upper-class intellectuals this new nationalism attracted support from other sectors. Young members of provincial elites saw in it a means to raise their status in relation to that of their more Europeanised counterparts in Buenos Aires. Likewise elite elements, seeing their political power undermined by the integration of the middle class and the apparently unbeatable electoral strength of the Radicals, believed that a restoration of elite rule ensured by force had become necessary. Finally, and perhaps most importantly, the new form of nationalism was one with great appeal for officers of the armed forces, especially the younger elements. Whilst cultural nationalism is generally the prerogative of civilians, economic nationalism is associated with both military and civilian groups. The experience of the First World War, and the consequent effect on Argentina's capacity to import the things she required, made the armed forces very aware of the problems they would face in acquiring *matériel* if they were actively involved in a war. Military emphasis on self-sufficiency began, therefore, in the 1920s.

This form of economic nationalism characterised the attitudes of many who supported the 1930 coup. Indeed, Uriburu took up the cause of the right-wing Catholic nationalist groups like the Liga Republicana. There is some debate concerning how far the effects of the Depression could be felt prior to Uriburu's coup, but, as Rock points out, declining agricultural prices on the world market and reduced levels of exports had resulted in an increasing balance of payments deficit throughout 1929. The withdrawal of US investment had exacerbated the situation as had the failure of the 1929–30 harvest, rising urban unemployment and cost of living.[49] The full effects felt after the coup merely contributed further to the spread of economic nationalism, and to increased disillusionment with representative popular government. (Some such nationalists still retained liberal elements in their policies, favouring a non-interventionist state, for example. Criticisms of labour organisation and activity were still couched in terms of *laissez-faire* economics.) However the internationalist perspective was too firmly established simply to disappear with the economic problems resulting from the Depression, and Uriburu's brief regime was a contest between what has been variously termed the 'new right' or 'right-wing nationalism', and the 'old right' or 'conservative liberalism', which had found a temporary coincidence of interests in opposing Yrigoyen's abuses of constitutional procedures.[50] The economic crisis at the same time enhanced disillusionment with capitalism and strengthened left-wing nationalism. This form of anti-liberalism is by no means easily distinguishable from the right-wing form, but tended to stress popular representation if not independent participation and the need for major social and political change. Some politically excluded middle-class elements embraced this form of nationalism. But in addition it spread further down the class structure as declining agricultural prices led to the displacement of rural workers, massive internal migration and the growth of urban shanty towns. Although in 1932 the nationalist orientation of Uriburu gave way to a conservative restoration which again placed government in the hands of the primarily European-oriented agro-export elite, nationalism in both its right- and left-wing forms continued to develop.

Both right- and left-wing nationalism saw Justo's acquisition of power as a return to the old, dependent politics. Both schools of thought were affronted by the apparent sell-out to foreign interests and especially the Roca–Runciman Pact of 1933 which spurred resentment of Britain. They were also alienated by the fraud and corruption of the Concordancia. The means of preserving the existing system were in effect generating forces opposed to its continuation. External events influenced both forms of nationalism too. The 'disastrous' experiment with republican government in Spain encouraged right-wing nationalism, whilst the 'success' of the first Five Year Plan in the Soviet Union contributed to leftist nationalism. But some left-wing nationalist groups were not inherently authoritarian. Young Radical intellectuals such as Luis Dellepiane, Arturo Jauretche and Raúl Scalabrini Ortiz set up Fuerza de Orientación de la Joven Argentina (FORJA) in 1935. FORJA combined belief in a popularly-elected government with economic nationalism. From a combination of such thought with other forms of nationalism, though more by accident than design, Peronism would emerge in due course.[51]

Although nationalist groups were never very powerful in the direct sense, because there were many of them with varying ideologies, small memberships and fragmented structures, nationalism itself was a potent indirect force during the successive internationalist regimes of the Infamous Decade. In a period in which liberal values were generally in decline and internationalist governments perched on very narrow support bases sought to remain in power, elements of domestic policy increasingly reflected not only authoritarian attitudes but also nationalism, expressing the continuing liberal and conservative tendencies within the elite itself. For example, the 1930s saw restrictions on public assembly and academic purges, as well as new immigration laws passed in 1932. Nationalist influence was especially marked in the sphere of foreign policy. Argentina backed Paraguay in the war with Bolivia, which was backed by Chile. She took part in regional conferences throughout the period, but failed to ratify most of the treaties and conventions which emerged from such gatherings. Her assertion of an independent foreign policy is most marked in her determination to remain neutral during the Second World War. Indeed a frequently cited explanation of the GOU coup in 1943 is the threat to this neutrality presented by the relatively pro-nationalist President Castillo's choice of Robustiano Patrón Costas as his successor.

As the United States perceived the growing totalitarian threat in Europe, she sought to develop the inter-American system. Argentina emphasised her traditional relationships outside the hemisphere and asserted her preference for neutrality. Whilst Pearl Harbor brought an immediate pro-US response from most of Latin America, Argentina merely accorded the United States non-belligerent status and remained the only Latin American state unwilling to reach a bilateral defence agreement with the United States during the Second World War. Despite pressures from the United States, she did not feel compelled to adjust her foreign policy, and indeed US Under-secretary of State Sumner Welles suggested that such pressures actually strengthened the GOU government.[52] Her independence of the United States was further asserted by Perón in a speech made in June 1944 in which he stated that whoever won the war was of no consequence to Argentina, provided that her government was sovereign over her national territory. When Argentina finally declared war on the Axis powers in January 1945, it was in order to ensure that she was not later excluded from the United Nations. Argentine neutrality was seen by the United States as reflecting the growth of fascism under the military government which had come to power in 1943. In fact, domestic right-wing nationalist groups were dissolved in 1944 (though exactly who took this action and the reasons for it remain contentious) and neutrality must be seen as having roots in the long-standing nationalist aspect of Argentine political history.

Despite the opposition of most right-wing nationalists to the social reforms and mass electoral base of Peronism, its appeal to working-class voters is frequently seen as a product of Perón's authentically Argentine image. However, the electoral consolidation of Peronism in February 1946 did not result in a new attitude to international relations, except in so far as it sought new relations outside the hemisphere to supplement the declining international position of Britain. Perón's Third Position made explicit the quest for national autonomy which had been a characteristic of Argentine foreign policy from the outset. It was officially an attempt to steer a uniquely Argentine course between the unbridled individualism of capitalism and the state collectivism of communism. In practice, Perón did not seek to leave the capitalist camp; internationalism remained a potent mode of thought and he reserved his fiercest ideological criticisms for communism. Nevertheless, the Third Position gave a philosophical base to a pragmatic foreign policy designed to achieve the best possible bargaining position for Argentina as the superpowers lined up their supporters at the beginning of the Cold War.

Rock's contention that Perón was a 'reluctant nationalist' whose behaviour was determined by domestic political constraints[53] appears to be borne out by the fact that his initial overt opposition to the United States gave way to 'intermittent conciliation for limited objectives',[54] and then, in his second term of office (1952–5), to vacillation between an integral nationalist and a kind of liberal internationalist economic policy. But this vacillation reflected Argentina's declining economic position and the consequent increasing

influence of an alternative cultural legacy. It enabled the
temporary unification of differently oriented military factions
which resulted in Perón's displacement. However, in his early
years in power, whilst the economic benefits of Argentina's
wartime neutrality lasted, the nationalist aspect of his foreign
policy was marked. Argentina asserted her independence of
the developing schism between the superpowers in a number
of ways. Perón established diplomatic relations with the Soviet
Union as early as June 1946 but continued to negotiate for
US military *matériel*. He refused to assist the United States
in isolating Franco's Spain in 1947.[55] In the same year,
Argentina agreed to take part in the Rio Conference and
the Rio Treaty which resulted from it, but Perón refused
to ratify the treaty until 1950. Even then Argentina did
not fall willingly into line with the United States and
abstained (along with Mexico) in the vote taken at the Tenth
Inter-American Conference in Caracas in 1954 which sought
to make communist infiltration a premise for the application
of the Rio Treaty. Argentina simultaneously sought to boost
her international standing by her independent line in foreign
affairs and through national development. Her foreign minister, J.A. Bramuglia, as President of the UN Security Council,
mediated between the United States and the Soviet Union in
the Berlin Crisis in December 1948. Argentina began her own
nuclear programme in 1950 when Perón created a national
commission for the purpose of developing atomic energy.[56]
But the increased international prestige Perón had hoped
for was not forthcoming and, when he left office in 1955,
a few months after the birth of the Non-Aligned Movement
at Bandung, Argentina's Third Position had left her largely
isolated. The military governments which followed were left
to re-establish international relations and did so with a clear
orientation to the West which had been strengthened by the
experience of Peronism.

Although Gerassi argues that Perón used right-wing
nationalism in his ascent to power and then effectively
destroyed it, he was ousted by a conjunction of forces
led by right-wing anti-liberals. The Lonardi government
was plagued, as Uriburu's had been, by the split between
the nationalist and liberal right. The latter faction emerged
as dominant, as it had in 1932, but it assumed a relatively

liberal form modified by the inherent nationalism of all political groups. Aramburu's dilemma was how to expunge the influence of Perón without appearing a traitor to his country. The liberal/anti-liberal division characterised the political parties as well as the military institution during the Aramburu government.

More overtly nationalist thought re-emerged with the election of President Frondizi in 1958. Frondizi's foreign policy was broadly neutralist, though domestic military pressure and economic necessity forced him to seek an accommodation with the United States. This was in spite of his rhetoric prior to gaining power, which included advocating Argentine non-adherence to the Rio Treaty. Despite believing that Argentine development rested on close relations with the West, and more specifically on US investment, Frondizi wished to preserve Argentina's independence in her international relations. To this end he accepted a loan from the Soviet Union in 1959, resisted US plans to make OAS sanctions on Cuba compulsory, and offered to mediate between the United States and Cuba during the Missile Crisis (this offer was rejected by both sides). Besides touring Latin America in an effort to win support for Argentine opposition to US intervention, Frondizi also visited extra-hemispheric developing nations, including India, emphasising Argentine neutrality.

Although Frondizi's failure to confront the increasingly left-wing and nationalist Peronists at home, and his refusal to comply with US policy to defeat the Left abroad, led the military to overthrow him, the nationalist perspective was merely temporarily concealed and regained ascendancy during the 1965–66 Dominican Crisis. President Illia initially sought to mediate in the crisis, but found himself subject to the pressures of strong domestic political opposition to US intervention in Latin America. The rare spectacle of comparative congressional consensus was achieved through the pervasive quality of nationalist feeling. Conservatives expressed their concern, Peronist deputies demanded the withdrawal of US forces, and the Socialists held that Argentina should leave the OAS in protest. Although the Socialists did not achieve their aim, Argentina did abstain in most votes on the issue.[57] However, contrary pressures were also at work. The dominant military factions opposed resistance to US policy and were soon to get their way as General Onganía supplanted Illia in June 1966.

The armed forces by definition have a nationalist role in defending the nation and when assuming political power they are asserting their capacity to realise the national destiny. Thus despite military internationalist thought, nationalism remains, especially so where a civilian nationalist political culture coexists with an internationalist perspective temporarily in the ascendancy. Thus Onganía's government could not steer a straightforward course favouring international economic and military linkages. Export earnings were limited, controls on new foreign investments tightened, the activities of foreign banks restricted and some foreign-owned firms nationalised. 'Plan Europa' sought to establish a domestic weapons production industry.[58] The dominant mode of thought amongst officers is also subject to change as factions shift and political options change. Such was the position by 1970 when Onganía's broadly pro-Western orientation had clearly failed to establish political order and economic development. Both during the brief presidency of the virtually unknown General Levingston (1970–71) and under General Lanusse (1971–73), the military sought a breathing space in which to achieve a more dignified and less absolute abdication of their political role. To do so, a change of orientation was necessary and nationalism became more overt.

Under Cámpora, Argentina joined other Latin American nations seeking to restructure the inter-American system and revise the Rio Treaty through the OAS. By the beginning of 1974, Argentina was making overtures to Cuba on trade. The return of Perón himself as president and his succession by his widow increased further the strength of Argentina's relations with developing nations outside the region and with the Soviet Bloc. Association with the Non-Aligned Movement was a means of counteracting feelings of lost status and powerlessness. This was also reflected in attempts to increase interest and pride in Argentina herself by means of such crude devices as Presidential Decree No. 587 in late 1973 which sought to ensure that at least half of published daily news was domestic.[59]

The military regime which replaced Isabel Perón in 1976 is perhaps the clearest example of changing security perceptions as a consequence of domestic political expediency which Ferrer colourfully describes as 'the unpredictability of an unconstitutional regime which one day serves the interest of American policy in Central America and the next is at war with NATO'.[60] To see the Falklands invasion as an anomalous act by a pro-Western military regime would be to misunderstand the strength of integral nationalism in Argentina. The two perceptions coexist and slight changes in the balance of these alternative orientations result in apparently major foreign policy oscillations. The 1976–83 military regime exhibited nationalism from the outset, but only when the conditions under which monetarist policies could appear to work disappeared did the necessary domestic pressures cause a change of emphasis. The officers who had won the support of many within the Reagan Administration never conceded their independence of action. For example in 1979 Argentina and the Soviet Union exchanged military delegations and in 1980 the Atomic Energy Commission sent a mission to the Soviet Union and succeeded in obtaining supplies of heavy water despite US opposition. Further contracts for nuclear services and supplies were signed in 1982. The need for a military regime espousing monetarist policies and seeking civilian austerity to justify its political position and economic cost was a more immediate consideration than the wishes of the United States, and Argentina's territorial disputes during the period, with Chile over the Beagle Channel and with Britain over the Falklands, must be seen in this light.

Although geopolitical considerations, especially access to Antarctica, have been suggested as factors for the Falklands invasion they were more a justification than a motive. The need for a regime suffering an unprecedented level of civilian criticism to distract popular attention from domestic problems remains the most likely explanation of the invasion and the use of a nationalist *cause célèbre* for this purpose seems an obvious tactic in retrospect. The Falklands dispute may be seen in terms of a continuing quest for national greatness. General Galtieri's seeking of US assistance by means of a warning to Alexander Haig that he had received offers of weaponry and personnel from non-Western sources such as Cuba reflects the strength of integral nationalism and the pragmatic use of an independent international position.[61]

NATIONALISM: DEPENDENCY

Domestic economic pressures have long provided a key to an understanding of changing emphasis on nationalist and internationalist perceptions in Argentina. Certainly they have led to the refinement of nationalist thought and to its increasing emphasis on dependency as an explanation of relative economic failure. It may be true that the slow process of the transfer of Argentine economic 'dependence' from Great Britain to the United States contributed to the questioning of that relationship, since the US economy was essentially competitive with that of Argentina. However, it is the sudden undermining of economic security as a consequence of the effects of the Great Depression which has pervaded economic nationalism since the 1930s. The myth of national greatness and economic prosperity, born out of the long and profitable trading relationship with Britain, was so abruptly destroyed that the whole tone of developing economic nationalism was altered. Economic nationalism prior to 1929 had recognised the state as the prime mover in the development process and domestic capital as the means by which development could be achieved. These attitudes were reflected in actions such as the establishment of YPF. However, economic nationalists at that stage saw such measures as complementing continued benefits from agrarian exports and most did not question the economic system's basis on comparative advantage. With the ending of free trade and the growth of protectionism, the primary export-based economy began to look precarious, subject to the whims of the world market and climatic factors. The declining availability of imports further contributed to a sense of economic vulnerability to external factors. The unpredictability of foreign capital inflow and external markets, and the affront to national pride consequent upon the foreign ownership of key industrial areas and utilities, gave rise to nationalist developmentalism reflected most clearly in the economic policies of Perón. This attitude was, however, so well-developed that post-Perón pro-Western orientated governments, despite some of them opening Argentina up further to foreign capital and multinational penetration, could not totally abandon developmentalist rhetoric or structures. For example, the state monopoly of agricultural marketing (IAPI), established by Perón though in accord with more limited earlier precedents, was not dismantled until 1976.

The light industrialisation of the early Perón era found theoretical expression in the structuralist economic explanations expounded by ECLA soon after its establishment in 1948. Stressing that industry was needed to generate foreign exchange as well as domestic investment, structuralism appealed to urban industrialists and nationalists in Argentina and Latin America generally. Economic nationalism was modified and strengthened by the two decades of stop–go economic activity, accompanied by spiralling inflation, which followed the Second World War. The extent of apparent Argentine economic vulnerability and indebtedness undermined the vision of national greatness established by the early twentieth century, when the nation was ranked alongside Canada and Australia in terms of both actual levels of and potential for development. Thus with the late 1950s, early 1960s crisis of import-substitution-industrialisation, an external explanation for this economic failure was sought and found in the concept of dependency, a leftist, though not necessarily Marxist critique of structuralism. It is no coincidence that much of the literature on dependency concerns itself with the Argentine case and that Argentines played a leading role in developing the concept.

Despite its very recent development, dependency theory has been retrospectively applied to the economic structure of Argentina both during the colonial era and throughout the national period. The role of nineteenth-century imperialism, for example, is seen as strengthening mercantile capitalism without promoting the growth of industry. The needs of the metropolis, Europe and especially Great Britain, are thought to have enabled the emergence of a European-oriented national bourgeoisie and encouraged the extreme levels of specialisation which led Argentina to become vulnerable to the vagaries of the international market. Indeed it is argued that by 1890, Argentina already had such a dependent economy that she was the worst hit of all the Latin American nations in consequence of the temporary slump which made itself felt in that year. Latin America in the nineteenth century is seen as lacking economic autonomy rather than political independence, in the sense of a limited capacity for taking independent economic action in relation to other international powers.

Clearly Argentine vulnerability and lack of autonomy is recognised as surfacing in the 1930s, having been largely hidden during most of the period of oligarchic domination and much of the Radical era. However it was the 1950s and 1960s development of multinational corporations and expansion of the international private financial system that produced in Argentina effects which spurred the development of structuralist and dependency explanations of the stagnating economy. These explanations offered the consolation of placing the blame for the national predicament elsewhere, i.e. with the Western industrialised nations. Argentina's need for international financial assistance has encouraged the development of integral nationalism for two main reasons. First, measures adopted in response to trade disequilibria 'necessitating' IMF assistance have reduced the industrial base as well as causing a massive decline in working-class living standards, most notably under the 1976–83 military government. Secondly IMF insistence on the adoption of such measures in return for aid has been seen as an affront to national sovereignty. The free flow of foreign capital into Argentina increased the foreign debt fourfold under the last military regime, and in 1984 it stood at US$48.5 billion. To service such a debt would require 60 per cent of Argentina's foreign exchange earnings, an impossible figure to meet without fundamental changes in the way Argentina conducts her economic affairs.

Argentine pride and the view that Argentina's potential greatness has been blocked by external factors have made dependency easy to accept as an explanation of national failure and frustrated aspirations. However, the acceptance of imperialism and dependency is frequently, though by no means always, defeatist, and reflects an endemic fatalism which pervades all aspects of Argentine life, not only attitudes to economic matters. Dependency theory under-estimates the importance of other factors, including culture. It sees Argentina as essentially weak and accords to the metro-politan powers, especially Britain, unchallengeable strength and uncanny foresight. Conil Paz and Ferrari write of this:

> Apart from being false and discouraging, such interpret-ation is nothing more than a timid attempt to cover, with a pious veil, the Argentine incompetence to resolve their most important problems. Such an approach can denote only the 'transference of faults', or the alienation of national problems and possibilities.[62]

The emphasis on one side as the driving force of the trading relationship between nations of the supposed 'periphery', such as Argentina, and those of the 'metropolis', such as Britain, which characterises much of imperialist and dependency theory, distorts reality. The contribution of primary exporters like Argentina to the establishment of the international economic system in the nineteenth century was as important as developments in European industry. Indeed, more flexible proponents of imperialist theory emphasise the importance of the collaboration of sectors within imperialised society. For them a process of negotiation, not imposed integration, is the source of an unequal economic relationship. With the value of Argentine exports increasing sixfold between 1880 and 1910, virtually the whole economic elite became committed to the primary export economy and this economic model became so widespread that few sectors questioned it until after 1930. This model cannot simply be seen as externally created and imposed, since it was in accord both with Hispanic economic values and attitudes which do not encourage the development of industry and with the availability of raw materials in Argentina. The nation's primary resource was the land. It was a combination of culture, availability of other raw materials and domestic decision-making as well as the question of chronology which resulted in the more impressive development of the United States, for example. In the early nineteenth century, US involvement in the international economic system had been that of a primary producer and exporter, and an importer of manufactured goods and foreign investment, just as Argentina's was to become from the late nineteenth century onwards.

The weakness of demand-side dominated economic explanations may also be illustrated by the selection of industrial products for reasons of national prestige. If demand were the main imperative, industrialisation policies should concentrate on low-cost industries where market opportunities already exist. Instead, for politico-cultural reasons national self-sufficiency has been sought in products with high fixed costs and relatively small national and/or congested international markets. For example, in the late 1960s, Argentina's costs for parts and materials for car production were 3.3 times as high as those of the United States. The same problem is illustrated in Argentina's recent attempts to develop a 'low-cost' car. Her version was expected to retail at between US$4000–5000 compared with Brazil's model which sells for US$2500.[63]

Unlike the weaker 'enclave' economies of some of the smaller Latin American nations where local elites were insufficiently developed and powerful to assert themselves against external forces, Cardoso and Faletto see Argentina (along with Mexico, Chile, Colombia and Brazil) as having, at least by the 1950s, the potential for autonomous development.[64] But, in fact, Argentina achieved such a position long before the mid-twentieth century. By the end of the nineteenth century, Argentina, like Canada and Australia, was sufficiently developed to ensure her integration into the world economy and to generate some economic diversification. All three nations would have been difficult to fit into either of the two poles of the dependency model; they were neither metropolitan nor clearly peripheral. Indeed, by the 1920s their living standards were more like those of the advanced capitalist countries of Europe than of other primary producers. As Waisman notes:

> ... the division of the world economy into center and periphery is too simple to account for empirical variation because there are different kinds of peripheries.[65]

Indeed dependency theory offers no explanation for the economic achievements of some apparently peripheral regions. Historically, one such example has been Japan. Though dependency theorists suggest that Japanese development points up her 'unsatellized' situation as more important than her relative impoverishment in terms of resources, Japan does not support their case. It was precisely foreign interference by the United States in 1853 which led to the Meiji Restoration and the development of modern industrial society. More recent economic growth in East Asia has also been a problem for dependency theory, especially so since Korea and Taiwan have experienced some limited improvement in income distribution to accompany this growth.

Comparisons of the relative economic achievements of Argentina, Canada, and Australia, further suggest weaknesses in the dependency model. For example, Canada's level of foreign economic penetration appears to have greatly exceeded that of Argentina. From 1914 to 1931 the level of foreign investment in Canada rose by 71 per cent compared to Argentina's 15 per cent for the same period. During the 1920s, the inflow of foreign capital was much more important to Canada. In addition, US involvement there was clearly much more extensive.[66] However, differential access to raw materials and foreign markets, as well as cultural features and domestic economic decisions have all contributed to Canada's much more impressive economic performance since the 1930s. Likewise, Argentina experienced fewer budgetary problems and lower debt service charges proportionate to the value of her exports than did either Canada or Australia during the 1930s. Australia suffered much more from the effects of the Depression since she experienced them on top of the effects of a domestic slump which had begun in 1927. Argentina was less hit by unemployment and the losses of her railways, being privately owned, did not constitute a cost to the national government. By 1934, Argentina was the only South American nation to have met her debts in full without dispute throughout the Depression. For Australia, servicing debts was much more problematic in consequence of national over-borrowing in the 1920s. Canada was better placed than Australia, though the Province of Alberta reluctantly defaulted in 1936.[67]

Similarly the assumption that the economic strength of the metropolis causes the economic weakness of Latin America is questionable. Inequality in trading relationships is the result, not the cause, of the respective strengths of the parties. In any case the 'metropolitan' capacity to penetrate Latin America has been seriously weakened during the twentieth century. The two world wars may be seen as weakening specifically the European role in Latin America, rather than dependency generally, although the expansion of Argentina's industrial base and the growth of economic nationalism suggest that in her case the effects of the wars were increased potential for autonomous economic action and a re-emergence of national assertiveness. Even if the view is taken that the world wars did not reduce dependency but rather contributed to the decline of European influence as the US role in Latin America increased, it must be recognised that the US role is now declining and Europe assuming an increasingly independent position within the Atlantic Alliance. It cannot be argued that in consequence Latin America will be subject to a renewed European imperialisation process, given Europe's continuing preference for close economic relationships within the Community, although Argentina has succeeded in retaining a higher proportion of her trade with the EC nations than other Latin American republics. Latin America generally enjoyed spectacular rates of economic growth during the 1960s and 1970s which were sustained by high rates of investment financed during the 1960s mainly by domestic capital. That foreign loans were sought was a domestic decision supported by Latin American economic nationalism which saw economic sovereignty as less threatened by such loans than by multinational encroachment.

Argentina's level of indebtedness may be seen by some as a threat to her economic sovereignty, but she does still have the capacity to continue to assert her independence, for example through her affiliation to the Non-Aligned Movement and her trade with non-Western powers. Indeed authors like Ferrer see Argentina as having great economic advantages and place the onus on the various sectors of Argentine society to work together to resolve the economic problems which beset the nation. Her relatively high average earnings, surplus of foodstuffs, virtual self-sufficiency in energy and comparatively low import needs suggest that national consensus on a new development strategy is what Argentina lacks. An economically unstable Argentina is of no use to external investors and they do not constitute the greatest threat to her autonomous economic growth. Confidence must be restored domestically in order to reduce interest rates and sustain an accord on the division of the national cake amongst the various sectoral interests. Though isolation from the world economy is impossible, as Argentina needs markets like every other interdependent trading nation, the resources for economic recovery are available within the national economy. She has spare industrial capacity and human resources and with the political cooperation of the disparate sectors, especially powerful pressure groups like the armed forces and high income elements, her government could in theory renegotiate loans, increase tax revenues, control imports and adopt such other measures, including further cuts in defence spending, as might prove necessary without severe reductions in living standards.

NATIONALISM: ITS FATALISTIC QUALITY

In a sense the idea of Argentina as a victim characterises both internationalist and nationalist thought, though in different ways. Internationalism carries with it the implicit assumption that Argentina is not strong enough to act autonomously and should tie herself ideologically to more powerful nations who can offer her protection and development. However, fatalism and pessimism have tended to be particularly associated with nationalist thought, growing in consequence of the end of the outward-oriented economic development in the era before 1930, and characterising those nationalist elements which might theoretically be expected to be most assertive and optimistic regarding the possibilities of an emerging developing nation. The restoration of confidence which Ferrer sees as necessary to autonomous development is precisely the feature hardest hit by the pervasive pessimism reflected in official economic figures, for example. As Wynia points out,

> Argentines take a perverse pleasure in their pessimism, always reminding each other how bad things are and how much worse they are bound to get.[68]

Pessimism was not the result of a simple transfer of Hispanic values during the colonial era which persisted despite the national experience. Rather such values were reinforced by national history and by the interaction of the influences of Iberian and European culture. The harsh isolated frontier experience could offer reinforcement to such beliefs, just as in North America it served to reinforce the opposite pre-existing attitudes by confirming Man's capacity to resist and control his environment. Sarmiento takes this view in suggesting that the insecurity of life in the early national period gave rise to a stoical acceptance of whatever might occur.[69] Economic and political factors have served as further reinforcements. Argentina's economic failure is so obvious given her apparent advantages, her temperate climate, her fertile soil, her high literacy and 'Europeanness', that some force must clearly have been acting against her interests and she exhibits

> ... a morose fatalism that depicts the country as an earthly paradise weighed down by some terrible suicidal curse ... [70]

In addition, the North American example is a slap in the face for Argentine pride, as is the status the nation once enjoyed as an economic outpost of Europe. Argentina feels herself to be in decline, having experienced a relatively recent period of prosperity and progress. Whether her past greatness be memory or myth, the future seems less bright. Blaming those external forces which gave once, but failed to maintain, the perception of national economic greatness is understandable, if unconstructive. Likewise the influence of European political models may be seen in a similar vein. The need for a constitutional façade shows the extent of their acceptance as an ideal. The failure to achieve this ideal, especially when the nation had apparently come so close to doing so with the electoral reform of 1912 and the election of Yrigoyen in 1916, leads to political defeatism and pessimism. This failure is in itself a double-edged sword. Not only does the fact of non-fulfilment give rise to pessimism, but in addition the operation of the alternative, non-electoral political system has an arbitrary quality which encourages a fatalistic attitude to the use of power.

Fatalism may not be entirely negative in its effects. It can be accompanied by an optimistic belief in good luck, as in the passion for lotteries, which has a very long history in Argentina. Indeed, Fillol sees fatalism as a source of confidence and optimism in Argentina since it suggests that a successful future may be given by God. However, he adds that such a belief saps the will to earn success. Human impotence in the face of unpredictable external events leads to the desire to remain uninvolved and to a lack of personal initiative and cooperation. The tendency then is to live in the present, not to plan for the future, as this remains beyond the individual's control:

> ... great success is obtained by waiting, by hoping, by the favour of the saints, or by luck – not primarily by thrift, work, and enterprise ... Where everything depends on the inevitability of future events, upon luck, or upon divine intervention, there is no need for active community enterprise.[71]

It has been suggested that the positive, optimistic appeal of gambling makes revolutions, which are tantamount to political lotteries, attractive to Latin Americans. This emphasises the wrong aspect of fatalism as a contributory factor to political instability. It is rather the negative aspect, 'la pareza criollo' in Bunge's terminology,[72] which is important. The positive side of fatalism may emerge when someone with emotional appeal appears who is believed to have the power to work the miracles that will resolve national problems, and such a figure was Perón, for some sectors at least. Nevertheless, it is more often in the form of resigned passivity that fatalism influences political stability. Most Argentines have certainly believed in the past that governments were fairly powerless to control events. They have accepted inefficiency and poor services. When such civilian government weaknesses have been used by military factions as reasons for their intervention in the political process, this has been met by passive resignation amongst the majority of the population. It is to be hoped that Jacobo Timerman's optimism that this trait has diminished since Alfonsín took power is not premature.[73]

NATIONALISM: ITS QUONDAM CHARACTER

As with fatalism, the tendency to look backward rather than to the future is associated with both internationalism and nationalism. This 'quondam orientation' is a generalised tendency rather than the specific quality suggested by Rodolfo Terragno (now Minister of Public Works in the Alfonsín government), who writes:

> No one could possibly imagine groups of Englishmen fighting each other in 1983 over Gladstone or Disraeli, or North Americans reviving the hatreds of the Civil War. Yet Argentines are capable of keeping alive the bitter confrontation between *rosistas* and *antirosistas* ... of prolonging the nineteenth-century debate between Federalists and Unitarists.[74]

Such a statement is inaccurate on two counts. First, it is selective in the opposing examples used and thus avoids mentioning the capacity of Irishmen to dwell on the outcome of the Battle of the Boyne, for example. Secondly, it exaggerates the emphasis on one specific period of conflict.

Internationalist thought emphasises its heyday in the late nineteenth and early twentieth century as the Belle Epoque of Argentine development and tends to see the period 1930–43 as the last era of sensible government. That the periods of internationalist ascendancy since then should be largely ignored in retrospect is a recognition of their explicit cultural impurity. The association of *de facto* non-electoral regimes with internationalism is in itself a negation of the European-oriented stream of influence. The content may have been internationalist, but the mode Iberian. However, the emphasis on Argentina's historical experience is much more clearly associated with nationalist thought because the past provides an image of the elusive national identity which nationalists would seek to protect and develop. Nationalist thought burgeoned from the insecurity of the post-First World War era and in consequence emphasised the past as the only source of security available. It was the failure of internationalism which was associated with modernity and Europeanness which promoted the greater introspection of quondam nationalism.

The quondam characteristic of aspects of Argentine nationalism is evident, with street names in Buenos Aires emphasising historic victories, such as Reconquista and Defensa. In state schoolrooms, paintings of national heroes adorn the walls and textbooks tell in cartoons the story of San Martín's ride across the Andes. However this 'obsession with the past'[75] precedes the growth of integral nationalism in the second and third decades of the twentieth century, which was accompanied by new trends in Argentine historiography. It has also been partial and rather more selective than the term 'obsession' suggests. Rosas's title 'Restorer of Laws', for example, may have implied a return to the hierarchical order and Hispanic values of the pre-revolutionary period, but his rule did not imply an enclave society or expulsion of European interests. As the military was professionalised, it was sympathetic to the emphasis on tradition of the European missions which assisted in the process. It saw the past as preferable to the present, and justified political intervention in such terms. Thus 1943 has been termed a 'gauchesque reaction',[76] and indeed on this particular occasion the intervention may be seen as the Iberian mode challenging the much-abused and only semi-legitimate European cultural stream. But from that time, historical precedent and justification became more complex.

Blanksten terms Perón's supporters the 'Quondam Faithful', and Kirkpatrick found her Peronist respondents to be much more willing to make comparisons with the past than to predict the future.[77] Nevertheless Perón's historical allusions and attempts to place his movement in a national historical context were much more confused and uncertain than this implies. Perón certainly evoked the memory of San Martín and of *Martín Fierro* (a copy of which he had been given by his father on the occasion of his graduation from the Colegio Militar in 1913).[78] But, despite Evita's likening of the Avellaneda meatpackers to the *gauchos*, he did not condemn the nineteenth-century liberals and cite Rosas as a mentor until long after, during his exile in Spain, at a time when a return to power seemed unlikely. In fact he identified himself with the opponents of Rosas by renaming the railway lines radiating out from Buenos Aires after Urquiza, Mitre, Sarmiento and Roca, and by likening the 1946 electoral victory to Caseros. Despite dealing a blow to the idealised image of 'old families and polo and romance down at the *estancia*',[79] he moved cautiously against agrarian interests and avoided direct confrontation with European-derived attitudes.

NATIONALISM IN HISTORIOGRAPHY AND BEYOND

Nineteenth-century Argentine nationalism changed its orientation as the century progressed. It was initially aimed at Spain, then later at the neighbouring states of Brazil, Paraguay and Chile as relationships deteriorated. Towards the end of the century resentment against the United States increased as economic and political rivalry intensified. This changing pattern is evident in historical writings and literature, and it indicates the absence of one clear national identity.

Thus, after 1830, the first major historiographical trend was to blame Spanish colonialism for Argentina's post-independence problems. This interpretation was found in the works of writers under European influence such as Sarmiento, Echeverría and other members of Joven Argentina. These writers established a tradition of seeing Rosas as wholly evil; as a dictator exploiting the rural masses to achieve personal power. That they should have interpreted the role of Rosas in this way reflects their association with the Unitarian cause, the fact that 'History was written by the victors . . . ,'[80] and their treatment by Rosas. For example, Echeverría was exiled in the 1840s and his attitude to the period is expressed in his story *El matadero*, which likens Argentina under Rosas to a gigantic slaughterhouse.[81] Likewise Sarmiento fought against Facundo Quiroga before going into exile in Chile and saw *caudillo* rule in Argentina as

> . . . the reign of brute force, the supremacy of the strongest, the absolute and irresponsible authority of rulers, the administration of justice without formalities or discussions.[82]

However not all writers on the subject of Rosas were so heavily under the influence of European thought. For example, Manuel Bilbao (1827–95), brother of the more famous

Francisco, defended Rosas on some counts and saw Federalism as being justified in the light of the colonial experience. By the end of the nineteenth century, the first balanced histories of Rosas were being published. Among these were Adolfo Saldría's *Historia de Rosas y su época* (Paris: 1881–7) and Ernesto Quesada's *La época de Rosas: Su verdadero caracter histórico* (Buenos Aires: 1898) which argued that criticisms of Rosas which separated him from his historical place were invalid and that his regime must be evaluated within its context.

But in the latter half of the century the dominant theme in historical writing remained the conflict between the two cultures, with most important writers taking the side of the European-oriented urban elite against the Iberian rural mass. Sarmiento makes his preference quite clear by referring to the former as 'civilisation' and the latter as 'barbarism'. In literature, too, the pro-European elitism was evident. José Marmol (1817–71), an exile in Montevideo under Rosas, for example, contrasts the vulgarity of Encarnación, Manuela and Mercedes and other members of Rosas's female entourage with the French manners, the sensitivity, delicacy and dignity of his heroine, Amalia Sáenz de Olabarrieta, in the novel *Amalia*.[83]

Mitre, though less influenced by the Black Legend and more willing to weigh historical evidence, was also subjected to criticism for the elitism of his work. His *Historia de Belgrano y de la independencia argentina*, first published in 1859,[84] included the suggestion that Belgrano had to whip up support for independence amongst the rural masses, whom he had written off as either hostile to or apathetic about independence. A series of critical articles were written by Dalmacio Vélez Sarsfield in *El Nacional*. The debate between Mitre and Vélez Sarsfield is seen by Ricardo Levene as a clash between elitism and a mass orientation, but may also be said to be an early challenge by Iberian-oriented nationalism against the European form.[85]

The development of this challenge was to occur in two main stages, although these may be seen as two distinct literary movements, not as parts of one revisionist school.[86] The first, beginning in the late nineteenth century, was to involve the romanticisation of the *gaucho*, who had previously been defined as racially inferior by authors under the influence of positivist thought, such as Sarmiento. The consolidation of the political power of the European-oriented liberal elite with the elevation of Mitre to the presidency and the declaration of Buenos Aires as the provisional capital in 1862, coincided with the beginning of the end of the *gaucho* lifestyle. As reflected in the historical and literary works of the era, a movement away from indigenous culture was considered to be the path to progress. In reality, economic progress caused the demise of aspects of indigenous culture. The *gaucho*'s mode of existence began to conflict with the changed interests of property owners. The move from pastoral to agricultural production and the need to produce quality meat for the European market spelled the end of the *gaucho*. The modernisation of ranching increased the social distance between owners/managers and their workers; legislation was used to ensure labour supplies and to contain the *gauchos*.[87] The growth of sheep farming, the need for fencing and railways and other aspects of the changing pattern of agriculture drew immigrants to the pampas. This alternative labour force contributed to the decline of the *gaucho*.

A reaction to the threat posed to tradition by the Europeanisation of culture began with a nostalgia for earlier days and a reinterpretation of the *gaucho*. The idea of the *gaucho* as a barbarian resisting the progress of civilisation in the form of city life gave way to a new view of the *gaucho* as representative of the real Argentina in opposition to the Europeanised urban elite. In 1872 José Hernández' (1834–86) *El gaucho Martín Fierro*[88] began the process of romanticisation. W.H. Hudson in *El Ombú* continued the theme, stressing the role of the *gauchos* in repulsing the English invasions.[89] *The Purple Land*, originally published in 1885 with the subtitle *That England Lost*, though emphasising the harshness of the life of the *gaucho* in the Banda Oriental, is nostalgic for his fast-disappearing skills and lifestyle.[90] By the end of the century, the *gaucho* had a new image, the noble savage corrupted and destroyed by contact with the process of development. Immigration had led to an assertion of *criollo* values which it was hoped would promote an authentic Argentine identity. Thus *Martín Fierro* was taken up initially by the Europeanised elite, and the references to social injustice were omitted from published versions of the text.[91] The changing image of the *gaucho*, as with the tango later, was strengthened by its functionality as an integrating myth for second-generation immigrants wishing to acquire a new cultural identity.[92]

The rehabilitation of the *gaucho* in historical and literary works was to encourage the growth of the liberal versus Rosista conflict in twentieth-century historiography. For example, Martiniano Leguizamón (1858–1935), although broadly critical of Rosas, kindled interest in the man through his use of nationalist themes, his analysis of *gaucho* history, which claimed that the *gaucho* originated in Argentina not Uruguay, and his publication for the first time of some of Rosas' papers.[93] Such works were characterised by pessimism and fatalism. They looked back at an era seen as 'good' which had passed. Thus they provide one source of the same qualities in later works.

Not all the literature of the 1930s was pessimistic. For example, the relative optimism of the nationalist, anti-semitic novels of Hugo Wast, who would become, albeit briefly, Minister of Justice and Education in 1943–44, made his work popular.[94] However, the general effect of 1930 on both historical and literary works was to deepen the pessimism, changing nostalgia to defeatism. Domestic economic and political events were not the only cause of the growing perception of Argentine history as a failure; ideas from abroad also contributed to this process. Oswald Spengler's *The Decline of the West*, although not specifically mentioning Argentina, was influential. It predicted the increasing decrepitude of Western civilisation, which would give way to a new era of 'Caesarism'.[95] Following his 1929 visit to Argentina, José Ortega y Gasset published an article criticising the lack of discipline, the incompetence and the narcissism of Argentine males. Count Hermann Keyserling's *South American Meditations* condemned as ludicrous the idea of building a neo-European culture in remote foreign parts, a theme which had impact on the gloomy quality of the work of Ezequiel Martínez Estrada amongst others.[96]

Indigenous intellectual currents reflected the obsession with failure and sought to explain it. A representative work was Eduardo Mallea's *Todo verdor perecerá*, which sees Argentines as isolated and depressed individuals incapable of communication with each other, existing in a hostile environment of drought and carcasses eaten by ants and magpies. Life is futile and beauty decays. Energy is beaten out of people by the harshness of failure. Similarly Mallea's *Fiesta en Noviembre* contrasts the violence and crudity of Argentina with the art and history of Europe (and also the East).[97]

Broad agreement existed that Argentina had taken a wrong course and that 1930 marked a sharp break in her history, but very different interpretations of why such a situation had arisen remained, reflecting the two cultures. Most intellectuals looked back to the pre-1930 period as a golden age, but found it so for different reasons. Most sought to identify the reasons for national failure, but differently oriented writers allocated historical blame to different sectors. Both schools of thought were characterised by defeatism, but writers under European influence, such as Mallea, saw the Argentine decline as reflecting the encroachment of America on high European standards whilst integral nationalists saw the impact of Europe as the source of the malaise. Thus a split emerged in literature and historiography which reflected the division between internationalist thought and nationalism, which was expressed in criticism of the national character on the one hand and in attacks on foreign influences on the other. The contribution of both schools to Argentine political culture has been largely negative. In recording the decline of national culture in the twentieth century without providing a blueprint for rectifying the situation or indeed any hope generally, they have contributed to the process of demoralisation.

This sense of failure was reflected in the changing quality of mass culture too. Originating in the nostalgic but not yet depressive years of the late nineteenth century, contemporary with the reinterpretation of the *gaucho*, the lyrical and romantic quality of the tango-*canción* survived into the 1920s but this gave way to the sense of futility characteristic of the 1930s. Tango lyrics continued to look back to a golden age of lost values, security and contentment, but a new bitterness and resentment was present. Feelings of national failure were expressed in lyrics concerned with individual, often sexual, failure. The misery of modern working-class existence in the *barrios* of Buenos Aires was a poor substitute for the imagined dignity of the Argentine male in the pre-1930 era, as Miguel Buccino's lyrics indicate:

> Pero algo vos darías
> por ser por un ratito
> el mismo compadrito
> del tiempo que se fue
> pues cansa tanta gloria.[98]

Cultural and economic pessimism was thus very widespread post-1930 and gave rise to historical revisionist trends critical of European cultural and economic influences in the period after the overthrow of Rosas. This view of history was not so much new as a modern re-emergence of the Iberian cultural stream albeit in an intellectual context, intellectualism having been previously primarily associated with the European-oriented urban elite. Although 1930 is widely seen as a benchmark, nationalist historiography did not emerge overnight. It had its antecedents in the growing sympathy for Spain and the undermining of the Black Legend consequent upon the US defeat of Spain in 1898. Thus Argentina was receptive to the spread of *Hispanidad* from Spain during the 1920s and its corollary, the growth of anti-imperialist thought. Likewise, the growing fear of US domination was already being expressed in the literature of the first three decades of the twentieth century in the works of writers such as Ugarte, José Ingenieros and Alfredo Palacios. Ugarte, for example, stressed the imperialist aspect of US policy in Latin America; he saw the latter as on the point of cultural absorption. However, the undermining of national political and economic confidence in 1930 increased receptiveness to revisionism, as national pride in Argentina's place as an outpost of Europe largely dissipated.

Although always a democrat, later an active and influential member of the UCR and author of a biography of Sarmiento,[99] Ricardo Rojas (1882–1957) was amongst the first important nationalist writers. In *La restauración nacionalista* (Buenos Aires: 1909), he emphasised that foreign cultural influences constituted a threat to Argentine traditions and that history should be taught in a manner which encouraged the development of nationalism. He coined the expression 'Argentinism' and suggested that Argentina's problems since independence reflected her cosmopolitanism; a solution, which was possible, could only be sought in her national past. There had been insufficient study of indigenous themes and Rojas aimed to express these in his work. Amongst the early nationalists emphasising the supremacy of Argentina's Hispanic stream of influence was Manuel Gálvez (1882–1962). Unlike Rojas, Gálvez saw democracy as ineffectual. As a Catholic nationalist, he welcomed the 1930 revolution as a means to restore order and saw it as Argentina beginning to take control of her own destiny after years of exploitation by British and US imperialism.

Gálvez was amongst those authors who comprised the revisionist historical school in the late 1930s and he contributed to the rehabilitation of Rosas, whom he saw as a popular hero caring for the masses. Most notable amongst those who re-interpreted the Rosas era was Carlos Ibarguren (1877–1956), who wrote the political programme for the coalition of conservative groups which opposed Yrigoyen in 1916 and who would later become a member of the GOU government. Like Gálvez and the other prominent nationalist intellectuals, Ibarguren came from a provincial upper-class background. As a traditionalist and a nationalist, his biography of Rosas praised the emphasis on order, hierarchy, property and religion, and stressed that tyrannical aspects of his regime were due not the machinations of Rosas but rather to the national situation at the time.[100] The same theme, that the violence and conflict of the Rosas period was the consequence of the activities of the liberal intellectuals and Argentina's foreign enemies, was also to be found in the work of Julio and Rodolfo Irazusta, amongst others. For the Irazustas, the post-Rosas era was one in which the European-oriented elite had succeeded in separating itself from the masses.[101] Thus, as Lynch points out, nationalists discovered new good in the Rosas regime and, rather than counteracting the imbalance of early liberal intellectuals who condemned him totally, they moved to the other extreme. Either way, the historical truth had been lost in ideological interpretation, and ' . . . much of the modern literature on Rosas speaks more of the present than it does of the past'.[102]

Much of this integral nationalist thought was absorbed into Peronist ideology, including Gálvez' concept of a 'New

Argentina'[103] and Ugarte's 'middle way' between socialism and capitalism which was to become the 'Third Position'. Popular culture flourished under Perón and Argentine film-makers emphasised cultural independence and the elevation of the masses. However, Peronism was essentially anti-intellectual, and much intellectual nationalist support was lost. Perón's reluctance to cite Rosas as a mentor, his praise for San Martín, the optimistic assertiveness of most of the Peronist period and its anti-elitism were offensive to many revisionist nationalists.[104] Gálvez was amongst those who remained with the movement, and some nationalist intellectuals became active in Peronist politics; for example Ernesto Palacio became a Peronist deputy in 1946. Julio Irazusta was amongst those who moved into the opposition to Perón and some of his later works are mere treatises against Peronism.[105]

The anti-intellectualism of Peronism led to the establishment of the Sociedad Argentina de Escritores (SADE), a literary society with a strong anti-Peronist orientation. This in turn generated a right-wing nationalist and pro-Peronist response in the form of the Asociación de Escritores Argentinos, led by Gálvez. The former group included, as might be expected, Jorge Luis Borges, Victoria Ocampo and Mallea. These writers were the heirs of the nineteenth-century liberals, and had been members of the 'Florida' group in the 1920s, but had since acquired a new pessimism and quondam orientation. They tended to be from upper-class backgrounds and regretted the passing of the old elitist, pro-European Argentina of the late nineteenth and early twentieth centuries. Their political thought, like their taste in literature and dinner-guests, was internationalist. Their attitudes are reflected in the cosmopolitan quality of the famous literary review, *Sur*, founded by Ocampo in 1931. Although frequently criticised for her preference for European culture, Ocampo did use the magazine to promote the work of Borges, the best known of this 'internationalist' literary set. For Borges, from a cultivated and wealthy background and educated in Europe, the 'civili-sation versus barbarism' theme continued with barbarism in the ascendancy. Immigration and the extension of the franchise contributed to the increasing decadence of Argentina. His stories and poems glorify an Argentina dominated by a

cultured and Europeanised intellectual and social elite, but
even they, or at least their heirs, have been barbarised by
contact with mass culture and the American environment.
Borges's preference for Europe and nostalgia for the past are
indicated when he writes:

> About 1946, Buenos Aires bore yet another Rosas, who
> was like our kinsman. In 1955, Córdoba rescued us, as
> Entre Ríos did in the century before. Now the situation
> is bad. Russia takes over the world; America limited by
> democracy cannot decide to be an empire. Every day our
> nation is becoming more provincial. More provincial and
> more false, as if it had its eyes closed. I would not be
> surprised if the teaching of Guaraní were substituted for
> Latin in our schools.[106]

Borges was among the writers selected to lunch with
President Videla in May 1976 in the hope of placating
intellectual criticism of the new government. He emerged
from the experience more enthusiastic about the regime than
his colleagues and reassured press and public that the junta
were 'gentlemen'.[107]

Although, like Borges, a member of SADE and an implacable opponent of Perón, Martínez Estrada sides with neither
the nationalist nor the liberal internationalist schools of
historiography and literature. He was an 'ambivalent' figure
forming, with Mallea, part of a diverging realist tendency
within the group, increasingly in conflict with the literary
aestheticism of Borges. This same feature characterises the
work of two authors who intially opposed Perón and were
part of the internationalist set, Ernesto Sábato and Julio
Cortázar. (Indeed, it was in association with Sábato that
Martínez Estrada found himself embroiled in a vicious and
very public literary slanging-match with Borges in 1956–57
over the latter's enthusiasm for the 'Liberating Revolution'
of 1955. Martínez Estrada and Sábato had come to recognise
that Perón was not a product of simple barbarism but rather
a response to working-class needs.)[108] Sábato, Cortázar and
Martínez Estrada all exhibit awareness of the duality of
Argentine culture and pessimism about the future. For
example, Martínez Estrada's *Radiografía de la pampa*, first
published in 1933, is seen as deterministic by some and

alternatively as not fully appreciating Argentine history. It is a catalogue of Argentine failure and provides little hope for the future. Thus the former criticism has some validity. But in recognising the adverse effects of the interaction of the two cultures, it could be said to appreciate Argentine history less selectively than the works of authors who adopt either a pro-European nostalgic approach or an Iberian revisionism.

For Martínez Estrada, Argentina was divided from the outset, the Europeanised urban elite having different motives for seeking independence from those which drove provincial elements. The competition of vested cultural and economic interests has perpetuated problems of poverty and underdevelopment. He sees, in the tradition established by Sarmiento though with a less clear preference, the city in opposition to the nation, a theme taken up most clearly in *Cabeza de Goliat* (1940).[109] The primary weakness of urban liberals both before and after Rosas was their failure to understand that Buenos Aires was not Argentina. Although subject to attacks from the revisionist school for his criticisms of Rosas,[110] whose rule he saw as 'systematised barbarism', Martínez Estrada believed the personalist regimes of Rosas and Yrigoyen (though not Perón) to be more representative of the people than those of urban liberals. Rosas, unlike his enemies, knew and understood the nation including the interior provinces. The revolution of 1930 Martínez Estrada believed to be more in accord with Argentine history and culture, more 'authentic' than 1880. Nevertheless, he was critical of the legacy of the colonial era. The Black Legend survives in his work and the experience of America debases and barbarises the Spanish conquerors. Shades of positivist thought also remain in his view of the *mestizo* as inferior to both the European and the Indian.

The overthrow of Rosas could not change the situation; it left effective control in the same hands though the old *caudillos* might have adopted a new orientation. It was not an 'Argentine' revolution, but rather a response to the changing economic needs of Europe and thus could not provide Argentina with what she lacked, a national identity and common values. The imposition of Europeanness is seen as wholly inappropriate for a nation so far away and so very different from Europe. It was an implant which could not take, remaining as a civilised and modern façade overlaid on and corrupting the essential barbarism of the Ibero-American reality. More specifically, laws and institutions can only be workable if they represent usual practice, thus the 'pseudostructures' borrowed from Europe and the United States merely encourage evasion and abuse. The reality for Argentina was the harshness of existence reflected in the *gaucho* lifestyle, and a frontier mentality in accordance with Turner's psychological model, as displayed by Martín Fierro. The interaction of the two cultures is detrimental in economics as well as politics, leading to the exaggeration of weaknesses already present in the Iberian legacy which had itself been first diminished by the Americas. For example, the European trading relationship contributed to the overvaluation of land and the ease of acquiring European capital encouraged the tendency to extravagance and 'misspending'. There never was, for Martínez Estrada, a golden age of Argentine development. The apparent optimism of the late nineteenth century was an illusion which reflected the aspirations of immigrants, which could never in any case have been satisfied. These immigrants reinforced the most marked Argentine trait, materialism. They came lacking the spiritual hopes and values which Argentina needed and brought her more of what she had in abundance already, venality.[111]

The persistence of Sarmiento's dichotomy of civilisation and barbarism in Argentine literary circles is illustrated by the response to Luna's *Los caudillos*, when it was first published in 1966. It met with a hostile reaction from both sides; from 'out and out liberals' accusing Luna of 'exalting barbarism' and 'raging revisionists' charging him with 'various heresies'.[112] That history should be a process of selective remembrance or, as Naipaul points out, of forgetting that which is inconvenient to one's perception of the past,[113] is made easier in a nation which has such varying cultural influences. More interesting is the recognition by Martínez Estrada that the strands of culture are interwoven and interact to produce the worst of both worlds.

THE INTERACTION OF NATIONALISM
AND INTERNATIONALISM

There has not been a consistent division between nationalist and internationalist elements in Argentine society. Each position has shown considerable flexibility in encompassing the other. This is inevitable in that each perspective must operate in an historical context not solely created by its own adherents. The internationalist orientation cannot sacrifice Argentine independence and cannot ignore popular hostility to the United States. The nationalist perspective is essentially pragmatic but still tends to accept an East–West division as well as a North–South division of the global order and remains tied to the idea of Argentina as a Western power. Both established traditions are permanently involved in policy-making and both pervade the military too. They constitute an entanglement of cultural features from which selection is made.

The coexistence of nationalist and internationalist thought expresses the two streams of cultural influence, the interaction of the two modes of thought reflects the pervasive quality of the cultural strands, neither of which could survive in a pure form because of the strength of the other and their welding together over time. In any case, each mode of thought would suggest an unrealisable ideal; its modification for practical purposes must be in the direction of the other option. Nationalism, aspiring to autonomous nation-statehood, cannot achieve its aims in an interdependent world. Internationalist thought, idealising the relationship with Europe in the past, cannot turn the clock back nor alter Argentina's geographical position. However, neither nationalism nor internationalism ever existed in a pure form despite the obvious association of the former with the Iberian legacy and the latter with European influences.

A strong internationalist tradition is a part of the Iberian legacy. The diffusion of Catholicism and Hispanic culture through the Spanish empire provides an international aspect to *criollo* culture. Thus despite the use of disputes with the French and later also the British, Rosas never sought to isolate Argentina completely. Although he owed more to the Iberian legacy, Rosas' regime was the outcome of both cultural influences and reflects his historical context. He could not restore colonial rule, even had he wished to do so; he therefore 'consolidated what the revolution had changed'[114] in his own inimitable style. He continued to allow some immigration, especially the importation of young Spaniards for domestic service. He did not exclude foreign interests; indeed foreigners were able to buy land in the Province of Buenos Aires quite cheaply and the French cited his apparent preferential treatment of the British as a factor for their blockade of the River Plate. After his defeat at Caseros, his liberal opponents also emphasised their nationalism and indeed they were political nationalists, seeking political sovereignty in the tradition of the American and French Revolutions. The cultural and economic internationalism of both the Generations of 1837 and 1880 was initially associated with the process of nation-building. It established the unifying 'agrarian myth' which would modify conflict during the late nineteenth and early twentieth centuries, and ensure that anti-imperialism in Argentina would frequently be a means employed to discredit the political opposition rather than an all-out attack on foreign interests. The relative success of this internationalism won the conditional support of most sectors, but the developmental processes it set in motion also supplied the basis for a deepening of the cleavage between the two cultural positions. The import of capital not only promoted the vision of a great and modern nation, it would also provide a focus for discontent when the dream turned sour. Likewise the import of labour encouraged the development of an industrial working class who, frustrated by political exclusion under mainly internationalist-oriented regimes, would later provide a support base for the primarily nationalist regime of Perón. The militancy of the descendants of these immigrants, although initially promoting the development of right-wing nationalism, would later strengthen the pro-Western model by contributing to fears of internal subversion, associated with the broadening of the support base of nationalism and its tendency to assume a popular form.

There has been a permanent ambivalence between the two views which has reflected a chronically fragmented society in which political pragmatism of a particular kind is at a premium. Despite a generalised disdain for political compromise prior to attaining power, once power is achieved the primary concern of office-holders in an unstable polity becomes the retention of position. The semi-legitimacy of both electoral and non-electoral political succession fails to guarantee a term in office and, as a result, the consideration of rapidly shifting power-bases becomes paramount. The retention of power involves appeal to elements holding either nationalist or internationalist perceptions or, more usually, both, since these perceptions are so pervasive. Government changes may obviously promote adjustments in the relative policy impact of the two positions, but there may also be shifts in emphasis within the duration of one regime, whether civilian or military. Such rebalancing clearly occurs universally when changes in the international situation require it, but in Argentina domestic considerations are more important. Oscillations in the economy are particularly potent sources of governmental delegitimisation which may require either new concessions to foreign capital to restore short-term economic equilibrium and therefore the public esteem of a regime, or perhaps a distraction to focus public interest on national prestige rather than economic problems. Variations in relative factional strength within the military establishment also constitute important threats to regime survival. Military factions frequently form according to differing attitudes to nationalism and internationalism, along with their related interpretations of order, as was the case in the Argentine army in the early 1960s. It was from just such factional infighting that Onganía emerged.

The impact of the two modes of thought has been seen as giving rise to inconsistencies in Argentina's international relations which are so marked that Milenky finds it impossible to write of Argentine foreign policy in the singular. Nevertheless, both perceptions carry with them one overriding aim, the enhancement of Argentina's place in the international order, though the interpretations of how this is to be achieved differ. The internationalist perspective has tended to emphasise the achievement of an important position in the Western political alliance and thus has sought to make Argentina indispensable to the United States in her battle against the forces of international communism. This political position has seen economic success as guaranteed by the linkage of the Argentine economy to the economies of the wealthiest capitalist nations. The nationalist attitude has been that Argentina must ensure her own success in the world economic order through pragmatism in her international relations and autonomous development. Thus she will carve for herself an important position amongst non-aligned states emerging as a third force independent of the two superpower-dominated blocs. The two perspectives may be mutually contradictory in the methods they advocate if not their aims, but neither alone can meet the needs of Argentina. On the one hand, she will not sacrifice her political independence, but on the other, the way in which this independence is perceived rests on her ability to obtain technology, military *matériel* and training from the West. Economic independence may be her goal, but Argentina's immediate economic needs may require Western cooperation if she is to attract foreign investment for development or, most recently, to re-negotiate repayment of her debts.

Argentine governments do not therefore exhibit the alternative perceptions in a pure form. Nevertheless, it might be said that internationalism and nationalism are exemplified most clearly by the military regime of 1976–83 which sought to establish itself firmly with the West and by the Perón governments of 1946–55 which emphasised the adoption of a 'Third Position' between capitalism and communism through a domestic alliance of capital and labour and through an independent foreign policy. But even these regimes could not and did not adhere consistently to their dominant modes of thought. In fact each of them represents in itself a combination of features, the electoral aspect of politics having derived from the influence of Europe and military intervention reflecting some elements of the Hispanic tradition.

The extent of Argentine nationalism is so great that internationalist-oriented regimes make appeals to it to retain support, and the ties to the West are so strong that nationalist regimes cannot dismiss them. Thus the legitimacy of the 1976–83 regime was heightened by nationalist pride in acting as host to and winning the 1978 World Cup. A similar nationalist legitimising process occurred in consequence of the Videla government's human rights record. A new level of *porteño* enthusiasm for the regime was achieved as cars in Buenos Aires were adorned with the legend 'Los argentinos somos derechos y humanos' (We Argentines are right and human) for the benefit of foreign visitors to the World Cup.[115] Despite the stress on comparative advantage, high levels of industrial tariff protection were maintained and conflicts arose within the regime. Videla and his successors sold vast quantities of wheat to the Soviet Union against the express wishes of the United States and moved into a situation of direct physical confrontation with part of the Western political alliance, Great Britain, over the Falkland Islands. Conversely, soon after his election, which rested at least in part on his stand against US imperialism, Perón stated that Argentina would support the United States in the event of a conflict with the Soviet Union,[116] and during his second term of office he granted extensive concessions to North American oil companies.

THE EFFECTS OF NATIONALISM (AND INTERNATIONALISM)

Since nationalism is a psychological quality, it is difficult to ascertain its effects. It may be argued that it should have an integrative function in an otherwise divergent society, but it is difficult to see Argentine nationalism in this light. It has alternatively been suggested that Latin American nationalism generally takes a weak and rhetorical form which does not fundamentally question dependence. This is partially true, but, at the same time, Argentina exhibits a strong negative nationalism built on what it opposes, not on a shared sense of national identity and tolerant pride, and thus it is not a force which unifies. It is imbued with a quest for explanation of thwarted national destiny, not with optimism for the future. It is ambiguous and unpredictable, as is indicated by the invasion of the Falkland Islands. Nationalism is one more point of division in an already divided society.

Whilst nationalism elsewhere may be seen as developing under nationally-oriented elites, in Argentina, as in other parts of Latin America, the modern form developed despite, and in at least rhetorical opposition to, elites displaying primarily internationalist objectives as a split within the political Right. The continuing existence of an internationalist orientation alongside developing nationalism may be seen as heightening social tensions and contributing to the intolerant quality of Argentine nationalism. The vertical divisions of society implied by growing economic nationalism in the 1930s were laid on top of horizontal divisions developing from the strengthening zero-sum model of Argentine society. The result was further fragmentation. The cohesion of the political elite was reduced by the increasing nationalism of elements within it. The political Right came to comprise an amalgam of liberal agro-export interests and nationalists. The political Left exhibited both forms of nationalism too, the internationalist Socialist and Communist Parties and the growing integral nationalist elements, parts of which would later join with some rightist nationalists to support Perón. It is worth noting that internationalist as well as nationalist elements overcame their political differences at the theoretical, if not practical, level to oppose Peronism. It is, of course, true that the coexistence of nationalism and internationalism reflects the fragmentation of Argentine society; that, for example, the continuation of modified internationalism amongst the dominant sections of the elite in the 1930s reflected an alluvial society with many different and not yet assimilated nationalities. Nevertheless, nationalism in Latin America generally has contributed to societal fragmentation, through its capacity to be used by different groups for their varying political purposes.

Without consensus on national identity, nationalism must by definition remain nebulous in its content, hence its failure to offer one coherent political programme and the relative unimportance in membership and voting strength of specifically nationalist groups. At the outset, integral nationalism was an oppositional position, developing against upper-class liberal internationalism and largely excluded from representation within mainstream Radicalism as a result of its association with Yrigoyen's ouster. In any case, as part of the Iberian rather than the European tradition, integral nationalism developed in a non-electoral form, until its 'popularisation' by Perón, being associated with Rosas, Uriburu and the GOU. As well as conflicting with democratic ideals, it also confronts social values within the Iberian strand of culture, such as individualism and thus indicates that not only do the different streams of influence conflict with each other (as well as reinforcing each other on occasion) but also that they are not internally consistent.

Although in conflict with, and generally unsuccessful in the formal political structure, nationalist feeling is so pervasive that all groupings must take account of it. Nationalism itself intensifies as different political groups use it to win popular support. Groups compete with each other to be more nationalistic, and the military, if they wish to assert it, have a head start in this competition.

9 Prospects for Political Stability

As a background factor for instability, political culture remains as a feature which could nurture potentially destabilising forces in Argentina's restored democracy. Optimism regarding prospects for the consolidation of democracy is largely based on the weakening of the military in relation to civil society. Is is therefore based on an acceptance of primarily military explanations of instability, although some changes in civilian political organisations have been acknowledged as important too.

Military explanations have emphasised the disposition/propensity of the institution to intervene. Alone such explanations must be seen as inadequate since intervention is a reactive and negative phenomenon; a rejection of the existing situation, not a precise programme for the future. The majority of attempted coups and a good proportion of successful interventions in Argentine politics have not been institutional. Indeed the possibility that coups may not only be factional affairs supported by civilian sectors, but in part accidental, has been specifically recognised.[1] Hence there is a continuing significant risk that Argentina's fragmented civil society with its ambiguous political culture may provide a backdrop against which factional in-fighting could lead to an 'accidental' attempt to wrest power from a civilian government.

The ousting of a civilian regime is neither an exclusively military affair nor is it epiphenomenal. In the terms suggested by non-military explanations of intervention, it must be said that Argentina still displays many characteristics which could theoretically promote instability. Although Argentina is a relatively developed country and structural inequality is less marked than in some 'stable' nations, she is still a modernising polity exhibiting economic frustration in many sectors of the population. Emergent sectors may

268

now be politically integrated, but it is by no means clear that the demands they voice are restrained by the cultural commitment to toleration that Dahl sees as essential to democratic stability.[2] Alfonsín is proud of the fact that during his presidency there has been no use of federal intervention against the provinces to eliminate political opposition. But whether this even-handed approach would continue under presidential hopefuls for 1989, the Peronist Carlos Menem or the Radical Eduardo Angeloz, remains open to question. It will depend on the challenges they face. As apparently insoluble challenges mount against any regime, its effectiveness is reduced and thus its legitimacy, especially so if governmental legitimacy is circumscribed to begin with. Legitimacy assumes shared expectations of what can properly be done and shared limits on the way that political change occurs. It rests on a widespread consensus on the 'rules of the political game' and this rests in turn on a credible belief that the government of the day can and will benefit its supporters. It does not necessarily imply a democratic form of politics, but it does require that institutions and procedures be seen to be coping with the challenges they face. Political succession through peaceful elections is usually seen as the most important feature of stable democracy. In order to be seen as fully legitimate procedures, elections must aggregate and modify demands to win widespread support, but at the same time they must generate sufficient governmental capacity to handle problems. Both modification of demands and the generation of capacity have traditionally been in short supply in Argentine politics.

All civilian governments since 1952 (with the brief but unhelpful exception of Cámpora) until the present one have been terminated by unconstitutional means. Survival of future governments will clearly depend on their ability to defuse potential challenges. In the past populistic forms and sequential appeasement of various key political sectors have deferred intervention, but in the longer term they have not stabilised democratic government. Argentina has long thought of herself as, and has been seen by outside commentators as, a nation of great social and economic potential thwarted by political incapacity. Now the dilemmas of democratic consolidation reverse the problem: political capacity is liable to be thwarted by economic weakness and social cleavages.

The military question played an important role in the election of Alfonsín. The economic and military failures of the armed forces paved the way for the restoration of civilian government with the chance to reform aspects of the military institution. Divisions between the discredited senior staff of the army and navy and their junior officers, as well as the air force disaffection with the other two services, suggested that an unique opportunity to get to grips with the political machinations of the armed forces was open to the civilian party or parties willing to grasp the nettle. The Multipartidaria grouping, initially permitted by President Galtieri in December 1981, embraced some 80 per cent of the electoral spectrum[3] including both the main political parties, and displayed considerable unity on the need to deal with the military question.

Despite the common elements of policy regarding reform of the armed forces exhibited by all bar the, then relatively weak, right-of-centre political groups, Alfonsín's election campaign stressed the political cultural differences. Radicalism was presented as liberal and democratic in comparison with the dictatorial and demagogic character attributed to Peronism. Mud, in the form of charges of collaboration with the military, was hurled at key orthodox/verticalist Peronists, and it stuck. In this the Radicals were helped by the behaviour of some of the leading lights of Peronism, most notably the inimitable Herminio Iglesias, who, at a televised rally at the culmination of the electoral campaign, used his cigarette lighter to set fire to a coffin symbolising the aspirations of Alfonsín and the UCR. Peronism was in any case tainted with the role of the Isabel Perón government in establishing that machinery of terror which became a mainstay of the Videla régime. The re-emergence of many of the same 'party hacks' during the election campaign did little to change the image of Peronism. Thus the apparent Radical threat to the military was enhanced and expectations of firm action were raised.

Optimism was the order of the day and the Radical government appeared to have a number of important advantages over previous civilian administrations which had succumbed to military ousters. Alfonsín had achieved some 50 per cent of the popular vote, and had a more secure base in the federal capital, where senior officers might reasonably be expected to notice it, than either Yrigoyen or Perón. The UCR had received support from sectors which had not previously voted Radical, the establishment of a broad-based mass political party which could beat the Peronists in elections appeared to have occurred. The relative weakness of the Peronist electoral base, a consequence of the erosion of the industrial sector under the military and the diminished influence of the unions, was seen as a good omen for the future, whilst at the same time the existence of the second mass party and the increased participation in both major parties was held to be indicative of a new pluralism. The old *caudillos* were dead and both main parties had a chance to leave behind personalistic, solidaristic forms in favour of modern, internally democratic electoral coalitions. Most importantly, the military 'image' was more tarnished than at any previous civilian restoration.

In practice, the new UCR government did take a number of steps the combined effect of which was to weaken the military base of power. The settlement by negotiation of the Beagle Channel dispute, under the auspices of Pope John Paul II, and the submission of the agreement to a referendum in which it achieved overwhelming popular support, removed one of the principal military arguments for a strong army, navy and air force, the fear of Chilean intentions in Patagonia and the South Atlantic. This in turn facilitated long-overdue reductions in the size of the armed forces and in their grossly inflated budget, which was reduced by US$800 million, though it was not followed, as some had hoped, by the complete ending of conscription (this was cut by more than two-thirds to an annual intake of some 30 000 conscripts), which had been, and remains, one of the most potent ways in which the armed forces impress their ideas on the general public. It also eased the way to treating as a purely economic question the splitting up of the military-owned industrial conglomerate, Fabricaciones Militares.[4]

To tackle the charges arising out of the arbitrary behaviour of the military forces during the 'dirty war', however, required detailed and systematic evidence, much of which was known to have been destroyed during the interim military government of General Bignone, who had been responsible for the transition. The President on 15 December 1983 established the National

Commission on the Disappearance of Persons, chaired by Ernesto Sábato.[5] Its objectives were to clarify the events of the 'dirty war', to receive accusations of disappearance or imprisonment of individuals during that period, and to make a report. This report, *Nunca Mas*, which was sent to the President in September 1984, appeared in print two months later and was reprinted four times within a month. The commission stated categorically that more than a thousand government security officers had been involved in the systematic violation of human rights, and so paved the way for civilian proceedings against those responsible.[6]

Most conspicuous of the new government's attempts to circumscribe the military role was the decision to bring members of the armed forces before civilian courts to face accusations of civil rights abuses during the 'dirty war', and in particular to press charges against the most senior officers who had comprised the succession of military juntas which had held power in the period 1976–83.[7] Despite repeated attempts on the part of the armed forces and their lawyers to evade or pre-empt these trials, the most senior officers involved were brought to justice. On 9 December 1985 ex-President Jorge R. Videla and Admiral Emilio E. Massera were sentenced to life imprisonment, and ex-President Roberto E. Viola, Admiral Armando Lambruschini and Air Force Brigadier-General Orlando R. Agosti to 17 years, 8 years and $4^1/_2$ years imprisonment respectively. The members of the third and final junta, ex-President General Leopoldo F. Galtieri, Admiral Jorge I. Anaya and Air Force Brigadier-General Basilio A.I. Lami Dozo, were acquitted on all human rights charges, but also faced charges of incompetence and maladministration which contributed to Argentina's defeat in the Falklands War of 1982, and for these in May 1986 they were sentenced to 12, 15 and 6 years imprisonment respectively. Clearly violations of human rights were seen as almost on a par with incompetence. During this period, moreover, despite some private initiatives, no successful prosecutions were brought against any junior personnel.

Finally at the end of 1987, after long consultations between the three services, a Defence Bill was passed by Congress. This had two complementary purposes: to establish a clear military role for the armed forces and to delimit the areas of responsibility of each of the services for the future. The bill specifically excluded the armed forces from a role in internal as opposed to external conflict, with a view to terminating the so-called 'national security doctrine' which the 1976 junta had used as the ideological justification for its intervention.[8]

Besides specific attempts to delimit the military role, the Alfonsín government further sought some restructuring of civilian society. This was essential not just because military intervention always occurs within a social context but also in consequence of the particular form taken by the preceding military regime. The Process of National Reorganisation sought to expunge communism through the re-creation of Argentine society within a particular interpretation of the 'Western Christian' tradition. The Process to some extent achieved the intended goal of total social penetration, proscribing certain books, films, people, ideas and life-styles. The restoration of broader cultural activity formed an important part of this government's policy and was exemplified by the opening-up of higher education, after the elitism and purges of the military period. The need to accommodate labour was also recognised to some extent, at least in the attempt to re-integrate Peronism into the national life with such important symbolic acts as the renaming of streets, squares and even whole towns in acknowledgement of the part played by the Peróns in the history of Argentina.

Nevertheless, despite attempts to circumscribe the military role in a democratic Argentina, at Easter 1987 simmering military discontent boiled over. Some officer factions felt they were not being accorded civilian respect for their victorious struggle against leftist subversion in the 'dirty war' of the 1970s; many felt, as did their counterparts in neighbouring Uruguay, that they should not have to appear before civilian courts to defend that role. The government in late 1986 had introduced the 'full stop' law. It was widely seen as a response to pressure from the Chiefs of Staff who felt that they could not maintain discipline unless there was an end to civilian prosecutions of military officers and men. The bill, rushed through Congress in less than 100 hours, put a time limit on prosecutions. Intended to defuse the issue, the rush to beat the deadline instead aroused fresh military irritation.

On Palm Sunday 1987 the Pope preached peace and

reconciliation to around a million people in Buenos Aires. But during his visit military chaplains also held masses for the 'victims of subversion' and then Army Chief of Staff General Héctor Ríos Ereñú called for understanding of the military role in the 'dirty war'. The following Tuesday an army Major, Ernesto Barreiro, failed to appear before the Federal Appeals Court at Córdoba, to answer charges concerning atrocities at La Perla Detention Centre.[9] The order that he be cashiered triggered off a revolt of the locally-garrisoned Airborne Infantry Regiment. As 200 000 people, who were brought from their homes by television appeals or bussed in from outlying districts, gathered in the square outside Congress in a beautifully stage-managed rally in support of democracy, Alfonsín told assembled representatives that no concessions would be made to military rebels. The revolt in Córdoba fizzled out, but instead a new and more serious rising erupted among some 150 officers at the infantry school at the Campo de Mayo just outside Buenos Aires.

The rebels, in camouflage uniforms and with blackened faces, led by the hitherto unknown Lieutenant-Colonel Aldo Rico, who had arrived the day before from Misiones, represented a cross-section of the Argentine army and were drawn in from bases all over the country. There was some obvious hesitation before the commander ordered to take matters in hand, General Ernesto Alais, was able to muster a thousand troops to quell the revolt. Neither the President nor the Chief of Staff seemed certain that sufficient support could be obtained. By Easter Day the city was gripped with tension, people seeking the latest news from passers-by with transistor radios clamped to their ears. At 3 p.m. the President told the huge crowds assembled in front of the Casa Rosada to wait for him while he went personally to the Campo de Mayo; at 6 p.m. he returned to wish them 'Happy Easter' and proclaim that the rebels had surrendered. In a fervour of enthusiasm for democracy old rivalries were temporarily suspended: Peronists cheered Radicals and Radicals Peronists, and a large banner across the Avenida de Mayo proclaimed 'Thank You Mr President'.

Government spokesmen heralded this outcome as the victory of democracy and claimed that no deals had been made. But the protracted period of inaction against the rebels remains inexplicable unless negotiations had in fact occurred, and the outcome gave the rebels almost all they wanted. The scent of victory inspired further brief risings in Salta and Tucumán. Many of the senior officers whose resignations had been demanded were retired, military trials were postponed and, despite the Justice Secretary's denials, a 'due obedience' bill was later introduced by the government majority in Congress.

Rico himself, placed under 'rigorous preventative arrest', allegedly for questioning which many months later had still failed to lead to proceedings against him, became the focus for continuing military discontent. At Christmas, while his supporters exchanged cryptic messages, he was allowed by the military command to be transferred to house arrest as part of a policy of not holding political prisoners over the festive season – a luxury denied to thousands of victims of the 'dirty war' who perished miserably and whose bodies have never been found. Worse still, while his supporters were escorting him to his new place of 'detention', one, a Lieutenant Maguire, threatened a reporter with his service revolver and subsequently rammed his car.[10]

These events caused a national sensation. Rico, ensconced at the Los Fresnos country club in a suburb of Buenos Aires, made it clear that if an attempt were made to return him to more rigorous confinement, he would resist. After the dismissal of three commanders for refusing to move their troops, a massive force of thirty tanks was sent to recapture him. Many of these tanks broke down as a consequence of a lack of servicing and shortages of spare parts. Those that were able to continue stopped for breakfast en route, giving Rico adequate opportunity to escape. Rumours flew that there had been a shoot-out and that Rico had been wounded, but it soon emerged that a friend (subsequently arrested) had flown him in a light plane to the military base at Monte Caseros, in the north-eastern Province of Corrientes, where he was supported in his defiance by some 50–130 troops. Monte Caseros, symbolic as the scene of the last stand of the nineteenth-century dictator Rosas, was very close to the borders of both Uruguay and Brazil and so convenient for a quick getaway. But this time the hesitations were not repeated. The town was surrounded and Rico recaptured by government forces, and the townsfolk spat on his supporters as they were led away.

The two Infantry Regiments in Corrientes supporting Rico (the 4th and 5th) were not alone however. Sympathetic revolts occurred all over the country: amongst the 19th Infantry Regiment in Tucumán, the 161st Anti-Aircraft Artillery Unit in San Luis, the 22nd Mountain Brigade in San Juan, the 35th Motorised Infantry Regiment in Santa Cruz and the 21st Mountain Infantry Regiment in Neuquén. Not only did army elements fail to obey 'the natural chain of command', but in addition some air force officers with civilian assistance briefly took control of Aeroparque, the domestic airport of Buenos Aires, from which they were soon dislodged by the police.

Only a tiny proportion of the 20 000 or so officers and NCOs in the Argentine army took part in these revolts, but ideological support for those who did is undoubtedly much more widespread despite tactical scepticism on this occasion. The military is slowly moving away from a largely defensive attitude to the charges brought against its members towards an increasingly strong desire for positive support and approval for its role in the 'dirty war'. The same national security ideology which sought to justify the military role in the 'dirty war' is now evident in the increasingly well-attended public meetings held by the Friends and Families of the Victims of Subversion (FAMUS). Rearmament, too, is returning as an issue and the military lobby is flexing its muscles over the question of its budget. There is even publicly-expressed nervousness about what the Chileans may be up to in Patagonia. Now that the Argentine military–civilian ratio has dropped to slightly below the Latin American average,[11] it is easier than it has been since 1983 to sustain the assertion that Argentina is inadequately defended against external threat.

It is also by no means clear that the Argentine military has recognised that its role should be confined to external threats as defined in the new Defence Law. Not only were unsuccessful attempts made by senior officers to introduce a very broad military role in the domestic context into the new legislation, but, when they failed to achieve these amendments, the intention of the civilian parties to keep the military out of a domestic counter-insurgency role was almost immediately ignored. In fact, at the Seventeenth Conference of

American Armies, opened in Mar del Plata on 16 November 1987 by President Alfonsín himself, the Argentine delegation proposed a motion recommending inter-American military anti-subversive action.[18]

Whether developing social attitudes reflect a new realism regarding the possibility of the principle of civil supremacy achieving hegemony in Argentina or a re-writing of recent Argentine history remains debatable. However it is worth noting that political groups once subject to accusations of collaboration, such as the Bloquistas of San Juan and UCeDe elements, not least the leader of the party, Deputy Alvaro Alsogaray, have been growing more outspoken in their support of the military role in suppressing 'communism'. Alongside former Buenos Aires Police Chief Ramón Camps, on trial for his part in the 'dirty war', and Commander-in-Chief of the Air Force Brigadier-General Ernesto Crespo, these civilian politicians defended the principle of 'due obedience' and anticipated the passage of the bill in the Chamber of Deputies on 16 May and the Senate on 5 June and its confirmation as constitutional by the Supreme Court on 23 June 1987. The law as passed exempts from trial, for past and future offences, all officers below the rank of lieutenant-colonel unless excesses were committed on their own initiative or for their own benefit. Due obedience pre-empts a judicial decision and goes against the UN Convention on Torture signed by Alfonsín in 1984. Its enshrining in law is a further blow against the already enfeebled civilian courts and, as the dissenting justices of the Supreme Court pointed out, violates several articles of the Argentine Constitution. More importantly it suggests a new revisionism because it wholly ignores the chaotic quality of the Process and the independence of action displayed by members of the security services during that period, an independence echoed in the activities of Barreiro, Rico and their supporters.

An Argentine adage has it that the country has no memory, but in reality selective remembrance, a universal human trait, is particularly well developed. As the military regime retreats into the past, comparisons with the present are more and more unfavourable to Alfonsín's civilian government. Rising recorded crime rates and reporting of other deviant activity, rather than being recognised as symptoms of a freer press and less harsh repression, are publicised as features reflecting the indiscipline and decadence of modern society in a manner that comes close to coup-mongering. Likewise, the decline in real wages, down by about 25 per cent since Alfonsín took office, is set against the expectations raised in the *plata dulce* (easy money) days of Martínez de Hoz, when the over-valued peso gave the Argentine middle class a very comfortable existence. Now thousand of pensioners are suing the government for full payment of what is due to them under a law which the government had first ignored and then tried to suspend. It could hardly pay up in a situation in which the annual trade surplus is only a quarter of the interest on the US$54.6 billion national debt. The fact that much of the debt is inherited from the military government itself, which squandered billions on impractical construction schemes (unfinished highways, the 'Russian mountains'),[13] subsidising financial speculation and personal corruption, is already largely lost in history.

The brunt of the austerity measures seen as the means to achieve economic stability has been borne by low-income groups. The consequences, as with the pensioners, have been lawsuits and more than 2000 strikes against the present government by white-collar and blue-collar workers, both Radical and Peronist unions alike. Meanwhile, much wealth (an estimated US$28.6 billion) remains hidden away abroad and tax evasion flourishes despite tax reforms designed to encourage the repatriation of capital. The DGI estimates the 'black economy' to cover some 40–60 per cent of all economic activity. If so, it probably embraces the greatest entrepreneurial capacities and fiercest competition exhibited nationally whilst the deficits of around 300 companies owned by the federal and provincial governments are colossal.

It is little wonder that an *extranjera* attitude still prevails, by which the foreign is rated above the domestic, whether for style, value or stability. Houses are priced in dollars. Some services in Argentina cannot be purchased with the national currency. Queues to change even small quantities of national currency into dollars are a permanent feature at *cambios*, and the government has to issue bonds in dollar values in order to try to harness the tendency to its own good. The flight of capital is accompanied by a flight of individuals. The return of an expatriate for a visit leads to delegations of prospective emigrants seeking information on how to follow him.

Argentines joke that theirs is 'the country of the future, always has been and always will be'. But Argentina seems to be living entirely in a present determined by various interpretations of the past, not in a present oriented towards the future. This strengthens the 'zero-sum' aspect of her political culture. Optimism since 1983 regarding a new capacity for compromise had some basis. The coalition on which Alfonsín's election rested was itself the product of compromise, most notably by those right-of-centre elements who saw Peronism as the greater threat. But since its foundation in 1982, the UCeDe has gone from strength to strength electorally. Tactical voting has been set aside and nothing in the attitude or words of Alsogaray suggests that he will compromise with Radicalism to ensure the continuation of non-Peronist government. The same must be said of the developing stance of the UCR itself. Although Alfonsín's successor as leader and party nominee, the Governor of Córdoba, Eduardo Angeloz, is in economic matters on the 'liberal' right of the party and therefore presumably more sympathetic to UCeDe policies, his public political statements have thus far set him firmly within the tradition of Radical intransigence.

The most hopeful sign, the reaction to Easter Week, was expressed in popular opposition to '*los milicos*' and in a new-found civility amongst the various caucuses in Congress. Even at the time, this unity was more apparent than real. Not only were some political groupings more sympathetic to the military than others, but amongst those which strongly condemned the risings other hostilities were never entirely suspended. On signing the sectoral pact in support of democracy on 19 April 1987, Saúl Ubaldini, as General Secretary of the CGT, made a stirring speech stressing that he was remembering working-class hunger and the plight of the pensioners, not offering support to the Radical government. Short-term expediency of this kind forestalls the emergence of real tolerance and compromise even amongst those most criticised for these very traits. Alfonsín himself, subject to much abuse from within his own party for not elevating party functionaries to the extent that the UCR might wish and for including opposition politicians in his government and in advisory groups, is not above jibing at the political Left from time to time. The '*zurdos*' ('commies') have been a handy scapegoat for the demonstrations and unrest occasioned by visiting foreign bankers, although Alfonsín is a more sophisticated politician than such statements suggest and must know that blaming the Left will merely feed subversion theories.

Certainly Alfonsín has shown himself sufficiently sophisticated to recognise and seek to rectify one of the main institutional features long seen by political analysts as a major weakness of Argentine politics, the presidential system. Potash's famous dictum that the military is the only force capable of ousting an unwanted president before his six-year term expires[14] remains a potent argument for constitutional reform. In the seamy world of Argentine politics, Alfonsín's preference for a parliamentary system with a figurehead president serving a repeatable four-year term has been widely assumed to reflect his personal desire to extend his term in office. Rumours about the President's current morale suggest nothing could be further from the truth but, in any case, through Carlos Menem, governor of La Rioja, the Peronist opposition have made it clear that a parliamentary system is one aspect of constitutional reform they will not accept. The all-or-nothing presidency will remain and it is likely that Menem will inherit it in 1989.

The ideal of a parliamentary system and loyal opposition would be difficult to sustain in the Argentine context. It is true that at the official establishment of Renewal Peronism on 21 December 1985 a document was released proposing reorganisation of the party. But, whilst there are strongly nationalist groups within the UCR and there has been some considerable agreement between the two main parties on policies such as the dismantling of the 'national security state', fundamental differences remain. Much policy accord reflects trade-offs in any case; most recently a tax reform package in return for certain labour legislation the Peronists sought. The major ideological differences remain; for example federalism (with seventeen out of twenty-one provincial governors Peronist) versus Radical centralism, and economic nationalism (with strong Peronist pressure for a debt moratorium) versus the Radical orientation to the Western international financial system. These differences represent real political cultural gulfs alongside class-based divisions over the question of the degree of redistribution of economic resources, and these may yet prove to be unbridgeable.

When Alfonsín came to power in December 1983 inflation was more than 300 per cent p.a., the foreign debt was some US$43 billion, 600 000 Argentines were unemployed – with a further $1^1/_2$ million underemployed.[15] Optimism regarding political stability was high, but perhaps unwarranted, since for Argentina democracy rests on economic stability in the longer term. Some factors for intervention have declined. Military morale, measured by their public statements, may be recovering but it is still lower, for example, than it has been during any previous civilian presidency. Resistance to working-class participation is no longer tactically appropriate. Such participation exists, and besides Peronism is seen as changed, less threatening to business interests though by no means welcome. Secondary organisations are stronger, political parties have vastly increased memberships, but there is no evidence that they are more capable of dealing with the high level of crisis that Argentine politics and economics generate. Other factors remain as ever: the messianic ideology of some military elements is still in evidence and the presidential system intact.

Argentina is still clearly not a 'stable democracy' since in such a system the president and commander-in-chief need not be cautious in how he seeks to quell a military revolt. The question of whether such stability can be obtained must remain open for two full presidential terms at least, and the period must include the peaceful constitutional handover of power from one civilian political party to another. That is an experience Argentina has not had since 1916.

Argentina's past aside, nobody who has experienced the warmth and hospitality of her people could other than hope for a brighter future. There remain many grounds for optimism. Argentina is still a vast and wealthy country by world standards, with immense productive resources. Her people have shown the capacity to endure and to re-orientate. Able and honest men have been elevated to office, not least amongst the present government and also the Peronist opposition.[16] Her political institutions may have been much abused, but the fact that they survive suggest that they are not fundamentally faulty, although modification may prove desirable. Further, cultural diversity can be enriching, and indeed Argentina's literary heritage exemplifies this point. Perhaps, with time, it will also prove to be so in the political sphere.

Notes

CHAPTER 1

1. For example, Roberto Cortés Conde and Ezequiel Gallo, *La formación de la Argentina moderna* (Buenos Aires: Paidos, 1967) p. 11; Gino Germani, 'Hacia una democracia de masas', in Torcuato S. di Tella, Gino Germani and Jorge Graciarena (eds) *Argentina: sociedad de masas* (Buenos Aires: EUDEBA, 1965) p. 206.
2. For example, Gerardo Duejo, *El capital monopolista y las contradicciones secundarias en al sociedad argentina* (Buenos Aires: Siglo XXI, 1973); and Guillermo O'Donnell, *Reflexiones sobre las tendencias generales de cambio en el Estado burocrático-autoritario* (Buenos Aires: Centro de Estudios de Estado y Sociedad, 1975).
3. For example, Félix Luna, *Las crisis en la Argentina* (Buenos Aires: Schapire Editor, 1976) p. 43; Malcolm Deas, 'Argentine Adam', *London Review of Books*, vol. VIII, no. 20, 20 November 1986, pp. 17–1; and Nicos P. Mouzelis, *Politics in the Semi-Periphery: Early Parliamentarism and Late Industrialisation in the Balkans and Latin America* (Basingstoke, Hampshire: Macmillan, 1986) p.213.
4. Ronaldo Munck, 'Cycles of class struggle and the making of the working class in Argentina, 1890–1920', *Journal of Latin American Studies*, vol. XIX, no. 1, May 1987, pp. 21–3.
5. Torcuato S. di Tella, 'Raices de la controversia educacional argentina', in Torcuato S. de Tella and Tulio Halperín Donghi (eds) *Los fragmentos del poder: de la oligarquía a la poliarquía* (Buenos Aires: Editorial Jorge Alvarez, 1969) p. 317.
6. José M. Gómez and Eduardo J. Viola, 'Transición desde el autoritarismo y potencialidades de invención democrática en la Argentine de 1983', in Oscar Oszlak (ed.) *'Proceso', crisis y transición democrática*, Vol. II (Buenos Aires: Centro Editor de América Latina, 1984) p. 35; Luis González Esteves and Ignacio Llorente, 'Elecciones y preferencias políticas en Capital Federal y Gran Buenos Aires: el 30 de octubre de 1983', in Natalio R. Botana, Luis González Esteves, Ignacio Llorente, Manuel Mora y Araujo and Susan Alterman (eds) *La Argentina electoral* (Buenos Aires: Editorial Sudamericana, 1985) p. 52; Virgilio R. Beltran, 'Comentarios as trabajo de L. González Esteves e I. Llorente', in ibid., p. 75; and Manuel Mora y Araujo, 'La naturaleza de la coalición alfonsinista', in ibid., p. 93.
7. Glen Dealy, 'Prolegomena on the Spanish American Political Tradition', *Hispanic American Historical Review*, vol. XLVIII, February 1968, pp. 37–42.
8. Editor's introduction in Harold Blakemore (ed.) *Latin America: Essays in*

Continuity and Change (London: The British Broadcasting Corporation, 1974) p. 7.

9. Mouzelis, p. 7.
10. Manuel Ugarte, *The Destiny of a Continent* (New York: Alfred A. Knopf, 1925) pp. 220, 271; and Francisco José Moreno, *Legitimacy and Stability in Latin America; A Study of Chilean Political Culture* (New York: New York University Press, 1969) p. xii.
11. For example, Barrington Moore, Jr, *Social Origins of Dictatorship and Democracy: Lord and Peasant in the Making of the Modern World* (Harmondsworth: Penguin, 1969) p. 438.
12. Ezequiel Martínez Estrada, *X-Ray of the Pampa* (Austin, Texas: University of Texas Press, 1971) p. 183.
13. Ignacio Llorente, 'Alianzas políticas en el surgimiento del peronismo: el caso de la Provincia de Buenos Aires', in Manuel Mora y Araujo and Ignacio Llorente (eds) *El voto peronista: Estudios de sociología electoral argentina* (Buenos Aires: Editorial Sudamericana, 1980) p. 313; Manuel Mora y Araujo, 'Las bases elstructurales del peronismo', in ibid., p. 433; Manuel Mora y Araujo and Peter H. Smith, 'Peronismo y desarrollo: las elecciones de 1973', in ibid., p. 450.
14. Edward S. Milenky, *Argentina's Foreign Policies* (Boulder, Colorado: Westview Press, 1978).
15. Víctor M. Sonego, *Las dos Argentinas: Pistas para una lectura crítica de nuestra historia* (Buenos Aires: Ediciones Don Bosca, 1983) pp. 15, 173 and 217.
16. Tulio Halperín Donghi, *Argentina en el callejón* (Montevideo: ARCA, 1964) p. 7.
17. José Roberto Dromi, *Democracias frustradas y revoluciones inconclusas* (Buenos Aires: Ediciones Ciudad Argentina, 1983) p. 91.
18. Oscar Oszlak, *La formación del estado argentina* (Buenos Aires: Belgrano, 1982) p. 241.
19. Felix Luna, *Los caudillos* (Buenos Aires: A Peña Lillo, 1971) pp. 31–3, 35.

CHAPTER 2

1. Jeane Kirkpatrick, *Leader and Vanguard in Mass Society: A Study of Peronist Argentina* (Cambridge, Massachusetts: Massachusette Institute of TEchnology, 1971) pp. 3, 13.
2. Seymour Martin Lipset, 'Values, Education, and Entrepreneurship', in Seymour Martin Lipset and Aldo Solari (eds) *Elites in Latin America* (New York: Oxford University Press, 1967) p. 8.
3. Ben G. Burnett and Kenneth F. Johnson, 'Foundations of Latin American Politics', in Ben G. Burnett and Kenneth F. Johnson (eds) *Political Forces in Latin America: Dimensions of the Quest for Stability* (Belmont, California: Wadsworth Publishing, 1968) p. 17.
4. Ronald H. Chilcote and Joel C. Edelstein, 'Alternative Perspectives of Development and Underdevelopment in Latin America', in Ronald H. Chilcote and Joel C. Edelstein (eds) *Latin America: The Struggle*

with Dependency and Beyond (Cambridge, Massachusetts: Schenkman Publishing, 1974) p. 36.

5. Alistair Hennessy, *The Frontier in Latin American History* (London: Edward Arnold, 1978) pp. 28–29.

6. Allison Williams Bunkley, *The Life of Sarmiento* (New York: Greenwood Press, 1952) pp. 4–5.

7. Editor's introduction in Hugh M. Hamill, Jr (ed.) *Dictatorship in Spanish America* (New York: Alfred A. Knopf, 1965) p. 13.

8. François Chevalier, 'The Roots of Personalismo', in Hamill, P. 48.

9. Carlos Octavio Bunge, 'Caciquismo in Our America', in Hamill, p. 121.

10. Max Weber, *The Theory of Social and Economic Organization* (New York: The Free Press, 1964) pp. 346–54.

11. Editor's introduction in Hamill, p. 19.

12. Francisco José Moreno, *Legitimacy and Stability in Latin America: A Study of Chilean Political Culture* (New York: New York University Press, 1969) p. 12.

13. C.H. Haring, review of John Lynch, *Spanish Colonial Administration, 1782–1810: The Intendant System in the Vice-Royalty of the Río de la Plata* (Fair Lawn, New Jersey: Essential Books, 1958), in *Hispanic American Historical Review*, vol. XXXIX, no. 3, August 1959, pp. 471–2; R.H. Humphreys, *Tradition and Revolt in Latin America* (London: Weidenfeld and Nicolson, 1969) p. 84; David Bushnell, *Reform and Reaction in the Platine Provinces, 1810 – 1852* (Gainsesville, Florida: University of Florida Press, 1983) p. 2; and James Lockhart and Stuart B. Schwartz, *Early Latin America: A History of Colonial Spanish America and Brazil* (New York: Cambridge University Press, 1983) pp. 347–58.

14. Jacques Lambert, *Latin America: Social Structure and Political Institutions* (Berkeley and Los Angeles: University of California Press, 1967) pp. 127–9.

15. Weber, pp. 346–54.

16. Moreno, pp. 23–4 and 28–9.

17. Ysabel F., Rennie, *The Argentine Republic* (New York: Macmillan, 1945) p. 29; and David Rock, *Argentina 1516–1982: From Spanish Colonization to the Falklands War* (Berkeley and Los Angeles: University of California Press, 1985) p. 88.

18. For example, Theodore Wyckoff, 'The Role of the Military in Contemporary Latin American Politics', *Western Political Quarterly*, vol. XIII, 1960, pp. 445–68; and Brian Loveman and Thomas M. Davies, Jr, 'Instability, Violence and the Age of the Caudillos', in Brian Loveman and Thomas M. Davies, Jr. (eds) *The Politics of Antipolitics: The Military in Latin America* (Lincoln, Nebraska: University of Nebraska Press, 1978) p. 25.

19. Lockhart and Schwartz, p. 359; and Rock, p. 47.

20. John J. Johnson, *The Military and Society in Latin America* (Stanford, California: Stanford University Press, 1964) p. 224.

21. Richard M. Morse, 'The Heritage of Latin America', in Howard J. Wiarda (ed.) *Politics and Social Change in Latin America: The Distinct*

Tradition (Amherst, Massachusetts: University of Massachusetts Press, 1974) p. 55.

22. Jorge Abelardo Ramos, *Revolución y Contrarevolución en la Argentina* (Buenos Aires: Editorial Plus Ultra, 1965) p. 14.

23. For example, André Gunder Frank, *Dependent Accumulation and Underdevelopment* (London: Macmillan, 1978) pp. 85–7.

24. Alberto Belloni, *Peronismo y socialismo nacional* (Buenos Aires: Ediciones Coyocán, 1962) p. 7.

25. Howard J. Wiarda, 'Social Change, Political Development, and the Latin American Tradition', in Wiarda, p. 11.

26. James Bryce, *South America: Observations and Impressions* (New York: Macmillan, 1914) p. 494.

27. William W. Pierson and Federico G. Gil, *Governments of Latin America* (New York: McGraw-Hill, 1957) p. 63.

28. Leopoldo Zea, *América en la historia* (Mexico: Fondo de Cultura Económica, 1957) p. 17.

29. José Ortega y Gasset, *Invertebrate Spain* (London: George Allen and Unwin, 1937) p. 34; and Roberto Fernandez Retamar, 'Debunking the Black Legend', *UNESCO Courier*, August–September 1977, p. 58.

30. Wiarda, in Wiarda, p. 12.

31. William S. Stokes, 'Social Classes in Latin America', in Peter G. Snow (ed.) *Government and Politics in Latin America* (New York: Holt Rinehart and Winston, 1967) p. 53.

32. Wiarda, in Wiarda, p. 12.

33. Editors' introduction in Joseph Maier and Richard W. Weatherhead (eds) *Politics of Change in Latin America* (New York: Frederick A. Praeger, 1964) pp. 3–4.

34. Kalman H. Silvert, 'The Politics of Social and Economic Change in Latin America', in Paul Halmos (ed.) *Latin American Sociological Studies* (Keele, Staffordshire: University of Keele, 1967) p. 51.

35. Tulio Halperín Donghi, *Politics, Economics and Society in Argentina in the Revolutionary Period* (Cambridge: Cambridge University Press, 1975) p. 3.

36. Wiarda, in Wiarda, p. 12.

37. Ibid

38. Antonio O. Donini, 'Religion and Social Conflict in the Perón Era', in Frederick C. Turner and José Enrique Miguens (eds) *Juan Perón and the Reshaping of Argentina* (Pittsburgh, Pennsylvania: University of Pittsburgh Press, 1983) p. 80/

39. Ivan Vallier, 'Religious Elites: Differentiations and Developments in Roman Catholicism', in Lipset and Solari, pp. 191–2.

40. Alexander T. Edelmann, *Latin American Government and Politics: The Dynamics of a Revolutionary Society* (Homewood, Illinois: The Dorsey Press, 1965) p. 158.

41. Lucio V. Mansilla, *Rozas: Ensayo histórico-psicológico* (Buenos Aires: Editorial Bragado, 1967) p. 79.

42. Michael Soltys, 'The road to separation of Church and state', *Buenos Aires Herald*, 25 October 1986, p. 8.

43. Charles A. Hale, 'The Reconstruction of Nineteenth Century Politics

in Spanish America; A Case for the History of Ideas', *Latin American Research Review*, vol. VIII, no. 2, Summer 1973, p. 64.

44. Marysa Gerassi, 'Argentine Nationalism of the Right: The History of an Ideological Development, 1930–1946', unpublished PhD thesis, Columbia University, 1984.

45. Arthur P. Whitaker, 'Nationalism and Religion in Argentina and Uruguay', in William V. D'Antonia and Frederick B. Pike (eds) *Religion, Revolution and Reform: New Forces for Change in Latin America* (New York: Frederick A. Praeger, 1964) p. 83.

46. Robert McGeagh, 'Catholicism and Sociopolitical Change in Argentina: 1943–1973', unpublished PhD thesis, University of New Mexico, 1974, p. 5.

47. Gerassi, p. 106; McGeagh, p. 32.

48. Peter G Snow, *Political Forces in Argentina* (Boston: Allyn and Bacon, 1971) pp. 82–3; c.f. McGeagh, pp. 52–3, 59–60, 84 and 88.

49. Robert J. Alexander, *The Perón Era* (New York: Russell and Russell, 1965) pp. 126, 127 and 130–1.

50. Snow, p. 83.

51. Arthur P. Whitaker, *Argentina* (Englewood Cliffs, New Jersey: Prentice-Hall, 1964) p. 141.

52. Robert J. Alexander, *Latin American Politics and Government* (New York: Harper and Row, 1965) p. 114; McGeagh, p. 166.

53. Guillermo A. Makin, 'The Military in Argentine Politics: 1880 – 1982', *Journal of International Studies*, vol.II, no. 1, Spring 1983, p. 55; and David Yallop, *In God's Name* (London: Jonathan Cape, 1984) p. 132.

54. John J. Kennedy, *Catholicism, Nationalism and Democracy in Argentina* (Notre Dame, Indiana: University of Notre Dame Press, 1958) pp. 208–9.

55. Luis González Esteves and Ignacio Llorente, 'Elecciones y preferencias políticas en Capital Federal y Gran Buenos Aires: el 30 de octubre de 1983', in Natalio R. Botana, Luis González Esteves, Ignacio Llorente, Manuel Mora y Araujo and Susan Alterman (eds) *La Argentina electoral* (Buenos Aires: Editorial Sudamericana, 1985) pp. 45–6.

56. Michael Dodson, 'The Catholic Church in Contemporary Argentina', in Alberto Ciria *et al.*, *New Perspectives on Modern Argentina* (Bloomington, Indiana: Indiana University Press, 1972) p. 57; and Michael Dodson, 'The Christian Left in Latin American Politics', in Daniel H. Levine (eda.) *Churches and Politics in Latin America* (Beverly Hills, California: Sage Publications, 1979) p. 120.

57. Snow, p. 86.

58. Whitaker, in D'Antonia and Pike, p. 85.

59. Dodson, in Ciria, pp. 60 and 62; McGeach, p. 326.

60. Dodson, in Levine, p. 121: and Donini, in Turner and Miguens, p. 91.

61. Russell H. Fitzgibbon and Julio A. Fernandez, *Latin America: Political Culture and Development* (Englewood Cliffs, New Jersey: Prentice-Hall, 1981) p. 307.

62. Jacobo Timerman, 'Choosing Silence Over Debate', *Newsweek*, 22 October 1984, p. 4; *Buenos Aires Herald*, 11 May 1985; and Emilio

F. Mignone, *Iglesia y dictadura; el papel de la iglesia a la luz de sus relaciones con el régimen militar* (Buenos Aires: Ediciones de Pensamiento Nacional, 1986).

63. Michael Soltys, 'September CoL fails to raise eyebrows', *Buenos Aires Herald*, 12 October 1986, p. 20; Michael Soltys, 'Camps court trial adjourns for 10 days', *Buenos Aires Herald*, 19 October 1986, p. 8; and Soltys, 26 October 1986, p. 8.
64   José Luis de Imaz, *Motivación electoral* (Buenos Aires: Instituto de Desarrollo Económico y Social, 1962) p. 25.
65. Bryce, p. 342.
66. McGeagh, pp 196–7.
67. Kirkpatrick, p. 128.
68. Richard Gillespie, *Soldiers of Perón: Argentina's Montoneros* (Oxford: Clarendon Press, 1982) pp. 52–3.
69. David McClelland, 'The Achievement Motive in Economic Growth', in Jason L. Finkle and Richard w. Gable (eds) *Political Development and Social Change* (New York: John Wiley and Sons, 1971) p. 97.
70   Roger E. Vekemans, 'Economic Development, Social Change and Cultural Mutation in Latin America', in D'Antonio and Pike, p. 139.

CHAPTER 3

1. Domingo F. Sarmiento, *Life in the Argentine Republic in the Days of the Tyrants (or Civilization and Barbarism)* (New York: Collier Books, 1961) p. 60.
2. José Luis Romero, *A History of Argentine Political Thought* (Stanford, California: Stanford University Press, 1963) pp. 69–70 and 83; and Jacques Lambert, *Latin America: Social Structure and Political Institutions* (Berkeley and Los Angeles: University of California Press, 1967) p. 122.
3. Víctor M. Sonego, *Las dos Argentinas: Pistas para una lectura crítica de nuestra historia* (Buenos Aires: Ediciones Don Bosca, 1983) pp. 37 and 154.
4. Romero, P. 82.
5. John J. Kennedy, *Catholicism, Nationalism and Democracy in Argentina* (Notre Dame, Indiana: University of Notre Dame Press, 1958) p. 31; and David Rock, *Argentina 1516–1982: From Spanish Colonization to the Falklands War* (Berkeley and Los Angeles: University of California Press, 1985) pp. 98–9.
6. Allison Williams Bunkley, *The Life of Sarmiento* (New York: Greenwood Press, 1952) pp. 22–3; and William H. Jeffrey, *Mitre and Argentina* (New York: Library Publishers 1952) p. 15.
7. Jonathan C. Brown, 'The Bondage of Old Habits in Nineteenth Century Argentina', *Latin American Research Review*, vol. XXI, no. 2, 1986, p. 20.
8. Kennedy, p. 33.
9. Sarmiento, p. 108.

10. Sonego, p. 17.
11. Carlos Ibarguren, *Juan Manuel de Rosas: Su vida, su tiempo, su drama* (Buenos Aires: Libreria 'La Facultad' de Juan Roldán y Cia., 1930) pp. 141 and 219.
12. John Lynch, *Argentine Dictator: Juan Manuel de Rosas 1829–1852* (Oxford: Clarendon Press, 1981) p. 114.
13. Romero, p. 132; Ezequiel Martínez Estrada, *Para una revisión de las letras argentinas* (Buenos Aires: Editorial Losada, 1967) p. 47; and George Camacho, *Latin America: A Short History* (London: Allen Lane, 1973) p. 108.
14. Bunkley, p. 118; Esteban Echeverría, *Dogma socialista y otros páginas políticas* (Buenos Aires: Angel Estrada y Cia, 1958); Arthur P. Whitaker, *Argentina* (Englewood Cliffs, New Jersey: Prentice-Hall, 1964) p. 61; Mark D. Szuchman, 'Continuity and Conflict in Buenos Aires: Comments on the Historical City', in Stanley R. Ross and Thomas F. McGann (eds) *Buenos Aires: 400 Years* (Austin, Texas: University of Texas Press, 1982) pp. 56–7; and Antonio Pagés Larraya, *Juan María Gutiérrez y Ricardo Rojas: Iniciación de la crítica argentina* (Buenos Aires: Universidad de Buenos Aires, 1983) p. 11.
15. Arthur P. Whitaker, *The United States and Argentina* (Cambridge, Massachusetts: Harvard University Press, 1954) pp. 75–6; and Peter Calvert, 'The Mexican Revolution: Theory or Fact?', *Journal of Latin American Studies*, vol. I. no. 1, May 1969, p. 52.
16. Tomás Roberto Fillol, *Social Factors in Economic Development: The Argentine Case* (Cambridge Massachusetts: Massachusetts Institute of Technology, 1961) p. 41; Torcuato S. di Tella, 'Raíces de la controversía educational argentina', in Torcuato S. di Tella and Tulio Halperín Donghi (eds) *Los fragmentos del poder: de la oligarquía a la poliarquía* (Buenos Aires: Editorial Jorge Alvarez, 1969) p. 292.
17. Sarmiento, pp. 33–4.
18. Romero, p. 137.
19. Romero, pp. 128, 136 and 141.
20. Ricardo Rojas, *El profeta de la pampa: Vida de Sarmiento* (Buenos Aires: Editorial Losada, SA, 1947) pp. 21–7 and 659; Bunkley, pp. 470–1; Carlos B. Quiroga, *Sarmiento: Hacia la reconstrucción del espíritu argentino* (Buenos Aires: Ediciones Antonio Zamora, 1961), pp. 8–11; Alain Rouquié (trans. Arturo Iglesias Echegaray), *Poder militar y sociedad política en la Argentina* (Buenos Aires: Emecé Editores, 1981) p. 60; and Ezequiel Martínez Estrada, *X-Ray of the Pampa* (Austin, Texas: University of Texas Press, 1971), p. 317.
21. Bunkley, p. 519.
22. Gino Germani and Kalman Silvert, 'Estructura social e intervención militar en América Latina', in Torcuato S. di Tella, Gino Germani and Jorge Graciarena (eds) *Argentina: sociedad de masas* (Buenos Aires: EUDEBA, 1965) p. 231.
23. Gino Germani, *Política y sociedad en una época de transición: de la sociedad tradicional a la sociedad de masas* (Buenos Aires: Editorial Paidos, 1962) pp. 220–1; Romero, pp. 142–3; Juan Bautista Alberdi, *Bases y puntos de partida para la organización política de la República Argentina* (Buenos Aires:

Editorial Plus Ultra, 1980) p. 237; and Guido di Tella, 'Economic Controversies in Argentina from the 1920s to the 1940s', in Guido di Tella and D.C.M. Platt (eds) *The Political Economy of Argentina 1880–1946* (Basingstoke, Hampshire: Macmillan, 1986) pp. 124–5.

24. Roberto Etchepareborda, 'La estructura socio-política argentina y la generación del ochenta', *Latin American Research Review*, vol. XIII, no. 1, Spring 1978, pp. 128–9.

25. Martínez Estrada (1971) p. 66.

26. Arturo Cambours Ocampo, *Verdad y Mentira de la Literatura Argentina: Bases Históricos de un Idioma Nacional* (Buenos Aires: Editorial A. Peña Lillo, 1962) p. 9; and Gustavo Sosa-Pujato, 'Popular Culture', in Mark Falcoff and Ronald H. Dolkart (eds) *Prologue to Perón: Argentina in Depression and War, 1930–43* (Berkeley: University of California Press, 1975) p. 137.

27. Martínez Estrada (171) p. 227.

28. George I. Blanksten, 'The Politics of Latin America', in Gabriel A. Almond and James S. Coleman (eds) *The Politics of Developing Areas* (Princeton, New Jersey: Princeton University Press, 1960) pp. 490–1.

29. Leopoldo Zea, *Ensayos sobre filosofía en la historia* (Mexico City: Stylo, 1948) pp. 181–2.

30. Editor's preface in Falcoff and Dolkart, p. xv.

31. Gabriel A. Almond and Sidney Verba, *The Civic Culture: Political Attitudes and Democracy in Five Nations* (Princeton, New Jersey: Princeton University Press, 1963) p. 5.

32. Howard J. Wiarda, 'Law and Political Development in Latin America: Toward a Framework for Analysis' in Howard J. Wiarda (ed.) *Politics and Social Change in Latin America: The Distinct Tradition* (Amherst, Massachusetts: University of Massachusetts Press, 1974) pp. 206–7; Arturo Merlo, *Argentina totalitaria* (Buenos Aires: Editorial Occidente, 1984) p. 28.

33. Glen Dealy, 'The Tradition of Monistic Democracy in Latin America', in Wiarda, pp. 72–3, 82–3 and 86.

34. Nicos P. Mouzelis, *Politics in the Semi-Periphery: Early Parliamentarism and Late Industrialisation in the Balkans and Latin America* (Basingstoke, Hampshire: Macmillan, 1986) p.18.

35. Oscar Cornblit, 'La opción conservadora en la política argentina', *Desarrollo Económico*, vol. XIV, January–March 1975, p. 609; Natalio R. Botana, *El orden conservador: la política argentina entre 1880 y 1916* (Buenos Aires: Editorial Sudamericana, 1977) pp. 71–3.

36. David Viñas, *Rebeliones populares argentinas: de los montoneros a los anarquistas* (Buenos Aires: Carlos Pérez Editor, 1971) p. 145.

37. Ronald Howard Dolkart, 'Manuel A. Fresco, Governor of the Province of Buenos Aires, 1936–1940: A Study of the Argentine Right and Its Response to Economic and Social Change', unpublished PhD thesis, University of California, 1969, pp. 77–80; Eduardo Crawley, *A House Divided: Argentina 1880–1980* (London: C. Hurst, 1984) p. 57; and Richard J. Walter, *The Province of Buenos Aires and Argentine Politics, 1912–1943* (Cambridge University Press, 1985) pp. 8–10.

38. Robert A. Dahl, *Polyarchy: Participation and Opposition* (New Haven:

Yale University Press, 1971) p. 137; and Tulio Halperín Donghi, 'The Argentine Export Economy: Intimations of Mortality, 1894–1930', in di Tella and Platt, p. 55; c.f. Anne L. Potter, 'The Failure of Democracy in Argentina 1916–1930: An Institutional Perspective', *Journal of Latin American Studies*, vol. XIII, no. 1, May 1981, p. 86.

39. Mouzelis, p.4.
40. Dahl, p. 136.
41. Charles W. Anderson, *Politics and Economic Change in Latin America: The Governing of Restless Nations* (New York: Van Nostrand Reinhold, 1967) p. 196.
42. Republic of Argentina, *Constitución de la Nación Argentina* (Buenos Aires: Torres Agüero Editor, 1981).
43. Lars Schoultz, *The Populist Challenge: Argentine Electoral Behavior in the Postwar Era* (Chapel Hill: University of North Carolina Press, 1983) p. 20.
44. Juan Carlos Torre, 'The Meaning of Current Workers' Struggles', *Latin American Perspectives*, vol. 1, no. 3, 1974, pp. 73–4; Robert R. Kaufman, 'Corporatism, Clientielism and Partisan Conflict: A Study of Seven Latin American Countries', in James M. Malloy (ed.) *Authoritarianism and Corporatism in Latin America* (Pittsburgh: University of Pittsburgh Press, 1977) p. 133; Louise Maureen Doyon, 'Organized Labour and Perón (1943–1955): A Study of the Conflictual Dynamics of the Peronist Movement in Power', unpublished PhD thesis, University of Toronto, 1978, p. 432; Daniel Maddison James, 'Unions and Politics: The Development of Peronist Trade Unions, 1955–66', unpublished PhD thesis, London School of Economics and Political Science, 1979, p. 5; Daniel James, 'Rationalisation and Working Class Response: the Context and Limits of Factory Floor Activity in Argentina', *Journal of Latin American Studies*, vol. XIII, no. 2, November 1981, p. 392.
45. Crawley, pp. 273–4.
46. Crawley, pp. 273–4.
47. Ricardo Rojas, *La literatura argentina, ensayo filosófico sobre la evolución de la cultura de la Plata* (Buenos Aires: 1925) cited in Kennedy, pp. 34–5.
48. Sonego, pp. 15, 173 and 217.
49. Martínez Estrada (1971) p. 199.
50. Jeane Kirkpatrick, *Leader and Vanquard in Mass Society: A Study of Peronist Argentina* (Cambridge, Massachusetts: Massachusetts Institute of Technology, 1971) pp. 198 and 201.
51. Crawley, p. 262.
52. Guillermo O'Donnell, *Modernization and Bureaucratic-Authoritarianism: Studies in South American Politics* (Berkeley: University of California Press, 1973) pp. 87 and 94.

CHAPTER 4

1. Douglas A. Chalmers, 'The Politicised State in Latin America', in James M. Malloy (ed.) *Authoritarianism and Corporatism in Latin*

America (Pittsburgh, Pennsylvania: University of Pittsburgh Press, 1977) p. 27.

2. Irving Louis Horowitz, 'The Norm of Illegitimacy: Toward a General Theory of Latin American Political Development', in Arthur J. Field (ed.) *City and Country in the Third World: Issues in the Modernisation of Latin America* (Cambridge, Massachusetts: Schenkman Publishing, 1970) pp. 28–9.

3. Richard M. Morse, 'The Heritage of Latin America', in Howard J. Wiarda (eda.) *Politics and Social Change in Latin America: The Distinct Tradition* (Amherst, Massachusetts: University of Massachusetts Press, 1974) pp. 52–3.

4. William Everett Kane, *Civil Strife in Latin America: A Legal History of US Involvement* (Baltimore: Johns Hopkins University Press, 1972) p. 176.

5. See Republic of Argentina, Comisión Nacional sobre la Desaparición de Personas, *Nunca Mas: Informe de la Comisión Nacional sobre la Desaparición de Personas* (Buenos Aires: EUDEBA, 1986).

6. Jacques Lambert, *Latin America: Social Structure and Political Institutions* (Berkeley and Los Angeles: University of California Press, 1967) p. 160.

7. William S. Stokes, 'Violence as a Power Factor in Latin American Politics', in Robert D. Tomasek (ed.) *Latin American Politics: Studies of the Contemporary Scene* (Garden City, New York: Doubleday, 1966) p. 251.

8. John J. Johnson, *The Military and Society in Latin America* (Stanford, California: Stanford University Press, 1964) p. 38.

9. Peter Calvert, *Latin America: Internal Conflict and International Peace* (London: Macmillan, 1969) p. 17.

10. Félix Luna, *Los caudillos* (Buenos Aires: A Peña Lillo, 1971) p. 19; John Lynch, *Argentine Dictator: Juan Manuel de Rosas, 1829–1852* (Oxford: The Clarendon Press, 1981) pp. 213–14.

11. Roberto Cortés Conde and Ezequiel Gallo, *La formación de la Argentina moderna* (Buenos Aires: Paidos, 1967) p. 51; James R. Scobie, *Argentina: A City and a Nation* (New York: Oxford University Press, 1971) p. 258; and Lynch, pp. 53–5.

12. Ezequiel Martínez Estrada, *X-Ray of the Pampa* (Austin, Texas: University of Texas Press, 1971) p. 48.

13. Andrew Graham-Yooll, *Small Wars You May Have Missed* (London: Junction Books, 1983) p. 119.

14. Jeane Kirkpatrick, *Leader and Vanguard in Mass Society: A Study of Peronist Argentina* (Cambridge, Massachusetts: Massachusetts Institute of Technology 1971) p. 201.

15. Julio A. Fernández, *The Political Elite in Argentina* (New York: New York University Press, 1970) p. 93.

16. Kirkpatrick, pp. 75 and 216.

17. Martin C. Needler, *Latin American Politics in Perspective* (Princeton, New Jersey: D. Van Nostrand, 1963) pp. 38–9 and 76.

18. Brian Barry, *Sociologists, Economists and Democracy* (London: Macmillan, 1970) pp. 49 and 51; Anne L. Potter, 'The Failure of Democracy in

Argentina 1916–1930: An Institutional Perspective', *Journal of Latin American Studies*, vol. XIII, no. 1, May 1981, p. 88.

19. Merle Kling, 'Violence and Politics in Latin America', in Paul Halmos (ed.) *Latin American Sociological Studies*, (Keele, Staffordshire: University of Keele, 1967) p. 128.

20. Gabriel A. Almond and G. Bingham Powell, Jr, 'A Developmental Approach to Political Systems: An Overview', in Jason L. Finkle and Richard W. Gable (eds) *Political Development and Social Change* (New York: John Wiley and Sons, 1971) pp. 56–7.

21. Gunnar Myrdal, *Asian Drama: An Inquiry into the Poverty of Natons* (Harmondsworth: Penguin, 1968) p. 66.

22. Charles W. Anderson, *Politics and Economic Change in Latin America: The Governing of Restles Nations* (New York: Van Nostrand Reinhold, 1967) p. 140.

23. Víctor Alba, *The Latin Americans* (New York: Frederick A. Praeger, 1969) p. 43.

24. Guillermo A. O'Donnell, *Modernisation and Bureaucratic-Authoritarianism: Studies in South American Politics* (Berkeley: University of California Press, 1973) p. 152.

25. Guillermo O'Donnell, 'Permanent Crisis and the Failure to Create a Democratic Regime: Argentina, 1955–66', in Juan J. Linz and Alfred Stepan (eds) *The Breakdown of Democratic Regimes: Latin America* (Baltimore: Johns Hopkins University Press, 1978) p. 140.

26. C.B. Macpherson, *The Real World of Democracy* (Oxford: Clarendon Press, 1966) pp. 11 and 20; and Kling, in Halmos, p. 120.

27. Kalman II. Silvert, 'The Costs of Anti-Nationalism: Argentina', in Kalman H. Silvert (ed.) *Expectant Peoples: Nationalism and Development* (New York: Vintage Books, 1967) pp. 258–9.

28. Horowitz, in Field, pp. 25–26.

29. Johnson, p. 46.

30. Winthrop R. Wright, *British-Owned Railways in Argentina: Their Effect on Economic Nationalism, 1854–1948* (Austin, Texas: University of Texas Press, 1974) pp. 17–18, 26 and 28–9; Colin M. Lewis, 'The British-Owned Argentine Railways, 1857–1947', unpublished PhD thesis, University of Exeter, 1974, p. 397.

31. Isaiah Berlin, *Four Essays op Liberty* (Oxford: Oxford University Press, 1969) pp. 122–34.

32. Irving Louis Horowitz, 'The Military Elites', in Seymour Martin Lipset and Aldo Solari (eds) *Elites in Latin America* (New York: Oxford University Press, 1967) p. 158.

33. Silvert, in Silvert, p. 352.

34. Kirkpatrick, pp. 162–3.

35. Morse, in Wiarda, p. 65.

36. José Enrique Miguens, 'Un análisis del fenómeno', in J.A. Paita (ed.) *Argentina 1930–1960* (Buenos Aires: Editorial SUR, 1961) p. 348.

37. O'Donnell, in Linz and Stepan, p. 162.

38. Guillermo A. Makin, 'The Military in Argentine Politics: 1880–1982', *Journal of International Studies*, vol. XII, no. 1, Spring 1983, p. 61.

39. Guillermo O'Donnell, 'Modernization and Military Coups: Theory, Comparisons and the Argentine Case', in Abraham F. Lowenthal (ed.) *Armies and Politics in Latin America* (New York: Holmes and Meier, 1976)p. 208.

40. George Camacho, *Latin America: A Short History* (London: Allen Lane, 1973) p. 26.

41. Anderson, pp. 94–109.

42. Oscar Cornblit, 'La opción conservadora en la política argentina', *Desarrollo Económico*, vol. XIV, January–March 1975, p. 637.

43. Guido di Tella, *Argentina under Perón, 1973–76: The Nation's Experience with a Labour-based Government* (London: Macmillan, 1983) pp. 199–200.

44. Russell H. Fitzgibbon and Julio A. Fernández, *Latin America: Political Culture and Development* (Englewood Cliffs, New Jersey: Prentice-Hall, 1981) p. 6.

45. José Luis de Imaz, *Motivación electoral* (Buenos Aires: Instituto de Desarrollo Económico y Social, 1962) pp. 3–4.

46. Kirkpatrick, pp. 162–3 and 168–9.

47. Vicente Reina Fernández, *Pensar en Argentina* (Buenos Aires: Ediciones Bodoni, 1983) p. 36.

48. Jürgen Habermas, *Legitimation Crisis* (London: Heinemann, 1976) p. 74.

49. James Neilson, 'The Approaching Pact', *Buenos Aires Herald*, 12 May 1983, p. 10.

50. Kirkpatrick, pp. 150–1.

51. Johnson, pp. 153 and 163.

52. James W. Rowe, 'Argentina's Restless Military', in Tomasek, p. 446.

53. Kirkpatrick, p. 125.

54. J.F. Torres, 'A New (and Partial) Approach to Measurement of Political Power', *Western Political Quarterly*, vol. XXVI, no. 2, June 1973, pp. 304–5.

55. *Buenos Aires Herald*, 22 December 1985, p. 17.

CHAPTER 5

1. Max Weber, *The Theory of Social and Economic Organisation* (New York: The Free Press, 1964) p. 328.

2. Weber, p. 328.

3. C.f. surveys of voting preferences for Alfonsín reported in Michael Soltys, 'Cat-and-mouse game fails to materialize', *Buenos Aires Herald*, 5 July 1987, p. 7.

4. Donna J. Guy, 'The Rural Working Class in Nineteenth Century Argentina: Forced Plantation Labour in Tucumán, *Latin American Research Review*, vol. XIII, no. 1, 1978, p. 135; and Frederick C. Turner, 'Entrepreneurs and *Estancieros* in Perón's Argentina: Cohesion and Conflict Within the Elite', in Frederick C. Turner and José Enrique Miguens (eds) *Juan Perón and the Reshaping of Argentina* (Pittsburgh, Pennsylvania: University of Pittsburgh Press, 1983) p. 226.

5. Liisa North, *Civil–Military Relations in Argentina, Chile and Peru* (Berkeley, California: University of California, 1966) p. 6.

6. Tulio Halperín Donghi, *Politics, Economics and Society in Argentina inthe Revolutionary Period* (Cambridge: Cambridge University Press, 1975) p. 65.

7. John Lynch, *Argentine Dictator: Juan Manuel de Rosas, 1829–1852* (Oxford: Clarendon Press, 1981) p. 124.

8. Félix Luna, *Los caudillos* (Buenos Aires: A Peña Lillo, 1971) . 20.

9. Miron Burgin, *The Economic Aspects of Argentine Federalism 1820–1852* (Cambridge, Massachusetts: Harvard University Press, 1946) p. 110.

10. Celso Rodríguez, 'Regionalism, Populism and Federalism in Argentina, 1916–1930', unpublished PhD thesis, University of Massachusetts, 1974, pp. v–vii.

11. Peter G. Snow, 'Argentina', in Ben G. Burnett and Kenneth F. Johnson (eds) *Political Forces in Latin America: Dimensions of the Quest for Stability* (Belmont, California: Wadsworth Publishing, 1968) pp. 399 – 400.

12. William S. Stokes, *Latin American Politics* (New York: Thomas Y. Crowell, 1959) p. 272.

13. Domingo Faustino Sarmiento, *Life in the Argentine Republic in the Days of the Tyrants (or Civilization and Barbarism)* (New York: Collier Books, 1961) p. 34.

14. George Pendle, *Argentina* (London: Oxford University Press, 1980) pp. 52–3.

15. David Crichton Jordan, 'Argentina's Nationalist Movements and the Political Parties (1930–1963): A Study of Conflict', unpublished PhD thesis, University of Pennsylvania, 1964, p. 55; Oscar Cornblit, 'La opción conservadora en la política argentina', *Desarrollo Económico*, vol. XIV, January–March 1975, p. 612: Natalio R. Botana, *El orden conservador: la política argentina entre 1880 y 1916* (Buenos Aires: Editorial Sudamericana, 1977) p. 17; David Rock, *Politics in Argentina 1890–1930; The Rise and Fall of Radicalism* (London: Cambridge University Press, 1975) pp. vii, 25 and 30.

16. Michael L. Conniff, 'Towards a Comparative Definition of Populism', in Michael L. Conniff (ed.) *Latin American Populism in Comparative Perspective* (Albuquerque, New Mexico: University of New Mexico Press, 1982) p. 23.

17. Maraysa Gerassi, 'Argentine Nationalism of the Right: The History of an Ideological Development, 1930–1946', unpublished PhD thesis, Columbia University 1984, p. 19.

18. Ezequiel Gallo and Silvia Sigal, 'La formación de los partidos políticos contemporaneos', in Torcuato S. di Tella, Gino Germani and Jorge Graciarena (eds) *Argentina: sociedad de masas* (Buenos Aires: EUDEBA, 1965) pp. 127–8.

19. Dario Canton, 'Military Interventions in Argentina, 1960 – 1966', in Jacques Van Doorn (eda) *Military Profession and Military Regimes: Commitments and Conflicts* (The Hague: Mouton, 1969) p. 265; Ezequiel Gallo, 'Santa Fé en la segunda mitad del siglo XIX; transformaciones en su estructura regional', in Torcuato S. di Tella and Tulio Halperín

Donghi (eds) *Los fragmentos del poder: de la oligarquía a la poliarquía* (Buenos Aires: Editorial Jorge Alvarez, 1969) p. 268; Alain Rouquié (trans. Arturo Iglesias Echegaray) *Poder Militar y sociedad política en la Argentina* (Buenos Aires: Emecé Editores, 1981) pp. 135–6; and Rock, pp. 42 and 45.

20. Rock, pp. 49–50.
21. Rock, p. 202.
22. Anne L. Potter, 'The Failure of Democracy in Argentina 1916–1930: An Institutional Perspective', *Journal of Latin American Studies*, vol. XIII, no. 1, May 1981, p. 101; c.f. Botana, pp. 129–134.
23. Rodríguez, pp. 43, 47–8, 56–7, 60, 76–8, 100, 111–3, 134–5, 284–5, 287 and 297.
24. Peter H. Smith, *Argentina and the Failure of Democracy: Conflict Among Political Elites, 1904–1955* (Madison, Wisconsin: University of Wisconsin Press, 1974) p. 95.
25. See Rodríguez.
26. Paul W. Drake, 'Conclusion: Reguiem for Populism?', in Conniff, p. 218.
27. Walter Little, 'Political Integration in Peronist Argentina, 1943 – 1955', unpublished PhD thesis, University of Cambridge, 1971, p. 12.
28. Walter Little, 'Electoral Aspects of Peronism, 1946–1954', *Journal of Inter-American Studies and World Affairs*, vol. XV, no. 3, August 1973, p. 274; and Robert H. Dix, 'Populism: Authoritarian and Democratic', *Latin American Research Review*, vol. XX, no. 2, 1985, pp. 35–6.
29. See Rodríguez; and Ronald Howard Dolkart, 'Manuel A. Fresco, Governor of the Province of Buenos Aires, 1936 – 1940: A Study of the Argentine Right and Its Response to Economic and Social Change', unpublished PhD thesis, University of California, 1969, pp. viii–x.
30. Thomas E. Skidmore, *Politics in Brazil, 1930–1964: An Experiment in Democracy* (New York: Oxford University Press, 1969) p. 67.
31. Gino Germani, *Authoritarianism, Fascism and National Populism* (New Brunswick, New Jersey. Transaction Books, 1978) p. 20.
32. Torcuato S. di Tella, 'Populism and Reform in Latin America', in Claudio Véliz (ed.) *Obstacles to Change in Latin America* (London: Oxford Universtiy Press, 1965) pp. 48–51.
33. Ernesto Laclau, *Politics and Ideology in Marxist Theory: Capitalism – Fascism–Populism* (London: NLB, 1977) p. 175.
34. Germani, p. 16.
35. Peter Worsley, 'The Concept of Populism', in Ghita Ionescu and Ernest Gellner (eds) *Populism: Its Meanings and National Characteristics* (London: Weidenfeld and Nicolson, 1969) p. 229.
36. Conniff, in Conniff, p. 7.
37. Germani, pp. 161–3.
38. Di Tella, in Véliz, p. 47.
39. Laclau, pp. 158–65.
40. Dix, pp. 30–5.

41. Laclau, pp. 157.
42. Alistair Hennessy, 'Latin America', in Lonescu and Gellner, pp. 28–9.
43. John D. Wirth's Foreword in Conniff, p. xi.
44. Lynch, pp. 2, 100 and 112–13.
45. Karen L. Remmer, *Party Competition in Argentina and Chile: Political Recruitment and Public Policy, 1890–1930* (Lincoln: University of Nebraska Press, 1984) p. 100.
46. Rock, p. vii.
47. Di Tella, in Véliz, p. 73.
48. Dix, pp. 30–1.
49. Germani, pp. 134–5.
50. Conniff, in Conniff, p 7; and David Tamarin, 'Yrigoyen and Perón: The Limits of Argentine Populism', in Conniff, p. 31.
51. Gallo and Sigal in di Tella, Germani and Graciarena, pp. 152–6.
52. Germani, p. 141.
53. Laclau, p. 183.
54. Rock, p. vii.
55. Germani, p. 143.
56. Oscar Cornblit, 'Inmigrantes y empresarios en la política argentina', *Desarrollo Económico*, vol. VI, January–March 1967, pp. 667–8; and Sergio Bagú, *Evolución histórica de la estratificación social en la Argentina* (Buenos Aires: Esquema, 1969) p. 82.
56. Tamarin, in Conniff, pp. 36–8.
58. Gallo and Sigal, in di Tella, Germani and Graciarena, p. 131; Paul B.Goodwin (trans Celso Rodríguez), *Los ferrocarriles británicos y la U.C.R., 1916–1930* (Buenos Aires: La Bastilla, 1974) p. 216; and Carl E. Solberg, *Oil and Nationalism in Argentina: A History* (Stanford, California: University of California Press, 1979) pp. 79 and 118.
59. Germani, p. 142.
60. Laclau, pp 182 and 190.
61. Germani, pp. 221–2; and Richard J. Walter, *The Province of Buenos Aires and Argentine Politics, 1912– 1943* (Cambridge: Cambridge University Press, 1985) p. 203.
62. Di Tella, in Véliz, p. 73.
63. Lars Schoultz, *The Populist Challenge: Argentine Electoral Behavior in the Postwar Era* (Chapel Hill, North Carolina: University of North Carolina Press, 1983) p. 25.
64. Gino Germani, *Estructura social de la Argentina: Análisis estadístico* (Buenos Aires: Editoral Raigal, 1955) pp. 254–60; and Germani (1978), pp. 162–3, 173 and 197.
65. Luis A.J. González Esteves, 'Las elecciones de 1946 en la Provincia de Córdoba', in Manuel Mora y Araujo and Ignacio Llorente (eds) *El voto peronista: Estudios de sociología electoral argentina* (Buenos Aires: Editorial Sudamericana, 1980) pp. 335–6; Mora y Araujo, 'La composición social', in ibid., p. 433; Manuel Mora y Araujo and Peter H. Smith, 'Peronismo y desarrollo: las elecciones de 1973', in ibid., pp. 448–9.
66. See Juan Domingo Perón, *El pueblo ya sabe de qué se trata* (Buenos Aires: 1946).
67. Juan Domingo Perón, *Perón Expounds His Doctrine* (New York: AMS,

1973) pp. 174 and 179; c.f. Jean Blondel, *Political Parties: A Genuine Case for Discontent?* (London: Wildwood House, 1978) pp. 53–4.

68. Tamarin, in Conniff, p. 40.

69. Di Tella, in Véliz, p. 72; Louise Maureen Doyon, 'Organized Labour and Perón (1943–1955): A Study of the Conflictual Dynamics of the Peronist Movement in Power', unpublished PhD thesis, University of Toronto, 1978, p. 646.

70. Jeane Kirkpatrick, *Leader and Vanguard in Mass Society: A Study of Peronist Argentina* (Cambridge, Massachusetts: Massachusetts Institute of Technology, 1971) p. 96.

71. Daniel Maddison James, 'Unions and Politics: The Development of Peronist Trade Unions, 1955–66, unpublished PhD thesis, London School of Economics and Political Science, 1979, pp. 85–6 and 124.

72. Alberto Ciria, 'Peronism and Political Structures, 1945–55', in Alberto Ciria *et al.*, *New Perspectives on Modern Argentina* (Bloomington, Indiana: Indiana University Press, 1972) pp. 2–3.

73. George I. Blanksten, *Perón's Argentina* (Chicago: University of Chicago Press, 1974) p. 65.

74. Little (1971) pp. 116, 126–7 and 132; Ciria, in Ciria *et al.*, pp. 3–5; Walter Little, 'Party and State in Peronist Argentina, 1945–1955', *Hispanic American Historical Review*, vol. LIII, no. 4, November 1973, p. 648; and Ernesto González, *Qué fue y qué es el peronismo* (Buenos Aires: Ediciones Pluma, 1874) pp. 36–7; Manuel Mora y Araujo, 'Introducción: La sociología electoral y la comprensión del peronismo', in Mora y Araujo and Llorente, pp. 49–50.

75. Di Tella, in Véliz, p. 71.

76. David Green *The Containment of Latin America* (Chicago: Quadrangle Books, 1971) pp. 153–4, cited in Eldon Kenworthy, 'Did the "New Industrialists" Play a Significant Role in the Formation of Perón's Coalition 1943–46?', in Ciria *et al.*, p. 15; and Torcuato di Tella, *El sistema político argentino y la classe obrera* (Buenos Aires: Editorial Universitaria de Buenos Aires, 1964) p. 55. See also Alberto Belloni, *Peronismo y socialismo nacional* (Buenos Aires: Ediciones Coyocán, 1962) p. 14.

77. Kenworthy, in Ciria *et al.*, p. 15.

78. Kenworthy, in Ciria *et al.*, pp. 15–16.

79. Thomas C. Cochran and Ruben E. Reina, *Capitalism in Argentine Culture: A Study of Torcuato Di Tella and S.I.A.M.* (Philadelphia: Univeristy of Pennsylvania Press, 1971) p. 225.

80. José Luis de Imaz, *Los qué mandan* (Buenos Aires: Editorial Universitaria de Buenos Aires, 1964) p. 23.

81. Horacio N. Casal, *La revolución del 43* (Buenos Aires: Centro Editor de América Latina, 1971) p. 11; and Tamarin, in Conniff, p. 42.

82. Little (1971), p. 8; Doyon, pp 111–12 and 123; David Rock, *Argentina 1516–1982: From Spanish Colonization to the Falklands War* (Berkeley and Los Angeles: University of California Press, 1985) p. 231; David Tamarin, *The Argentine Labor Movement, 1930–1945: A Study in the Origins of Peronism* (Albuquerque: University of New Mexico Press, 1985) pp. 30–1; Guido di Tella, 'Economic Controversies in Argentina from

the 1920s to the 1940s', in Guido di Tella and D.C.M. Platt (eds) *The Political Economy of Argentina 1880–1946* (Basingstoke, Hampshire: Macmillan, 1986) p. 125; and Tim Duncan and John Fogarty, *Australia and Argentina: On Parallel Paths* (Carlton, Victoria: Melbourne University Press, 1986) p. 26.

83. Miguel Murmis and Juan Carlos Portantiero, *Estudios sobre los origenes del peronismo*, Volume One (Buenos Aires: Siglo XXi Argentina Editores, 1974) p. 79; and Doyon, p. 121.

84. Félix Pérez and Juan Taccone, 'Sindicalismo argentino', in di Tella and Halperín, pp. 480–1; Imaz, P. 213; and Rodolfo Puiggrós, *El peronismo: Sus causas* (Buenos Aires: Carlos Pérez Editor, 1971) pp. 51–2.

85. Roberto Cortés Conde, 'Partidos politícos', in J.A. Paita (eda) *Argentina 1930–1960* (Buenos Aires: Editorial SUR, 1961) p. 138; and Gino Germani, 'Hacía una democracía de masas', in di Tella, Germani and Graciarena, p. 225.

86. Gino Germani, 'El surgimiento del peronismo: el rol de los obreros y de los migrantes internos', in Mora y Araujo and Llorente, pp. 105–6; Eldon Kenworthy, 'Interpretaciones ortodoxas y revisionistas del apoyo inicial del peronismo', in ibid., pp. 193–7; and Tulio Halperín Donghi, 'Algunas observaciones sobre Germani, el surgimiento del peronismo y los migrantes internos', in ibid., pp. 225–6.

87. Germani, in di Tella, Germani and Graciarena, p. 226.

88. Guido di Tella, *Argentina Under Perón, 1973–1976: The Nation's Experience With a Labour-Based Government* (London: Macmillan, 1983) p. 22.

89. Little (1971), pp. 9–10; Peter H. Smith, 'La base social del peronismo', in Mora y Araujo and Llorente, pp. 74–5; Kenworthy, in ibid., p. 201; Dix, pp. 37–8.

90. Charles W. Anderson, *Politics and Economic Change in Latin America: The Governing of Restless Nations* (New York: Van Nostrand Reinhold, 1967) p. 123.

91. Tomás Roberto Fillol, *Social Factors in Economic Development: The Argentine Case* (Cambridge, Massachusetts: Massachusetts Institute of Technology, 1961) p. 85.

92. Germani (1978), pp. 158–69; Germani, in Mora y Araujo and Llorente, pp. 105–6, pp. 109, 111, 115 and 116–27.

93. Gino Germani, *Política y sociedad en una época de transición: de la sociedad tradicional a la sociedad de masas* (Buenos Aires: Editorial Paidos, 1962) p. 244.

94. Carl Taylor, *rural Life in Argentina* (Baton Rouge, Louisiana: Louisiana State University Press, 1948)) p. 118.

95. Walter Little, 'The Popular Origins of Peronism', in David Rock (ed.) *Argentina in the Twentieth Century* (London: Duckworth, 1975) pp. 164 and 168; cf. Germani in Mora y Araujo and Llorente, p. 109, p. 111 and p. 115.

96. Little (1971), pp. 45–6; Doyon, pp. 215–16 and 436; Little, in Rock, pp. 168–9; Halperín, in Mora y Araujo and Llorente, p. 236; and José Enrique Miguens, 'The Presidential Elections of 1973 and the End of

an Ideology', in Turner and Miguens, p. 158. See also Rodríguez.
97. Germani (1955), pp. 254–60.
98. Little, in Rock, pp 164–6.
99. Kenworthy, in Mora y Araujo and Llorente, pp 206–7; Miguens, in Turner and Miguens, p. 158.
100. Miguens, in Turner and Miguens, pp. 148–50.
101. Imaz, p. 9.
102. Juan E. Corradi, 'Between Corporatism and Insurgency: The Sources of Ambivalence in Peronist Ideology', in Morris J. Blachman and Ronald G. Hellman (eds) *Terms of Conflict: Ideology in Latin American Politics* (Philadelphia Institute for the Study of Human Issues, 1977) p. 109; Ignacio Llorente, 'Alianzas políticas en el surgimiento del peronismo: el caso de la Provincia de Buenos Aires', in Mora y Araujo and Llorente, pp. 393–4; Manuel Mora y Araujo, 'Las bases estructurales del peronismo', in ibid., p. 431; Mora y Araujo and Smith, in ibid., P. 489; and James F. Petras, 'Terror and the Hydra: The Resurgence of the Argentine Working Class', in James F. Petras, Morris H. Morley, Peter de Witt and A. Eugene Havens, *Class, State, and Power in the Third World* (London: Zed Press, 1981) p. 261.
103. Kirkpatrick, p. 41; and Miguens, in Turner and Miguens, p. 152.
104. Weber, pp. 358–9.
105. Julie M. Taylor, *Eva Perón: The Myths of a Woman* (Chicago: University of Chicago Press, 1979) pp. 4–7.
106. Miguens in Turner and Miguens, p. 160.
107. Turner, in Turner and Miguens, pp. 226 and 230.
108. Kirkpatrick, p. 212; Little (1971), p. 28.
109. Carlos Octavio Bunge, 'Caciquismo in our America', in Hugh M. Hamill, Jr (ed.) *Dictatorship in Spanish America* (New York: Alfred A. Knopf, 1965) p. 122.
110. Robert Michels, *Political Parties: A Sociological Study of the Oligarchical Tendencies of Modern Democracy* (New York: The Free Press, 1962) p. 92.
111. Seymour Martin Lipset, *Political Man* (London: Mercury Books, 1963) pp. 97–176.
112. Germani, in di Tella and Halperín, pp. 474–5.
113. Jacques Lambert, *Latin America: Social Structure and Political Institutions* (Berkeley and Los Angeles: University of California Press, 1967) pp. 359–60.
114. Kirkpatrick, pp. 200, 216–17 and 221–2.
115. James Neilson, 'The Approaching Pact', *Buenos Aires Herald*, 12 May 1983, p 10.
116. T.W. Adorno, E. Frenkel-Brunswick, D.J. Levinson and R.N. Sanford, *The Authoritarian Personality* (New York: Harper and Row, 1950) pp. 255 –7.
117. Little (1971), p. 59; Juan Carlos Torre, 'The Meaning of Current Workers' Struggles', *Latin American Perspectives*, vol. I, no. 3, 1974, p. 74; Doyon, pp. 205–6; James (1979), pp. 35–8, 55, 80, 98, 124 and 167 – 9; and Daniel James, 'Rationalisation and Working Class Response: the Context and Limits of Factory Floor Activity

in Argentina', *Journal of Latin American Studies*, vol. XIII, no. 2, 1981, p. 375.

118. Jordan, pp. 149–50; Little (1971), pp. 14 and 119–25; Doyon, pp. 290, 397–9, 409 and 418; Marysa Navarro, 'Evita's Charismatic Leadership', in Conniff, pp. 53–4.

119. Little (1971), pp. 33 and 60; Doyon, pp. 259 and 263; James (1979), pp. 2–3 and 5.

120. Little, in Rock, pp. 172–4.

121. Torcuato S. di Tella, 'Working Class Organisation and Politics in Argentina', *Latin American Research Review*, vol. XVI, no. 2, 1981, p. 48.

122. Wayne S. Smith, 'The Return of Peronism', in Turner and Miguens, p. 138.

123. Weber, pp. 361 and 363–5.

124. Navarro, in Conniff, p. 55.

125. V.S. Naipaul, *The Return of Eva Perón* (London: André Deutsch, 1980) p. 96.

126. Navarro, in Conniff, p. 50.

127. Perón (1973), p. 97.

128. Francis G. Castles, 'Political Stability and the Dominant Image of Society', *Political Studies*, vol. XXII, 1974, pp. 293–5.

129. Hennessy, in Ionescu and Gellner, p. 34.

130. Castles, pp. 295–6.

131. E.g. John William Cooke, *La lucha por la liberación nacional; El retorno de Perón; La revolución y el peronismo* (Buenos Aires: Granica Editor, 1973) p. 9.

132. Irving Louis Horowitz, 'The Election in Retrospect', in Richard R. Fagen and Wayne A. Cornelius, Jr. (eds) *Political Power in Latin America: Seven Confrontations* (Englewood Cliffs, New Jersey: Prentice-Hall, 1970) p. 131.

CHAPTER 6

1. E.g. Lawrence E. Harrison, *Underdevelopment is a State of Mind: The Latin American Case* (Lanham, Maryland: University Press of America, 1985) pp. 4–6.

2. José Ortega y Gasset, *Invertebrate Spain* (London: George Allen and Unwin, 1937) p. 35.

3. Editor's introduction in Hugh M. Hamill (ed.) *Dictatorship in Spanish America* (New York: Alfred Knopf, 1965) p. 13.

4. 'Myself first, my family second, the world third', Edward S. Milenky, *Argentina's Foreign Policies* (Boulder, Colorado: Westview Press, 1978) pp. 50–1.

5. Charles Gibson, *Spain in America* (New York: Harper and Row, 1966) p. 213.

6. Salvador de Madariaga, 'Man and the Universe in Spain', in Hamill, pp. 31–3.

302 *Notes*

7.   Salvador de Madariaga, *Englishmen, Frenchmen, Spaniards* (London: Oxford University Press, 1931) pp. 80 and 140–1, cited in Harrison, p. 143.
8.   Diana Balmori, Stuart F. Voss and Miles Wortman, *Notable Family Networks in Latin America* (Chicago: University of Chicago Press, 1984)) pp. 8 and 28–9.
9.   Arnold Strickon, 'Class and Kinship in Argentina', *Ethology*, no. 4, October 1962, p. 512; Juan Carlos Agualla (trans. Betty Crouse), *Eclipse of an Aristocracy: An Investigation of the Ruling Elites of the City of Córdoba* (University of Alabama Press, 1976) pp. 2–3, 7–8, 28–31 and 77; and Balmori, Voss and Wortman, pp. 38–50, 150–2 and 183–4.
10. C.f. Mark D. Szuchman, 'Household Structure and Political Crisis: Buenos Aires, 1810–1860', *Latin American Research Review*, vol. XXI, no. 3, 1986, p. 79.
11. Kalman H. Silvert, *The Conflict Society: Reaction and Revolution in Latin America* (New York: American Universities Field Staff, 1966) p. 8.
12. David C. McClelland, *The Achieving Society* (Princeton: New Jersey: D. Van Nostrand, 1961) pp. 178–90.
13. But c.f. Strickon, p. 506.
14. McClelland, pp. 76–8, 100–1, 167–9, 187 and 289.
15. Francisco José Moreno, *Legitimacy and Stability in Latin America: A Study of Chilean Political Culture* (New York: New York University Press, 1969) pp. xvii–xviii.
16. Rosita Forbes, *Eight Republics in Search of a Future: Evolution and Revolution in South America* (New York: Frederick A. Stokes, n.d.) p. 131.
17. Martin C. Needler, *Latin American Politics in Perspective* (Princeton, New Jersey: D. Van Nostrand, 1963) p. 12; Charles W. Anderson, *Politics and Economic Change in Latin America: The Governing of Restless Nations* (New York: Van Nostrand Reinhold, 1967) pp. 151–2; S.M. Lipset, 'Values, Education and Entrepreneurialship', in Seymour Martin Lipset and Aldo Solari (eds) *Elites in Latin America* (New York: Oxford University Press, 1967) p. 17; John William Freels, 'Industrial Trade Associations in Argentine Politics', unpublished PhD thesis, University of California, 1968, pp. 2 – 3; and James F. Petras, 'Terror and the Hydra: The Resurgence of the Argentine Working Class', in James F. Petras, Morris H. Morley, Peter De Witt and A. Eugene Havens, *Class, State and Power in the Third World* (London: Zed Press, 1981) p. 201.
18. D.W. McElwain and W.J. Campbell, 'The Family', in A.F. Davies and S. Encel (eds) *Australian Society: A Sociological Introduction* (London: Pall Mall Press, 1965) p 135.
19. Anderson, p. 141.
20. Kenneth F. Johnson and Ben. G. Burnett, 'Stability–Instability in Latin American Politics', in Ben G. Burnett and Kenneth F. Johnson (eds) *Political Forces in Latin America: Dimensions of the Quest for Stability* (Belmont, California: Wadsworth Publishing, 1968) p. 517.
21. Ivan Vallier, 'Religious Elites: Differentiation and Developments in Roman Catholicism', in Lipset and Solari, p. 214.

22. Simón Bolívar, *Mirada sobre América española* (Quito: 1929), cited in J. Fred Rippy, 'The Anguish of Bolívar', in A. Curtis Wilgus (ed.) *South American Dictators During the First Century of Independence* (New York: Russell and Russell, 1963) p. 22.

23. Ortega y Gasset, p. 44.

24. Gabriel A. Almond and Sidney Verba, *The Civic Culture: Political Attitudes and Democracy in Five Nations* (Princeton, New Jersey: Princeton University Press, 1963); and Jeane Kirkpatrick, *Leader and Vanquard in Mass Society: A Study of Peronist Argentina* (Cambridge, Massachusetts: Massachusetts Institute of Technology, 1971) p. 117, 120 and 321–3.

25. Tomás Roberto Fillol, *Social Factors in Economic Development: The Argentine Case* (Cambridge, Massachusetts: Massachusetts Institute of Technology, 1961) p. 3.

26. Anderson, pp. 145–6; c.f. Thomas C. Cochran and Ruben E. Reina, *Capitalism in Argentine Culture: A Study of Torcuato Di Tella and S.I.A.M.* (Philadelphia: University of Pennsylvania Press, 1971) pp. 266–7.

27. Michael Redclift, 'Social Structure and Social Change', in Harold Blakemore (ed.) *Latin America: Essays in Continuity and Change* (London: British Broadcasting Corporation, 1974) p. 81.

28. Peter G. Snow, 'The Cultural Background', in Peter G. Snow (ed.) *Government and Politics in Latin America* (New York: Holt, Rinehart and Winston, 1967) p. 38.

29. Robert A. Dahl, *Polyarchy: Participation and Opposition* (New Haven, Connecticut: Yale University Press, 1971) p. 152.

30. Ysabel F. Rennie, *The Argentine Republic* (New York: Macmillan 1945) p. 6.

31. Rennie, p. 14.

32. Ezequiel Martínez Estrada, *X-Ray of the Pampas* (Austin, Texas: University of Texas Press, 1971) p. 51.

33. Domingo F. Sarmiento, *Life in the Argentine Republic in the Days of the Tyrants (or Civilization and Barbarism)* (New York: Collier Books, 1961) p. 54.

34. Martínez Estrada, p. 29; and Leopoldo Lugones, *El payador* (Buenos Aires: Huemul, 1972) p. 57, cited in Richard W. Slatta, *Gauchos and the Vanishing Frontier* (Lincoln, Nebraska: University of Nebraska Press, 1983) p. 63.

35. Theodore H. Moran, 'The "Development" of Argentina and Australia: The Radical Party of Argentina and the Labor Party of Australia in the Process of Economic and Political Development', *Comparative Politics*, vol. III, October 1970, p. 71.

36. Dan L. Adler, 'Matriduxy in the Australian Family', in Davies and Encel, pp. 153–4; Agulla, pp. 17–18.

37. Víctor Alba, *The Latin Americans* (New York: Frederick A. Praeger, 1969) p. 337.

38. *Buenos Aires Herald*, 14 April 1987, p. 11.

39. Jo-Ann Fagot Aviel, 'Political Participation of Women in Latin America', *Western Political Quarterly*, vol. XXXIV, no. 1, March 1981, pp. 161 and 171.

40. V.S. Naipaul, *The Return of Eva Perón* (London: André Deutsch, 1980) p. 157.
41. Fillol, pp. 14–15; and Thomas F. McGann, *Argentina: The Divided Land* (Princeton, New Jersey: D. Van Nostrand, 1966) p. 100.
42. Alexander M. Haig, Jr, *Caveat* (London: Weidenfeld and Nicolson, 1984) p. 280. See also O.R. Cardoso, R. Kirschbaum and E. van der Kooy, *Malvinas: La trama secreta* (Buenos Aires: Sudamericana-Planeta, 1986) pp. 131–55.
43. Richard D. Mallon and Juan V. Sourrouille, *Economic Policymaking in a Conflict Society: The Argentine Case* (Cambridge, Massachusetts: Harvard University Press, 1975) p. 166.
44. Silvert, p. 85.
45. Richard W. Weatherhead, 'Traditions of Conflict in Latin America', in Joseph Maier and Richard W. Weatherhead (eds) *Politics of Change in Latin America* (New York: Frederick A. Praeger, 1964) p. 37.
46. Moreno, pp. xvii–xviii.
47. James D. Theberge and Roger W. Fontaine, *Latin America: Struggle for Progress* (Lexington, Massachusetts: Lexington Books, 1977) p. 129.
48. John Lynch, *Argentine Dictator: Juan Manuel de Rosas 1829–1852* (Oxford: Clarendon Press, 1981) p. 31.
49. Germán Arciniegas, 'Is a Caudilla Possible? The Case of Evita Perón', in Hamill, p. 189.
50. Glen Dealy, 'The Tradition of Monistic Democracy in Latin America', in Howard J. Wiarda (ed.) *Politics and Social Change in Latin America: The Distinct Tradition* (Amherst, Massachusetts: University of Masschusetts Press, 1974) pp. 73–6.
51. Julio A. Fernández, *The Political Elite in Argentina* (New York: New York University Press, 1970) p. 11.
52. Jacinto Oddone, *Historia del socialismo argentino*, Volume Two (Buenos Aires: Centro Editor de América Latina, 1983) pp. 161 and 167.
53. Michael J. Francis, *The Limits of Hegemony: United States Relations with Argentina and Chile During World War II* (Notre Dame, Indiana: University of Notre Dame Press, 1977) p. 45.
54. Marvin Goldwert, *Democracy, Militarism and Nationalism in Argentina 1930–1966: An Interpretation* (Austin Texas: University of Texas Press, 1972) p. 11.
55. Hubert Herring, *A History of Latin America from the Beginnings to the Present* (New York: Alfred A Knopf, 1955) p. 635.
56. George I. Blanksten, *Perón's Argentina* (Chicago: University of Chicago Press, 1974) p. 294.
57. Ronald C. Newton, 'On "Functional Groups", "Fragmentation" and "Pluralism" in Spanish American Political Society', in Wiarda, p. 132.
58. Daniel Maddison James, 'Unions and Politics: The Development of Peronist Trade Unions, 1955–66', unpublished PhD thesis, London School of Economics and Political Science, 1979, p. 105.
59. Guillermo A. O'Donnell, *Modernization and Bureaucratic Authoritarianism: Studies in South American Politics* (Berkeley, California: University of California Press, 1973) p. 152.

60. Eduardo Crawley, *A House Divided: Argentina 1880–1980* (London: C Hurst, 1984) pp. 251–2.

61. Fernández, p. 95.

62. Frederick C. Turner, 'Entrepreneurs and *Estancieros* in Perón's Argentina: Cohesion and Conflict Within the Elite', in Frederick C. Turner and José Enrique Miguens (eds) *Juan Perón and the Reshaping of Argentina* (Pittsburgh, Pennsylvania: University of Pittsburgh Press, 1983) pp. 228–9 and 234.

63. See Juan Carlos Torre, 'The Meaning of Current Workers' Struggles', *Latin American Perspectives*, vol. 1, no. 3, 1974.

64. Jacobo Timerman, *Prisoner Without a Name, Cell Without a Number* (Harmondsworth: Penguin, 1982) pp. 14–15.

65. Timerman, p. 15.

66. Guillermo O'Donnell, 'Democracia en la Argentina: Micro y macro', in Oscar Oszlak (ed.) *"Proceso", crisis y transición democrática*, Volume I (Buenos Aires: Centro Editor de América Latina, 1984) pp. 14–15.

67. Altaf Gauhar interviewing Raúl Alfonsín in Buenos Aires in August 1984, *Third World Quarterly*, vol. VII, no. 1, January 1985) p. 2.

68. Walter Little, 'Civil–Military Relations in Contemporary Argentina', *Government and Opposition*, vol. XIX, no. 2, 1984, pp. 208 and 218; Torcuato S. di Tella, 'The October 1983 Elections in Argentina', *Government and Opposition*, vol. XIX, no. 2, 1984 pp. 188–9 and 192; Virgilio R. Beltran, 'Comentarios al trabajo de L. González Esteves e I. Llorente' in Natalio R. Botana, Luis González Esteves, Ignacio Llorente, Manuel Mora y Araujo and Susan Alterman (eds) *La Argentina electoral* (Buenos Aires: Editorial Sudamericana, 1985) p. 75; and Manuel Mora y Araujo, 'La naturaleza de la coalición alfonsinista', in ibid., pp. 89, 90, 93 and 101.

69. Ronaldo Munck, 'Democratization and Demilitarization in Argentina, 1982–1985', *Bulletin of Latin American Research* vol. IV, no. 2, 1985, pp. 86–7.

70. Guido di Tella, *Argentina under Perón, 1973–1976; The Nation's Experience with a Labour-Based Government* (London: Macmillan, 1983) pp. 14–15.

71. Kirkpatrick, pp. 200 and 233.

72. Martin Weinstein, *Uruguay: The Politics of Failure* (Westport, Connecticut: Greenwood Press, 1975) p. 15.

73. Frederick B. Pike's introduction in Frederick V. D'Antonio and Frederick B. Pike (eds) *Religion, Revolution and Reform: New Forces for Change in Latin America* (Tenbury Wells, Worcestershire: Fowler Wright Books, 1964) p. 8.

74. Harrison, p. 8.

CHAPTER 7

1. See Miron Burgin, *The Economic Aspects of Argentine Federalism 1820 – 1852* (Cambridge, Massachusetts: Harvard University Press, 1946).

2. Robert A. Potash, *The Army and Politics in Argentina 1928–1945:*

Yrigoyen to Perón (Stanford, California: Stanford University Press, 1969) p. 283.

3.   Max Weber, *The Protestant Ethic and The Spirit of Capitalism* (London: Unwin University Books, 1965); Charles W. Anderson, *Politics and Economic Change in Latin America: The Governing of Restless Nations* (New York: Van Nostrand Reinhold, 1967) p. 82; Economic Commission for Latin America (ECLA) *Social Change and Social Development Policy in Latin America* (New York: United Nations, 1970) p. 29; Carlos Díaz Alejandro, *Essays on the Economic History of the Argentine Republic* (New Haven, Connecticut: Yale University Press, 1970) p. xiii; and Lawrence E. Harrison, *Underdevelopment Is a State of Mind: The Latin American Case* (Lanham, Maryland: University Press of America, 1985) pp. xvi–xvii.

4.   Seymour Martin Lipset, 'Values, Education and Entrepreneurship', in Seymour Martin Lipset and Aldo Solari (eds) *Elites in Latin America* (New York: Oxford University Press, 1967) p. 3.

5.   Ezequiel Gallo, *Agrarian Expansion and Industrial Development in Argentina (1880–1930)* (Buenos Aires: Instituto Torcuato di Tella, May 1970) p. 10; and Ronaldo Munck, 'Cycles of class struggle and the making of the working class in Argentina, 1890–1920', *Journal of Latin American Studies*, vol. XIX, no. 1, May 1987) pp. 20–21.

6.   ECLA, p. 29.

7.   Anderson, p. 82.

8.   W.H. Hudson, *Far Away and Long Ago* (London: J.M. Dent, 1962).

9.   James Bryce, *South America: Observations and Impressions* (New York: Macmillan, 1914) p. 343.

10. Karl Marx, *Capital: A Critical Analysis of Capitalist Production*, Vol. 1. (London: Lawrence and Wishart, 1974) p. 340.

11. Ezequiel Martínez Estrada, *X-Ray of the Pampa* (Austin, Texas: University of Texas Press, 1971) p. 62.

12. Carlos Octavio Bunge, *Neustra América: Ensayo de psicología social* (Buenos Aires: Vaccaro, 1918) p. 149; Manuel E. Río, *Córdoba: Su fisonomía, su misión: Escritos y discursos* (Córdoba, 1967) p. 95, cited by Mark D, Szuchman, *Mobility and Integration in Urban Argentina: Córdoba in the Liberal Era* (Austin, Texas: University of Texas Press, 1980) p. 77; and Martínez Estrada, p. 33.

13. Domingo F. Sarmiento, *Life in the Argentine Republic in the Days of the Tyrants (or Civilization and Barbarism)* (New York: Collier Books, 1961) pp. 30–1.

14. Carl Solberg. *Immigration and Nationalism: Argentina and Chile, 1890 – 1914* (Austin, Texas: University of Texas Press, 1970) pp. 96–100.

15. Thomas C. Cochran and Ruben E. Reina, *Capitalism in Argentine Culture: A Study of Torcuato Di Tella and S.I.A.M.* (Philadelphia: University of Pennsylvania Press, 1971) p. 265; and interview, July 1987, with Gerald Wakeham, architect of the Banco de Londres, Buenos Aires.

16. Torcuato S. di Tella, 'Raíces de la controversia educacional argentina', in Torcuato S. di Tella and Tulio Halperín Donghi (eds) *Los fragmentos del poder: de la oligarquía a la poliarquía* (Buenos Aires: Editorial Jorge

Alvarez, 1969) p. 294; Solberg, pp. 7–8 and 14; Carl E. Solberg, 'Land Tenure and Land Settlement: Policy and Patterns in the Canadian Prairies and the Argentine Pampas, 1880–1930', in D.C.M. Platt and Guido di Tella (eds) *Argentina, Australia and Canada: Studies in Comparative Development 1980–1965* (London: Macmillan, 1985) p. 63; and Carlos F. Díaz Alejandro, 'Argentina, Australia and Brazil Before 1929', in Platt and di Tella, pp. 102–3.

17. Ovidio Mauro Pipino, *1947–1955: La década fatal; origen del colapso nacional* (Córdoba, Argentina: private publications, 1979) p. 15.

18. Díaz Alejandro, p. 11.

19. Díaz Alejandro, pp. 217 and 299–8; Gallo, p. 13; and A. O'Connell, 'Free Trade in One (Primary Producing) Country: the Case of Argentina in the 1920s', in Guido di Tella and D.C.M. Platt (eds) *The Political Economy of Argentina 1880–1946* (Basingstoke, Hampshire, Macmillan, 1986) pp. 87–8. Cf. John William Freels, 'Industrial Trade Associations in Argentine Politics', unpublished PhD thesis, University of California, 1968, pp. 17–18.

20. Oscar Cornblit, 'Inmigrantes y empresarios en la política argentina', *Desarrollo Económico*, vol. VI, January–March 1967, pp. 680–4; Roberto Cortés Conde and Ezequiel Gallo, *La formación de la Argentina moderna* (Buenos Aires: Paidos, 1967) p. 103; Solberg, pp. 31–2, 35, 57 and 60; Gallo, pp. 17 and 19; Theodore H. Moran, 'The "Development" of Argentina and Australia: The Radical Party of Argentina and the Labor Party of Australia in the Process of Economic and Political Development', *Comparative Politics* vol. III, October 1970, pp. 84–7; Cochran and Reina, p. 33; and David Rock, *Politics in Argentina 1890–1930: The Rise and Fall of Radicalism* (London: Cambridge University Press, 1975) p. 271.

21. Douglas A. Chalmers, 'The Politicised State in Latin America', in James M. Malloy (ed.) *Authoritarianism and Corporatism in Latin America* (Pittsburgh, Pennsylvania: University of Pittsburgh Press, 1977) pp. 32–3.

22. James Lockhart and Stuart B. Schwartz, *Early Latin America: A History of Colonial Spanish America and Brazil* (New York: Cambridge University Press, 1983) p. 5.

23. Frederick C. Turner, 'Entrepreneurs and *Estancieros* in Perón's Argentina: Cohesion and Conflict Within the Elite', in Frederick C. Turner and José Enrique Miguens (eds) *Juan Perón and the Reshaping of Argentina* (Pittsburgh, Pennsylvania: University of Pittsburgh Press, 1983) p. 226.

24. Guillermo A. O'Donnell, *Reflexiones sobre las tendencias generales de cambio en el Estado burocrático-autoritario* (Buenos Aires: CEDES, 1975) p. 2.

25. Jeane Kirkpatrick, *Leader and Vanguard in Mass Society: A Study of Peronist Argentina* (Cambridge, Massachusetts: Massachusetts Institute of Technology, 1971) pp. 199–200.

26. Russell H. Fitzgibbon and Julio A. Fernández, *Latin America: Political Culture and Development* (Englewood Cliffs, New Jersey Prentice-Hall, 1981) p. 307.

27. Lewis Hanke, *South America* (Princeton, New Jersey: D. Van Nostrand, 1959) p. 163.
28. Anderson, p. 145.
29. James R. Scobie, *Buenos Aires: Plaza to Suburb, 1870–1910* (New York: Oxford University Press, 1974) p. 218; and Susan M. Socolow, 'Buenos Aires at the Time of Independence', in Stanley R. Ross and Thomas F. McGann (eds) *Buenos Aires: 400 Years* (Austin, Texas: University of Texas Press, 1982) pp. 26–7.
30. Martínez Estrada, p. 5.
31. Juan Carlos Agulla (trans. Betty Crouse) *Eclipse of an Aristocracy: An Investigation of the Ruling Elites of the City of Córdoba* (University of Alabama Press, 1976) pp. 17–18.
32. Tomás Roberto Fillol, *Social Factors in Economic Development: The Argentine Case* (Cambridge, Massachusetts: Massachusetts Institute of Technology, 1961) p. 3.
33. See Isabel Laura Cardenas, *Ramona y el robot: el servicio doméstico en barios prestigiosos de Buenos Aires (1895–1985)* (Buenos Aires: Ediciones Búsqueda, 1986).
34. See Weber; and David C. McClelland, *The Achieving Society* (Princeton, New Jersey: D. Van Nostrand, 1961).
35. Weber, pp. 26–7.
36. Richard D. Mallon and Juan V. Sourrouille, *Economic Policymaking in a Conflict Society: The Argentine Case* (Cambridge, Massachusetts: Harvard University Press, 1975) p. 80.
37. Edward Shaw, 'No willing partners for reactivation', *Buenos Aires Herald*, 10 August 1986, p. 2; and Manuel Tanoira, 'World economic trends viewed sharply', *Buenos Aires Herald*, 4 January 1987, p. 2.
38. José Ortega y Gasset, *Invertebrate Spain* (London: George Allen and Unwin, 1937) pp. 152–3.
39. David McClelland, 'The Achievement Motive in Economic Growth', in Jason L. Finkle and Richard W. Gable (eds) *Political Development and Social Change* (New York: John Wiley and Sons, 1971) p. 94.
40. Fred W. Riggs, *Administration in Developing Countries: The Theory of Prismatic Society* (Boston: Houghton Mifflin, 1964) p. 148; Colin M. Lewis, 'The British-Owned Argentine Railways, 1957–1947', unpublished PhD thesis, University of Exeter, 1974, pp. 397–8.
41. See Gino Germani, *Política y sociedad en una época de transición: De la sociedad tradicional a la sociedad de las masas* (Buenos Aires: Editorial Paidos, 1962) p. 172; Gustavo Beyhaut, Roberto Cortés Conde, Haydée Gorostegui and Susana Torrada, 'Los inmigrantes en el sistema occupacional argentino', in Torcuato S. di Tella, Gino Germani and Jorge Graciarena (eds) *Argentina: sociedad de masas* (Buenos Aires: EUDEBA, 1965) p. 118; Sergio Bagú, *Evolución histórica de la estratificación social en la Argentina* (Buenos Aires: Esquema, 1969) pp. 125–6.
42. Dale L. Johnson, *The Sociology of Change and Reaction in Latin America* (Indianapolis: Bobbs-Merrill, 1973) p. 7.
43. José Luis de Imaz, *Los que mandan* (Buenos Aires: Editorial Universitaria de Buenos Aires, 1964) pp. 136–8 and 160.

44. Andrew Graham-Yooll, *The Forgotten Colony: A History of the English Speaking Communities in Argentina* (London: Hutchinson, 1981) p. 240.

45. Graham-Yooll, p. 242.

46. Weber, pp. 35 39–40, 112, 157–8 and 162.

47. Karl Kautsky, *Foundations of Christianity* (New York: Russell, 1953).

48. Weber, pp. 35–6.

49. Tulio Halperín Donghi, *Politics, Economics and Society in Argentina in the Revolutionary Period* (Cambridge: Cambridge University Press, 1875) p. 31.

50. Víctor Alba, *Nationalists Without Nations: The Oligarchy Versus the People in Latin America* (New York: Frederick A. Praeger, 1968) pp. 53–9.

51. Fernando H. Cardoso, 'The Industrial Elite', in Lipset and Solari, pp. 110–13.

52. Fillol, pp. 58–9.

53. Federico Debuyst, *Las clases sociales en América Latina* (Madrid: FERES, 1962) p. 46; Bagú, p. 136; and Enrique Oteiza, 'La emigración de ingenieros da la Argentina: un caso de "brain drain" latinoamericano', in di Tella and Halperín, p. 504.

54. Di Tella, in di Tella and Halperín, p. 315.

55. James W. Wilkie and Adam Perkal (eds) *Statistical Abstract of Latin America*, vol. XXIV (Los Angeles: UCLA Latin American Center, 1985) pp. 145 and 148.

56. Bagú, p. 54.

57. Agulla, p. 18; Juan Carlos Tedesco, *Educación y sociedad en la Argentina (1800–1900)* (Buenos Aires: Ediciones Punnedille, 1970) pp. 94 and 96–7.

58. Charles Gibson, *Spain in America* (New York: Harper and Row, 1966) p. 131.

59. Eduardo A. Rocca, *Argentina: Los grupos dirigentes* (Buenos Aires: Editorial Palestra, December 1966) pp. 51–2; Tedesco, p. 83. See also Agulla, p. 36.

60. Guillermo A. O'Donnell, *Modernization and Bureaucratic-Authoritarianism: Studies in South American Politics* (Berkeley, California: University of California Press, 1973) pp. 44 and 46.

61. Alexander T. Edelmann *Latin American Government and Politics: The Dynamics of a Revolutionary Society* (Homewood, Illioois: The Dorsey Press, 1965) pp. 267–8. See also Oteiza, in di Tella and Halperín, pp. 506–21.

62. Bryce, p. 346.

63. Cardoso, in Lipset and Solari, pp. 109–10.

64. Fillol, p. 20; José Luis Romero (intro, and trans. by Thomas F. McGann) *A History of Argentine Political Thought* (Stanford, California: Stanford University Press, 1963) p. 181; Laura Randall, 'Income Distribution and Investment in Argentina', *Latin American Research Review*, vol. XII, no. 3, 1977, pp. 137–8; and Laura Randall, *An Economic History of Argentina in the Twentieth Century* (New York: Columbia University Press, 1978) p. 30.

65. ECLA, pp. 29–30.

66. Weber, pp. 51, 53 and 58–60.

67. H.S. Ferns, *Argentina* (London: Ernest Benn, 1969) p. 138.
68. Bryce, p. 318.
69. William S. Stokes, 'Social Classes in Latin America', in Peter G. Snow (ed.) *Government and Politics in Latin America* (New York: Holt, Rinehart and Winston, 1967) pp. 55 and 65.
70. Carlos F. Díaz Alejandro, *Exchange-Rate Devaluation in a Semi-Industrialised Country: The Experience of Argentina 1955–1961* (Cambridge, Massachusetts: Massachusetts Institute of Technology, 1965) pp. 61 and 63.
71. Cornelia Butler Flora, 'Photonovels', in Harold E. Hinds, Jr, and Charles M. Tatum (eds) *Handbook of Latin American Popular Culture* (Westport, Connecticut: Greenwood Press, 1985) pp. 151 and 159.
72. Weber, p. 172.
73. Gilbert Wilson Merkx, 'Political and Economic Change in Argentina from 1870 to 1966', unpublished PhD thesis, Yale University, 1968 pp. 315–16.
74. Díaz Alejandro (1970) p. 32; Solberg (1970) pp. 49–50; Peter Alhadeff, 'Public Finance and the Economy in Argentina, Australia and Canada During the Depression of the 1930s', in Platt and di Tella, p. 174.
75. Díaz Alejandro (1965) p. 100.
76. Aldo Ferrer, *Living Within Our Means: An Examination of the Argentine Economic Crisis* (Boulder, Colorado: Westview Press, 1985) p. viii.
77. Tulio Halperín, 'The Argentine Export Economy: Instimations of Mortality, 1894–1930', in di Tella and Platt, p. 43.
78. Jonathan C. Brown, *A Socioeconomic History of Argentina, 1776 – 1860* (New York: Cambridge University Press, 1979) p. 3.
79. John Lynch, *Argentine Dictator: Juan Manuel de Rosas 1829–1852* (Oxford: Clarendon Press, 1981) pp. 21–2; and David Rock, *Argentina 1516–1982: From Spanish Colonization to the Falklands War* (Berkeley and Los Angeles: University of California Press, 1985) p. 99.
80. Richard W.Siatta, *Gauchos and the Vanishing Frontier* (Lincoln, Nebraska: University of Nebraska Press, 1983) p. 96.
81. Lynch, p. 89.
82. Brown, pp. 158–9; Solberg, in Platt and di Tella, pp. 54–5 and 61–2; José Pavlotzky, *Historia clínica de mi país: Argentina 1930 – 1982* (Buenos Aires: Corregidor, 1983) p. 27; and Carlos H. Waisman, 'Population and Social Structure in Argentina', *Latin American Research Review*, vol. XXI, no. 2, 1986, pp. 256–7.
83. Roberto Cortés Conde, *El progreso argentino, 1880–1914* (Buenos Aires: Editorial Sudamericana, 1979) p. 167; Debuyst, p. 46; Bagú, p. 76; Alberto J. Pla, *La burquesía nacional en América Latina* (Buenos Aires: Centro Editor de América Latina, 1971) p. 63; Brown, pp. 147 and 158–9; and Nicos P. Mouzelis, *Politics in the Semi-Periphery: Early Parliamentarism and Late Industrialisation in the Balkans and Latin America* (Basingstoke, Hampshire: Macmillan, 1986) p. 17.
84. Martínez Estrada, p. 10.
85. E.R. Wolf, *Sons of the Shaking Earth: The People of Mexico and Guatemala– Their Land, History and Culture* (Chicago: The University of Chicago Press, 1959) . 204.
86. Burgin, p. 29; André Gunder Frank, *Capitalism and Underdevelopment*

in Latin America: Historical Studies of Chile and Brazil (Harmondsworth: Penguin, 1969) pp. 13–14; André Gunder Frank, *Latin America: Underdevelopment or Revolution* (New York: Monthly Review Press, 1970) p. 14; Slatta, pp. 93 – 4; and Dale L. Johnson, 'Class Roots of Dictatorship in South America: Local Bourgeoisies and Transnational Capital', in Dale L. Johnson (ed.) *Middle Classes in Dependent Countries* (Beverly Hills, California: Sage Publications, 1985) p. 205. Cf. Agulla, p. 18.

87.   Roger Gravil, 'State Intervention in Argentina's Export Trade between the Wars', *Journal of Latin American Studies*, vol. II, no. 2, 1970, p. 150.

88.   James H. Street, 'The Internal Frontier and Technological Progress in Latin America', *Latin American Research Review*, XII, no. 3, 1977, p. 40.

89.   Samuel P. Huntingon, *Political Order in Changing Societies* (New Haven, Connecticut: Vale University Press, 1968) p. 66.

90.   Halperín Donghi, p. 389.

91.   Scobie, p. 234.

92.   Robert J. Alexander, *Juan Domingo Perón; A History* (Boulder, Colorado: Westview Press, 1979) pp. 146–7.

93.   Pierre F. de Villemarest, *The Strategists of Fear* (Geneva: Editions Voxmundi, 1981) p. 44; Joseph A. Page, *Perón: A Biography* (New York: Random House, 1983) p. 342; and Eduardo Crawley, *A House Divided: Argentina 1880–1980* (London: C. Hurst, 1984) pp. 167–8 and 174.

94.   David Yallop, *In God's Name* (London: Jonathan Cape, 1984) pp. 118–19 and 312.

95.   Huntington, p. 61.

96.   E.g. Claude Ake, 'Political Integration and Political Stability: A Hypothesis', *World Politics*, vol. XIX, April 1967, p. 581.

97.   Fillol, p. 8.

98.   Charles Wagley, *Latin American Tradition: Essays on the Unity and Diversity of Latin American Culture* (New York: Columbia University Press, 1968) p. 66.

99.   Ake, p. 581.

100.   Anderson, pp. 141–2.

101.   Edward Shaw, 'García: lone crusader up against tough odds', *Buenos Aires Herald*, 17 August 1986, p. 7.

102.   Michael Soltys, 'Integration to bring sub-tropical weather?', *Buenos Aires Herald*, 3 August 1986, p. 3.

103.   Alhadeff, in Platt and di Tella, pp. 163–4.

104.   Edward Shaw, 'Future outlook brighter than forecast', *Buenos Aires Herald*, 17 August 1986, p. 3; and Edward Shaw, 'Fair chance of placing economy in high gear', *Buenos Aires Herald*, 31 August 1986, p. 2.

105.   Ferrer, pp. 3–4.

106.   Fillol, pp. 19–20 and 60–1.

107.   Merkx, pp. 325–6.

108.   Ferrer, p. 4.

312 *Notes*

109. Edward Shaw, 'Argentina looking good from the outside', *Buenos Aires Herald*, 7 September 1986, p. 2.

CHAPTER 8

1. Kalman H. Silvert, 'The Strategy of the Study of Nationalism', in Kalman H. Silvert (ed.) *Expectant Peoples: Nationalism and Development* (New York: Vintage Books, 1967) p. 19.
2. Arthur P. Whitaker, *The United States and Argentina* (Cambridge, Massachusetts: Harvard University Press, 1954) pp. 14–15.
3. K.R. Minogue, *Nationalism* (London) Methuen, 1969) p. 23.
4. Jeane Kirkpatrick, *Leader and Vanguard in Mass Society: A Study of Peronist Argentina* (Cambridge, Massachusetts: Massachusetts Institute of Technology, 1971) p. 15; and Oscar Oszlak, *La formación del estado argentina* (Buenos Aires: Belgrano, 1982) p. 244.
5. Whitaker, p. 86.
6. Manuel Ugarte, *The Destiny of a Continent* (New York: Alfred A. Knopf, 1925) p. 212.
7. Paul Webley and Katharine Cutts, 'Children, war and nationhood', *New Society* 13 December 1985, pp. 451–3.
8. Michael Soltys, 'CGT prepares pots-n-pans general strike', *Buenos Aires Herald*, 28 September 1986, p. 8.
9. Jorge Estomba quoted by Edward Shaw, 'To be or not to be – the Argentine dilemma', *Buenos Aires Herald*, 22 September 1985, p. 14.
10. Shaw, p. 14.
11. Víctor Alba, *Nationalists Without Nations: The Oligarchy Versus the People in Latin America* (New York: Frederick A. Praeger, 1968) pp. 12–16.
12. Leopoldo Zea, *Latin America and the World* (Norman, Oklahoma: University of Oklahoma Press, 1969) p. 83.
13. Hubert Herring, *A History of Latin America: From the Beginnings to the Present* (New York: Alfred A. Knopf, 1955) p. 215.
14. D.C.M. Platt, 'Domestic Finance in the Growth of Buenos Aires, 1880–1914', in Guido di Tella and D.C.M. Platt (eds) *The Political Economy of Argentina 1880–1946* (Basingstoke, Hampshire: Macmillan, 1986) p. 4.
15. James Bryce, *South America: Observations and Impressions* (New York: Macmillan, 1914) p. 315.
16. Robert A. Potash, *The Army and Politics in Argentina 1945–1962: Perón to Frondizi* (London: The Athlone Press, 1980) p. 82.
17. Martin C. Needler, 'United States Government Figures in Latin American Military Expenditure', *Latin American Research Review*, vol. VIII, no. 2, 1975, pp. 101–3.
18. John Duncan Powell, 'Military Assistance and Militarism in Latin America', *Western Political Quarterly*, vol. XVIII, 1985, p. 385.
19. Irving Louis Horowitz, 'The Military Elites', in Seymour Martin Lipset and Aldo Solari (eds) *Elites in Latin America* (New York: Oxford University Press, 1967) p. 180.

20. Gary W. Wynia, *The Politics of Latin American Development* (New York: Cambridge University Press, 1978) p. 328.

21. William C. Smith, 'Reflections on the political economy of authoritarian rule and capitalist reorganisation in contemporary Argentina', in Philip O'Brien and Paul Cammack (eds) *Generals in Retreat: The Crisis of Military Rule in Latin America* (Manchester: Manchester University Press, 1985) p. 49.

22. Quoted by David Jessel in 'Heart of the Matter' on Chile, BBC Television, February 1983.

23. Potash, p. 81.

24. Guido di Tella, *Argentina Under Perón, 1973–76: The Nation's Experience with a Labour-Based Government* (London: Macmillan, 1983) p. 38.

25. John Keegan, *World Armies* (London: Macmillan, 1983) pp. 20 and 609; and Walter Little, *Military Power in Latin America* Institute of Latin-American Studies, Working Paper 4 (Liverpool: University of Liverpool, 1986) p. 46.

26. John Gerassi, *The Great Fear in Latin America* (New York: Collier Books, 1963) p. 66.

27. Richard Gillespie, *Soldiers of Perón: Argentina's Montoneros* (Oxford: Clarendon Press, 1982) p. 223.

28. *The Times*, 4 January 1978, cited by Gillespie, p. 229.

29. Smith, in O'Brien and Cammack, p. 50.

30. Louis L. Snyder, *The Meaning of Nationalism* (New Brunswick, New Jersey: Rutgers University Press, 1954) pp. 116–17, cited by Marvin Goldwert, *Democracy, Militarism and Nationalism in Argentina 1930 – 1966: An Interpretation* (Austin, Texas: University of Texas Press, 1972) p. xviii.

31. Salvador de Madariaga, 'Man and the Universe in Spain', in Hugh M. Hamill, Jr (ed.) *Dictatorship in Spanish America* (New York: Alfred A. Knopf, 1965) p. 31.

32. Alain Rouquié (trans. Arturo Iglesias Echegaray), *Poder militar y sociedad política en la Argentina* (Buenos Aires: Emecé Editores, 1981) p. 56.

33. Mark Falcoff, 'Argentina', in Mark Falcoff and Frederick B. Pike (eds) *The Spanish Civil War 1936–39: American Hemispheric Perspectives* (Lincoln, Nebraska: University of Nebraska Press, 1982) p. 293.

34. Thomas F. McGann's introduction in José Luis Romero, *A History of Argentine Political Thought* (Stanford, California: Stanford University Press, 1963) p. x.

35. Whitaker, p. 108.

36. Miron Burgin, *The Economic Aspects of Argentine Federalism 1820 – 1852* (Cambridge, Massachusetts: Harvard University Press, 1946) p. 22; Joseph S. Tulchin, 'The Impact of U.S. Human Rights Policy: Argentina', in John D. Martz and Lars Schoultz (eds) *Latin America, the United States, and the Inter-American System* (Boulder, Colorado: Westview Press, 1980) pp. 209 – 10; and John Lynch, *Argentine Dictator: Juan Manuel de Rosas 1829–1852* (Oxford: Clarendon Press, 1981) p. 37.

37. Arthur P. Whitaker, 'Nationalism and Social Change in Latin America', in Joseph Maier and Richard W. Weatherhead (eds)

Politics of Change in Latin America (New York: Frederick A. Praeger, 1964) p. 90.

38. Lynch, p. 55.
39. Richard W. Slatta, *Gauchos and the Vanishing Frontier* (Lincoln, Nebraska: University of Nebraska Press, 1983) p. 170.
40. Domingo F. Sarmiento, *Life in the Argentine Republic in the Days of the Tyrants (or Civilization and Barbarism)* (New York: Collier Books, 1961) p. 38.
41. Thomas F. McGann, *Argentina, the United States, and the Inter-American System 1880–1914* (Cambridge, Massachusetts: Harvard University Press, 1954) p. 108; and W. Raymond Duncan and James Nelson Goodsell, *The Quest for Change in Latin America: Sources for a Twentieth Century Analysis* (New York: Oxford University Press, 1970) pp. 9–10.
42. Alejandro Dabat and Luis Lorenzano, *Argentina: The Malvinas and the End of Military Rule* (London: Verso, 1984) p. 14.
43. Paul B. Goodwin (trans. Celso Rodríguez), *Los ferrocarriles británicos y la U.C.R., 1916–1930* (Buenos Aires: La Bastilla, 1974) p. 216.
44. Richard J. Walter, *The Province of Buenos Aires and Argentine Politics, 1912–1943* (Cambridge: Cambridge University Press, 1985) p. 9.
45. Arthur P. Whitaker and David C. Jordan, *Nationalism in Contemporary Latin America* (New York: The Free Press, 1966) p. 3; Peter H. Smith, *Politics and Beef in Argentina: Patterns of Conflict and Change* (New York: Columbia University Press, 1969) p. 29; and Goldwert, p. 16.
46. Sandra McGee Deutsch, *Counterrevolution in Argentina, 1900–1932: The Argentine Patriotic League* (Lincoln, Nebraska: University of Nebraska Press, 1986) pp. 3–4, 36–8, 81, 98–9, 166, 174–7, and 220–5; Ronald Howard Dolkart, 'Manuel A. Fresco, Governor of the Province of Buenos Aires, 1936–1940: A Study of the Argentine Right and Its Response to Economic and Social Change', unpublished PhD thesis, University of California, 1969, pp. 20, 23–5 and 29; and Carl Solberg, *Immigration and Nationalism: Argentina and Chile, 1890–1914* (Austin, Texas: University of Texas Press, 1970) p. 113.
47. José Carlos Chiaramonte, 'La crisis de 1866 y el proteccionismo argentino de la decada del 70', in Torcuato S. di Tella and Tulio Halperín Donghi (eds) *Los fragmentos del poder: de la oligarquía a la poliarquía* (Buenos Aires: Editorial Jorge Alvarez, 1969) p. 173; John William Freels, 'Industrial Trade Associations in Argentine Politics', unpublished PhD thesis, University of California, 1968, p. 27; Winthrop R. Wright, *British-Owned Railways in Argentina: Their Effect on Economic Nationalism, 1854–1948* (Austin, Texas: University of Texas Press, 1974) p. 81; and Smith, pp. 29–30.
48. Carl E. Solberg, *Oil and Nationalism in Argentina: A History* (Stanford, California: University of California Press, 1979) pp. viii and 29.
49. David Rock, *Politics in Argentina 1890–1930: The Rise and Fall of Radicalism* (London: Cambridge University Press, 1975) pp. 252–3.
50. David Crichton Jordan, 'Argentina's Nationalist Movements and the Political Parties (1930–1963): A Study of Conflict', unpublished PhD thesis, University of Pennsylvania, 1964, pp. 64–5; Falcoff, in Falcoff and Pike, p. 301.

51. Marysa Gerassi, 'Argentine Nationalism of the Right: The History of an Ideological Development, 1930–1946', unpublished PhD thesis, Columbia University , 1964, pp. 16–32; Mark Falcoff, 'Intellectual Currents', in Mark Falcoff and Ronald H. Dolkart (eds) *Prologue to Perón: Argentina in Depression and War 1930–1943* (Berkeley, California: University of California Press, 1975) pp. 126–7.
52. Sumner Welles, *Where Are We Heading?* (New York: Harper and Row, 1946, pp. 200–3, cited in O. Edmund Smith, Jr, *Yankee Diplomacy: US Intervention in Argentina* (Dallas: Southern Methodist University Press, 1953) p. 112.
53. David Rock, *Argentina 1516–1982: From Spanish Colonization to the Falklands War* (Berkeley and Los Angeles: University of California Press, 1985) p. 280.
54. Donald C. McKay's introduction in Whitaker, p. x.
55. Edward S. Milenky, *Argentina's Foreign Politics* (Boulder, Colorado: Westview Press, 1978) p. 13.
56. Alberto A. Conil Paz and Gustavo E. Ferrari, *Argentina's Foreign Policy 1930–1962* (Notre Dame, Indiana: University of Notre Dame Press, 1966) pp. 177–8; F. Parkinson, *Latin America, the Cold War, and the World Powers 1945–1973: A Study in Diplomatic History* (Beverley Hills: Sage, 1974) pp. 15–16; and James D. Theberge and Roger W. Fontaine, *Latin America: Struggle for Progress* (Lexington, Massachusetts: Lexington Books, 1977) pp. 135–6.
57. Parkinson, pp. 208–9.
58. Jorge I. Domínguez, 'Business nationalism: Latin American national business attitudes and behaviour towards multinational enterprises', in Jorge I. Domínguez (ed.) *Economic Issues and Political Conflict: US–Latin American Relations* (London: Butterworth, 1982) p. 45; and Heraldo Muñoz, 'Beyond the Malvinas Crisis: Perspectives on Inter-American Relations', *Latin American Research Review*, vol. XIX, no. 1, 1984, p. 160.
59. Marvin Alisky, *Latin America Media: Guidance and Censorship* (Ames, Iowa: Iowa State University Press, 1981) pp. 3 and 179.
60. Aldo Ferrer, *Living Within Our Means: An Examination of the Argentine Economic Crisis* (Boulder, Colorado: Westview Press, 1985) p. 40.
61. Alexander M. Haig, Jr. *Caveat* (London: Weidenfeld and Nicolson, 1984) pp. 263 and 278; and Guillermo Makin, 'Argentina: The Authoritarian Impasse', in Christopher Clapham and George Philip (eds) *The Political Dilemmas of Military Regimes* (London: Croom Helm, 1985) p. 164.
62. Conil Paz and Ferrari, p. 23.
63. Edward Shaw, 'Prospects rise for radical state overhaul', *Buenos Aires Herald*, 23 November 1986, p. 2.
64. Fernando Henrique Cardoso and Enzo Faletto, *Dependency and Development in Latin America* (Berkeley, California: University of California Press, 1979) pp. 3 and 69–73.
65. Carlos H. Waisman, 'Population and Social Structure in Argentina', *Latin American Research Review*, vol. XXI, no. 2, 1986, p. 256.
66. Roberto Cortés Conde, 'Some Notes on the Industrial Development of Argentina and Canada in the 1920s', in D.C.M. Platt and Guido di Tella (eds) *Argentina, Australia and Canada:*

Studies in Comparative Development 1870–1965 (London: Macmillan, 1985) p. 155.

67. Peter Alhadeff, 'Public Finance and the Economy in Argentina, Australia and Canada During the Depression of the 1930s', in Platt and di Tella, pp. 164–70.

68. Gary W. Wynia, 'Argentina: The Frustration of Ungovernability', in Robert Wesson (ed.) *Politics, Policies, and Economic Development in Latin America* (Stanford, California: Hoover Institution Press, 1984) p. 15.

69. Sarmiento, p. 26.

70. Eduardo Crawley, *A House Divided: Argentina 1880–1980* (London: C. Hurst, 1984) p. 3.

71. Tomás Roberto Fillol, *Social Factors in Economic Development: The Argentine Case* (Cambridge, Massachusetts: Massachusetts Institute of Technology, 1961) pp. 9–14.

72. Carlos Octavio Bunge, *Nuestra América: Ensayo de psicología social* (Buenos Aires: Vaccaro, 1918).

73. Jacobo Timerman, 'Stopping the Generals', *Newsweek*, 8 October 1984, p. 22.

74. Rodolfo H. Terragno's introduction, in Crawley, p. xviii.

75. Vicente Reina Fernández, *Pensar en Argentina* (Buenos Aires: Ediciones Bodoni, 1983) p. 34.

76. Ysabel F. Rennie, *The Argentine Republic* (New York: Macmillan, 1945) p. viii.

77. Jeane Kirkpatrick, *Leader and Vanguard in Mass Society: A Study of Peronist Argentina* (Cambridge, Massachusetts: Massachusetts Institute of Technology, 1971) pp. 215–16; and George I. Blanksten, *Perón's Argentina* (Chicago: University of Chicago Press, 1974) pp. 306–56.

78. Crawley, p. 26.

79. V.S. Naipaul, *The Return of Eva Perón* (London: André Deutsch, 1974) p. 147.

80. Félix Luna, *Los caudillos* (Buenos Aires: A Peña Lillo, 1971) p. 20.

81. Esteban Echeverría, *La cautiva* (Buenos Aires: Editorial Sopena Argentina, 1962) pp. 80–96.

82. Sarmiento, p. 30.

83. José Marmol, *Amalia* (Buenos Aires: Editorial Sopena Argentina, 1964).

84. Bartolomé Mitre, *Historia de Belgrano y de la independencia argentina* (Buenos Aires: Félix Lajouane Editor, 1887).

85. Ricardo Levene, *Mitre y los estudios historicos en la Argentina* (no details), p. 88, cited in Jack Ray Thomas, *Biographical Dictionary of Latin American Historians and Historiography* (Westport, Connecticut: Greenwood Press, 1984) p. 51.

86. Clifton B. Kroeber, 'Rosas and the Revision of Argentine History, 1880–1955', *Revista Interamericana de Bibliografía*, vol. X, January–March 1960, pp. 5–6.

87. Carlos Alberto Leumann, *La literatura gauchesca y la poesía gaucha* (Buenos Aires: Editorial Raigal, 1953) p. 9; and Slatta, pp. 1, 4–6, 30, 47 and 90.

88. José Hernández, *El gaucho Martín Fierro y la vuelta de Martín Fierro* (Buenos Aires: Editorial Sopena Argentina, 1956).

89. Leumann, pp. 171–3.
90. W.H. Hudson, *The Purple Land: Being the Narrative of One Richard Lamb's Adventures in the Banda Orientál, in South America, as Told by Himself* (London: Duckworth, 1929).
91. John King, *Sur: A Study of the Argentine Literary Journal and its Role in the Development of Culture, 1931–1970* (Cambridge: Cambridge University Press, 1986) p. 12.
92. Julie M. Taylor, 'Tango: Theme of Class and Nation', *Ethnomusicology*, vol. XX, no. 2, May 1976, p. 275.
93. Thomas, pp. 230–1.
94. Kroeber, pp. 14–15; Falcoff, in Falcoff and Dolkart, pp. 116–17; Robert Weisbrot, *The Jews of Argentina: From the Inquisition to Perón* (Philadelphia: The Jewish Publication Society of America, 1979) pp. 227–9.
95. Oswald Spengler, *The Decline of the West* (New York: Alfred A. Knopf, 1939) p. 507. See also King, p. 36.
96. Ezequiel Martínez Estrada, *Para una revisión de las letras argentinas* (Buenos Aires: Editorial Losada, 1967) pp. 53 and 65; Martin S. Stabb, *In Quest of Identity: Pattern in the Spanish American Essay of Ideas, 1890–1960* (Chapel Hill: University of North Carolina Press, 1967) pp. 68 and 163; Arthur P. Whitaker, 'An Overview of the Period', in Falcoff and Dolkart, pp. 2 and 27–8; and King, pp. 36–7.
97. Eduardo Mallea, *Fiesta en Noviembre* (Buenos Aires: Club del Libra A.L.A., 1938); and Eduardo Mallea, *Todo verdor perecerá* (Buenos Aires: Editorial Espasa-Calpe, 1941).
98. 'But you would give a lot/to be for just one moment/again the same *compadrito*/of times past/for so much glory tires'. Julio Mafud, *Sociología del tango* (Buenos Aires: Editorial Américalee, 1966), pp. 25 and 280; Gustavo Sosa-Pujato, 'Popular Culture', in Falcoff and Dolkart, pp. 138–9; Taylor, pp. 273–80; and Gerard Béliague, 'Popular Music', in Harold E. Hinds, Jr, and Charles M. Tatum (eds) *Handbook of Latin American Popular Culture* (Westport, Connecticut: Greenwood Press, 1985) p. 4.
99. Ricardo Rojas, *El profeta de la pampa: Vida de Sarmiento* (Buenos Aires: n.p., 1945).
100. Carlos Ibarguren, *Juan Manuel de Rosas: Su vida, su tiempo, su drama* (Buenos Aires: Libreria 'La Facultad' de Juan Roldán, 1930).
101. Tulio Halperín Donghi, *El revisionismo histórico argentino* (Buenos Aires: Siglo XXI Editores, 1970), p. 14.
102. Lynch, p. 2.
103. Manuel Gálvez, *La tragedía de un hombre fuerte* (Buenos Aires: Compañía General Fabril Editora, 1961) pp. 36 and 90–122.
104. Kroeber, pp. 18–19.
105. For example, Julio Irazusta, *Perón y la crisis argentina* (Buenos Aires: La Voz del Plata, 1956).
106. Jorge Luis Borges, *El librole arena* (Buenos Aires: Ermecé Editores, 1975) p. 5.
107. Andrew Graham-Yooll, *A State of Fear: Memories of Argentina's Nightmare* (London: Eland, 1986) p. 112.

108. Ernesto Sábato, *El túnel* (Buenos Aires: Editorial Sudamericana, 1967); Martin S. Stabb, 'Argentine Letters and the Peronato: An Overview', *Journal of Inter-American Studies and World Affairs*, vol. XIII, nos., 3 – 4, 1971, pp. 449 and 455; Julio Cortázar, *Libro de Manuel* (Buenos Aires: Editorial Sudamericana, 1973); Stephen Boldy, *The Novels of Julio Cortázar* (Cambridge: Cambridge University Press, 1980) pp. 2, 33–4 and 172; John King, 'The Latin American Novel in Translation: Mapping the Field', *Bulletin of Latin American Research*, vol. IV, no. 2, 1985, p. 129; and King (1986) pp. 54, 86–7 and 188–9.

109. Ezequiel Martínez Estrada, *Cabeza de Goliat: microscopía de Buenos Aires* (Buenos Aires: Club del Libro A.L.A., 1940).

110. For example, Arturo Jauretche, *Los profetas del odio* (Buenos Aires: Ediciones Trafac, 1956).

111. Ezequiel Martínez Estrada, *Muerte y Transfiguración de Martín Fierro: Ensayo de interpretación de la vida argentina*, vol. II (Buenos Aires: Fondo de Cultura Económica, 1958) p. 291; and Ezequiel Martínez Estrada, *X-Ray of the Pampa* (Austin, Texas: University of Texas Press, 1971) pp. 5, 37, 43, 62, 72, 133, 160, 172, 178–80, 199, 317–18, 341 and 347–8.

112. Luna, p. 9.

113. Naipaul, p. 166.

114. H.S. Ferns, *Argentina* (London: Ernest Benn, 1969) p. 85.

115. The present authors found one of these stickers still on a shop window in Buenos Aires in 1987.

116. Parkinson, p. 15.

CHAPTER 9

1. Morris Janowitz and Roger W. Little, *Sociology and the Military Establishment* (Beverly Hills, California: Sage Publications, 1974) p. 10; Alain Rouquié (trans. Arturo Iglesias Echegaray), *Poder militar y sociedad política en la Argentina* (Buenos Aires: Emecé Editores, 1981) pp. 17–19.

2. Robert A. Dahl, *Polyarchy: Participation and Opposition* (New Haven: Yale University Press, 1971) pp. 7 and 38–9.

3. Torcuato S. Di Tella, 'The October 1983 Elections in Argentina', *Government and Opposition* vol. 19, no. 2, 1984, p. 189.

4. For details of the role of Fabricaciones Militares under the military governments see Jimmy Burns, *The Land That Lost its Heroes: the Falklands, the Post-War and Alfonsín* (London: Bloomsbury, 1987) pp. 15–16.

5. Sábato had accompanied Borges to the notorious meeting with General Videla in 1976 after which Borges had declared that he was happy that Argentina was in the hands of 'gentlemen'. See *inter alia* Andrew Graham-Yooll, *A State of Fear: Memories of Argentina's Nightmare* (London: Eland, 1986) p. 112. Sábato had made it quite clear that he did not share this view.

6. Argentina: Comisión Nacional sobre la Desaparición de Personas, *Nunca Mas* (Buenos Aires: EUDEBA, 1986).
7. See *Nunca Mas*, pp. 264–5.
8. *La Nación*, 29 December 1987.
9. *Nunca Mas*, pp. 80–1 and 202–3, where the clandestine detention centre, located on RN20 from Córdoba to Villa Carlos Paz, is stated to have been comparable in importance with the Campo de Mayo or ESMA.
10. *La Tarde de Tucumán*, 31 December 1987.
11. *Buenos Aires Herald*, 27 December 1987, editorial, p. 14.
12. *Buenos Aires Herald*, 22 November 1987, pp. 3 and 8.
13. A nickname for the vast amusement park planned but not finished by the military government. The reference is to the 'Potemkin villages' constructed to fool the Empress Catherine the Great.
14. Robert A. Potash, *The Army and Politics in Argentina 1928–1945: Yrigoyen to Perón* (Stanford, California: Stanford University Press, 1969) p. 202.
15. Eduardo Crawley, *A House Divided: Argentina 1880–1980* (London: C. Hurst, 1984) p. 445.
16. Interviews in April 1987 with Arnaldo Musich, leading businessman and former Ambassador to the United States under the Videla government, and others.

Index